Li
3 G

ni
bef

JUN

22.

8 Ma

9 Ma

Ju

5

HISTORY OF THE
LONDON DISCOUNT MARKET

HISTORY OF THE LONDON DISCOUNT MARKET

by

W. T. C. KING

With an Introduction by

T. E. GREGORY

FRANK CASS : LONDON

Published in Great Britain by
FRANK CASS AND COMPANY LIMITED
67 Great Russell Street, London WC1B 3BT, England

and in United States of America by
FRANK CASS AND COMPANY LIMITED
c/o International Scholarly Book Services, Inc.
P.O. Box 4347, Portland, Oregon 97208

Library of Congress Catalog Card No. 71–171824

ISBN 0 7146 1231 6

First edition	1936
New Impression	1972

Printed in Great Britain by
Fletcher & Son Ltd, Norwich

CONTENTS

INTRODUCTION

Good wine needs no bush, and it requires no words of mine to stress the technical merits of this book. Mr. King, as well as being a trained economist, is himself a financial journalist in daily contact with the Money Market. He has utilized to the full the wonderful store of information contained in the British Parliamentary Papers (a by-product, but what a striking one, of our system of Government) and in the daily and periodical press of a century past, to produce the first full and consistent account of that Discount Market, without which neither our commercial banking system nor the working of our Central Bank can be properly understood. He has carried out his self-appointed task supremely well and his book will take its rightful place as one of the indispensable tools of the student of British banking and currency.

Nevertheless, it is a surprising fact that we should have had to wait so long for the historian of the Discount Market. For the London Discount Market is unique, and its existence has contributed more than any other single factor to the elaboration of what may legitimately be called the Anglo-Saxon tradition in Central Banking technique. The bill of exchange has existed for centuries: the Bank of England, itself by no means the first to be created of the great European Central Banks, antedated the Discount Market in its classical late Victorian form by many decades. Yet in no other country in the world did quite the same relationships evolve between the Central institution and the Money Market. The bill of exchange became, in France and Germany, in Holland and Scandinavia, the instrument of re-discounting—the typical earning asset of the Central Bank. Yet, by and large, over the whole Continent, the bill was bought by the Central Bank either from its own circle of private customers or—with the added safety of an endorsement by a banker—from the Commercial banks. Nowhere in the world was the " Open Market " precisely what it was in London—a market living by borrowing liquid funds for the purpose of investment in bills of exchange, with the right of recourse, in times of need, to the Central Bank. Elsewhere, the " Open Market ", in so far as it existed at all, was a market lending short-term funds to the Stock Exchange (as in Holland or in New York), or it consisted essentially in dealings between banks themselves. The English system, a product of happy accident and circumstance, the uniqueness of which was barely understood even here in England, evolved slowly and painfully and it is not certain whether the future will ever again see it functioning with that smoothness and delicacy which was its pre-War characteristic. For the moment, at any rate, the disastrous decline in the international trade of the world has largely eliminated the international bill on London, upon which the market lived, and which was its real *raison d'être*. To know the credit-standing of the drawers and acceptors of bills, to provide the Commercial banks with the maturities they required, to take from them their short-term moneys and to repay if need be by loans or re-discounts from the Central Bank meant a most happy marriage between the needs of the business and the financial worlds. If the international bill is not to survive, if the Discount Market in future is to live on dealings in short-dated Government securities and in Treasury Bills, then it may well be that the relationships which have hitherto been the real essence of the " Open Market " may undergo changes as profound as those which changed the Discount Market at an earlier date, as Mr. King tells us, from a conduit-pipe between local banks, some with excess deposits and some with deficient resources, into a great International Market, the boss upon which turned the vast volume of pre-war international trade. It is easy to imagine an evolution in the direction of the elimination of the Discount Market altogether: for the Treasury Bill is a standard instrument of credit, to handle which requires no special knowledge. The short-loan investments of the banks might easily be replaced by larger holdings of Treasury Bills, and the relations between the Central Bank and the outside market might undergo fundamental changes. It appears clear that the business community on the whole prefers the elasticity of the overdraft system to the greater constraint of the bill of exchange, so that a revival of the internal bill market, so ardently advocated in many quarters in recent years, is hardly likely. Present tendencies, then, are not entirely satisfactory—and yet it is hardly possible to imagine the London money market without the Discount Market. Certainly the disappearance of that market would revolutionize our whole concept of the technique of Central Banking.

For nothing is more remarkable in the practical literature of Central Banking, inspired by English sources, than the constantly expressed conviction of the necessity for an " Open Market " if a Central Bank is to function efficiently. Where an " Open Market " does not exist, then, it seems, it has to be created. But if that is impossible? Then the Central Bank is driven into cultivating direct relationship with the Commercial banks—or creating indirect relationships of control and command by means of Foreign Exchange operations and the possession of the Government Accounts. English economists and bank officials, who have grown up to regard the London Money Market as the ideal to which to point, must always submit to a painful effort of the imagination before they can deal with situations which appear to make it impossible to create conditions even remotely analogous to those obtaining in London. And yet, whilst the attempt is being made to adapt the tradition of London to the circumstances of Canada or South Africa or India, a revolution may be taking place at home. On these matters, it is useful to speculate but equally useless to predict.

Meanwhile, here is Mr. King's book to reinforce some useful lessons. The Discount Market has never been quite the same in successive decades: its relations to the Central Bank have not always been friendly and its functional significance has been very different at different times. In the main, the market was built up, and has altered its operations from time to time, under the pressure of necessity. From this point of view we are presented by a triumph of pure empiricism—for the Discount Market has been less directly affected by the enactments of positive law than any other part of the Money Market, once the Usury Laws were got out of the way. But, as the book also makes clear, nothing is more untrue than to suppose that no creative thought was in the past expended upon the working of the market or to suppose that practical instinct alone furnishes the key to the history of the response of form to function. In each decade City men have reflected on the problems of their time and day: and what passes as English monetary and banking theory has been largely the product of the reflection of City men themselves. Echoes of ancient controversies sound through the pages of this book: the controversies were none the worse for having been initiated and carried through by City men themselves. I most warmly recommend this book —the more so as it is the product of the pen, not of a " professional " economist, but of one who is " something in the City " himself.

T. E. GREGORY.

THE LONDON SCHOOL OF ECONOMICS.
October 7, 1935.

AUTHOR'S PREFACE

FROM the days of Bagehot to those of the Macmillan Committee, successive authorities have recognized that it is to her possession of a specialized discount market that London largely owes her supremacy as an international financial centre. "That essential link and cog in the [financial] machine which we call the Discount Market," said Mr. Montagu Norman some months ago, "invented and brought to perfection a side of business peculiar to the City of London, and unknown practically in other places . . . without which the City would never have reached the position of international eminence which it undoubtedly has reached." London's supremacy has not, however, been confined to the international sphere in which her financial organization first became famous: in no other centre in the world can vast financial transactions be carried through with such speed or with so little disturbance of the general credit structure; in no other centre is control by the central bank exercised, or the need of the Treasury provided, so smoothly or so rapidly. In recent years, when London has faced a challenge in the international sphere, this second aspect of her pre-eminence has been more than ever emphasized by experience in other markets, where even comparatively unimportant operations can cause violent rate fluctuations and disconcerting reactions upon the exchanges, to the inevitable discomfort of trade. This "domestic" superiority of the London market, certainly no less than her international supremacy, is attributable to the peculiar structure and efficiency of her Discount Market. This, too, has come to be generally recognized, and in the past six or seven years different financial centres have sought to copy this particular part—almost the only *unique* part—of London's financial equipment.

The object of these attempts, it is interesting to note, has not always been the same. New York and Paris have both sought to establish specialized discount houses as a means of attaining new power in the international sphere ; others have coveted the smooth effectiveness of London's discount and call loan markets as mechanisms of purely internal finance, with the special facilities they afford for the exercise of central bank control ; and yet a third group has aspired primarily to ease of Treasury financing, especially at short-term. These various efforts at imitation, each emphasizing a different aspect of the value of the London Discount Market, point to a growing interest in the means by which London came to acquire so distinctive a mechanism. Of this interest I have found first-hand and tangible evidence in repeated discussions with overseas bankers, notably with those from " young " countries which are only now beginning to develop an organized money market.

It therefore seemed that a history of the London Discount Market might conceivably serve a strictly utilitarian and practical purpose. Although several excellent histories of the London Money Market, viewed in its broadest sense, have long been available, to my knowledge no previous attempt had been made to trace the evolution of the London Discount Market as such. It would be foolish, however, to pretend that this utilitarian object provided my main motive when I began to delve into the origins of London's discount business. In fact, my first object was simply to collect sufficient historical material to enable me in a practical and mainly descriptive work to show the modern discount market in perspective. Completion of this other book has been postponed temporarily, for researches into the history revealed much material which seemed to be valuable for its own sake. In particular, I felt that this material shed a certain amount of new and possibly important light, not only upon the contemporary working and growth of the general banking system during the past 150 years, but upon the evolution of that central banking technique which has made the Bank of England's system and practice the model for other central banks throughout the world. That alone seemed a sufficient justification for presenting the history in a separate book. In addition, it appeared that because of the absence in the past of a separate survey of the evolution of the Discount Market, inadequate attention had been paid to the part which the bill brokers and the discount houses played in nineteenth-century banking generally.

Until the last quarter of the century the English banking system remained what is known as a " unit " banking system. At a time when the financial needs of different districts differed even more widely than they do now, a localized banking system could function efficiently only through a sort of central pool by means of which the credit surpluses of one type of district (the agricultural areas) and the credit deficiencies of the other type of district (the industrial areas) could find their level. The Discount Market (and its ultimate corollary, the short-loan market) provided such a pool, as well as the conduit-pipes by which it was tapped and fed. It is hardly an exaggeration, therefore, to say that the Discount Market occupied a key position in the nineteenth-century banking structure; it was literally indispensable to that particular structure. Without the discount houses and the bill brokers, the evolution of the banking machine must perforce have followed a very different course. The difference would profoundly have affected the modern structure, not merely of the money market, but of the deposit banks themselves.

The actual history of the Discount Market itself thus forms only one theme of the book. Other and no less prominent themes are:

> The all-important relationship between the Discount Market and the general banking structure;
>
> The contribution which the peculiar development of the Discount Market made to the distinctive final form of the British banking system and of the London Money Market;
>
> The progressive utilization of the Discount Market as a mechanism of Treasury finance; and
>
> The evolution, step by step, of the market technique of the Bank of England, first as competitor with the discount houses, and later as controller of the whole market and credit situation.

In emphasis, this last theme, the growth of central banking technique, is roughly co-equal with the first, the growth of the Discount Market itself.

I have sought throughout to develop these various ideas from a practical point of view, being concerned more with the precise means by which each successive problem was overcome than with the theoretical implications of these problems. Theoretical aspects, or contemporary theoretical controversies, are discussed only where they were vital to an understanding of the development of the financial system at the time. The treatment is mainly chronological, and for that reason each chapter should be regarded more as a convenient grouping of contemporaneous material around a central theme than as a strictly homogeneous whole.

I have tried to make the book easily intelligible to the general reader, first by avoiding technical phraseology; and, secondly, by including a brief note of explanation, in really simple terms, of the nature of bills and bill discounting. The use of a considerable number of footnotes has proved inevitable, but, with the object of minimizing the somewhat ponderous form which they must give to any book, I have generally cited the full title of each source or book once only, and have thereafter used a system of abbreviations and cross-references ; full titles of books, etc., and the reference indices of Parliamentary Papers, will be found in a short bibliography of principal sources.

As the material is drawn very largely from first-hand sources—chiefly from contemporary publications and official inquiries, fully detailed in the text—my acknowledgments here need not be extensive. The brief sketch of the antecedents of the Discount Market, up to about 1750, is, however, based almost entirely upon the excellent and painstaking researches of the late Dr. Ellis T. Powell, of *The Financial News*, and Dr. R. D. Richards. To those two writers I owe a special debt, as well as to Mr. L. H. Jenks, whose stimulating and splendidly documented book on capital movements I found invaluable when dealing with the growth of the international money market. Of my numerous personal obligations, to friends in the Discount Market, in the banks and elsewhere, only a few can be specifically, and none adequately, acknowledged here. My special thanks are due to Mr. W. M. Dacey, who read the whole book both in typescript and in proof and whose meticulous care saved me from many pitfalls and inaccuracies ; to Miss I. Shrigley, who as Librarian of the Institute of Bankers responded unstintingly to my often extreme demands upon her patience ; to Mr. Collin Brooks, whose long-sustained interest in the book has been a source of constant inspiration. Above all, and most warmly, I thank Professor Gregory—for lending the weight of his pen to introduce the book ; for reading the typescript chapter by chapter ; for many invaluable suggestions, made over a period of years and at almost every stage of the work. It remains to add that neither he nor the others who have so willingly helped can be in any way responsible for textual inaccuracies or for the arguments and opinions expressed. Responsibility for these, as for the many deficiencies of the book, is entirely mine.

W. T. C. K.

20, BISHOPSGATE, E.C.2.
October, 1935.

AN EXPLANATORY NOTE

ANY discussion of the Discount Market must involve the use of terms with which the lay reader may be unfamiliar. Few of these lend themselves to definition in the language of everyday, though all are readily definable in the jargon of the market or of the economist. But definitions which themselves require definition, though possibly impressive, are not helpful. In a purely descriptive work, this difficulty of simple definition can be avoided by explaining each term fully as it arises; but in an historical work, especially where source references are at all frequent, repeated interruption of narrative or argument by explanation must impair both readability and clarity. In the following pages, technicalities have been avoided wherever possible, but where they occur the context has been left to afford an explanation. This will generally be sufficient, but the lay reader may possibly welcome a little additional assistance. For his benefit, it is proposed to give here a really simple explanation of what the Discount Market is.

In any discount market the tangible commodity is the bill of exchange. This, in its crudest form, is simply a written acknowledgment of the existence of a debt—virtually an "I.O.U." which embodies the debtor's undertaking to pay at a specified time. Some bills are payable on demand; but a discount market deals usually only with those payable at a definite future date. These "usance" bills (the usance, currency or tenor of a bill is the period between its creation and maturity) arise in many ways, but an illustration of one will suffice. A merchant agrees to sell £100 worth of goods on three months' credit, and seeks to embody the transaction in a bill of exchange. To achieve this he sends written instructions to the buyer to pay to him, or to any person he may name or subsequently "order", the sum of £100 in three months' time. These instructions constitute the bill, which might take the following (simplified) form:

London, January 1, ——

To a Buyer,
Glasgow.

Three Months after date please pay to John Smith, or Order, the sum of ONE HUNDRED POUNDS, *for value received.*

A Seller.

On receipt of this bill, the buyer acknowledges his debt by " accepting " the bill, which he does by writing across its face the word " Accepted ", adding his signature. Until that moment he is merely the " drawee " of the bill, with no liability upon it; but as soon as he signs he becomes its " acceptor ", the person who is primarily responsible for its due payment. If, however, he should default, then any third party who has taken the bill in settlement of a debt and who still holds it can at once proceed against the " drawer ", the original seller of the goods. In the above example, John Smith could so proceed. But if John Smith had himself transferred the bill to his own creditor, then that creditor could proceed not only against the drawer but also against John Smith. Similarly, any subsequent transferee could proceed not only against the drawer and John Smith, but against any intermediate holders who, when transferring the bill, had also endorsed it.

In this, its modern, form the bill of exchange is therefore something more than an acknowledgment of a debt: it is also a legally binding undertaking to pay the debt, which is guaranteed by all " parties " to the bill—the acceptor, drawer, and endorser(s). It is, moreover, indisputable evidence that the debt exists, and is therefore an instrument upon which a holder can base a legal action, even against parties with whom he has no direct contractual relations. Finally, it is what is known as a " negotiable " instrument, which means that a person who takes it in legitimate circumstances achieves (except where there is forgery) an unassailable right to it, even though his transferor had no such right. These legal attributes of the bill, which largely explain its great commercial and financial value, are now set out formally and fully in a " codifying " statute, the Bills of Exchange Act of 1882; but for many years dealings in bills were governed solely by the customs of merchants. These, indeed, formed the basis of the modern code, for the bill was used for the acknowledgment of indebtedness between merchants, as a simple I.O.U., and even for making payments to third parties, long before its existence was recognized by the law, and long before there was any kind of discount market.

At a very early date, however, these purely mercantile uses of bills were extended to financial uses. Financial dealings in bills arise when they are used, not merely as acknowledgments of indebtedness or for payments to trade creditors, but as a means of raising money by the sale of the bills (and the debts which they represent) to third-party financiers. Such a financier is necessarily out of his money until the date when the bill (and the debt) falls due and is paid. He therefore charges interest to the seller of the bill for that part of its life or currency which is still unexpired. Nowadays, this interest is almost invariably paid in advance, so that the sum which the seller of the bill actually receives is the amount of the debt (or bill) *minus* the interest. Interest so paid is known as " discount ", and the rate at which it is calculated is the " rate " of discount, always expressed as so much per cent. *per annum*. Thus the higher the rate of discount, the lower is the price which the seller of the bill obtains and the buyer pays.

This is a potential source of confusion to those accustomed to ordinary market dealings, for in the Discount Market the only " price " quoted is a rate of discount. Hence " discounts " are said to be " firmer " (dearer) when the rate of discount rises and when, therefore, the " price " of bills falls—an apparent inversion of the usual state of affairs. In reality, there is no inversion : although the tangible commodity *in* the Discount Market is the bill of exchange, the commodity in which the market *deals* is not bills, but loans made by the purchase of bills. If this point be firmly grasped there will be no confusion, for it will be seen that when the " price " in the market—the rate of discount—rises, the price of loans also rises ; and when the discount rate falls, the price of loans falls. Thus the true sellers in the market are the sellers of loans, the buyers or discounters of bills ; and the true buyers are the buyers of loans, the sellers of bills.

A body of third-party discounters, some or all of whom are ready at all times to lend money by discounting bills, is the first requisite of a discount market in any sense of the term. But bill discounters are not of themselves sufficient to constitute such a market, for a market in any commodity must possess some degree of cohesion and organization, whether natural or self-imposed. In particular, its operations must be conducted with such publicity and such free competition as will ensure that within its bounds at a given moment there cannot be any marked differences in the prices which different sellers charge and different buyers pay. The other requisite of a discount market is therefore such competition among discounters, and among those with bills for discount, as will ensure virtual uniformity of discount rates. Where these two conditions are satisfied, there is a discount market in the broadest sense of the term. In this sense, the market embraces all those competing parties—bankers and merchants—who lend money by the purchase of bills, and all those traders (and bankers) who borrow money by the sale of bills.

It is not in this broad sense, however, that the term " discount market " is most commonly used. The term is usually restricted to the operations of certain specialized financial intermediaries which act as the connecting link between the ultimate borrowers and the ultimate lenders. In the London Money Market those borrowers and those lenders are to-day, and have been for many years, domiciled in all parts of the world : the intermediaries who comprise the London Discount Market strictly so-called are, without exception, localized in London. They are, indeed, compendiously referred to as " Lombard Street ". Of these intermediaries, by far the most important are the London discount houses. These houses, unlike the few firms known as " running brokers ", are not, however, pure agents. Their function is to make available for borrowers the funds of lenders, but in so doing they interpose their own credit and responsibility between the ultimate parties. Instead of merely bringing together lenders and borrowers—the buyers and sellers of bills—and then leaving the parties to strike a bargain, as the true bill " broker " would do, they take upon themselves the risk of the loans which they grant in buying bills. Moreover, they procure the funds which they lend by themselves borrowing, as principals and not as agents, from the banks and other houses which constitute the remaining part of the London Money Market. In other words, they are intermediary discounters or dealers, who utilize borrowed money to finance the bills which they buy and hold. In market parlance, they " run a book " and finance a bill portfolio ; and both upon the loans which they contract and upon the bills which they re-sell (with their endorsement or guarantee) they incur full legal liability.

This is the Discount Market whose history forms one of the several main themes which are developed in the following pages. Its limits, as will appear, can be clearly defined, but its operations are inseparably inter-woven with those of all other discounters and lenders of short-term funds. The activities of all who come within the sphere of the market in its broadest sense will therefore require detailed examination. This broader survey, however, will be pursued only so far as is necessary to show in true perspective the operations of Lombard Street, and the part it plays and has played in the banking system in particular and in the national economy in general.

HISTORY OF THE LONDON DISCOUNT MARKET

CHAPTER I

THE RISE OF THE BILL BROKERS

In its modern form, the London Discount Market is hardly more than three-quarters of a century old. There were, it is true, a few houses which worked on the modern principle, financing bill portfolios with borrowed funds, even as long ago as the early eighteen-thirties. For many years, however, these intermediary discounters or bill dealers were outnumbered by bill brokers and firms that were virtually bill brokers—the bill "jobbers", who bought and sold as principals, but who did not finance bills to any important extent. The discount market of to-day is therefore of comparatively recent origin. Nevertheless, it can trace its ancestry right back to the earliest forms of money-dealing in this country. Discounting is one of the earliest banking functions, and was a well-recognized practice by the time of the goldsmith-bankers. Indeed, the surviving ledgers of Alderman Edward Backwell,[1] covering the period from 1663 to 1671, include some accounts which appear to have related exclusively to discount business. It is not, however, through such operations that the bill market's ancient lineage can be established, for the early discounters worked mainly with their own resources, and sought bills merely as suitable investments, in days when investment media, except in land, were few. The second stage in discounting operations began when the merchants or goldsmiths started to buy bills with deposits left with them by their friends or business acquaintances. Even this was not true "intermediary" discounting as practised by the modern discount house, for the deposits of these early discounters came from commercial or private sources,

[1] Cited by R. D. Richards, *Early History of Banking in England* (1928), pp. 27–8. Backwell stopped payment in 1682.

and not from banking sources as does the bulk of the market's funds to-day. In short, it is the agency function of the market, and not its discounting function, which must be stressed in tracing its evolution: it is among financial intermediaries that its origins must be sought.

Growth of Financial Intermediaries

There is abundant proof that financial intermediaries were common at a very early date; and although it is less certain that the earliest brokers or money-dealers were actually *bill* brokers, there is no doubt that their functions were closely analogous to those of the nineteenth-century bill brokers from whom the discount houses directly sprang. The essential function of these "procurers" or "inducers", as they were called, was that of arranging loans between merchant and merchant or between merchants and titled gentry—the former being generally the lenders! Such brokers certainly existed in pre-Tudor times, and their dealings were even then sufficiently recognized to be regulated by Statute. An Act passed in the early years of Henry VII, restricting the business of exchange to brokers holding the King's licence, adjured even "englisch brokers and estraungers brokers which be named and assygnet to occupie lefull brocage" not to be "ynducers and bargeyne makers of unlefull chevysaunce and usurie",[1] thus plainly indicating that the business of procuring was widespread. These early money-dealers went under various names, but it is difficult to assign a distinctive function to each, for most of them seem to have performed much the same kind of business, essentially that of procuring. Of the various types, the "money-scrivener" or "scrivener" is probably the most important for the present purpose. A scrivener, as the word implies, was originally a writer, whose function was the preparation and writing of contracts, bonds, or bills obligatory for his less literate principals, the merchants and monied men. From the nature of his calling, he came to acquire a considerable insight into the credit-standing, resources and business of his clients, and learnt to distinguish those who had funds to spare from those who had need to borrow. Such knowledge once acquired, it was but a short step [2] from the business of scribe to that of financial inter-

[1] Cited by Ellis T. Powell, *Evolution of the Money Market*, p. 24.
[2] See H. C. Gutteridge, *Origin and Historical Development of the Profession of Notaries Public*, for details of the transition.

mediary who offered, for a consideration in the shape of commission (brokerage), to bring borrower and lender together.

In later statutes the scrivener is coupled with the broker and " solicitor ", and this is particularly noticeable in the early Usury Laws, which shed much light on the antecedents of the bill market. Thus in 1623 [1] an Act passed to reduce the maximum legal rate of interest from 10 to 8 per cent. forbade scriveners, brokers, solicitors and drivers of bargains, under penalty of a forfeit of £20 or imprisonment for " halfe a yeare ", to take more than 5*s*. per cent. for *arranging* a loan, or more than 12*d*. per cent. for securing the renewal of the loan ; and a similar clause is to be found in the Act of 1660.[2] Nevertheless, there is no doubt that much higher rates were frequently charged, and Richards affirms that procuration charges often exceeded 5 per cent. Even that exorbitant charge must frequently have formed no larger proportion of the total cost of a loan than did the nineteenth-century bill broker's commission (when money rates were low), for lenders' charges were extortionate in the extreme. For example, the author of the tract of about 1676 entitled *The Mystery of the New Fashioned Goldsmiths or Bankers*, after referring to the goldsmiths' " running cashes ", states that—

> They begun to accommodate men with moneys for Weeks and Months, upon extraordinary gratuities, and supply all necessitous Merchants that overtraded their Stock, with present Money for their Bills of Exchange, discounting sometimes double, perhaps treble, interest for the time, as they found the Merchant more or less pinched.

It is not surprising that the scriveners, and money-lenders generally, were not the best-loved persons in the society of the fifteenth, sixteenth and seventeenth centuries ; they were attacked on religious, humanitarian, economic and sociological grounds. But the great number of tirades [3] against them is in itself evidence of their growing importance in the body economic.

[1] 21 Jac. I, c. 17 ; brokers and " drivers of bargaynes " are also dealt with in 13 Eliz., c. 8 (1571), which repealed an Act of 1552 that sought to prevent the payment of any interest at all.

[2] This statute confirmed the maximum legal rate of interest at 6 per cent.

[3] Richard Porder's sermons, especially his Whitsun Monday sermon at St. Paul's in 1570, contain many such attacks. David Jones, in his farewell sermon at St. Mary Woolnoth in 1692, declared, however, that the intermediaries were allowed only to scratch where the banker himself took care to bite (Ellis Powell, p. 135). The author of *A New Discourse on Trade*, almost certainly Sir Josiah Child, writing before

It is beyond question, then, that money-dealers acting as pure intermediaries existed at a very early date, and that by the seventeenth century, if not before, their activities had become really widespread. Indeed, it seems quite probable that they preceded even the function of discounting, though probably not the bill of exchange itself, for even in England the bill as an instrument of credit is of great antiquity. Instruments closely resembling letters of credit were in use in 1191, and references to them are to be found in the Crusade papers.[1] Bills of exchange were certainly known before that time, and actually figured in the courts as far back as 1300.[2] The first statutory reference occurs in 1379, to " letteres d'eschange ",[3] but there was apparently no legal decision directly affecting them until 1603.[4] Indeed, for many years their use was deliberately discouraged by the law. Thus Byles, writing in 1829, states :

> At the first introduction of bills of exchange, the English Courts of Law regarded them with a jealous and evil eye, allowing them only between merchants ; but their obvious advantages soon compelled the Judges to sanction their use by all persons ; and of late years the policy of the Bench has been industriously to remove every impediment, and add all possible facilities to these wheels of the vast commercial system.

This early attitude of the law is of special significance, for by seeking to check the use of bills except as between merchants, the law denied facilities essential to the *discounter* of bills, since a financier who took a bill could not be a *party* to it, and hence was denied the full legal rights of an endorser, and may even have been penalized as a holder. It is for this reason that one can surmise that the money-dealer preceded the discounter, for the absence of legal protection must have exerted a strong deterrent to financial operations in bills. At all events, it is certain that the first money-dealers, though they clearly performed

1669, attacked all money-dealing and usury on the grounds that it diverted funds from trade and from the country, and made people reluctant to buy or improve land. He also thought that " this new invention of cashiering " (goldsmith-banking) had " bettered the usurers' trade 1 or 2 per cent. per annum ".

[1] A. P. Usher, " Origin of the Bill of Exchange ", *Journal of Political Economy*, XXII, p. 566.

[2] A. H. Thomas, *Calendar of Early Mayors' Court Rolls*, cited by Richards.

[3] *Byles on Bills*, Preface to first edition (3 Rich. II, c. 3).

[4] *Martin* v. *Boure*, 1603, Cro. Jac. 6, cited by Byles.

functions which in the economy of the time closely paralleled those of later bill brokers, were not mainly dealers in bills.

This is confirmed by yet another characteristic of the early bills. The bill of exchange did not originate in England, and the first bills traceable in this country grew out of overseas trade. The so-called " outland " bill was therefore in general use long before the inland bill made its appearance. The money-scriveners' business was primarily domestic in character, and it is therefore reasonable to assume that their dealings in bills could not have been important until early in the seventeenth century, when the bill first began to play an appreciable part in purely domestic business. From that time, the work of the intermediaries in arranging bill finance must have become increasingly important, for internal bills were common by the end of the seventeenth century, and by 1750 their use was really general. Adam Smith, in 1776, made it clear that loans could be obtained against bills of exchange (by discount, presumably) more easily than upon any other security, and this was evidently true for many years before Smith wrote. He says :[1]

> The customs of merchants, which were established when barbarous laws of Europe did not enforce the performance of their contracts, and which during the course of the last two centuries have been adopted into the laws of all European nations, have given such extraordinary privileges to bills of exchange that money is more readily advanced upon them than upon any other species of obligation, especially when they are made payable within so short a period as two or three months after their date.

While financial intermediaries must have played an important part in such discount operations, it is clear that the bill brokers before Smith's time differed in at least one noteworthy respect from those of the early nineteenth century. Before 1750, or thereabouts, they appear to have acted largely, though not exclusively, between merchant and merchant, rather than between banker and banker or banker and merchant. But the transition from money " scrivening " to bill broking, properly so-called, was already far advanced in the first half of the eighteenth century. It was completed by the rise of the country banks.

Brokers as Agents for Country Banks

The essential characteristic of any money-broking business was and is the linking-up of those in need of funds and those

[1] *Wealth of Nations*, Vol. I, p. 274.

with funds to spare. So long, however, as the principals were mainly private traders on the one hand, and individual capitalists or merchants on the other, the brokers' business remained comparatively limited. But when individuals gave place to financial institutions as the major prospective lenders and borrowers, the possible scope of the bill broker's activities was enormously enlarged. Such a change resulted from the establishment of the country banks. So long as such banking as existed was concentrated within the metropolis, the problem of finding suitable employment for " surplus " deposits presented no extreme difficulties, and could usually be solved without the employment of a bill broker. Country banking, on the contrary, implied localized banking, and banking localized in districts which, from the nature of their economic life, provided the banker either with an excess of deposits for which no local use could be found, or with a preponderance of prospective borrowers over depositors. In the early stages of their development, country bankers more commonly experienced the former source of embarrassment, and often found employment for their funds simply through their London banker agents; though a few of them preferred to utilize the services of the London bill brokers.

When, however, with the beginnings of industrialization and the growth of trade, banks grew up in districts where borrowers predominated, the services of the bill broker became indispensable. His primary function then quickly came to be that of receiving bills from the " industrialist " banker and arranging for their discount either in London or by the " agriculturalist " country bankers; for, except at harvest-time and certain other seasons, the bankers in agricultural areas invariably had a substantial surplus to employ. This, indeed, was to be the major function of the bill market for roughly a hundred years—until, in fact, the amalgamation and branch movement in banking began to destroy the original localized system.

As will emerge clearly later, many different influences have contributed to the moulding of the discount market into its present form—a form which (until recently, at least) is unique among the world's money markets, which has been described over and over again as one of the main reasons for London's supremacy, and which has been assiduously copied, though with little success, by her rivals. Of these various influences, none is more important than the localization of country banking. It is no digression, therefore, to examine briefly the reason for that localization.

There is no doubt that almost the sole cause was the peculiarity of English banking legislation. In the early stages, no doubt, localization would have occurred under any system of law and regulation, for banking, like any other form of commerce, must have small beginnings in an old-established[1] country. But, in the absence of special impediments, one would have expected a steady enlargement of the sphere of operations; and such extension would have been stimulated by the very circumstance which so encouraged the brokers—the varied needs of particular districts. In England, however, there *were* special impediments, in the shape of the theory and practice of the Bank of England monopoly, which was protected by the prohibition of note-issuing by any other bank having more than six partners. This prohibition was embodied in the Acts of 1708 and 1742,[2] and had the greater force and effect by reason of a delusion, universal for many years, that it applied to *all* banking functions, and not solely to that of note-issuing. The delusion was natural, for, until the second quarter of the nineteenth century, note-issuing, practically speaking, *was* banking. Hence the country banks, being note-issuing institutions, had to remain small, and therefore localized, firms. The bill broker, as the vital connecting link, thus came to be an integral part in the banking machinery down to the latter part of the nineteenth century.[3]

The date at which country banking first developed is generally put at about 1740, although no exactitude can be claimed for it, as many of the first banks undoubtedly grew out of merchant houses, which only gradually forsook their merchanting for their banking functions.[4] The major development of independent country banks, however, occurred after 1750, for Burke[5]

[1] In the "young" countries, banking development followed different lines. For an excellent account of such development by joint-stock and chartered banks in the Dominions, see A. J. S. Baster, *Imperial Banks*.

[2] 7 Anne, c. 7, and 15 Geo. II, c. 13, s. 5.

[3] A similar argument will be found in Bagehot's evidence before the 1875 *Select Committee on Banks of Issue,* Minutes, Q. 7999. Bagehot, in a closely reasoned analysis, declared that the restrictions upon corporate note-issue "created" the money market (and also the English system of deposit banking), since localization was the cause of that "wonderful superfluity of money which we have in London".

[4] Powell traces the origin of a number of famous firms, including Smith, Payne & Smith's; Twining's; and Jones, Loyd. See also Martin, *Stories of Banks and Bankers*.

[5] *Regicide Peace*, Works, Vol. V, p. 291.

stated that in that year there were not twelve " bankers' shops " outside London. Under the stimulus of the industrial revolution, development from that time onwards was very rapid. Bisschop affirms that there were 150 by 1776 and 350 by 1790 [1]; while John Henton Tritton, a partner in the London house of Barclay & Co. (London banking agents for several country banks), stated before the Bullion Committee of 1810 [2] that in 1797 the number was 230; in 1808, over 600; and in 1810, 721.

There is good reason to believe that the beginning of bill broking on true nineteenth-century lines was contemporaneous with this very rapid growth of country banking: that bill brokers proper began to operate for banks shortly after 1750. Several such firms certainly existed in the last quarter of the century, for Thomas Richardson, detailing in 1810 [3] the operations of brokers as agents for country banks, declared that similar dealings were current before the suspension of cash payments (1797); while Samuel Gurney explained in 1848 [4] that Benjamin and Abraham Goldsmid acted as bill brokers before he did, *i.e.*, before 1807. This firm, established about the middle of the century by Aaron Goldsmid, a German Jew, at 25, Leman Street, and later continued by his two sons, apparently dropped bill dealing in its later years, for in 1792 the brothers removed to Capel Street, opposite the Bank, and during the Napoleonic Wars did a lucrative business in floating and jobbing in Government loans.[5] It is uncertain, too, whether, in its bill broking days, the firm dealt with country banks, although this seems quite probable, for Gurney always regarded his country banking connection as so vital a part of his business that otherwise it is unlikely that he would have considered Goldsmids' business as the same as his own.

Despite these early examples, it is clear that the development of country banking did not give any marked fillip to bill broking until after the " restriction " of cash payments at the Bank of England in 1797. Before that date, and probably for some short time afterwards, the London bankers invariably allowed interest on the balances left with them by the country banks

[1] *Rise of the London Money Market*, 1640–1826.

[2] *Select Committee on the High Price of Bullion*, 1810, Minutes, p. 141.

[3] See Bullion Committee, Minutes, p. 123.

[4] 1848 *Committee of House of Lords on Commercial Distress*, Minutes, QQ. 1337, 1344.

[5] For details of the Goldsmids, see Fox Bourne, *English Merchants*, Vol. II, p. 235; Jenks, *Migration of British Capital*, p. 19; Lawson, *History of Banking*; and early issues of the *London Directory*.

for whom they were agents. After the suspension, however, the inflation of the Bank of England note-issue,[1] the increase in the number of private issuers, and the credit excesses which they permitted, produced a fall in interest rates and created great difficulty in the employment of funds. The effect was especially marked on the price of Exchequer bills, then a favourite channel for the investment of surplus bank resources, with the result that the London bankers discontinued the allowance of interest on country bank balances.[2] This change was undoubtedly one of the most important early factors making for an increase in the activities of the bill brokers, for so long as interest was allowed, most country bankers were well content to leave the bulk of their surplus with their banking agents, thus avoiding the trouble and anxiety which the selection of securities involved. The cessation of London interest enforced a more energetic policy upon the country banks, and, as George Carr Glyn, a partner in the famous London bank of Glyn, Mills & Co.,[3] later explained, the country bankers began increasingly to employ their funds through a bill broker or in Government securities.[4]

Bill Broking in 1810

By 1810, as Richardson's evidence before the Bullion Committee [5] very plainly shows, the bill broker agency system for the country banks was widespread. Richardson's house [6] *received* bills " to a considerable amount from Lancashire in particular ", and these bills were sent for discount to Norfolk, Suffolk, Essex, Sussex and (small sums) to some parts of Yorkshire. For bankers in these districts his firm employed on discount (he had " no transactions whatever but which relate to discount ") no less a sum than between seven and eight millions annually, mainly for Norfolk houses, and had about £1,500,000 lent for them at

[1] See footnote to p. 27, *post*.

[2] The firm of Jones, Loyd & Co., however, continued to allow interest at 4 per cent.—See evidence of Lewis Loyd and Samuel Gurney before the 1819 *Commons' Committee on the Resumption of Cash Payments by the Bank*.

[3] The style of the firm in 1832 was Sir Richard Carr Glyn, Bart., Hallifax, Mills & Co., even then at 67, Lombard Street.

[4] See 1832 *Committee of Secrecy on the Renewal of the Bank of England Charter*, Minutes, p. 225.

[5] Minutes, p. 122.

[6] Richardson, Overend & Co.; see *post*, p. 17, *et seq*.

any one time. Richardson, Overend & Co.'s experience was not, however, typical, for they were by far the largest bill broker agents for the country banks. Richardson himself declared that there were several other houses conducting a similar country bank agency business in 1810, but considered that their operations for country banks would not amount to one-third of his own country bank turnover. It appears, then, that the bill market as a whole employed at that date about £10,000,000 annually for the country banks.

Country bank agency business, however, was still not the major portion of the London bill brokers' business. Richardson & Overend themselves had a large merchant connection; and, indeed, much of their country business was dependent upon it, for at that time the volume of bills sent to them from the "industrial" parts of the country fell substantially short of the demand for bills from other parts. But the firm had not the lion's share of the merchant business, for Richardson told the Committee that there were "a great many" who carried on "similar transactions for mercantile houses in London, and obtain money on discount from London bankers". He thought that these operations for merchants were in the aggregate "much greater" than those for country bankers; although there is some doubt whether he meant the total operations for country bankers (bill purchases as well as bill sales), or simply the aggregate of bills discounted *for* them. If he meant the former, it is clear that the aggregate annual turnover of the London brokers must have been substantially more than twenty millions, *i.e.*, substantially more than double the £10,000,000 which the market as a whole employed each year for the country bankers, plus an unknown (though certainly much smaller) turnover of bills which it received from the banks for discount. However, from the context of his statement, it seems more probable that he referred only to bills sent for discount, meaning that the brokers discounted many more bills for merchants than they did for country banks, in which case his estimate affords no precise guide to the aggregate operations of the market. Even so, it is unlikely that the figure would be very much *less* than twenty millions per annum, or five millions outstanding at any one time.

Despite the wide extent of their operations in 1810, the brokers' methods of transacting business had not then become crystallized into the standard form which they assumed a few years afterwards, and which continued almost down to the present time. Their brokerage charges, for example, were comparatively variable. Although the recognized charge was $\frac{1}{8}$ per cent. on a three months' bill, or $\frac{1}{2}$ per cent. per annum, levied on the person bringing the bill for discount, the rate was apparently raised whenever a higher charge could reasonably be justified by the exigencies of the moment. Indeed, Lewis Loyd, father of the more famous Samuel Jones Loyd, declared in 1819 [1] that he had heard of " no regular or fixed price " for brokerage, which he thought was fixed " arbitrarily " according to the prevailing value of money and the negotiability of the bills. Loyd, however, had never employed a bill broker, so that his evidence on this point may not be wholly reliable. At all events, the guiding principles which he cites hardly justify his claim that the brokers' charges were " arbitrary ". Nevertheless, there is no doubt that variations from the rule were fairly common. In the early years of the century, some country bankers even *paid* commission (usually $\frac{1}{4}$ per cent.) to brokers to procure bills for them,[2] and this (payment by the lender) was apparently the usual procedure by London *banker* agents when dealing with the country banks.

This practice had probably disappeared by 1810, at least so far as *broker* agents were concerned; it was certainly never followed by Richardson, Overend & Co. Thomas Richardson's evidence [3] on the point is worth quoting in full:

> Do you guarantee the bills you discount, and what is your charge per cent.?—No, we do not guarantee them; our charge is one-eighth per cent. brokerage upon the bill discounted; but we make no charge to the lender of the money.
>
> Do you consider that brokerage as a compensation for all the skill which you exercise in selecting bills, which you thus get discounted?—Yes, for selecting the bills, writing letters, and other trouble.
>
> Does the party who furnishes the money give you any kind of compensation?—None at all.
>
> Does he not consider you as agent, and in some degree responsible for the safety of the bills which you give him?—Not at all.
>
> Does he not prefer you on the score of his judging that you will give him good intelligence on the subject?—Yes, he relies upon us.
>
> Do you then exercise a discretion as to the probable safety of the bills?—Yes, if a bill comes to us which we conceive not to be safe, we return it.

---

[1] 1819 Commons' Committee, Minutes, p. 165. But *cf.* 1857 *Select Committee on the Bank Acts*, Minutes, QQ. 4420–6.

[2] *e.g.*, Gurney & Co., of Norwich; see p. 18, *post*.

[3] Bullion Committee, Minutes, p. 123.

But even though the brokers' commission may have been liable to variation, the discount rate, paradoxically, was not. Except for a few isolated instances before 1797, discount was at an invariable 5 per cent. throughout the country, and this fixed rate, the maximum allowed under the Usury Laws, prevailed for some years after 1810. Hudson Gurney, a partner in Gurney & Co. of Norwich, whose connection with Samuel Gurney, both in business and by birth, gave him a special knowledge of bill broking, told the Lords' "Resumption" Committee [1] that "there never was an instance" of discount by private banks at under 5 per cent. until 1817.[2] Samuel Gurney, asked by the Commons' Committee if lower rates had been charged before the war, replied that he had "heard it used to be done in former years".[3]

The question of discounting below the legal rate would, of course, have arisen but for the rigidity of the policy of the Bank of England, which invariably charged the maximum rate: Bank rate remained at 5 per cent. from 1746 until 1822. Quite unwittingly, the Bank helped the brokers in another respect—by the stringency of its discount regulations. This stringency could not harm the brokers, for they had never then known the privilege of discounting at the Bank; but it did seriously penalize the country bankers. First, the Bank would not take bills of more than 65 days' currency. Secondly—and this was the more onerous restriction—it always insisted that every bill should bear two *London* names, whereas the majority of bills never had more than one London name. These two provisions together ruled out more than two-thirds of the paper sent to London by the country banks.[4] Thus, despite the large resources of the Bank of England, the bill brokers and private bankers were able successfully to compete with the Bank's discount department.

The bill brokers, indeed, were actually employed in circumventing the Bank's regulations. It was the general practice of country banks to pay for bills remitted to them by brokers in short bills having three or four days to run, and payable in London, or in orders for cash on their London bankers. In some

[1] 1819 *Lords' Committee on the Resumption of Cash Payments by the Bank*, Minutes, p. 95.

[2] *Cf.* D. B. Chapman, before the 1857 Committee, QQ. 5258–70, and also Twells, QQ. 4420–6.

[3] 1819 Commons' Committee, Minutes, p. 178.

[4] See Richardson's evidence before Bullion Committee.

cases, however, the country bankers drew for longer dates (within the 65 days' limit) on their London agents, and remitted these bills to the brokers, who carried them to the Bank for discount on behalf of the country bank (the brokers presumably procuring an endorsement to make the second "London" name). This practice emerges clearly from the evidence of Whitmore and Pearse, respectively Governor and Deputy-Governor of the Bank in 1810; and their evidence also shows that the Bank tried to discourage these operations by rejecting such paper, whatever its "solidity", when it reached an "unreasonable height".[1] The principal method of discouragement was to place a limit upon the discounts by any one house, a form of credit control initiated, though in a somewhat different character, in 1795.[2] This rule, however, operated for merchants as well as for bankers, and in consequence diverted much discount business to private channels which might otherwise have gone to the Bank. As Richardson explained, the business of some houses arose principally at one period of the year, when they made their sales. Such houses thus could never get complete discount accommodation from the Bank at the period when they most needed it: they therefore resorted to the brokers, whose business benefited accordingly.

The London private bankers, on the other hand, generally relied upon the Bank of England. They were allowed to open accounts at the Bank some years before 1797, but it was not until the restriction of payments that they were allowed to discount in their own names.[3] Throughout the war they freely availed themselves of this privilege, keeping their reserves mainly in Exchequer bills, and re-discounting at the Bank whenever they were seriously short of cash.[4] In consequence, they tended to employ their resources much more closely than did the London banks of later years. They therefore had less need of the services of the bill brokers than had the country bankers, and were not usually willing to lend at call or for very short periods. But for this circumstance, bill brokers might have started to "run a book" rather earlier than they actually did.

[1] Bullion Committee, Minutes, pp. 119–20.

[2] See App. 14 of the 1797 Report of the *Committee of Secrecy on the Restriction of Payments by the Bank*, for the actual announcement posted at the Bank. (See also *post*, pp. 71–2.)

[3] 1797 Committee, Evidence of Giles and Bosanquet.

[4] See Glyn's evidence before 1848 Lords' Committee (Q. 1916); Gilbart, *Logic of Banking* (1865), p. 555; and Ellis Powell, *op. cit.*, p. 331.

Despite the absence of an organized call loan market, there is evidence to show that bill brokers even then did a " jobbing " business in money, as opposed to bills, as a side-line to their major operations. Richardson, declaring in 1810 that the London bankers kept about one-eighth less notes in proportion to their " payments " than they had eight years previously, attributed this economy of cash largely to " the more ready method in which they can borrow bank notes for the day, through the means of brokers ". Richardson himself was often an intermediary in such cases, " not unfrequently to the amount of twenty or thirty thousand pounds a day ", and remarked that " from our general intercourse with them, we can borrow of one to pay the other at an hour's notice ".

Discount Rates and the Usury Laws

At times, the services of the brokers in this respect must have been of very great value to the bankers, for in 1810 the Bank had not developed even the rudiments of an " open market " stabilizing policy, and sudden spasms of monetary stringency were frequent. These were naturally most severe when tax-payments were flowing in to the Bank just before the quarterly payments of the Government dividends. At such periods in particular, both bankers and bill brokers were greatly handicapped in their business by the Usury Laws, especially as the *normal* market rate was also the maximum rate. This meant that the rate could not be raised to attract fresh lenders without breaking the law; and while many persons in trade undoubtedly paid little heed to the legal rate in difficult times, it seems that the bill brokers were generally very circumspect. London bankers were often able to evade the law by such devices as selling stock for cash and buying it back for " time " (generally at exorbitant rates),[1] but no such loop-holes were open to a broker with bills to sell for a client.. All he could do was to retain the bills until the pressure had passed, meanwhile running the risk of gravely offending, as well as inconveniencing, his customers. The following letter, written by Hudson Gurney

[1] One interesting method, adopted by country bankers, was thus described by Hudson Gurney in 1814: " Sneaths have hit upon one new scheme of banking, viz., buying corn themselves at higher than market price, paying in their own notes, and selling said corn in London for what it would fetch, to procure the ready." (See Bidwell, *Annals of an East Anglian Bank*, pp. 101–7.) And *cf. post*, p. 29.

to Simon Martin (both of Gurney & Co.) on December 11, 1812, is illuminating :

> Richardson, Overend & Co. are not distressed *other than in mind*, which they seem greatly, as they have £100,000 of the very primest paper lying in their cases which they can get no money for anywhere, all are so poor, and they greatly fear losing their best connections from not being able to keep the channel open.[1]

The inevitable effect of the Usury Laws was, indeed, to check the volume of accommodation obtainable during a pressure, and at the same time to *increase* the rates of interest charged. So long as the rate of interest is free, it is tolerably certain that a rise in the discount rate will always attract discounters from somewhere, and will also check the offerings (if not also the creation) of bills. With a controlled rate, however, the only course open to the law-abiding lender, once demands for loans exceeded his ability to meet them, was to refuse accommodation altogether, irrespective of the standing of the customer and the quality of the paper which he had to offer. The result was that merchants, when unable to secure assistance through the bankers or bill brokers, sought help from less reputable lenders, who were not merely enabled thereby to dictate their own extortionate terms, but could argue with some force that they merited a liberal compensation for the risks they ran of incurring the considerable penalties imposed by the law. This vicious operation of the usury legislation is vouched for over and over again by contemporary commentators, while even in periods of comparative ease in money one reads frequently of short spells of stringency in which it was very difficult, and sometimes impossible, to secure cash for " even the most unexceptionable " bills.

Another source of difficulty at this time, and indeed throughout the " Restriction " period, arose from the dubious credit to which over-issue had reduced many bankers. Bank failures were so alarmingly frequent that each successive pressure brought a violent revulsion from all bank acceptances, whether those of issuers or not. Hudson Gurney's letters, again, give a graphic picture. In August, 1812, he wrote :

> On the whole, there is a thorough want of confidence in bankers in Town, and all are so poor, they cannot get a bill discounted with a day to run, and all the bill brokers, R. O. & Co. excepted, quite fast, the payments of Government and the general sinking of

[1] Bidwell, *op. cit.*

> balances the supposed causes; those who have money are all buying stock, which has been the reason of the funds' rise, and those who come to discount to Richardson, Overend & Co. throw out the bankers' acceptances as assiduously as they used to pick them out.[1]

A few days later he remarked that "the day of grievous pressure is on the London bankers, whose acceptances are in the worst credit of any kind of paper . . . this they wish not to be spoken of, as they think that if one or two more go . . . the consequences will be incalculable . . . many great houses are fighting through from day to day".

The bill broker's lot in such conditions was hardly enviable, but despite these various handicaps his importance in the financial machine steadily increased. The Bullion Report, referring to the increased operations of brokers in the four or five years before 1810, pointed out that the improved discount facilities available in London had tended to increase the business of the country manufacturer, by enabling him to turn over his capital more quickly[2]; and it also instanced the economy in London bankers' cash, already mentioned, as one of the beneficial results of the new facilities which the brokers afforded. Again, the marked decrease in losses sustained on bills by country bankers (which had been very heavy before the Restriction) was attributed to the work of the bill brokers. Richardson thought that "many of the country bankers have made losses by taking bills themselves; but those who do their business in London by means of a broker who understands it, have but few losses".[3] This, he firmly believed, was the sole reason for the improvement. He was, of course, commending his own business, but he was able to say that on bills procured by his house there had been no losses "except to a very small amount indeed". That this was no idle boast was confirmed by the independent and unsolicited testimony of Richardson's most important clients.[4]

[1] Bidwell, *op. cit.*

[2] Discount accommodation generally cost the country manufacturer 6 or 6½ per cent. per annum—5 per cent. for discount, ½ per cent. for brokerage, and ½ or 1 per cent. for obtaining the bill on the banker in London (in effect, an acceptance commission). See Bullion Report, pp. 26–7.

[3] Bullion Committee, Minutes, p. 124.

[4] Hudson Gurney, arguing in 1813 that paper "fortified at both ends, and plaistered behind" (commercial bills with many endorsements)

By the time of the Bullion Report, therefore, the foundations of the modern Bill Market had been firmly laid. The subsequent half-century was destined to witness an enormous expansion, and the rise of one firm—Richardson's own—to an eminence unrivalled even by the great discount houses of to-day. These developments, however, apart from the vital transition from pure broking to dealing, were mainly a question of the scale of operations, and not of fundamental changes in the nature of the business itself. Bill broking proper, even in Bagehot's time, was essentially the same operation as that originally performed by its outstanding pioneer—Thomas Richardson.

The origin of Richardson's house is therefore worth special study, not merely because of the great importance it assumed in later years,[1] but because its early history epitomizes the whole evolution of the market in its first fifty years or so. It also sheds a flood of light upon the operations of the country bankers. No apology is needed, then, for the minor repetitions which must arise in an attempt to trace the story in some detail.

The Origin of Overend, Gurney and Co.

The foundation of the bill broking firm which ultimately became the famous house of Overend, Gurney & Co. is directly traceable to the evolution of a family merchanting business in the wool trade into a large and powerful country banking business—that of Gurney & Co. of Norwich. The Gurneys, one of the oldest families in the kingdom, tracing their descent from Hugh de Gournay, a Norman nobleman who came to England with William the Conqueror and was granted land in Norfolk, had for centuries conducted a prosperous business in the East Anglian wool trade.[2] From very early times, and certainly from the reign of James I, they had combined banking with merchanting functions, first by taking deposits from, and making loans to, friends and persons with whom they were connected in trade, and later as capitalist "entrepreneurs" of the char-

was better than Exchequer bills, pointed out to his partners that of £1,800,000 currently employed in bills through Richardson, only £12,000 had been returned unpaid. (The question of holding Exchequer bills had arisen from the difficulty of negotiating bank paper.) (See Bidwell, *op. cit.*, pp. 104–8.)

[1] As the famous house of Overend, Gurney & Co.

[2] See Fox Bourne, *op. cit.*, pp. 340, 356–64.

acteristic " domestic system " type. This aspect of their operations, as well as the great importance of the family in East Anglia, is very clearly brought out in the following extract:

> The collecting of yarns from . . . manufacturers of the East of England and holding them in stock to supply those who are employed in weaving . . . was a very lucrative business, and we deliberately question whether the Gurneys did not at one time derive from it an annual income greater than is obtained by any bank in the Island of Great Britain. . . . In the course of dealing with the worsted spinners for their yarn, this family began to supply them with cash to pay the wages of labour, and enable them to carry on their operations in business. Out of these circumstances arose the great banking operations of this family, who in London and the country may now be described as exercising an influence and a power inferior to that of no banking establishment in Great Britain, that of the Bank of England alone excepted.[1]

It was not until 1775, however, that a separate banking business was established, when the brothers, John and Henry Gurney, both strict Quakers, founded the Norwich and Norfolk Bank.[2] This bank, and possibly the merchanting house before it, was unable to employ all its resources locally, and accordingly sought the help of one Joseph Smith, a London wool factor whose firm had for years had trade connections with the Gurneys. Smith, from the nature of his business, was in a position to obtain many bills of exchange, mainly drawn by the wool trade, and these he furnished to the Norwich bank on payment of a commission of $\frac{1}{4}$ per cent. on the amounts involved. And he apparently remained the main channel through which the Gurneys obtained their bills for at least a quarter of a century.

Meanwhile, his financial business proved so prosperous that he gradually dropped wool-dealing and began bill broking proper. The firm first appears in the list of London bankers in 1799, as Joseph Smith & Co., of 60, Old Broad Street, and, two years later, as Smith & Holt.[3] The business was not, however, run

[1] *Circular to Bankers*, October 5, 1838.

[2] The name was changed in 1779 to Richard, Bartlett & Joseph Gurney on the death of John Gurney (Henry had died in 1777) and the family name remained prominent in the title until the bank was absorbed by Barclays in 1896.

[3] Smith died about 1818, but William Holt continued the business until 1824, when it became Drewett & Fowler, which amalgamated in 1852 with Barnard & Co., later, Dimsdale, Drewett, Fowler & Barnard.

on the usual lines. Influenced by his connection with Gurneys', which had begun before there was any recognized course of dealing by bill brokers, Smith invariably regarded himself as the agent for the lenders, and accordingly looked to them for commission.

This peculiarity is important, for it was the direct cause of the foundation of the first " true " bill broking firm. In 1802, Thomas Richardson, one of Smith & Holt's clerks, drew his employers' attention to the fact that it was customary for merchants in London who had bills for discount to pay brokerage to the bill brokers who secured accommodation for them. This, he suggested, would be a better method of business for Smith & Holt, for not only would their country bank connections, relieved of the commission, probably take more bills, but the fact that money was then scarce would enable the change to be made with the minimum of offence to those who supplied the bills. This suggestion did not appeal to Smith & Holt, and, upon their refusal to change their mode of dealing, Richardson elected to leave the firm and start a bill broking business of his own on the new principle. He was already known to the Gurneys, and promptly wrote to them to inquire whether he might send bills to them for discount, *without* the charge of commission. Gurneys', satisfied from Richardson's account of the circumstances of his resignation that there had been no bad blood between him and his late employers, began to share their business between the two firms. Thus began the largest discount business of the first half of the nineteenth century.

Richardson's business was quite legitimate, but, so far as the Gurney connection was concerned, he was definitely undercutting Smith & Holt. Joseph Smith was naturally annoyed, and voiced his grievance to the Norwich bank, tactlessly insinuating that the Gurneys had inspired Richardson's resignation. This, however, failed to ruffle the partners of the bank, whose honesty and kindliness were well known, and they sent the following courteous reply,[1] dated June 14, 1803:

JOSEPH SMITH—

Esteemed Friend,—The subject of thy letter has occupied our serious consideration, and no part of it has struck us with more surprise and pain than that it should be possible for thee to entertain of us the opinion that we should be capable of so dishonourable a conduct as to prepare the mind of Thos. Richardson for leaving

---

[1] Quoted by Matthews and Tuke, *History of Barclays Bank*, p. 110.

his situation with thee and adopting his present plans ; we entirely disclaim so unworthy a conduct ; the opposite was the fact, for nothing ever passed from us but what was calculated to induce him to retain his situation.

This, however, was not enough for Smith & Holt, who, fearing that they might lose their most valuable connection, and possibly other business too—should Gurneys' elect to "push" Richardson—suggested that his judgment of bills might not be wholly dependable. These fears, it seems, were unfounded, for Gurneys' again poured oil on the troubled waters by arranging that all bills supplied by Richardson should first be submitted to and approved by Smith & Holt. The arrangement was embodied in a letter to Smith dated June 22, when Gurneys' wrote :

> . . . to remove the difficulties thee and thy partner seem to apprehend with regard to T. R.'s application as *our friend.* In the first place, we shall introduce him only in the character of one who may offer good bills and such as you exclusively shall approve, submitting them to every scrutiny you think reasonable, and we trust we can depend that such scrutiny will not be influenced by other motives than simply to ascertain the credit of the paper, for you may depend on our not listening to captious complaints against you, but we rely still more upon your fears being groundless, or nearly so, from the complexion of the paper Richardson has sent us.[1]

Gurneys', it will be seen, came out of the tussle very satisfactorily, for they had arranged without any additional expense that two independent firms should overlook their paper, and for every bill that they received from Richardson (for which they paid no commission) Smith & Holt's reputation was just as much at stake as Richardson's. Moreover, it was certain that the older firm, in their desire to protect their connection with Norwich, would scrutinize Richardson's bills at least as carefully as they did their own, for they would naturally wish to reject as many of the former as possible.

Richardson, however, must have given them but few opportunities for rejection, for his business with Gurney & Co. increased steadily. Two years later—in 1805—he was joined by one John Overend,[2] and the style of the firm became Richardson,

[1] Bidwell, *op. cit.*, p. 80. A similar letter, dated June 25, was sent to Richardson.

[2] According to Gilbart (*op. cit.*, p. 553), Overend, too, had been a clerk in Smith & Holt, and it is suggested that it was he who was responsible for Smith's turning bill broker in the first instance. On this point, however, Gilbart is almost certainly unreliable, for he errs when he gives the date of Overend's entry as 1807, and also when he

Overend & Co.[1] Shortly afterwards, the partners sought to increase their business by an ingenious scheme to induce Gurneys' to take more of their bills. This took the form of a proposal that if the Norwich house would instruct their London agents (apparently Smith & Holt, and possibly also Barclay, Tritton & Bevan) to discount a certain number of bills on their behalf for Richardson, Overend & Co., the latter firm would allow to Gurneys' a part of the commission received from the sellers of the bills. The offer was attractive, for while Gurneys' had always *paid* Smith & Holt for procuring bills, they were now offered bills not merely without charge (as Richardson had done previously) but with a payment for their services in taking them. However, the Gurneys' scrupulous honesty led them to question the transaction on the grounds that it might infringe the Usury Laws, for discount rates, as already noted, were then always at the legal maximum of 5 per cent. Their suspicions were confirmed by Counsel's opinion, which declared :

> . . . Such a transaction would undoubtedly be usurious. Though the holder of a bill payable at a future date may properly pay to *any person* a recompense under the name of brokerage, commission or any other name, for his time and labour in procuring the bill to be discounted ; yet, if any part of such recompense, through any channel, or by any contrivance, gets into the pocket of the person discounting the bill at five per cent., such part, however small, will make the transaction usurious.[2]

This opinion was a sufficient warning to the Gurneys, but the matter did not end there, for Richardson's proposal had brought home to them that their earlier mode of dealing had been needlessly expensive, and had set them thinking of possible alternative schemes for saving commission. Counsel was next presented with a proposition which differed from the first only in form : Richardson, Overend & Co. were to open an account current with Gurneys' by remitting bills to them (these to be paid for by an equal amount, less discount, of return orders on London), and at the settlement of the account the bill brokers were to be

states that Richardson was originally a clerk in Smith, Wright & Gray (later Esdaile & Co.). Somewhat similar accounts of the early years of the firm were given by the *Economist* (1858, p. 305) and by Martin, *op. cit.*, (1865), but it is probable that both of these were based on Gilbart.

[1] About this time, the firm moved from 6, White Lion Court to 14, Birchin Lane. In 1808 there was a further change, to 23, Lombard Street. (And see, *post*, p. 26 *n.*)

[2] Cited by Bidwell, *op. cit.*, p. 84.

charged a commission of $\frac{1}{8}$ per cent. This scheme, needless to say, Counsel dismissed as emphatically, and for the same reasons, as he had disposed of the first.

Even then Gurneys' were not satisfied. If they themselves could not participate in the commission, it was clear that their best course was to concentrate their business with the firm which charged commission only to the sellers of bills, *i.e.*, Richardson, Overend & Co., but this, it appears, they were unwilling to do if another equally profitable method could be found. Their reticence was presumably due to consideration for their lengthy connection [1] with Joseph Smith, and possibly also to a feeling that their conduct towards him might be judged less honourable than their business dealings ordinarily were. At all events, Counsel was confronted with yet another scheme, suggesting that the London agents, " bankers in a limited way ", should in sending bills to the country be remunerated by charging only the sellers of bills, as a bill broker would do. Even this suggestion was discouraged by Counsel, for although he declared that " as the proposition is now put " it could not subject the London agents to prosecution for usury, and agreed that bankers could also act as brokers, he pointed out that " the circumstance of a party so discounting a bill being by trade a banker, might, and probably would, have much weight in impressing a jury with a belief that the defendants did not act as *bona fide* brokers without further interest in the discount ".[2]

This third opinion, by convincing Gurneys' at last that there was no legitimate way of continuing business with Smith & Holt except upon the original expensive terms, apparently turned the scale definitely in favour of Richardson, Overend & Co. Gurneys' made no further attempt to secure a share of the commission, and from that time, or shortly after, the proportion of their discount business transacted by the new London firm steadily increased. As an isolated fact, Gurneys' decision may seem a mere trifling incident in the everyday conduct of banking affairs. Actually, it proved to be of fundamental importance in the history of the bill market, for Gurneys' substantial business was undoubtedly the major, if not the sole, cause of the rapid and successful growth of Richardson, Overend & Co. : without such a buttress the firm might never have risen beyond the level of

[1] Gurneys' desire to avoid offence to Smith was clearly shown in their correspondence with Richardson when they first agreed to take his bills. (See Bidwell, *op. cit.*, p. 80.)

[2] Bidwell, *op. cit.*, p. 84.

mediocrity. Seven years later the partners admitted their indebtedness in the plainest terms. In a letter to Gurneys' they wrote [1]:

> We must allow that our connection with your house has been the great means of establishing us and making us what we now are, and of giving us far greater power and command of money than any other house in the line, or even in London.

Samuel Gurney Comes to London

It was not, however, until 1807 that the Gurney family was represented in the London firm. In 1802, John Gurney, a partner at Norwich, had sent his son, Samuel Gurney, to join the banking and tea-importing business of Joseph Fry (John Gurney's brother-in-law) at St. Mildred's Court.[2] The ability which was later to make the young clerk as familiar and respected a figure in the City as Nathan Rothschild was quickly apparent: his cousin, who afterwards became his biographer, declared of his entry to the firm that " he took to business and liked it; in the counting-room he was exceedingly amiable and cheerful, and was liked and beloved by the whole establishment ".[3] Five years later, his apprenticeship served, he was introduced by his father to the bill broking firm, after a searching investigation of its business. The inquiry was evidently completely satisfactory, for not only Samuel Gurney, but also his brother John, shortly became partners, although John continued to spend the greater part of his time at Lynn, apparently seeking Norfolk bills for the firm, and arranging return remittances from Norwich.

The effect of this infusion of Gurney blood is plainly seen in the growing proportion of the bank's business which passed to the new partnership, which by August, 1808, was supplying no less than 42 per cent. (and Smith & Holt the balance) of Gurneys' London-acquired portfolio, including that of its branches.[4] By the middle of the following year, despite an expansion of the

[1] *Ibid.*, p. 78.

[2] This firm first appears in the list of London bankers in 1807, and (later as Fry's & Chapman) conducted a noteworthy banking business with Quakers. Its stoppage in 1828 gave Lewis Loyd, senior partner of Jones, Loyd & Co., the opportunity for an amusing quip: when a Quaker client transferred his account to the more sophisticated house, Loyd remarked, " You are right, Friend; it is wiser to place thy money with a rich sinner than with a poor saint." (See Hilton Price, *Handbook of London Bankers*, p. 62.)

[3] *Memorials of Samuel Gurney*, by Mrs. T. Geldart.

[4] See Bidwell, *op. cit.*, p. 88.

portfolio from under £1,100,000 to over £1,450,000, Richardson, Overend & Co. was transacting the whole of the business. As an indication of the great dependence of country banks of this type upon the London market for employment of their funds, it is worth noting that at this date Gurneys' deposit and other liabilities, excluding those of their (comparatively small) branches, were about £1,000,000, showing that local assets, apart from cash, must have been very small.

Despite the precautions which had been taken, in 1809 the Usury Laws again obtruded themselves in the relationships between the two houses. John Gurney, senior, died, and John Gurney, junior, was to succeed him as partner at Norwich. The question therefore arose whether the son could legitimately continue as partner of Richardson, Overend & Co. Counsel was again called in, and gave his opinion that there would be no infringement of the Usury Laws by John's partnership both in the bill broking and in the banking house, provided that his share of the brokerage were " kept to his separate use ", and was not " carried into account with his banking partners in the Norwich house ".[1] Fortified by this opinion, John became a partner in both houses, but his health failed after the premature death of his wife in 1808, and he soon relinquished his connection with the London firm.[2] This may explain why by 1813, if not earlier, Gurneys' *as a firm* were sharing directly in the profits of the bill broking business. The participation is shown in the statement of accounts transmitted by Richardson, Overend & Co. to Gurneys' in 1814.[3]

This statement, reproduced on the succeeding page, is peculiarly interesting, for it not only shows that even at this early stage bill broking was a distinctly lucrative business, but affords a close guide to the firm's turnover. On the assumption that the average currency of bills discounted by Richardson, Overend & Co. was three months, carrying brokerage of $\frac{1}{8}$ per cent. (actual), their turnover of bills in 1813 must have been over £17,500,000. This is a surprising figure, for, only three years earlier, the firm's annual employment of money of country bankers was only about seven or eight millions, and it is unlikely that at this date the connection with merchant houses would have brought the aggregate turnover to much more than ten millions.

[1] Bidwell quotes all of these various opinions in full.

[2] John Gurney died in 1815, when Samuel Gurney succeeded him as partner at Norwich, though he never resided there.

[3] Bidwell, *op. cit.*, p. 109.

LONDON, *4th Mo.* 6, 1814.

GURNEYS & Co.

We annex a short statement of our Profit and Loss Account for this year, and credit you £5,500 accordingly, and are

Your assured Friends,

RICHARDSON, OVEREND & Co.

	£	*s.*	*d.*
To expenses for the year	1,582	17	10
T. Richardson	6,000	0	0
Jno. Overend	6,000	0	0
S. Gurney	5,500	0	0
Gurneys	5,500	0	0
Reserved for expenses now due, including property duty	3,729	19	11
	£28,312	17	9

	£	*s.*	*d.*
By amount of Commission	22,198	7	3
By Noble Hunt on Woolffs & Co., paid in full	5,000	0	0
By profit on interest account	1,114	10	6
	£28,312	17	9

Another noteworthy point in the statement is the writing-back of the £5,000 provision which had clearly been made in a previous year for a dishonoured bill, " Noble Hunt on Woolffs & Co ", the loss on which had been made good in full in the year covered by the accounts. The significance of this is that it strongly suggests that the firm was already acting in a small way as dealers, and not merely brokers, despite subsequent assertions by its partners [1] that they conducted a purely agency business until the late 'twenties. The reason for this supposition is that a broker *qua* broker, who at law is only a " transferor by delivery ",[2] would suffer no loss if a bill which had passed through his hands were dishonoured; the loss would fall wholly on the buyers of the bill.[3] It is, of course, possible that the firm undertook to

[1] Chapman's Evidence before 1857 Committee, see *post*, p. 64.

[2] A " transferor by delivery " is one who passes on a bill without endorsing it, and who, therefore, cannot be a party to it. He cannot in consequence be liable *on the bill*, although he warrants that it is " what it purports to be " (*i.e.*, a valid bill), and thus is liable in the event of prior forgery. In the case in question, forgery is improbable, for if forgery had occurred the phrase, on recovery of the money, would hardly have been " *paid* " in full.

[3] See *ante*, p. 11.

shoulder the loss in some special case, but the considerable sum earned on "Interest Account" also points to a business other than pure brokerage. Even the profits from the incidental "money-jobbing" business already mentioned (see p. 14) ought properly to have been included as commission, and not as interest, if the firm were in this respect acting as pure intermediaries, and not as principals borrowing and lending on their own behalf. Nevertheless, for practical purposes, there is no doubt that bill broking proper accounted for virtually the whole of the firm's operations for rather more than a decade after this date.[1] And, whatever the precise nature of its business in 1813, it is equally clear that by then the house had successfully borne all the difficulties of adolescence, and had firmly established itself as by far the biggest bill broking firm of the day—a supremacy it was to retain for another fifty years.[2] For the greater part of that period, at least until shortly before Samuel Gurney's death in 1856, it was to be renowned almost as much for the scrupulous honesty and straightforwardness of its dealings as for their extent and importance. Great wealth never turned Samuel Gurney's head, and never led him to forget the daily observance of the principles of his religious creed. "He is the only man I have seen," declared the Rev. Henry Tracey, "who has passed through the burning fiery furnace without the smell of it in some way hanging about his garments."

Rapid Spread of the Bill Broker System, 1810–25

The period after 1810, as Richardson, Overend & Co.'s 1814 accounts indicated, witnessed a marked expansion of bill market business, both with country banks and with merchants. Increased business from the former arose partly from the continued growth in their number, which reached 940 in 1814; but the main influence was undoubtedly the great expansion of their note

[1] Richardson estimated the annual turnover at £20,000,000 in 1823, remarking that his business was "very much beyond" that of any of his competitors. (See his evidence before the Enquiry into the Law of Pledges and Loans on the Security of Goods, cited by Ricardo, in his *Plan for the Establishment of a National Bank* (1824).)

[2] The name "Overend, Gurney & Co." was not adopted until 1827, after the death of Thomas Richardson. The address was then 23, Lombard Street, but some six years later was changed to 65, Lombard Street, the famous site at the corner of Birchin Lane and Lombard Street which the firm occupied until its collapse in 1866. For many years the firm was known in the City as the "Corner House".

issues. In addition, a growing appreciation of the facilities afforded by the "new" bill brokers was leading many banks to substitute bills for Government securities (and other, less desirable, assets) as the principal means of employing their surplus funds.[1] Thus the volume of money sent to the brokers rose even more rapidly than did banking resources as a whole. Moreover, with the advance of industrialization, and the consequent spread of banking in the industrial areas, country bankers were beginning to regard the bill market not only as a channel for the investment of money (as most had done in 1810), but also as a means of procuring it; and after 1810 re-discounting through brokers became increasingly important. This tendency was of great value to the brokers, for it meant that they could always be certain of a supply of bills in bulk, instead of being compelled to seek them in small quantities from among hundreds of individual merchants.

Dealings with merchants and industrialists, however, also expanded markedly, and the bill brokers began to establish direct connections in all the principal industrial districts. This movement, it seems, was in the first place due not so much to the enterprise of the brokers themselves as to the rigidity of the country bankers' discount policy. These banks maintained an almost invariable rule of discounting for local customers at 5 per cent., whatever the condition of the London market, and this practice also applied to Scotland. Until about 1817, the same held good for the London bankers and bill brokers, but after the Peace the over-issue of notes[2] and the general credit inflation produced a great glut of money, and London private discounters were compelled to discount below 5 per cent. Traders and manufacturers in the "great manufacturing and mining districts" were not slow to observe the differential, and thus began to send their bills direct to Lombard Street,[3] which had already become the recognized home of the discount market.

[1] See Hudson Gurney before 1819 Lords' Committee, Minutes, p. 94.

[2] At the time of the suspension of cash payments in 1797, the Banks' note issue was below £10 millions; by 1800 it had reached £16·8 millions, and by 1810 it was around £25 millions. The total remained between £23 and £25 millions until the middle of 1814, when it rose rapidly to over £28 millions. A further three years of comparative stability then occurred, but in 1817 there was a steep rise to £29·5 millions. The ensuing five years saw a moderately steady fall, as the holding of Public securities declined, until by 1822 the circulation was back to £17·5 millions. Detailed figures are to be found in the appendices to the Report of the 1832 Committee.

[3] *Cf. Economist*, 1858, p. 305

Samuel Gurney stated in 1819 [1] that his business had " very much increased since the Peace ", and, when asked whether the expansion had resulted from larger business with country bank connections or from " the general increase in discounts ", declared that both factors had contributed; but there is no doubt that the currency inflation was the major influence. " With the increased circulation," he said, " we got a very extensive business indeed ", complaining that money became so abundant that bills had to be taken at 4½ per cent. Even at that almost unprecedented [2] rate the volume of bills offered was insufficient to meet the demand, and Gurney had unwillingly to employ part of his principals' money in " fluctuating Government securities ", which previously he had resolutely shunned. The plethora, he states, was such that " all the great bankers and dealers in money in the country found great difficulty in using their money at all; they had such an abundance of bank notes always in their drawers, they could not use them ".

As Bank rate remained throughout at 5 per cent., the fall in market rate diverted a large part of the Bank of England's discounts to private discounters. During the Restriction period, the Bank's bill portfolio had risen very rapidly to wholly abnormal figures, reaching a peak in the third quarter of 1810, when its quarterly average of £21,482,400 was actually the highest for the whole period from 1797 to 1831, notwithstanding the enormous accommodation granted during the 1825 crisis. That figure, however, was quite exceptional, and there had followed a decline to under £12 millions in 1814, with a recovery to £16·5 millions by the third quarter of 1815. From that time onwards, the effect of the inflation and of the consequent competition from private discounters was very marked, for in every quarter throughout 1816 and 1817 the average dropped quickly, reaching only £2,541,200 at the end of the second year, at which level it remained fairly constant until the middle of 1818.[3] During the whole of this period, therefore, many millions of discounts which for years had gone to the Bank were being placed through the

[1] Evidence before 1819 Commons' Committee.

[2] Gurney had " heard " of lower rates than 5 per cent. before the war.

[3] 1832 Committee, App. 56 and 57. The actual figures from 1816 to 1819 are as follows:

	Jan.–March.	April–June.	July–Sept.	Oct.–Dec.
1816 . . .	£14,315,900	£13,380,400	£10,569,400	£7,399,800
1817 . . .	5,823,500	4,148,300	3,329,300	2,541,200
1818 . . .	2,976,900	2,847,800	4,610,400	6,865,700
1819 . . .	8,363,700	6,632,300	6,021,600	5,042,200

discount market proper.[1] In such circumstances, the increase in Richardson's business after the Peace is hardly surprising, but some may wonder at the relative scarcity of bills which he found so troublesome. The explanation is to be found mainly, though not wholly, in the fact that the decline in the Bank's bill portfolio was not at once fully reflected in its *note issue*, which, though it declined appreciably in 1818, did not begin to fall rapidly until the latter part of 1819. Thus Gurney stated in the first half of 1819 that "when there was a large circulation a year since, we were very glad in our business to discount bills for our friends at 4½ per cent. interest; consequently nobody would, without a charge of commission, send them to the Bank, and pay them 5 per cent." In such cases, he declared, other discounters would always be served before the Bank of England.

Towards the end of 1818, however, the reduction of Bank of England credit began to have its effect on the discount market, and in the ensuing nine months Gurney's turnover was reduced by one-fifth or one-sixth, and he was satisfied that other bill brokers had suffered at least as serious a contraction. Indeed, by the middle of 1819, he was complaining of a shortage, not of bills, but of money, which he attributed to the inadequacy of the circulation:

> . . . when I am in that situation in my business, that if I want to borrow £10,000 till the following day (a situation, *from the wants of others*, which it is my business to supply, I am frequently placed in) I cannot do it; that there is not a banking house in London that will part with £10,000 till the following day; then I say that there is too little of the circulating medium in the city; this has been the case several times lately. . . .[2]

Actually, he explained, he had been handicapped in his efforts to place all his bills at 5 per cent. by the ability of bankers to obtain more than the legal rate by lending on stock "in what is called continuation"; *i.e.*, by the purchase of stock for cash with an obligation upon the seller to buy back in the future at an inflated price. Gurney's comments on this point are interesting in that they indicate that even at that time the discount market was recognized as a distinct entity in the money market, entirely separate from the other principal component, the stock market. It is also worth noting that Gurney did not fall into the error, not infrequently current even to-day, of assuming that, because

[1] See 1819 Lords' Committee, Report, pp. 9–10.
[2] 1819 Commons' Committee, Minutes, p. 173.

the money supply in Lombard Street is diminished, the real supply of bank credit must also be reduced:

> . . . it should be recollected that the circulating medium in the city is in the hands of the bankers, and though there is that operation [loans on stock], it does not diminish or increase the circulation at all; they equally have it in their own hands in the afternoon, some may have it, though others may part with it; it is an operation by which large sums are drawn from the market in which I am, into the stock market.

Which goes to prove that the short loan fund, though much smaller in 1819 than it now is, was then scarcely less volatile, even though "call" loans in the modern sense were almost unknown. It may be noted in this connection that, a few years previously, the mobility of funds in the market had been increased by a change of practice on the part of the Bank, which formerly had always required bills which it held on other London bankers to be paid in its own notes, and before twelve o'clock on each day. To assist the private bankers, the Bank postponed its demands until between three and four o'clock, and also intimated that it would accept payment in drafts on itself.[1] This change, as John Smith, a London banker, explained to the 1819 Committee,[2] was of "very material importance" to the bankers, and also produced an appreciable economy of cash.

Widespread Use of the Domestic Bill

Such technical details as these are, perhaps, of little significance in themselves, but they indicate plainly that the London money market was rapidly becoming a well-organized and clearly defined unit in the financial system. Its importance, even at this early stage, was to a great extent due to the popularity of the bill of exchange as an instrument of internal credit. Both the 1810 and the 1819 Enquiries, and a mass of contemporary pamphlets and books, afford abundant evidence of the high esteem in which the bill was held. The growing preference for bills as a channel for the investment of bank funds has already been mentioned. But bills acquired through a bill broker or London agent by no means accounted for the whole of a banker's bill portfolio. The

[1] These drafts were issued by the Bank to those whose bills it had discounted, the discounter then paying them into his account with a London banker.

[2] 1819 Commons' Committee, Minutes, p. 221.

bill was, in fact, the main instrument of bank accommodation: bank loans, although fairly common, were in most districts always much smaller than local discounts, while (except in Scotland) the overdraft system was practically unknown. Nor was there any demand for such facilities (the principal merit of which is that they enable the borrower to pay cash for his purchases), for in most industrial districts the standard business "terms" were for payment by bill at a given date—the period varying according to the district and the trade.

From this it will be appreciated that one of the main functions of the local banker was to turn his customer's bills into cash, or, alternatively, to give him usance drafts on London in exchange. And as the local bills were necessarily often drawn for very small sums, a substantial country banker would receive hundreds in the course of a day. Much of this paper, from its nature, was not negotiable except within a few miles of the district in which it was drawn (and/or accepted), unless backed by the banker's endorsement, when it could generally be placed in the London market. In districts where the parties were known, however, the bills passed from hand to hand with the freedom of currency. Indeed, they *were* currency, and formed the recognized mode of payment at many fairs and market towns, provided that they complied with the customary requirements of each place.[1]

In Lancashire, in fact, they for many years formed by far the greater part—in Lewis Loyd's opinion, at least 90 per cent.—of the circulation, and such was the preference for them that local bankers refrained from issuing notes. One consequence of this was that Bank of England notes enjoyed a larger circulation and better credit in Lancashire than in most other country districts, for they were required for such purposes as wage-payments. The following examples of the use of bills generally, given by Henry Thornton in 1802,[2] may be regarded as representative:

> They not only spare the use of ready money, they also occupy its place in many cases. Let us imagine a farmer in the country to discharge a debt of £10 to his neighbouring grocer, by giving him a bill for that sum, drawn on his corn factor in London, for

---

[1] Lewis Loyd, who had seen bills with 120 endorsements, declared that it was customary for purchasers to go to market with bills ready drawn in their favour (generally by the local banks on their London agents, at up to 2 months' date), often for round amounts. (1819 Lords' Committee, Minutes, QQ. 11–16.)

[2] Article on "An Inquiry into the Nature and Effects of the Paper Credit of Great Britain", in the first number of the *Edinburgh Review*.

xxx Impt

grain sold in the metropolis; and the grocer to transmit the bill, he having previously endorsed it, to a neighbouring sugar baker, in discharge of a like debt, and the sugar baker to send it, when again endorsed, to a West India merchant in an out-port, and the West India merchant to deliver it to his country banker, who also endorses it, and sends it further into circulation. The bill, in this case, will have effected five payments, exactly as if it were a £10 note payable on demand to bearer. It will, however, have circulated chiefly in consequence of the confidence placed by each receiver of it in the last endorser, his own correspondent in trade. . . . A multitude of bills pass between trader and trader in the country in the manner described; and they evidently form, in the strictest sense, a part of the circulating medium of the Kingdom. . . . The amount of bills in existence may . . . be at all times greater than the amount of all the bank notes of every kind, and of all the circulating guineas. Liverpool and Manchester effect the whole of their larger mercantile payments, not by country bank notes, of which none are issued by the banks of those places, but by bills at one or two months' date, drawn on London. The bills annually drawn by the banks of those towns amount to many millions.[1]

The position thus described was substantially the same in 1819,[2] except that after 1815 a large increase in the stamp duties had discouraged the use of very small bills (under £20), especially in Lancashire and in the West Riding woollen industry.[3]

For all but very small sums, therefore, bills remained the principal means of payment. In such circumstances, the services of the bill broker were indispensable. No great knowledge, perhaps, was required for the appraisal of drafts by reputable country bankers; such drafts could safely be taken by the banks in London and elsewhere without the hall-mark which a good broker's approval implied. But, save possibly in Lancashire, bank drafts were far outnumbered by merchant acceptances; and the worth

[1] It was to facilitate such drawings that Joseph Jones, of Manchester, first set up in London, establishing the famous house of Jones, Loyd & Co., upon which the Manchester house thereafter drew. For an excellent account of the whole system of country bank drafts on London, see James Taylor, *A Letter to William Leatham: Money, a Servant of the People, etc.* (1842).

[2] See especially John Gladstone's evidence before 1819 Commons' Committee, Minutes, p. 105.

[3] See William Leatham's *Letters to William Raynor Wood, On the Currency*, written in 1840. Leatham, a Wakefield banker, made an exhaustive investigation into the bill circulation, and estimated that in 1815 aggregate drawings amounted to £650 millions. (See also William Beckett before 1832 Committee, Minutes, p. 100.)

of these only the specialist broker, whose business it was to know something of the standing of most of the major parties whose acceptances found their way to London, could judge. Regular customers invariably relied upon the bill broker's judgment, and would take from him paper which would have been rejected unhesitatingly had it been sent direct. Thus the bill brokers, although they gave no guarantee, rendered negotiable vast numbers of bills which otherwise could not have been placed at all. And even with the finest paper there could have been no really extensive discounting without the bill broker, as the vital link between the place of origin and the place of discount.

Gurney's evidence [1] suggests that the brokers discriminated pretty closely against certain classes of paper, for he explained that the bills which he took were "drawn chiefly upon houses in London; but the bills we discount are not confined to bills on bankers, they are drawn on houses in London, or houses in the country, payable in London; but that [the second type] is the sort of bill we do not much countenance". The brokers were less particular, however, about the tenor of bills, for sometimes bills were taken with two or three years to run. "There are very long bills drawn in particular lines," declared Gurney, "but we do not often discount bills which have longer than a year to run; in some trades they draw regularly at 12 months, in others 6, in others at 9, in others at 3 and 4." Even so, most of Gurney's bills were under 65 days (the maximum currency then accepted at the Bank of England), but the firm never looked to the length of the bill, "only to the quality". The Bank of England, it is interesting to note, did not regard even quality as the major factor, so long as a bill were not drawn to finance speculation:

> . . . The bank is always ready to lend on commercial paper, that is legitimate in its origin, and is not carried to too great an extent by the parties who apply for discount. . . . The bank does not always look to the security, but they look to the origin of the bills, and they look to the extent of the account of the person who applies.[2]

[1] 1819 Commons' Committee, Minutes, p. 173, *et seq.*

[2] Evidence of George Dorrien, Governor of the Bank, before Commons' Committee (Minutes, p. 26). The deputy-Governor, Charles Pole, thus classified bills: "A speculative bill, carrying with it a tendency to monopoly . . . will carry with it, almost immediately, the appearance, the acceptors or drawers of the bill being principally brokers, or persons of that description, to a very large extent; whilst the bill founded on a fair and commercial transaction would be principally upon the con-

Despite this apparently generous interpretation of its functions, the Bank was frequently attacked on the grounds that its rigid limitation as to currency operated harshly against certain trades, where long drawings were unavoidable. Import bills, in particular, had to be carried by private banks for long periods before they became eligible. Samuel Thornton explained to the Lords' Committee [1] that " Articles of import are, many of them, sold at a Credit, varying from 4 to 9 Months, and the Bills passed for such Imports are generally discounted by private Banks, and held by them till they become due, within the Period of two Months, at which alone the Bank will take them ; added to this circumstance, every Merchant, when Money is not scarce, gives preference in offering his Discounts, to his private Banker, before he will come to the Bank."

The Bank's policy was, indeed, very illogical in some respects, for at times it was finding real difficulty in securing sufficient bills to maintain its issues at the level which it deemed desirable. The obvious course in such a case, failing a reduction of Bank rate, was to ease the discount regulations. What the Bank actually did, for a short period after the American War, was to apply a differential rate to bills drawn from abroad, discounting such paper at 4 per cent., although purely domestic bills were never taken below 5 per cent., the official Bank rate.

sumer, and become a fair bill." He admitted, however, that if the speculator had sufficient means, his bills would not be rejected, unless he were dealing in the " necessities of life ". This apparently explains the discrimination against brokers' (not *bill* brokers) bills, since these afforded evidence of speculations on *borrowed* capital. In evidence before the Lords' Committee (Minutes, p. 32), Dorrien listed the factors which he considered rendered bills objectionable in their *origin* : " The Monopoly of any particular Article ; Speculations in Corn ; Foreign Loans ; and Bills of that Description. That is, Bills drawn or accepted by Persons who the Bank suspects are engaged in such Speculations." (See also Lewis Loyd before 1819 Lords' Committee, Minutes, p. 294.)

[1] Minutes, p. 77.

CHAPTER II

THE 1825 CRISIS AND ITS RESULTS

THE year 1825 is one of the few key-dates in Bill Market history, for the great crisis of that year wrought changes in the banking structure which were responsible for every major influence upon market evolution in the succeeding twenty years. The crisis itself can be briefly dismissed, for its immediate impact upon the bill brokers, though sufficiently unpleasant at the time, is of only passing interest. Its principal cause was widespread speculation, stimulated partly by a series of good harvests, partly by the low yields on Government securities,[1] but especially by improvident finance on the part of the country banks. To a great extent, the banking excesses were traceable to an error of judgment by the Government, which in 1822 had unexpectedly announced that country bank notes of less than £5, which were to have been forbidden in 1823, could be issued for another ten years. This step invited over-issue, especially as the Bank of England, in an imprudent effort to employ the very large reserves it had accumulated against the expected reduction of the country circulation, promptly reduced its rate to 4 per cent. and extended the currency of eligible bills from 65 to 95 days. Abundant credit was thus made available to finance the many speculative projects which were afoot,[2] and especially the numerous " development " schemes for the newly established South American Republics.[3]

[1] Two important conversions were effected in 1822 and 1824.

[2] Nathan Rothschild's evidence before the 1832 Committee contains a graphic account of commodity speculation, notably in wool, spelter, corn and cotton, and also of the enormous volume of bills drawn from abroad in consequence. He himself received up to £1½ millions of such bills within two months. The normal volume of foreign drawings may be gauged from the following passage : " The bills drawn on wine and brandy are of no consequence ; they may amount to a couple of millions or thereabouts ; but, in times of quiet, I purchase regularly, week by week, from £80,000 to £100,000 worth of bills, which are drawn for goods shipped from this country."

[3] Twenty loans for foreign states, representing about £40,000,000 (nominal) were issued in London from 1822 to 1825, apart from the

The inevitable results were a precarious position in many commodity markets, an adverse trend of the exchanges, and an ominous drain of gold.

Early in 1825 the Bank scented the trouble which should have been evident months before, and sought a belated corrective by refusing to discount. This merely added to the general alarm, and by the end of the year the difficulties of Sir Peter Pole & Co.,[1] which carried the accounts of no less than forty-four country banks, precipitated a panic. A complete collapse of the currency system was averted only by the sudden reversal of the Bank's restrictionist policy.[2] Jeremiah Harman declared that—

> We lent . . . by every possible means, and in modes that we never had adopted before; we took in stock as security, we purchased Exchequer bills, we made advances on Exchequer bills, we not only discounted outright, but we made advances on deposits of bills to an immense amount; in short, by every possible means consistent with the safety of the Bank; and we were not on some occasions over-nice; seeing the dreadful state in which the public were, we rendered every assistance in our power.[3]

This description was supplemented by J. Horsley Palmer, who explained that considerable sums were also lent on title-deeds, and that "every sort of security was tendered, without much enquiry as to its nature" provided that it was deemed "eventually" secure. In addition, between £300,000 and £400,000 was lent on the Bank's behalf, mainly against goods, by commissioners in each of five or six districts outside London.[4] These measures allayed the panic, but failed to prevent the collapse of numerous banks and widespread commercial distress.

The lessons of such a crisis could not easily be forgotten, for, as one contemporary commentator remarked, the country had

numerous ridiculous company projects—one sought to drain the Red Sea to recover treasure abandoned after the crossing of the Jews. (See *Journal of the Statistical Society*, Vol. xli, pp. 313 *et seq.*)

[1] An excellent description of this failure is given by Lawson.

[2] Credit for the successful change was claimed by Thomas Joplin, who, at the height of the panic, inspired a leading article in the *Morning Courier* (of December 14), advocating liberal lending as the only possible means of removing the public's frenzied fear. (Joplin, *An Examination of the Report of the Joint Stock Bank Committee*, including an appendix on the 1825 crisis.)

[3] 1832 Committee, Minutes, p. 154.

[4] The Bank's discounts in January, 1826, averaged £13,673,600, the largest monthly average between 1824 and 1831. (See 1832 Committee, App. 55.)

been "within twenty-four hours of barter". Resolute steps were at once taken to improve the banking system. It was perceived that the major source of weakness lay in the fact that the bulk of the banking business outside London was in the hands of a vast number of small banks with purely local experience and (generally) with inadequate reserves. Many of them, indeed, were no more than jumped-up shopkeepers, with no knowledge whatever of banking principles. This evil, it was argued with some force, was directly attributable to the Bank's monopoly of joint stock banking. Pressure was therefore brought to bear upon the Bank to assent to the authorization of joint stock banks outside a radius of 65 miles from London, provided that they had no office in the metropolis. The bank directors agreed,[1] but it seems questionable whether they would have done so had they not been offered a weapon with which they might hope to fight the expected competitors—permission to establish branches. Both provisions were incorporated in an Act [2] passed in May, 1826, and both were destined to have important consequences for the Bill Market.

These were not, however, the only immediate changes produced by the crisis. The position of the London bankers had been rudely shaken, the more so as the catastrophe had been precipitated by the suspension of one of their number. In the past they had generally pursued a policy of using their resources to the full, freely re-discounting at the Bank of England whenever needs for cash were pressing. But the events of December, 1825, had brought home to them the fact that in time of acute crisis the Bank of England had to bear the discount demands of practically the whole country,[3] and that in such circumstances even its superior resources might not suffice for their own urgent needs. From this realization there arose the central reserve system [4] which for many years was a unique feature of the London Money Market, for after the crisis the London bankers dropped their practice of re-discounting, and it has never been resumed. Instead, they began to establish adequate cash reserves

[1] They had refused an identical proposal in 1823, although in the previous year Joplin had exposed the fallacy of the view that the clause of the 1742 Act which forbade joint stock issues thereby prohibited joint stock *deposit* banking. (See Joplin, *Essay on Banking*, 1822.)

[2] 7 Geo. IV, c. 46.

[3] Private discounts were stated to have "ceased entirely" at one time during the crisis.

[4] Glyn even went so far as to advocate a central *gold* reserve. (See 1832 Committee, Minutes, p. 221.)

of their own, holding them partly in Bank of England notes and partly in a balance at the Bank itself. George Carr Glyn, asked in 1832 [1] in which of the two forms London reserves were usually held, replied that the London banker " holds it in both ways ; he holds a portion necessarily always at home, in Bank of England paper, and a small portion in gold ; but it is our custom, and I believe it is so likewise *now* with nearly every Banking house, to keep also a large deposit in the Bank of England ".

Meanwhile, the Bank of England had awakened to a greater sense of its responsibilities. The directors had been forcibly reminded of the great reliance placed upon them by the mercantile and banking community, and had also discovered that the safe conduct of their affairs under a Gold Standard [2] required a degree of prudence which they had never been called upon to exercise during the Restriction period. From this standpoint, the crisis must clearly be regarded as a milestone in the history of central banking, for the Bank began to follow a much more cautious policy in the management of its issues and in the maintenance of reserves, and gradually assumed functions which are now considered as the ordinary duties of a central bank. It is doubtful, however, whether any of the more fundamental innovations was made on grounds of public interest ; more probably the directors were thinking mainly in terms of their own security, which happened to be precisely what was needed from the broader viewpoint. This interpretation of their motives derives support also from the aggressive attitude of the Bank in other spheres, especially in its desire to push its circulation in the country, and in its open hostility to the joint-stock banks.

Recapitulating, it may be said that from the standpoint of the Bill Market the 1825 crisis produced four major lines of change in the banking structure—the beginnings of joint stock banking ; the establishment of Bank of England branches ; the cessation of re-discounting by the London private banks ; and the assumption of certain central banking functions by the Bank of England. Each of these must be considered in turn.

[1] See 1832 Committee, Minutes, Q. 2870.

[2] The " Resumption " Act of 1819 (59 Geo. III, c. 49) contemplated a gradual restoration of cash payments, and full convertibility as from May 1, 1823 ; but, actually, full resumption was achieved on May 1, 1821, under the authority of a second enabling Act (1 and 2 Geo. IV, c. 26).

The Beginnings of Joint Stock Banking

Joint stock banking as we know it to-day and the bill broker system as it first operated in this country are mutually exclusive phenomena. But the joint stock banking of the second and third quarters of the nineteenth century was vastly different from that of the twentieth century; and it is no exaggeration to say that it was for close upon fifty years the most important single buttress of the original form of the bill market. Integrated joint stock banking later meant the death of the bill broker agency system; disintegrated banking was utterly dependent upon it. The fundamental reason for this dependence was that banking, although after 1825 increasingly conducted by joint stock institutions, long remained *localized* banking. That, however, does not explain why the provincial joint stock banks were more dependent upon the bill broker than were the older private banks.

The explanation is to be found in the differences between the two systems. Private banking was based upon the issue of notes, the attraction of deposits being only a secondary aim. Joint stock banking, on the other hand, was primarily deposit banking.[1] Thus the joint stock banks, which *began* as deposit banks, had from the outset to attract depositors either from the existing private banks or from among the many who had still to learn the utility of a banking account. The obvious (and, indeed, almost the only) method of doing this was to offer substantial rates of interest on all balances. This was, in fact, one of the main distinguishing features of the new system: the joint stock banks competed frantically among themselves, many of them offering extravagant rates of interest on current as well as on deposit accounts. In its early stages the system was grossly abused, and the new methods shocked the more experienced private bankers, who declared that such banks could not pay their way and could not long remain solvent. Many of them did neither, but it was clear that if banks of this kind were to succeed, they could do so only by keeping their resources very fully employed.

This necessity had two results, each of which redounded to the benefit of the bill brokers. In the first place, many of the country joint stock banks kept virtually no cash reserves, except the bare minimum required for till money, relying upon re-discounting to

[1] Many joint stock banks which started with note-issues relinquished these after a few years; the *London* joint stock banks, necessarily, were exclusively deposit banks.

provide cash when required. These re-discounts were almost invariably arranged through the London brokers, whose business prospered accordingly. Some of the private banks, it is true, had re-discounted on an appreciable scale, but until the advent of the joint stock deposit institutions, most bankers had regarded the re-sale of bills as an operation to be undertaken only in times of stringency, or at special seasons of the year; and as the bigger private banks generally kept a reasonable reserve, their applications to London were comparatively infrequent. With the joint stocks, however, re-discounting became a daily occurrence, as much a part of their routine operations as the discount of local paper for customers. And the more intense the fight for deposits, the greater became the demand for re-discount facilities, for the early joint stock bank manager or director rarely gave due consideration to the fact that he was contingently liable on all bills re-sold until they had been duly paid at maturity. If competition forced him to raise his deposit allowances, there seemed to be a heaven-sent method of making good the resultant inroad into profit-margins: all he had to do was to speed up his despatches of bills to the London brokers, and increase proportionately his local discounts. As may be imagined, on such occasions he was not always over-particular about the quality of the paper which his clients tendered, so long as he knew that his endorsement would make it acceptable to the London bill broker.

The second consequence of the joint stock banker's need for a very full employment of his resources was a strong preference for bills of exchange as a means of investment. As already noted, bills had become popular with some of the private banks, and became increasingly so, as bill market facilities improved and were better understood; but there remained many private bankers who held a fair proportion of their investments in Government securities. Before the repeal of the Usury Laws in so far as they applied to bills of exchange, this was, indeed, a very desirable practice.[1] But to a banker whose business was so conducted

[1] ". . . When not more than 5 per cent. could by law be given on bills of exchange, it was an established principle that Bankers, particularly Country Bankers, should hold Government securities, by the sale of which, though at a great sacrifice, they could raise money in periods of emergency. They frequently on such occasions had to sell their stock, etc., at from 5 to 10 per cent. loss, which, if they only wanted the money for a month, was raising at the rate of from 50 to 100 per cent. for that period. But the Usury laws having been altered as regards bills of exchange, and the Banks being thus enabled on such securities to give a higher rate of interest, if necessary, appear to think that they

that his assets had to be realizable at an hour's notice on any day in the year, Government securities were far from appropriate: bills were the only possible securities. The joint stock banker in agricultural districts, where deposits generally exceeded demands for accommodation, thus employed almost the whole of his available resources in the purchase of bills through a bill broker. And even the banker in districts where the demand for accommodation was less sluggish sent money to London whenever he had a surplus, even though he knew that the funds might be needed locally within a short period. In similar circumstances most private bankers, unaccustomed to re-discounting, would be content to witness a temporary increase in their cash reserves; the joint stock banker, on the other hand, knew that he could always reverse the operation and procure immediate cash without any departure from his normal practice or principles. Thus the rise of the joint stock banks brought a substantial increase in both sides of the bill brokers' business, the one balancing the other.

It was, in fact, during this period of localized joint stock banking, extending roughly from about 1830 until the 'sixties or 'seventies, that the bill market as an agent for the *domestic* distribution of credit reached its highest point, in terms both of the scale of operations and of importance in the body economic. The system was essentially the same as that of the first quarter of the century; but in that period, for reasons that should now be apparent, the dealings of the private country banks with the bill brokers never assumed very large figures, whereas the joint stock banks in the later period, owing partly to the general expansion of trade and industry, dealt with them on an enormous scale. Again, while in the earlier period the bill broking facilities formed a very valuable adjunct to the country banking organization, they were never a wholly indispensable part of it. If at that time there had been no brokers, country banking would undoubtedly have been less efficient and less profitable, and money would have been spread far less evenly throughout the country, but the country banks would have managed tolerably well through their normal London banker agents. During the

will obtain money on them at any time at a less sacrifice than by holding stock, and they consequently keep all their reserve in bills of exchange. . . ."—Joplin, *Examination of the Report of the Joint Stock Bank Committee* (James Ridgway, 1837). The alteration in the law which Joplin discussed was effected by the Bank Charter Act, 1833, section 7. (See *post*, p. 68.)

later period, however, at least in so far as joint stock banking was concerned, bill broking could quite legitimately be considered an integral part of the country banking system. But for the existence of the brokers, it is certain that provincial joint stock banking, in its first forty or fifty years at least, would have assumed a totally different form, and that difference would as surely have left its mark until the present day. In short, the bill broker, *qua* broker, then became a really important person; he reached an eminence in the social and banking hierarchy which he will never again attain. Yet, even while joint stock banking was still in its infancy, the seeds of the decay of the true broker system had been sown: for, shortly after 1825, there had arisen a new type of operator in bills, the dealer who carried bills on his own account, and who was ultimately to supplant the broker proper as the principal constituent of the Discount Market.

This innovation in bill market practice is best considered under a later heading [1]; but it demands mention at this stage because the new type of business, once begun, derived much stimulus from the joint stock banks. The reason will be readily appreciated: the bill dealer's ability to run a portfolio of bills in his own name depended, primarily, upon his ability to secure deposits at rates of interest below current rates of discount. Many private bankers, however, would not dream of lending at such rates; they kept what they deemed an adequate reserve of idle cash, and on all other assets expected to earn at least as much as was returned on bills. Most joint stock banks were differently placed: they used their resources up to the hilt, and were very willing to employ a fluctuating margin of funds at rates below those they secured on bills, so long as such funds could be turned into cash at very short notice and with the minimum of trouble. They therefore became important lenders of "short money" to the new class of discount dealers, and their custom was undoubtedly a very big factor in the noteworthy growth of bill dealing after the early 'thirties.

Provincial Joint Stock Bank Re-discounts

Such were the major influences of early joint stock banking upon the Bill Market. Their precise operation must now be examined chronologically, and in greater detail. The first joint stock banks followed almost immediately upon their authoriza-

[1] See *post*, pp. 62–69.

tion by the Act of 1826. Indeed, six banks were established in the same year.[1] All, however, seem to have been birds of passage, for they were entirely over-looked by the 1832 Committee, to whom it was stated that the first joint stock banks were the Huddersfield Banking Co., the Bradford Banking Co., and the Lancaster Banking Co., all established in 1827. In the following year the Bank of Manchester, the first non-issuing joint stock bank, was formed, although it did not commence business until 1829. Three formations in 1830, including the Bank of Liverpool, brought the total up to nineteen, and the number was almost doubled in the ensuing two years.[2] Really intensive development, however, did not begin until 1833, when the Act which renewed the Bank of England Charter [3] confirmed the fact that *non-issuing* joint stock banks could legally be set up in the metropolis. London formations began at once, the London and Westminster starting business in 1834, the London Joint Stock in 1836, and the Union and the London & County Banks three years later. This same period also witnessed active development in the provinces: in these seven years no fewer than 87 joint stock banks were formed in England and Wales.[2]

With the development proceeding at so amazing a rate [4]—an average of more than one new bank per month—it is small wonder that the discount brokers also made rapid strides. Gurney declared in 1836 [5] that the discount business of London had doubled in the preceding five years; his own turnover had greatly increased, and in the two months before the date of his evidence (July 22, 1836) it had been larger than ever before in his experience. The expansion was not, however, wholly attributable to the joint stock banks. Gurney was very explicit on this point, and explained that there had also been a large expansion in the discounts offered in London, though he admitted that there had "possibly" been a bigger increase in bills sent from the country. It is possible, however, that his caution was due to a desire not to offend his best customers, the country joint stock banks, for the chairman of the Committee was quite

[1] 1857 Committee, App. 21. [2] *Ibid.*

[3] 3 and 4 Wm. IV, c. 98.

[4] A very detailed and careful account of the origin, development and practice of the early joint stock banks will be found in Dr. S. E. Thomas's *Rise and Growth of Joint Stock Banking* (1934), which would have saved the present writer much toilsome and lengthy research had it appeared a few months earlier.

[5] Evidence before *Secret Committee on Joint Stock Banks*, 1836, QQ. 2551–618.

evidently hostile to them, on account of their re-discounting operations, which Gurney, in a wordy quibble, did his best to screen. Ultimately, he was forced to admit that the "larger proportion" of the "very great extension" of bill market business came through these institutions, and to agree that they re-discounted in London much more freely than the private banks had done.[1]

These reluctant admissions [2] of the importance of joint stock re-discounts found abundant confirmation in the evidence of other witnesses. Samuel Jones Loyd stated with pride in 1832 [3] that his house never re-discounted ("we do not consider it to be the act of a banker of first-rate character and conduct, by any means"), but that the Manchester Joint Stock Bank regularly did so, from which he inferred that that institution had not "materially succeeded as a bank of deposit." Henry Moult, of the ill-fated Northern and Central Bank, gave evidence from the opposite angle,[4] remarking that "a great part of the business of joint stock banks" was "to give out money in the country and procure it on discount in London". Indeed, he declared that the facility of obtaining discounts in London had been the principal reason for his own bank's extension of branches, as well as for the premium at which he (and other joint stock bankers) had been able to issue new shares to finance these developments. These discount facilities, he believed, were the fundamental cause of the boom in joint stock flotations. The Northern and Central Bank, it is worth noting, actually had a standing arrangement with bill brokers whereby the latter guaranteed to take a fixed quantity of bills each week, and if they failed to do so the contract was to be terminable instantly.

Such evidence of the widespread nature of the re-discounting habit could be multiplied; but the recitation would not add much to the above, which can be regarded as representative. One other extract, however, is useful as indicating the re-discounting practice even of bankers who normally had a surplus

[1] Gurney's final effort at evasion was to remark that re-discounts for private bankers had been "very large" between 1808 and 1815!

[2] *Cf.* Gurney's evidence before 1832 Committee (QQ. 3743, 3744). At this earlier date he was far less guarded, and stated that some joint stock banks were in districts which provided great surplus cash, but "others, under equally good management, find it answer their purpose to take advantage of the low rate of interest in London . . . we discount sometimes for the first houses in this island, and the most wealthy".

[3] 1832 Committee, Minutes, p. 234.

[4] Second Report of Committee on Joint Stock Banks, Minutes, Q. 840.

of deposits. Charles S. Forster, a Walsall banker, thus described his system [1]:

> Our practice is, that we have no unemployed money, to send it all to London, and supposing an extra demand arises in the country at a higher rate of discount [than in London], we then discount bills in London, or wait their coming into cash, and employ it in the country ; and the practice of making notes enables us to carry on both systems, because the time we get by the circulation of the notes enables us to get the London bills paid, so as to meet the extra demand in the country.

The note issuing bankers,[2] necessarily, tended generally to be less dependent upon re-discounts, partly for the reason which Forster cited, and partly because, as the chairman of the 1836 Committee [3] pointed out, the non-issuers sometimes had to pay more for their " circulation ". By this he meant the cost of securing notes from the Bank of England by special arrangement,[4] on the one hand, and the cost of attracting deposits, on the other.

There can be no doubt that the adoption of re-discounting as a regular practice greatly enlarged the volume of bills that were *discountable.* Gurney endeavoured to prove that it merely changed the channel by which bills reached the market—through the banks instead of coming direct from the holders. That in itself was a change of some importance ; but it was not the principal one. In many cases, no doubt, bills with local commercial names upon them might, with a good bill broker's approval, become re-discountable with banks in other districts, and a great deal of credit was certainly mobilized by this method, especially in the early years of the century. But there were a great many more local bills which not even the bill broker would have cared to approve, for he could not know the credit of *every* acceptor or drawer, and his own reputation or his resources were at stake in every case.[5] These bills, however, assumed a

[1] 1832 Committee, Minutes, Q. 1570.

[2] Forster took a great pride in his note issue, which he held to be the one thing which raised him above the level of the bill brokers, for whom he had no great esteem. " When a banker abandons his circulation, he degrades into a bill broker."

[3] 1836 Committee, Minutes, Q. 593. [4] See *post*, pp. 56–7.

[5] During the first quarter of the century, as has been explained, the brokers, when acting strictly as such, did not guarantee the bills or endorse them. By 1836, however, they frequently gave guarantees (presumably when acting as dealers), although they rarely endorsed. See evidence of John Harding, a private banker of Burlington, before 1836 Committee, Minutes, Q. 2255.

totally different character in the eyes of the discount market when they were backed by the endorsement of a joint stock bank, and these banks almost invariably endorsed the bills which they re-sold. Gurney's evidence [1] shows the broker's standpoint very clearly:

> Do you think that, speaking generally, there has not been a large amount of joint stock paper discounted on the London market which it might have been difficult to discount without the endorsement of those large institutions?—There has been paper discounted in the London market, that would not have been current without the endorsement of joint stock or private banks; this arises from the parties to the bill residing in the country, and not being known in London. The paper may, however, be of equal character.

He refused to agree, however, that the joint stock banks had endorsed and re-discounted paper which would have been rejected by the private banks, but admitted that he had a faith in the endorsement which he would not have had in the bills themselves.

From the narrowest standpoint, there was real justification for this faith, even where the bills were suspected of being intrinsically unsound, for to the re-discounter a joint stock bank endorsement was frequently more valuable than that of a private bank, not because the corporate body was necessarily more substantial or more credit-worthy (it often was *less* credit-worthy!), but simply because in the event of trouble the holder was protected, even though the bank were without assets, by his right to proceed against the separate estates of the many proprietors—the principle of limited liability was not applied until 1858. This circumstance was undoubtedly one of the principal causes of the wide re-discount facilities afforded to the new banks.

It is also worth noting that whether or not the early joint stock banks were less rigorous in their judgment of bills than were the private banks, they did in practice endorse and re-discount much more largely; and for the purpose of explaining and assessing the growth of the bill market it is immaterial whether the increase in bills offered in London was, or was not, due partly to the inclusion of indifferent paper. One last witness, this time before the 1841 Committee, may be cited in support of this assertion [2]:

[1] Before 1836 Committee, Minutes, Q. 2577.

[2] *Select Committee on Banks of Issue*, 1841, Evidence of I. C. Wright, a private banker at Nottingham, Q. 1632.

. . . It is not the practice of private banks to re-discount their bills; and we should not do so. It is the case certainly with some banks, particularly with joint stock banks, that when they are banks of issue they also habitually re-discount their bills in the market, but that is a system which we have not considered it respectable to act upon.

To sum up, it can be said that the re-discounting operations of the provincial joint stock banks increased the supply of bills in London and the business of the brokers for the following reasons—(1) They operated in many areas not previously "banked"; (2) by their willingness to resell bills, they were able to take much business, even in districts where private banks were already established, which the private banker who avoided re-discount would have been obliged to reject; (3) their endorsements gave negotiability to many bills which the brokers, though they may have had direct connections with the districts in question, would not otherwise have countenanced; and (4) they not infrequently gave a more liberal credit than the private bankers had done, thereby stimulating the creation of bills, and their ultimate re-sale in London.

Early Joint Stock Bank Call Loans

The second main influence of the early joint stock banks upon the bill market—through their practice of lending at call—can be more briefly traced, for until the 'fifties it was of less importance than their re-discounting operations. It arose, however, from the London, as well as from the provincial, joint stock banks, whereas re-discounting had been confined almost exclusively to the latter. So far as the provincial banks were concerned, the custom of lending to brokers at call was undoubtedly closely bound up with re-discounting operations, and probably originated from them. It has already been noted that the Northern and Central Bank had an undertaking from brokers to take a certain amount of bills per week, and it is highly probable that other banks made similar arrangements. Local cash requirements, however, would not be uniform week by week, and would often be below the amount of bills which the brokers had agreed to accept, for this figure would tend to be fixed close to maximum needs. But since the banks could demand that the brokers should take the agreed amount, they would naturally feel obliged to remit up to the limit even though at times smaller re-discounts would have sufficed; for otherwise the brokers would have had a legitimate cause for complaint. In such circumstances there could be no better way of employing the short-term surplus thus achieved in London than by leaving it with the brokers to be " called " for when required, provided that the brokers themselves had channels in which the funds could be employed. Overend, Gurney & Co., in particular, had many such channels, through their numerous connections with banks and traders in London and throughout the country, and they accordingly secured the lion's share of the new type of business.

When exactly the practice began is uncertain, but it is clear that by 1836 it was quite well developed. Thus Cassels,[1] of the Northern and Central Bank, stated in that year that it was not uncommon for his bank to have £100,000 with Overend, Gurney & Co., as a result of surpluses left from re-discounts. In this particular case, the arrangement with Gurney's was that, instead of discounting the bills immediately they arrived, and then allowing a " call " rate of interest on the funds retained, they did not charge the discount at all until the money was drawn out.

This may have been a special case, but it serves to illustrate one of the ways in which provincial call loans began; and there is no doubt that the habit once formed would tend to spread. It was greatly stimulated, just as were the bill purchases of the private country banks in earlier times, by the fact that the joint stock banks could secure no interest on deposits left with their London banker agents. The latter were therefore kept as bare of funds as possible, any surplus being immediately transferred to the bill brokers. The broker's account, as Cassels emphasized, was always regarded as the first source of cash. This was true even in 1832,[2] for George Carr Glyn, as London agent for provincial banks, when asked whether he arranged for the employment of the country banks' funds in London, replied that it was always done " directly with the bill broker ". The country bank, he explained, gave the bill broker a credit with the London agent for any surplus funds that might accumulate with the latter. Gilbart confirmed this, stating that the country banks used a direct account with brokers to feed the account with London banker agents, transferring funds from the former to the latter only as necessary.

Another factor in the extension of the call loan market, and

[1] 1836 Committee, Minutes, Q. 1758.
[2] 1832 Committee, Minutes, QQ 2936, 2937.

one which became increasingly important after the middle 'thirties, was the diminishing popularity of Exchequer bills. At one time these had been the main channel for all types of short-term investors, but with the growth of trade and of commerce, and an improving Stock Exchange organization, new and competitive securities had arisen, which came to be preferred by the private investor, with the result that Exchequer bills became less readily negotiable.[1] For many years there was to be heated controversy [2] on the question whether they were, in fact, more negotiable—in good times and in bad—than bills of exchange, but many bankers made up their minds quickly, and turned away from the Exchequer bill market in the early 'thirties, substituting bills of exchange bought through brokers, and call loans with them. Thus Daniel Robertson, of the National Provincial Bank, in 1837 [3]:

> We found it more convenient to lend the money that we kept in reserve to bill brokers [than to buy Government securities] . . . we got a higher rate . . . and the money was at our command. . . . We lend a certain sum of money to them, payable on a day or two's notice, and they give us in return the security of bills of exchange.

J. Gibbins, too, a banker of Birmingham and Gloucester, referred [4] to his reserves in London in "money with the bill brokers, at interest at call, and in bills that we have from them".

Even the Scottish joint stock banks preferred bills of exchange and call loans to Government securities. J. A. Anderson, of the Glasgow Union Banking Co., stated in 1841 [5] that his bank regularly kept a large part of its reserves in "money in bill-brokers' hands, secured by bills or otherwise". This preference greatly helped the brokers, for discount rates in Scotland were maintained at a uniform rate which did not always con-

[1] And see *post*, pp. 115, 116.

[2] *Cf*. Stuckey, "I have known more than one period when we could not discount at all for 3 or 4 days; in 1825, in the panic, it was so" . . . ". . . I have not found that with a good bill, even of the House of Baring, I could get money more easily than on Government stock" (1836, Minutes, QQ. 1436, 1376), and Paul Moon James, "I have known Exchequer bills to fail, but I have never known bills of exchange to fail; I am alluding to the panic of 1825; I could not sell Exchequer bills for several hours at that time" . . "at that time money was obtained upon bills of exchange on the same day on which I could not get money for Exchequer bills" (1841, Minutes, QQ. 1485, 1486).

[3] 1837 *Committee on Joint Stock Banks*, Minutes, QQ. 2338–9.

[4] 1836 Committee, Minutes, Q. 994.

[5] 1841 Committee, Minutes, QQ. 2411–69.

form with rates in London, and Anderson found, especially in the winter of 1840–1, that he could frequently get " as much by lending our money to bill-brokers in London, sometimes more, than from our customers in Glasgow ". He thought that if there were in fact any limit to the money which could be thus employed in London, it would be " a very wide one ". The older, and more conservative, Scottish chartered banks, however, strongly opposed the new practice. Alexander Blair, Treasurer of the Bank of Scotland, was asked[1] whether he approved the holding of reserves " with the great discount brokers in London, Overend, Gurney & others, revocable on demand, or in bills of exchange, so as to be capable of being called into the general action of the business when needed " ? He replied, logically enough—

> that such a reserve would be secure only because the practice is not general ; if it were, all banks would be calling in funds or selling, or failing to renew, bills at the same time, which would lessen the supply of discount precisely at the time when it ought to be maintained.

and argued that in lending to brokers a banker trusted an individual rather than the public credit of the country, which he would be doing if he bought Exchequer bills. Anderson was not impressed by such arguments, and commented cynically that when the chartered banks were first established and their habits formed, there were no bill brokers !

The London joint stock banks adopted the system of lending at call from the outset, for they were exclusively deposit banks, paying interest on a large part of their resources, which normally could not find the necessary full employment in financing customers' needs. It was not, however, until the late 'forties that their call money came to be a really important part of the total call loans to brokers, partly because only a few banks were firmly established before 1844, and partly because the system of taking deposits at interest did not become acutely competitive in the early years. Detailed examination of their relations with the bill market is therefore best deferred to a later stage.

The Bank of England Branches

It is an interesting paradox that branch banking, which in later years was to destroy the bill market's traditional " agency "

[1] 1841 Committee, Minutes, QQ. 1965–9.

business with the country banks, and to restrict its direct business with merchants, should, when practised by the Bank of England, have failed to damage the first, and have greatly stimulated the second. This establishment of Bank of England branches—which forms the second major line of banking change after 1825—followed even more quickly upon the enabling Act of 1826 than did the first joint stock banks. The first branch was opened within two months,[1] followed by three more before the end of the year, and by 1834 twelve branches were working.[2] Their establishment, as Timothy A. Curtis, Governor of the Bank in 1838, explained, was suggested by the Government, and their avowed objects were to provide greater banking facilities in the provinces and, above all, to improve the circulating medium. The overriding consideration in their management, therefore, was the extension of the Bank's local circulation. This they achieved principally through the medium of discounts, for loans were usually unimportant (the Bank would not lend against land, then the commonest banking security) and overdrafts forbidden.

The mechanism of discount operations was strictly prescribed,[3] and herein lies the main reason why the Bank's entry into competitive country discounting did not injure the brokers' business. Ordinary commercial discounts were available at the new branches only to those (of " supposed credit ") who opened a " discount account ", which had first to be sanctioned by London, whither the applications were despatched in weekly batches. The authority sanctioning the " name " of the prospective customer was accompanied by a discount limit, although when the customer presented commercial bills of which he was the holder, instead of bills originating from himself (as drawer), the manager was allowed some discretion in observing the limit.[4] Promissory notes were not accepted, no matter what endorsements they bore, nor were any bills of more than three months to run, while in every case at least two " good " names were essential. Moreover, all bills had to be approved by London. These onerous, though indisputably " sound ", rules were apparently followed with meticulous care, for we find Joseph C. Dyer, a director of the Manchester Joint Stock Bank, complaining in

[1] At Gloucester in July, 1826.

[2] See 1838 *Committee on Joint Stock Banks*, Minutes, Q. 43, *et seq.*; 1836 Committee, App. 1; and 1832 Committee, App. 51.

[3] See 1838 Committee, Evidence of T. A. Curtis, and 1832 Committee, Minutes, p. 110.

[4] See 1838 Committee, Evidence of Samuel Turner, Minutes, Q. 262.

1832 [1] of the formalities of the methods of the Bank's Manchester Branch, and declaring that it made a " minute examination ", regularly objecting to " certain proportions " of the bills sent in. Paul Moon James, similarly, remarked in 1841 [2] that the Bank of England branches were " very particular ", explaining that bills that would pass current in general were occasionally rejected by the Bank of England, though " always for some good reason ". Their prudence was, indeed, beyond reproach. James, praising their support for " sound principles of trade in regard to bills ", stated that he had found " both in regard to the limit of circulation and the refusal of discount and in their examination of bills, that they have always exercised a sound discretion, that they have never acted from caprice " ; while Thomas Attwood, a Birmingham banker, declared that the Birmingham branch had done a great service—

> . . . by discounting generally all the best bills, none of the bad ones and none of the difficult ones . . . I have no doubt that the country banks would have discounted those bills, but the distress would have been so great that they would have had neither the power under that issue nor the will ; as it is, they have got all the bad bills left in their hands, and all the locked up debts, all the dangerous and doubtful and difficult affairs are left as legacies of ruin in the hands of the old bankers.[3]

Such rules are becoming to a central bank at any time, but the Bank was seeking to push its facilities (and thereby its issues) in competition with commercial banks, and, for normal commercial business, restrictions of this kind would be onerous even to-day. They were much more so in the 'thirties of the last century, which were not remarkable for purist principles in matters of bill finance.[4] It is scarcely to be wondered, then, that much private discount business went elsewhere, or that the aggregate Branch Bank discounts would have been quite small but for certain special arrangements with other bankers.[5] Even James [6] was forced to conclude his eulogy of the Bank's methods by the remark that " they are not altogether adapted to the

[1] 1832 Committee, Minutes, p. 306.

[2] 1841 Committee, Minutes, Q. 1431.

[3] 1832 Committee, Minutes, p. 453.

[4] See *post*, p. 91, *et seq.*

[5] In 1831, the first year in which discounts for bankers were shown separately, the Branch Banks' aggregate discounts averaged £1,718,000, of which £844,077 was for bankers. The Bank's *total* discounts amounted to £3,245,000 (1832 Report, Appendices, 41, 42 and 56).

[6] 1841 Committee, Minutes, Q. 1518.

general trade of the country ", while the Governor of the Bank himself (J. Horsley Palmer), admitted that the private banks often afforded a better service to the public than did the Bank's branches :

> I am most decidedly of opinion that all banking business is better done by private bankers than by public bodies ; there are more facilities afforded in the way of credit by a private banker than can be offered *under existing regulations* by a Branch of the Bank of England, which gives no credit to anyone ; and there are forms required to be adhered to in acting with the Bank, which are extremely inconvenient in conducting private business.[1]

Possibly the most objectionable regulation, from the trader's point of view, was that which restricted the tenor of discountable paper to three months, for in many trades the usance was much longer, as, for example, in the South Wales iron trade, where bills were drawn at six months, and in the import trades.[2] Another source of grievance arose from the fact that, shortly after their establishment, the branches initiated a system of bill classification,[3] dividing bills into two classes—" A 1 " and " A 2 " —according to the standing of the parties, and charging $\frac{1}{4}$ per cent. more for the discount of bills of the second class. This was regarded as an injustice, for " the second-class parties, considering the business they transacted, and the more limited engagements they came under, were equally responsible with parties who were called A 1 ". Such objections ultimately led to the abandonment of the scheme, and to the adoption of a uniform rate—Bank rate—for all private discounts.

These various impediments to a free discount business, and especially the general " red tape " associated with the Branch Banks, prevented the diversion of any very substantial volume of discounts from the commercial banks. Had this occurred, the brokers' business might have suffered appreciably, for the Bank of England never re-discounted. The Branch Banks did, however, succeed in cheapening the cost of local discount accommodation, for they always worked without commission,[4] whereas nearly all the country bankers had been accustomed to charge 5*s*. or 6*s*. per cent. in addition to the discount, and sometimes

[1] 1832 Committee, Minutes, Q. 478.

[2] *Ibid*., Evidence of J. P. Wilkins, p. 110 ; and P. M. James before 1841 Committee, Minutes, Q. 1509.

[3] 1848 Lords' Committee, Evidence of A. H. Wylie, Q. 2088.

[4] 1832 Committee, Minutes, p. 39.

a "postage" charge as well.[1] Competition led to the abatement, and finally to the abandonment, of these commissions.[2]

Apart from this indirect benefit, the value of the Branch Banks to the commercial community lay not in any accommodation they might afford to the few who could satisfy the various conditions, but in the facilities offered for the transmission of funds from place to place, and especially to and from London. Before the establishment of the branches, remittances were costly, difficult to arrange, and dangerous, so that in practice only those provincial traders and industrialists who worked on a considerable scale, or who had distant trade agencies, were able to conduct their financial operations outside their own towns. All others were effectively cut off from the London market, and were therefore at the mercy of the local banker. The Branch Banks, however, set themselves out to provide every facility for the free transmission of funds,[3] affording "complete access to the London market, and to the lower rate of interest which prevails in the Capital". For customers with drawing accounts, they would make payments to accounts at the parent Bank, or any branch, without charge, and would charge only postage for payments to persons without accounts. Moreover, they would perform similar services for any member of the public, charging only a small commission.

It was through these facilities that the Branch Banks most helped the bill market. Once the difficulty of arranging a return remittance had been thus overcome, many persons who formerly had been unable to discount in London began to do so: they remitted their bills direct to a London bill broker, instructing him to pay the proceeds into the Bank of England, for their credit at one or other of the Branch Banks, the remittance being achieved simply at the cost of postage to London.[4] S. J. Loyd was forced to admit that this practice had deprived his firm's Manchester house of some of its best customers, although he contended that the new mode of dealing was due more to the reduction of the rate of interest and to "the many increased facilities of obtaining discounts in London" than simply to the establishment of the Branch Bank at Manchester.[5]

[1] See Gilbart, *A Practical Treatise on Banking* (1828), p. 31.

[2] See Evidence of Charles S. Forster, of Walsall, before 1832 Committee (p. 104).

[3] 1832 Committee, Minutes, p. 7.

[4] See evidence of William Beckett, a Leeds banker, before 1832 Committee, Q. 1436.

[5] *Ibid.*, QQ. 3343–5.

He agreed, however, that the major factor had been the great improvement in the facilities for the transference of funds from London to Manchester—a significant admission, in view of his own firm's special advantages for remittance business in comparison with purely local country bankers.

Samuel Gurney confirmed the existence of the new practice, but, as usual, his confirmation was a little more cautious than the facts (which he admitted) seemed to warrant :

> Have you not found that the establishment of the Branch Banks has brought you, as a bill broker, more immediately in contact with the traders and manufacturers in the large towns ?—It has in some measure ; my business has not been injured by it.
>
> Do not the manufacturers and merchants that formerly sent their bills to a banker for discount, now send them to you for discount ?—Yes, we do a vast deal of that description of business.[1]

Connections of this kind were invaluable in the seven or eight years after 1826, when the brokers' main problem was rather to find sufficient good bills than sufficient buyers of them.[2] Moreover, the link with manufacturers, once established, was not readily broken.

Effects upon Country Bank Re-discounting

In one respect, however, the Branch Banks may have injured the brokers' business, for in some districts they tended to reduce the volume of bank re-discounting in London. Owing to the comparative failure of their own private discount business, they sought other methods of forcing Bank of England notes into provincial circulation. From the outset, as G. W. Norman, a director of the Bank since 1821, explained to the 1840 Committee, they refused to open discount accounts for any *issuing* banker, whether private or joint stock.[3] This rule was ostensibly designed to prevent excesses by private issuers—

> . . . It was conceived the duty of issuing bodies, especially under ordinary circumstances, to be prepared to preserve the convertibility of their notes, from their own resources, and that mischief

[1] *Ibid.*, QQ. 3785, 3786.

[2] See Gurney's Evidence before 1832 Committee, Minutes, p. 258.

[3] 1840 Committee, Minutes, p. 34. The rule was partly modified from Sept., 1828, to Feb., 1834, to facilitate withdrawal of £1 and £2 notes, discount facilities being given to a limited extent for this purpose, and also to those banks which assisted in the collection of the revenue, proportionately to the assistance given.

> would arise were the Bank to hold out an expectation of being able to afford aid at periods when a superior duty to the public would perhaps compel it to withhold assistance.

but in practice it eventually became a weapon with which to fight competitive note issues in general, and those of the joint stock banks in particular. Thus fortified, the Bank let it be known that it would consent to abandon its rule in favour of particular banks, provided that they relinquished their issues. The usual arrangement was that a country banker who agreed to substitute Bank of England notes for his own should obtain discount accommodation from the Branch Bank equivalent to the size of the note issue withdrawn, these advances being made at 3 per cent., *i.e.* 1 per cent. under Bank rate.[1] In such cases the country banker had a " fixed amount " assigned to him—he could not take more than a certain amount, and had always to take a certain minimum, the two limits (having on the average a spread of about 14 per cent.) being determined by the seasonal oscillations of his own note issue in the past.[2] Once the upper limit was reached he could apply for discount accommodation only on the usual terms, the Bank naturally having the right to refuse further assistance, just as it could refuse any ordinary private application. Accommodation given under these special arrangements was generally described as a loan, secured on approved bills—always endorsed by the discounter—having a maximum currency of 90 days [3] ; but the Bank bought the bills outright, and the borrower could not substitute fresh bills for those already " pledged ".[4] There were slight variants of this general scheme. One bank, for example, received £10,000 without charge, £50,000 (with a minimum of £43,000) at 3 per cent., and an annual payment from the Branch Bank of £350, to cover the expense of actually procuring the notes.[5] Other banks had no fixed amounts assigned, but agreed to suspend their issues in return for general discount facilities and a ready contact with the London market. By 1831 twenty-four country

[1] See J. Horsley Palmer before 1832 Committee, Minutes, p. 32. Also Timothy A. Curtis before 1838 Committee, Minutes, p. 8 ; and Appendices to both Reports. The arrangements were usually terminable at a year's notice.

[2] See Timothy A. Curtis before 1838 Committee, Minutes, pp. 6, 7.

[3] The maximum was given as 90 days by Horsley Palmer in 1832, and as 95 days by Curtis in 1838.

[4] 1841 Committee, Minutes, Q. 1432, *et seq.*

[5] See Evidence of I. C. Wright, a Nottingham banker, before 1848 Lords' Committee. His bank's arrangement was made in 1837.

banks had been induced to relinquish issue by one or other of these methods, eleven banks having fixed amounts assigned, aggregating £786,000.[1] Special discount facilities of similar kind were also extended to several banks in Liverpool and Manchester which had never issued notes.[2]

The effect of these various arrangements upon the discount "markets" of the towns affected[3] was naturally considerable. Banks which had arranged to secure funds on such favourable[4] terms began to take local bills freely at low rates, undercutting the uniformly high rates maintained by their less fortunate competitors. Charles S. Forster complained that the Branch Banks had not only enforced discounting without an additional commission charge, but in his own town (Walsall) had reduced the rate of discount from 5 to 3½ per cent., and at times even to 3 per cent., compared with the ruling Bank rate of 4 per cent.[5] Where rates of discount were forced down in this fashion, the Branch Banks must have damaged the London bill brokers' connections with provincial traders and industrialists. This may be inferred from Samuel Gurney's emphatic opposition to the "substitution" schemes.[6] He declared that they had lowered the rate of interest, and produced the "strongest competition among money-dealers [he included non-issuing bankers under this heading] in those towns; I think it is altogether a wrong proceeding". In some instances, he said, the local rate had fallen below the market rate in London.

The brokers' loss of business on this account, however, was probably not very serious on balance. It was only in Lancashire, broadly speaking, that the weakening of local discount

[1] Appendix to 1832 Report.

[2] Appendix to 1838 Report.

[3] Special discount accommodation was furnished by the Branch Banks of Gloucester, Swansea, Birmingham, Newcastle, Hull, Portsmouth, Liverpool and Manchester.

[4] Some bankers, however, contended that their issues had cost less than 3 per cent., and that they therefore lost by the substitution; other witnesses declared that these bankers were thereupon forced to expand their turnover by increased re-discounting.

[5] Forster himself scorned to give up his issue for the advantages which the Branch Banks afforded, and jeered at his competitors for so doing. "When a banker issues notes," he declared, "and pays those notes honourably, he retains a much more important station in the commercial world; when he discounts bills with the paper of another establishment, and sends his bills to that establishment, he has become an agent of theirs, in fact, more a bill broker than a banker." (1832 Committee, Minutes, Q. 1504, *et seq.*)

[6] *Ibid.*, QQ. 3774–9.

rates became really acute; for as the banks of Liverpool and Manchester had never issued notes, any special discount accommodation enabled them to take a larger turnover, and did not merely replace a note issue which in some cases might have cost less than the 3 per cent. charged by the Bank. Moreover, the note-issuing bankers, as a class, had never been among the largest re-discounters, and some of them had always refused to countenance the practice. The concentration of their discount business at the Branch Banks, therefore, could not greatly have diminished the aggregate re-discounting in London, although it must have caused some reduction. It is possible, too, that the re-discounts of those Lancashire banks which had no special Branch Bank facilities may actually have been increased, owing to their desire to make up in increased turnover what they lost in lower rates, so long as the brokers, in their turn, would consent to work at a smaller profit-margin. Meanwhile, in towns where no special substitution arrangements had been made, the Branch Banks worked only at 4 per cent., their rate for *private* business in all towns, and also the rate charged normally by the other provincial bankers, despite the lower market rate in London.[1] In these districts, therefore, the brokers' connections tended to increase, under the stimulus of easier return remittances.

Even the extreme fall in discount rates in Lancashire must have had its compensations for the London market, for in this county, as already noted,[2] there was an abnormally large floating supply of bills. For dealings in raw cotton and yarn the price was always based on three months' credit, but if cash were paid an interest rebate of 5 per cent. was allowed (the rate was 6 per cent. for cotton manufactures). Thus, so long as the banks charged 5 per cent. for discounts (plus the commission), the bills tended to remain in circulation until maturity. When, however, local discount rates fell below 5 per cent., it became profitable for the trader to discount bills which he held, in order to pay cash and secure the rebate for fresh purchases. This process had begun in 1827, when the Bank of England rate, and therefore also local private discount rates, had been reduced to 4 per cent.,[3] but it was greatly increased when the Branch Bank discount facilities began to force local rates down

[1] See Gurney before 1832 Committee, Minutes, QQ. 3775–7.
[2] See *ante*, p. 31.
[3] Except for the period from 1822 to 1825 (*ante*, p. 35), Bank rate stood at 5 per cent. from 1746 until 1827.

below Bank rate.[1] The consequence was a marked reduction of the bill circulation in Lancashire,[2] and a marked increase in the volume of discounts; and it is a reasonable supposition that some part of the increase found its way to London, either through direct discounts, or through re-discounts. Another reason for the contraction of the bill circulation—though this is of less significance from the bill market standpoint—was the fact that those banks which accepted accommodation from the Branch Banks were forbidden to pay away bills to their customers. An exception was made in favour of bills of 21 days or less, as these were used primarily for distant remittance purposes, and consequently did not compete with Bank of England notes as currency.[3]

All factors considered, it seems that the special "substitution" schemes could have done little to offset the advantages to the bill market of the general facilities provided by the Branch Banks. Moreover, these special arrangements did not always work smoothly, and, where difficulties arose, the banks promptly sought the aid of the bill brokers. One witness complained that the Branch Banks not only scrutinized very closely all bills tendered as security, and frequently rejected some, but that they could not be relied upon to maintain the agreed accommodation at all times. Indeed, Samuel Turner, the Agent at the Liverpool Branch Bank, stated quite frankly that in times of acute pressure the joint stock banks were sometimes told that the usual 3 per cent. discounts would be withheld, and that money could be found for these banks only if obtained, at their expense, in the London market in the normal way.[4] Dyer, of the Manchester Joint Stock Bank, declared that the Branch Bank had caused him grave inconvenience by refusing discounts without any warning. His bank had naturally considered that the main value of the agreement with the Branch Bank was the apparent assurance of obtaining accommodation at reasonable rates at all times; when it found that there was, in fact, no

[1] S. J. Loyd, asked in 1832 when his house in Lancashire would charge commission as well as discount on local discounts, and whether commissions were customary prior to the establishment of the Branch Banks, replied that "discount transactions are a custom that has grown up in the last six or seven years, since the comparative cheapness of money". (1832 Committee, Minutes, QQ. 3356, 3357.)

[2] See 1832 Committee, Minutes, Q. 4421, and 1838 Committee, Minutes, Q. 289.

[3] See P. M. James before 1841 Committee, Minutes, Q. 1432 *et seq.*

[4] 1838 Committee, Minutes, p. 17.

such assurance, it turned instead to the London market, and passed its business through the bill brokers.[1]

Discrimination against Joint Stock Issuers' Paper

In the middle 'thirties, yet another aspect of Bank of England policy tended to throw the joint stock banks into the hands of the brokers. In this case, however, it was only the issuing bankers which were affected. The Bank, apparently not satisfied with its attack on the joint stock issuers through the policy of assisting non-issuers, adopted an even more aggressive attitude by refusing, both in London and at the branches, to discount any bill bearing the endorsement of the former class of joint stock bank.[2] This rule was aimed at joint stock re-discounting in the London market, and could have been justified as a prudent, though somewhat drastic, measure if it had included *all* joint stock endorsements, for the large volume of re-discounts in London was indisputably one cause of the unhealthy credit inflation and speculative excesses of the period.[3] But the desire to restrain such activity could hardly have been the dominant reason for the Bank's action, for the issuing joint stock banks, as a class, were not the worst offenders.

The restriction naturally had a salutary effect upon the banks concerned, for even the London bankers, who were not accustomed to re-discount at the Bank of England, were not anxious to take bills which were not re-discountable, and thus began to refuse the banned paper. Many country bankers adopted a similar attitude, especially in times of actual or expected money pressure. At times the joint stock issuers experienced the utmost difficulty in securing London re-discounts, as the following evidence by J. W. Gilbart [4] shows:

> Do you mean to say that with respect to bills unexceptionably good in themselves, with respect to which a bill broker would have no hesitation, that even those bills were difficult to discount if it were known that they had the endorsement of a joint stock bank of issue ?—Yes, it is known to be the rule that the Bank of England will not discount bills which have the endorsement of any joint stock bank of issue, and instances have occurred of the acceptances of the first bankers in London being refused on that account.

---

[1] 1832 Committee, Minutes, p. 306.

[2] See 1840 Committee, Evidence of J. B. Smith, and 1841 Committee, Minutes, Q. 1310.

[3] See *post*, p. 91, *et seq.*

[4] 1838 Committee, Minutes, Q. 2008.

Thomas Joplin, complaining also of the Bank's rule which limited discountable bills to those drawn direct on London, strongly opposed the new restriction [1]:

> The rule [against bills drawn upon country acceptors, even though payable in London] of the Bank of England may be a very proper one, as regards their own private trade; but inasmuch as it impedes the intercourse which subsists between bankers, it is very injurious to the commerce of the country, it ought not to exist with reference to bankers who find it necessary to apply to them in cases of emergency. They ought to understand most clearly that the Bank will discount for them in such event whatever good bills payable in London they may possess. So far, however, from this being the case, the Bank have actually adopted another rule which is far worse—they have resolved not to discount any bills upon which the endorsement of a Joint Stock Bank not issuing Bank of England notes is to be found, even though it may be in other respects in conformity with their rules and regulations. The consequence is that the Deposit banks have been obliged to refuse the paper of the Joint Stock Banks, and the wonder is that the latter have not all stopped payment. Had the rule produced all the effects intended, in preventing these banks obtaining discounts, there is no doubt that such would have been the result.
>
> Had the Bank refused to discount for them itself, perhaps much objection could not have been made; nor would the Joint Stock Banks have cared for such a determination. But to throw a barrier between them and the Deposit banks is a proceeding of which they and the country have a right to complain—as it is clear that the power thus possessed by the Bank is entirely derived from their monopoly. If they had to gain their business by competition with other establishments, such a rule would lose them their connections, for nobody would deal with a bank which refused the best bills of the country.

In periods of money stringency the operation of the new restriction must have reacted adversely upon the bill brokers, by reducing the volume of paper which could be placed; but in general it undoubtedly benefited them, by making their services even less dispensable to the joint stock issuers. Direct re-discounting by the latter through London banker agents or with other country banks had been made almost impossible. Joint stock issuers who had not previously employed brokers therefore began to do so, while existing connections were more firmly cemented; for the brokers, with their many contacts with merchants as well as bankers, could place bills where the joint stock banks themselves

[1] Joplin, *The Money Pressure of 1836*.

could not. Moreover, the larger firms, such as Gurney's, which conducted a dealing as well as a broking business, could if necessary carry a certain proportion of the paper themselves. A banker who bought bills in the market regarded them as a reserve, and therefore sought to ensure that practically the whole of them could in the last resort be tendered to the Bank of England ; but a large discount dealer, except in the worst money pressure, could consider himself secure if only a substantial proportion of his portfolio were thus re-discountable. Indeed, it seems not improbable that the large dealers actually preferred to hold a certain quantity of these bills, for, owing to the disability attaching to them, they were obtainable at comparatively favourable rates, without any corresponding loss of intrinsic quality.

The End of London Bank Re-discounting

From the standpoint of the bill market, the third main line of banking change which arose from the crisis of 1825—the cessation of re-discounting by the London private bankers—produced effects which were farther-reaching, and more fundamental, than those of either the development of the joint stock banks or of the Bank of England branches. These two tendencies increased the size of the market ; the third changed its form. It not only stimulated the growth of a new type of intermediary bill business, in principle that of the modern discount house, but was a major determinant of the distinctive and superior framework of the London Money Market as a whole. The importance of the altered practice of the London banks was not, however, fully appreciated at the time : in the short run, the change was definitely less spectacular than either of the other developments, both in its operation and in its impact upon Lombard Street ; and it probably did not yield any immediate or rapid increase in market turnover.

The reason for the London banks' step—the realization that it was imprudent to rely for cash resources unduly upon the Bank of England—has already been explained.[1] The change itself can be briefly described in the words of two contemporary observers. Glyn, a London private banker himself, told the 1848 Lords' Committee [2] that " in 1825 it is a notorious Fact that the Bankers of London, pressed upon by their Country Connexions, discounted with the Bank of England. Since that Period the private Bankers never have discounted with the Bank of England ". In conse-

[1] *Ante*, p. 37. [2] Minutes, Q. 1916.

quence, they began to establish cash reserves of their own,[1] and in order to avoid holding an unduly large proportion of idle barren funds, sought employment for a proportion of these in really short-term securities. Previously, they had employed in Government securities most of the funds which they could not use in discounts or loans to customers; after 1825 they turned instead to first-class bills of exchange bought through the London bill brokers ("brokers' bills", as they were called). But not even a three months' bill, despite its self-liquidating character, was a sufficiently liquid security for a non-issuer's banking reserve, if the banker was to be sure that he need never be forced to rediscount; for the clientèle of the City bankers, in contrast to that of the West End and Fleet Street bankers (and of some country bankers), consisted largely of business and commercial customers, whose accounts were very active in proportion to their size. The City bankers therefore sought to employ a part of their surplus in secured loans repayable on demand, necessarily at a proportionately lower rate than that obtainable on bills, and found that they could do so with the larger bill broking firms. The transition is thus described by Gilbart[2]:

> A London banker never considers as a part of his reserve the bills he has discounted for his customers. Nothing could damage his credit more than any attempt to rediscount these bills. During the war, the London bankers had discount accounts with the Bank of England; and in the panic of 1825, it is well known that they discounted largely with that establishment. But since that period they have not done so, and their endorsements are never seen in the money market. The practice is now more general of lodging money at call with the large money dealers. And it is in this way that the London bankers make provision for any sudden demand. It is rarely, however, that any large demand comes so suddenly as to occasion any inconvenience. And it may be observed that such bankers as are members of the Clearing-house [all the principal private London banks were members] have the whole day to make preparation—one of the circumstances which enables them to lock up at night with a smaller amount of cash.

In another passage,[3] Gilbart states that "after this event [the 1825 crisis] the London bankers changed the mode of their invest-

[1] See also Glyn's evidence before 1832 Committee, Minutes, Q. 2870. (*Ante*, p. 38.)

[2] A. S. Mitchie's edition of Gilbart, *The History, Principles and Practice of Banking* (1882), p. 301.

[3] *Logic of Banking* (1859), p. 555.

ment. Instead of employing their surplus funds in the purchase of Government securities, and discounting at the Bank of England, they placed their surplus funds on deposit with the bill brokers, and ceased to discount with the Bank." Thus began the vital change in bill market practice which was ultimately to revolutionize the market structure.

In 1825, however, few bill broking firms were big enough, or sufficiently well-connected, to justify them in assuming the responsibilities involved in thus employing borrowed funds to finance bills bought on their own account, nor was the credit of many of them strong enough to induce the bankers to lend. At the outset, Gurney's was probably the only house which was trusted in this way, and even after others had come into the business, its " book " for many years easily surpassed that of all of its competitors combined. But to those who could command the trust of the bankers, the new type of business was well worth while, for profits from the re-sale of bills, if not also from " running " them, could far exceed those obtainable from a simple brokerage connection.

Nevertheless, not even Gurney's could have embarked on bill dealing but for the fact that money rates after the 1825 crisis were well below the legal rate. The Usury Laws, fixing a maximum rate of 5 per cent., were a great handicap to all forms of banking business, but they made bill dealing by a specialist dealer virtually impossible. David Barclay Chapman, who succeeded Samuel Gurney as senior partner of Overend, Gurney & Co. in 1856, explained to the 1857 Committee that this restriction had severely hampered his firm even when it acted solely as brokers; and when asked whether he was ever able to charge more than 5 per cent. while the Act was in force, declared:

> No, we had very great difficulty. In the first place, we were prevented keeping capital in the house; I am speaking of 30 years ago; we acted then as brokers, and were obliged to act as brokers until that Act [the Usury Law] was repealed.[1]

Actually, his explanation was incomplete: there was nothing in the Usury Law which *forbade* a broker from also acting as dealer and " keeping money in the house "; but so long as the current rate of discount was equal to the legal rate, the restriction had this effect in practice.

There were several reasons for this. The first was that to take " deposits " and run a book even on a small scale seriously

[1] Minutes, Q. 4881.

endangered the more important brokerage business. So long as a firm acted solely as brokers, it could take bills at the legal rate of 5 per cent. discount, passing them on to the buyer at the same rate, and could in addition exact its own commission of ½ per cent. per annum (⅛ per cent. actual on a three months' bill) for "procuring". In theory, it could also accept deposits (if obtainable at less than 5 per cent.), and make a "running" profit by employing them in buying bills on its own account at 5 per cent., without any brokerage charge. Neither of these transactions would be in itself usurious, but if the two sets of operations should be in any way combined, the law would be infringed. Thus any house which had conducted business on these lines would have exposed itself to the constant risk of prosecution under the Act. If in fact the two operations had been strictly segregated (this would have been no easy matter in practice), the firm could, *prima facie*, have produced a complete defence by proving that no bill which had been taken at 5 per cent., plus brokerage, had been retained in portfolio. But, in practice, it would have been very difficult to convince a jury that this was the case, as Counsel's opinion given to Gurneys' of Norwich on an almost identical point plainly showed.[1] In the circumstances, the risk was not worth taking, for there were other serious obstacles to be considered as well. The most serious of these was that the twofold method of dealing would easily cause trouble among the firm's clients. These would readily sell their bills to the firm at 5 per cent. without a commission charge, but it would have been difficult to reimpose the commission once it had been relinquished. Sellers of bills would quite naturally have been resentful had they been told on one day that their discounts would cost them 5 per cent., and on the next that the cost would be 5½ per cent., not because of any change in the value of money, but simply because the discounters on the second occasion were acting as brokers. Yet such arbitrary variations of practice would have been necessary to preserve any profit at all on broking business.

A further important reason why the Usury Laws prevented bill dealing when the rate was 5 per cent.—apart from the obvious fact that there was then no possibility of a re-sale profit—was that a bill market house dare not carry bills on borrowed money unless it was virtually certain that most of them would be rediscountable in an emergency. But if a banker could secure a return of 5 per cent. on bills in normal times, it was most unlikely that he would be willing to buy them at that rate in a pressure,

[1] See *ante*, p. 22.

even though he had funds to spare, which most bankers at such moments had not. For in periods of real stringency, much higher rates could almost invariably be secured in other ways, such as by " continuation " loans on stock.[1] The holder of bills who desired to sell was thus greatly hampered by his inability to attract buyers by offering a high rate, and although various eminent witnesses [2] declared that bills could be sold even at the height of the 1825 panic, the uncertainties were too great to leave an adequate safety margin to the firm whose whole reputation and business depended upon its ability to repay call loans at a moment's notice.

The initiation of bill dealing business after 1825 was thus due as much to the fact that market rates were below 5 per cent. as to the willingness of the London bankers to lend funds at call. Before that date, as has been explained, the rate was generally a fixed 5 per cent., except for a short period in 1817 and 1818, and again in 1822–5. The 5 per cent. rate was, in fact, often quite arbitrary, as was the Bank rate; bankers expected 5 per cent. on discounts, and they got it, for except when an increase in the Bank of England's issue produced an extreme glut of money, there was no attempt to cut rates. " When I first came to the business," [3] said Chapman,[4] " and for several years afterwards, we charged the Bank rate,[5] and $\frac{1}{8}$ per cent. commission; the Bank rate was a uniform rate, and did not fluctuate for several years afterwards; it generally stood at 5 per cent., and we charged a commission for transacting the business . . . we charged one uniform rate of 5 per cent." But after the firm adopted a dealing business, it dealt " according to the true value of money ":

> When the system altered with you, and you charged under the legal rate, did you then charge a commission; suppose, for instance

---

[1] See *ante*, p. 29. [2] *Ante*, p. 49 *n*.

[3] Chapman joined Gurney's in 1817.

[4] 1857 Committee, Minutes, Q. 5265.

[5] Chapman's memory was at fault to some extent, for his house (according to Gurney in 1819) charged $4\frac{1}{2}$ per cent. for a short period in 1818. His evidence in 1857 is in places actually contradictory; and he implied that the rigid 5 per cent. rate ruled right up to the time when the firm began to act as dealers (which he asserted quite definitely was after 1825), although a table of rates which he produced showed that $3\frac{1}{2}$ per cent. was charged throughout 1824, and well into 1825, when it rose to 4 per cent., and eventually to $4\frac{1}{2}$ per cent., plus commission in each case. The passages quoted, however, seem to be reliable, apart from the small error first noted.

> you charged 4 per cent. ?—No ; our business assumed a totally different character ; we departed from the business of brokers to the business of dealers ; we dealt, according to the true value of money, with the public. It is a very rare thing indeed that we charge a commission ; it must be a very exceptional case.[1]

Bank rate did, in fact, remain at the legal maximum until July 5, 1827, but the effects of the crisis, so far as money rates were concerned, had passed by June, 1826, when the market rate of discount for first-class paper dropped to 4½ per cent. From that time onwards, Bank rate became increasingly ineffective, for by June, 1827, the market rate had reached 3 per cent., remaining at that level until the end of 1828. With such a comfortable margin between the current rate and the legal maximum, Gurney's were able to take full advantage of the new willingness of the London private banks to lend funds at call.

From the moment when they did so, there began that divorce of the commercial banks from the Bank of England which has since become one of the most important features of the structure of the London Money Market. In other less highly organized money markets an increased demand upon the commercial banks for cash leads them to increase their re-discounts with the central bank. Moreover, an increase in the aggregate of these re-discounts, and therefore of central bank credit, may occur temporarily even at times when there is no real shortage of available credit ; for as a banker will not ordinarily re-discount with other commercial banks, an application to the central bank in these markets may be caused simply by a momentary unevenness in the distribution of the credit supply. One bank may be re-discounting, while its competitors have more funds than they can readily use.[2] Anomalies of this kind cause fluctuations in market rates, and rapid swings from ease to stringency, which cannot occur in the London market. In London an increased public demand for cash is met simply by a calling-in of short loans from the bill " brokers ", who immediately discover whether one bank can lend the equivalent of what another has called. Only when it is apparent that the fresh loans will not balance the withdrawals is there any re-discounting with the Bank of England, and then it is the bill " brokers ", and not the bankers, who thus apply for assistance. One of the most important advantages of this system is that the discount market, strictly so-called, becomes

[1] 1857 Committee, Minutes, Q. 5267.

[2] The operation of the Federal Reserve System in recent years has provided repeated examples of this sort of credit " wastage ".

a kind of "buffer" or shock-absorber, lessening the impact of major changes in the credit position upon the trade and commerce of the country, and always ensuring that there shall be no application for increased central bank credit unless and until the need for it is clearly demonstrated.

This vital change of practice in London did not, of course, become effective immediately—or, indeed, for many years—after 1825, for although the London private banks, by refraining from re-discounts and by lending at call, began in principle to operate in exactly the same fashion as they do to-day, banks in the provinces, as has already been explained, continued and actually increased their re-discounting operations. Nor was there any rapid alteration in the bill market mechanism, despite the fact that within a few years a number of provincial joint-stock banks also became ready lenders of funds at call.[1] Apart from the fact, previously noted, that few bill brokers were then of sufficient standing to attract such loans, there were two important reasons for this slow growth. The first was the restriction imposed by the Usury Laws, for although these were in practice inoperative so long as money rates remained low, there was always the contingent danger that a sudden rise in rates might make the limitation again effective. To guard against this risk of embarrassment, the prudent operator was obliged to refrain from carrying more than a moderate portfolio, and therefore would not accept deposits on any extensive scale. This handicap to bill dealing, as opposed to bill broking, was not removed until 1833, when, as a result of the strong agitation of witnesses before the 1832 Committee, bills of exchange of up to three months were exempted from the legal restriction. The exemption was granted by section 7 of the Bank Charter Act of 1833.

The second impediment to the growth of bill dealing in its first few years arose from the fact that until 1830 bill market houses were not allowed to have discount accounts with the Bank of England. In these circumstances, the London bankers naturally preferred not to commit themselves too heavily in call loans to the market. In normal times there was virtually no risk in such loans, so long as they were restricted to substantial and reputable houses, for a dealer could ordinarily borrow from one banker to repay another, and in the last resort could re-sell bills; but the bankers fully realized that in a time of pressure all banks would probably be calling simultaneously, and that, in

[1] See *ante*, pp. 42, 47–50.

addition, the country banks would prefer not to increase their bill portfolios. At such a period, not even the best bill broker connection could afford much protection, and not even the most credit-worthy of bill market houses could guarantee that it would not be compelled to default on its undertaking to repay at " call ". The only ultimate guarantee would have been an ability to go to the Bank of England and demand notes against bills; and, as the brokers were denied this right, the London bankers, had they lent very heavily at call, would have run the risk of being obliged, in time of pressure, to break their rule and approach the Bank direct.

The actual alteration in the Bank of England's practice in this respect will be considered in the succeeding section.[1] Here it is sufficient to record that after 1833 the bill market both had rediscounting facilities and was freed from the yoke of the Usury Laws. The purely technical obstacles to the rise of the new type of bill business had been removed, and the system made steady progress from that time onwards. Before 1844, however, it remained a comparatively small part of the activities of the market, which was still engaged primarily in broking business. Brokers far outnumbered dealers, and it is certain that even the latter carried portfolios which were much smaller than the aggregate volume of their operations. To judge from Gurney's experience, dealing and broking businesses were not conducted simultaneously, for Chapman explained that his business " assumed a totally different character ", by which he clearly meant that the firm began to buy all bills for its own account, acting always as a principal. But there is no doubt that, for a number of years after the change, a very large proportion of the bills which it bought was re-sold *immediately*, so that no question of financing them arose. In these " jobbing " operations, the significance of the change in practice was not very apparent. The only differences were that, under the new system, profits came from the margin between the rate of discount at which the various houses bought and the rate at which they re-sold, instead of from a fixed commission; and that, as endorsers, they became contingently liable on all bills which passed through their hands, whereas as brokers they had incurred no legal liability whatever.

The fourth, and last, major change which sprang from the 1825 crisis—a new attitude of the Bank of England towards its responsibilities and functions—was also of fundamental, rather than

[1] See *post*, pp. 88–90.

immediately spectacular, importance in the evolution of the banking system and the discount market. To appreciate its significance, however, demands a knowledge of the relationships between the Bank of England and the market in the preceding years. The whole transition is therefore best discussed in a separate section, which immediately follows.

CHAPTER III

GROWTH OF CENTRAL BANKING FUNCTIONS

There is abundant evidence to show that at a very early date the Bank of England recognized that its special position, as banker to the Government and as sole London note-issuer, demanded that its affairs should be managed on different principles from those which governed the activities of a purely " private " bank. Even before the close of the eighteenth century, as the evidence before the 1797 inquiry reveals, the Bank was groping towards a rudimentary species of general credit control. During the Restriction period, as has been shown, it operated regularly in the discount market on competitive terms ; but it is clear that these activities were dictated only partially by motives of private profit.

In the first place, its resources were indispensable to the market. Except on the comparatively rare occasions when a plethora of funds forced outside rates below the 5 per cent. Bank rate, the commercial world and " private " discounters alike relied upon the Bank for substantial discount accommodation. This reliance, indeed, was very marked even before the Restriction period, as the intense opposition aroused by a contractionary policy adopted in the pressure of 1793, and again in December, 1795, plainly demonstrated. On the second occasion, when the Bank announced that it would reject a proportion of each discount application whenever total demands exceeded the sum " it shall be resolved to discount on that Day ",[1] public feeling was so strong that a meeting of London merchants resolved to issue their own joint promissory notes against deposits of cash, bank bills and commercial paper.[2] The scheme did not materialize, but a year later, just after the suspension of cash payments, we find similar meetings [3] protesting against renewed restrictions, and finally resolving—

[1] The text of the Notice will be found in App. 14 to the 1797 Report, p. 224.

[2] See Powell, *op. cit.*, p. 237.

[3] Meetings at the London Tavern on March 16, 24, and 31, 1797. (See 1797 Report, App. 18, pp. 228–30.)

> That the Committee . . . are of opinion that it is important to the Mercantile Interest of the Country . . . that the Practice of Discounts should be extended to and continued upon the Scale stated . . . and that, therefore, if the Bank of England be incompetent [owing to the large extent of its advances to the Treasury] to afford this necessary and reasonable Aid, it will be requisite that some other Public Establishment should be created to supply the Deficiency ; at the same time wishing that this Assistance may be derived through the old and customary Channel, the Bank of England.

These protests, together with the fact that outside discounts were almost unobtainable when the Bank was restricting,[1] clearly indicate the degree of dependence. " When the Bank of England discounts readily all good Bills," declared Boyd in 1797,[2] " Merchants, Bankers, and individuals of every description having the command even for a very short time of sums of money, readily employ such money in discounting such Bills of Exchange, because they know, that at any future day when they have occasion for their money again, they have only to send in to the Bank the same bills they had discounted."

Early Efforts at Credit Control

This dependence, however, does not wholly explain the Bank's constant activities in the market, for provided that it had increased its issues in other ways, and so long as it was an *ultimate* source of discount assistance, the needs of business could easily have been almost wholly supplied by private discounters. Actually, the Bank regarded active discount operations as an essential part of its system of credit control, preferring always to make its issues against commercial bills rather than against Government securities. One reason for this preference, as the Governor, Daniel Giles, explained in 1797,[3] was the self-liquidating and short-dated character of investments in bills, which gave the Bank greater elasticity in expanding or contracting its issues, and also enabled it to grant a larger accommodation with safety than it could have

[1] Henry Thornton, describing the pressure of December, 1795, declared, " I believe that private Discounts had at that time nearly ceased, if not entirely so—I do not mean by private Discounts the Discounts of Bankers, who in general discount for their Customers in all Periods—I mean by private Discounters, individual Merchants, or Monied Men, who lend out Money upon Bills." (Evidence before 1797 Committee, p. 140.)

[2] 1797 Lords' Committee, Minutes, p. 67. [3] *Ibid.*, p. 68.

done against Government paper.[1] But the principal reason was the belief that by lending on bills the Bank could always ensure that the business situation was kept within proper bounds. "When the money is lent on discount," said George Dorrien, Governor in 1819,[2] "the directors are enabled to check any improper speculations, or any circumstances that they think injurious to the country." When money was lent against securities, he argued,[3] the discounts would be made by private discounters, so that speculations might be financed which the Bank would not notice, or might in any event be unable to check.

These facts—the public reliance on the one hand, and the attempt to prevent speculation on the other—demonstrate clearly that even before 1825 the Bank had some conception of the functions of a central bank, upon whom there was a duty imposed to protect and assist the public. But although this principle was becoming dimly recognized by the Bank board, its application was crude in the extreme. The central theory which governed the Bank's credit policy was a conviction that it was impossible to over-issue notes so long as the issues were made by commercial discounts, and for legitimate business only. The working-rule was, "Let the public act upon the circulation": the public would apply for notes when they were required, and would always repay its loans when less notes were required, to the extent of the excess. The Bank never "forced" its circulation, said the Governor in 1810,[4] with apparent pride. It thus professed to follow a purely passive policy, in the placid faith that it could safely comply with all demands upon it, provided that it was satisfied that these came from "solid" merchants for bona-fide and not speculative transactions.[5] At the time of the Bullion Report, even the level of discount rates was held to be irrelevant to the volume of speculative or legitimate activity, and thus, also, to the safety of the Bank's position. Both the Governor and Deputy-Governor contended[6] that the security against an additional issue would be "precisely the same" whether it was made by discounts at 5 per cent., 4 per cent., or 3 per cent.; and there were traces of this belief even in 1819.[7]

[1] By 1810 it was a recognized principle that the Bank's portfolio should always include some bills falling due on every day. (See Bullion Committee, Evidence of Whitmore, p. 80.)

[2] 1819 Commons' Committee, Minutes, p. 26.

[3] 1819 Lords' Committee, Minutes, p. 32.

[4] Bullion Committee, Minutes, pp. 96, 97.

[5] *Ibid.*

[6] *Ibid.*, Evidence of Whitmore and Pearse.

[7] 1819 Commons' Committee, Evidence of Dorrien, p. 145.

A natural corollary to this general principle of credit control was a complete indifference both to the state of the foreign exchanges and to the price of gold. Whitmore said in 1810 [1] that he " did not advert to the circumstance of the exchanges " in regulating the amount of his loans and discounts, " it appearing upon a reference to the amount of our notes in circulation, and the course of the Exchange, that they frequently have no connexion ", which ingenuous remark he amplified by saying that his personal opinion was that the amount of the circulation had " no reference " to the exchange.[2] His views on the price of gold appeared at first sight to be more discerning, for he did advert to the difference between the mint and market prices ; but any credit for astuteness which this statement might have gained him must have been sadly diminished by the explanation which followed [2]—" inasmuch as we do not discount, *at any time*, for those persons who we know or have good reason to suppose export Gold ". And that was all : both he and Pearse, who humbly " concurred ",[2] were convinced that exchanges and gold prices were hidden mysteries quite irrelevant to discount policy. Nine years later the same opinions were still current in the Bank parlour. Dorrien, asked by an apparently incredulous Sir Robert Peel,[3] whether the Bank's sole criterion of control was the " nature " of the business offered, without any regard for the exchanges, promptly pointed out that—

> If a house, which is in the constant habit of dealing in exchanges, were to send in a large sum for discount, at a time that the exchanges were unfavourable to the country, it certainly would become a part of the consideration.

In such a case, however, the exchanges would be considered because they might affect the credit of the house in question ; in other cases, they were " made a consideration only in a general way ". It is only fair to note that Dorrien showed greater powers of penetration before the Lords' Committee,[4] for in an interesting passage (which indicated that even then the " differentials " between discount rates in different foreign markets were beginning to have important effects) he explained that the pressure in the Paris market, in other " great Continental commercial towns ", and in America towards the end of 1818 began to affect the ex-

[1] Bullion Report, p. 16, and Minutes, p. 96.
[2] *Ibid.*, Evidence of Whitmore and Pearse.
[3] 1819 Commons' Committee, Minutes, p. 33.
[4] Minutes, p. 33.

change adversely because discount rates abroad were mugh higher than in London. But he was unable to reckon the par of exchange with France, as it was not his " line of business ".[1]

The Bullion Committee itself had exposed these fallacies, and had shown that in its credit policy the Bank did not even adhere to its professed rule [2]; but the advice which might have averted the 1825 crisis was not followed. Nor, from the Bank's standpoint, did there seem to be any pressing reason why it should have been followed, for since the Committee's recommendation of an early return to specie payments was equally ignored, the Bank directors remained free from the one restriction which could not have failed ultimately to reveal to them the danger, as well as the fallacy, inherent in their policy.

To the discount market, the significance of this policy was not only that it resulted in constant and sometimes intense competition from the Bank for discount business, but that it tended to endanger the stability of all bill dealings by actually stimulating the growth of unsound and speculative paper. The Bank authorities no doubt honestly attempted to discriminate against speculative paper, but the test of whether or not an application was " bona-fide " was not easily applied, and when in doubt they clearly preferred to err on the side of leniency. In consequence, the Bank frequently discounted beyond the point at which, even on the basis of its own inadequate rule, fresh discounts ought to have ceased. Two passages are specially illuminating. Sir Francis Baring, attacking the whole theory that issues could be regulated solely on the basis of the volume of good bills offered for discount, gave some glaring instances of abuse [3]:

[1] Horsley Palmer, it is worthy of note, was in 1832 no less observant of the rules of professional etiquette, for although he " imagined the Bank of England to be the only body which has knowledge of the actual state of the Foreign Exchanges ", he could not say how the par of exchange was to be " defined in figures ". He preferred the surer method of testing the rate by watching to see whether gold would be withdrawn from, or offered to, the Bank. (1832 Committee, Minutes, p. 14).

[2] " The Bank," declared the Committee, quoting Whitmore and Pearse, " ' does not comply with the whole demand upon them for discounts, and they are never induced, by a view to their own profit, to push their issues beyond what they deem to be consistent with the public interest ' ; in other words, they do not act up to the principle which they represent as perfectly sound and safe, and must be considered therefore as possessing no distinct and certain rule to guide their discretion in controlling the amount of their circulation." (See 1810 Report, p. 16, *et seq.*)

[3] 1810 Committee, Minutes, p. 132.

. . . there are many instances of clerks not worth £100 establishing themselves as merchants, and receiving (since the restriction) an accommodation from the Bank, by discounting what is called good bills to the amount (probably) of five or £10,000; such a demand, I am inclined to consider as created by the Bank, and not arising out of a regular course of trade, such as would exist if the restriction were removed. . . .

The second extract, from the evidence of William Ward,[1] a director of the Bank, a "cambist" and a Mediterranean merchant, can be left to speak for itself:

In the event of Mercantile Embarrassment, might not Bills which would otherwise be considered as good, become so discredited as to oblige the Bank to refuse to discount them?

It would have that effect on the Bills of great Speculators, but not with others; because the Principle upon which the Bank acts, is to render its discounts as beneficial as possible to the Public; and from a *Spirit of Kindness* it would probably extend the same Indulgence as usual, whenever it could discriminate between Speculators and regular Traders.

Would the Bank then be induced to discount the Bills of regular Traders, although under the supposed case of general Mercantile Distress they might not be considered as safe?

They would not do so if they were decidedly considered as unsafe; but there being always Two and sometimes more Securities, they would *hope for the best*, and discount liberally; because if each party could pay 10*s*. in the Pound the Bank would not ultimately lose.

It might have been expected that the policy of keeping always in touch with the discount market, and of invariably holding a large proportion of total securities in commercial bills, would have produced a highly-variable Bank rate policy. But in fact the Bank board believed that an alteration in the rate would never affect the volume of legitimate bills tendered.[2] "Demand," said Dorrien, "proceeds from the wants of the public," and these, he believed, could not be altered by any variation in the cost of satisfying them. "The experience and constant attendance of the directors . . . enable them to judge what is a sufficient accommodation to the real wants of the trade of the country, and that is always supplied." [2] The Bank therefore maintained a constant rate, and was undoubtedly assisted in so doing by the almost equal rigidity of private bank discount

[1] 1819 Lords' Committee, Minutes, p. 60.

[2] 1819 Commons' Committee, Minutes, pp. 145–6. See also, *ante*, p. 73.

charges. In 1817, however, the decline in discount applications [1] at the Bank did lead to a suggestion that the rate might be lowered, but Jeremiah Harman, the Deputy-Governor, was convinced that the board acted rightly in opposing a change because, although a reduction " might have been consistent with the existing state of things then, in all probability we should have had to raise it again "—two years later.[2] Needless variations in rates, then as now, were generally regarded as detrimental to trade, but the theory seemed to have been followed a little slavishly. Harman, who endorsed all Dorrien's theories, nevertheless denied that the Bank " was run on mechanical principles ".[2]

Even the resumption of cash payments did not at once force the Bank board to realize the error of its ways. It is true that a more cautious policy was followed from 1819 to 1821, but this was due solely to the need for conserving reserves in preparation for the return to full convertibility—scheduled at first to take place in 1823, but actually achieved in 1821—and not to any better grasp of fundamental principles. That this was so is apparent from the reckless lending policy after 1822, when the Bank found that it had a large surplus reserve. It required the crisis of 1825 to point the moral, but even then, as will be seen, the lesson was not fully learned.

The Policy of a " Fixed and Uniform " Bank Rate

The experience gained in that year, when the Bank was actually forced to seek assistance from the Bank of France, did, however, bring home to the board the dangers which could arise from ignoring the foreign exchanges, and shortly afterwards—about 1827—the Bank began to take official cognizance of them in determining its credit policy.[3] But the old principle of " letting the public act upon the issues " was not abandoned : the new theory was grafted on to the old, and a fresh rule evolved, under which the Bank professed to aim at backing its liabilities—deposits as well as notes—as to one-third in gold and the balance in securities.[3] The aim was then to keep the securities as constant as possible, as by so doing the Bank would ensure that its note issue would fluctuate only through the action of the public in

[1] *Ante*, p. 28.
[2] 1819 Commons' Committee, Minutes, p. 146 ; and see 1797 Committee, Minutes, pp. 15–16.
[3] See Horsley Palmer's evidence before 1832 Committee, Minutes, Q. 72.

paying in or withdrawing gold, which action would in turn be governed by the state of the exchanges. A natural corollary to this principle—Horsley Palmer's famous "Rule of 1832", so-called because he first propounded it in public to the Committee of that year—was that the Bank should no longer be a regular or substantial source of discounts. Had Bank rate been maintained in close touch with market rates, the Bank, except in times of stress, would have had no excuse for rejecting any legitimate discount demand which might be made upon it, and in that event it would have been impossible to keep the volume of securities stable (except, possibly, by constant equalizing operations in Government stocks), and the old troubles would have recurred.

Accordingly, the Bank definitely relinquished its theory that discount operations had to be a central part of its credit control. In this respect, it substituted an exactly opposite principle. Horsley Palmer declared that so long as the Bank was well supplied with other readily marketable securities, private discounts were one of the "worst means" of regulating issues, for they interfered with the action of the London private banks and tended to an extension of the circulation which might be prejudicial to the Bank. The board therefore preferred that its rate should be generally above the market rate, "thereby not to interfere with the employment of money actually in existence", and argued that the Bank should be "a bank of discounts" only in times of emergency. The underlying theory of Bank rate technique from 1825 to 1844 cannot be better explained than in Palmer's own words [1]:

> . . . in ordinary times the leading functions of the Bank of England have been to furnish, upon a stated principle, an adequate supply of paper money convertible into coin and bullion upon demand, and to act as a bank for safe deposit of public and private money, and in so acting, that it is not deemed to be desirable to attempt to regulate the amount of issues of the Bank in London through commercial discounts, but that there are occasions and circumstances when the functions of the Bank as a bank for commercial discounts in the Capital have been and must ever be of the first importance to the country . . . when a scarcity of money or discredit exists in the London commercial money market. . . . The reasons which appear to me to exist against the regulation of the

[1] 1832 Committee, Minutes, p. 37. See also 1848 Commons' Committee, Evidence of James Morris (Q. 2641) and of S. J. Loyd; and 1848 Lords' Report, pp. xxxiii and xxxiv.

amount of the issues through commercial discounts in London, arise from the magnitude of the deposits in the possession of the bankers of London and other individuals, seeking employment with which the Bank ought not, in my opinion, to interfere. The Bank, fixing a public rate of interest at which it may be willing to discount all approved bills of a given description, and being the only body issuing money *ad libitum*, within the sphere of the circulation of such bills, thereby fixes the *maximum* of the rate of interest during the existence of such notice, and consequently all persons having money already in existence to employ, must necessarily offer to lend it under the Bank's public rate, except in times of actual scarcity or deficiency of money currency. If the Bank were required to hold no other securities than commercial bills, they would be under the necessity of acting in common with all other parties, *viz.*, by competition in the purchase of bills of exchange at the existing market rate of interest. It is that competition with private bankers and individuals in London which seems to me to be so objectionable. . . .

This principle, it will be observed, represented a substantial advance upon those followed before 1825. On all fundamental points, it differed but little from what has since come to be regarded as the classic principle of orthodox central bank credit control. Unfortunately, it was not rigidly pursued, for the Bank did *not* keep its securities at a constant level, neither did it regularly maintain one-third of its liabilities in bullion.[1] One reason for this was that the activities in the provinces, particularly the operation of the special " substitution " schemes, were in direct conflict with the general theory. The Bank rate aspect of the new principle was, on the other hand, strictly followed : the Bank *did* maintain its rate above market rate, and in London did, therefore, cease to conduct any substantial volume of regular

[1] Between 1832 and 1840 the " difference between the highest and lowest amount of deposits was £12,384,000 ; securities, £10,804,000 ; bullion, £8,178,000 ; whilst the difference between the highest and lowest amount of circulation is only £3,334,000 ; the securities, which were to have been kept even, varied to the extent of nearly £11,000,000, and the circulation, which ought to have varied with the influx or efflux of bullion, varied only to the extent of rather more than £3,000,000. The result of the action of the Bank was to keep their circulation even, and to let their deposits, securities, and bullion vary ".—Chairman of the 1840 Committee before the House of Commons during the debate on the 1844 Act. See *House of Commons Debates*, Vol. LXXIV (Series 3), May 20, 1844, cited by Professor T. E. Gregory in his *British Banking Statutes and Reports, 1832–1928* (Vol. I, p. xviii). The latter work contains a reasoned analysis of the evolution of central banking theory and technique throughout the century.

discount business. This is plainly demonstrated by the following table :

BANK RATE AND MARKET RATE, 1824–1844.*

(Yearly Averages)

Year.	Bank Rate. (*a*) %	Market Rate. (*b*) %	Excess of (*a*) over (*b*). %
1824	4·00	3·50	0·50
1825	4·05	3·88	0·17
1826	5·00	4·50	0·50
1827	4·52	3·25	1·27
1828	4·00	3·04	0·96
1829	4·00	3·38	0·62
1830	4·00	2·81	1·19
1831	4·00	3·69	0·31
1832	4·00	3·15	0·85
1833	4·00	2·73	1·27
1834	4·00	3·38	0·62
1835	4·00	3·71	0·29
1836	4·39	4·25	0·14
1837	5·00	4·44	0·56
1838	4·13	3·00	1·13
1839	5·10	5·12	−*0·02*
1840	5·07	4·98	0·09
1841	5·00	4·90	0·10
1842	4·27	3·33	0·94
1843	4·00	2·17	1·83
1844†	4·00	1·97	2·03

* The market rates are those charged by Overend, Gurney and Co., and are calculated from the table of *monthly* average rates which Chapman laid before the 1857 Committee (1857 Report, App. C).

† First 8 months only : period before passing of Bank Act of that year.

These figures graphically substantiate S. J. Loyd's statement [1] that before 1844 the Bank rate " was 4 or 5 per cent. ; if the market rate of interest was below 4 per cent., the Bank ceased to discount till it got up again to that point ". This policy was said to have prevented violent fluctuations in market rates. Actually, there were considerable fluctuations, but there is no doubt that they would have been more marked had the Bank competed for discount business. Thus the Lords' Committee of 1848 declared [2] that the practice of the Bank (before 1844) to discount " at a rate nearly fixed and uniform "—

> . . . must necessarily have checked the Fall in the Rate of Discount, when already low, which the active competition of the Bank

[1] Before 1848 Commons' Committee, Minutes Q. 5262.

[2] Report, pp. xxxiii–xxxiv.

> of England must have produced, and on the other hand must have checked the Tendency upwards which would have been the result of a reduction in the number of lenders. . . . In the one case the Bank was kept out of the Discount Market ; in the other it obtained almost the command of that market. In both cases the effect was to produce steadiness and diminish fluctuation.

The Committee's reference to a " uniform " as well as a " fixed " rate was to the fact that the Bank did not discriminate between various classes of eligible paper. The principle of the " minimum rate ", so well known to-day, had yet to be introduced : the published Bank rate was applied whatever the currency of the bills, and whatever the standing of the parties to them or of the applicants for accommodation. Except for comparatively short periods in times of stringency, the maximum usance was 95 days, and the rate charged " was invariably the same whether the bills were good or whether they were indifferent. I do not mean to say that bad bills were done, but supposing the bills were passed, they were done at the same rate," explained Morris in 1848.[1] One result of the whole policy was that the Bank generally secured only second-class paper, but Horsley Palmer considered that the practice helped many people to secure finance who could not otherwise have done so, as their bills, though " good ", were not acceptable to the market.[2]

An inevitable consequence of the rigidity of Bank rate policy was that in time of pressure the Bank relied entirely upon restriction of discount facilities to check demands upon it. James Morris admitted that before 1844 this was virtually the only " weapon " employed : the Bank either curtailed the volume of discounts absolutely, by limiting the amount available for each applicant, or shortened the permissible currency.[3] The first method generally aroused the greater public outcry, and was hardly employed after the resumption of cash payments—Horsley Palmer stated that it had never been the " general practice " of the Bank, unless the demand were " to an extravagant extent ".[4] Limitation of the *échéance* was almost equally objectionable, for in practice it amounted to a refusal of assistance to holders of a very large part of the total bill circulation, and operated with especial harshness against those trades where usances were necessarily long. In consequence, these measures often increased commercial discredit at the very time when public alarm was

[1] *Ibid.*, Minutes, Q. 480.
[2] 1832 Committee, Minutes, QQ. 170–2.
[3] 1848 Lords' Committee, Minutes, Q. 534. [4] *Ibid.*, Q. 896.

most dangerous. Loyd, writing in 1844,[1] declared that "a rate of discount by the Bank of 8 or 10 per cent. would have been considered preferable to some of the limitations which prevailed".

Before the exemption of three months' bills from the Usury Laws, one or other of these methods of control was inevitable, but their disadvantages were generally recognized by the Bank. Thus Palmer pointed out in 1832[2] that, if Bank rate had reached the maximum, the authorities might be compelled, if the foreign exchanges were adverse, "to limit the quality or description of bills to be tendered for discount . . . as the only resource left . . . either of which measures would be equally detrimental to the commerce of the country".[3] But despite the relaxation of the Usury Laws in 1833 (the concession was extended to bills of all dates a few years later), the Bank retained the *échéance* weapon. Until June 20, 1839, Bank rate never rose above 5 per cent.,[4] and even when the rate weapon was then brought into play, it was accompanied by exceptionally stringent limitations, the eligible currency being restricted temporarily to no more than 30 days.[5] It was quickly restored to 95 days, but in the following year the restrictive policy was again employed, this time as an alternative to an increase in the rate.

[1] *Thoughts on the Separation of the Departments* (1844). Loyd, however, discussing the limitation of *échéance* to 65 days, was "not at all prepared to say that there are not some advantages attending this more severe mode of limitation". He considered that it was desirable to warn the commercial community against over-trading by periodically making it difficult, or less facile, to realize the best securities.

[2] 1832 Committee, Minutes, p. 37.

[3] But *cf*. G. W. Norman before the same Committee (Q. 2437): "What do you think is the best way of diminishing the issues upon discounts, do you not think it is better to raise the rate of discount than to do it by a capricious rejection of a portion of the paper that is offered for discount?—Most decidedly so; the inconvenience then falls on those best able to bear it. I consider the attempt to reduce discounts in general, by rejecting the bills of any particular persons, as a plan likely to fail, and to be productive of great public inconvenience, and that it ought never to be adopted except in cases of the very last necessity. Under certain circumstances, we might *without much inconvenience* diminish the limit beyond which bills offered for discount shall not run, from three months to two months, for instance, as it was formerly."

[4] The rate was raised to 5½ per cent. on June 20, and to 6 per cent. on August 1, 1839.

[5] See Morris's evidence before 1848 Commons' Committee, Minutes, QQ. 4431, 4432.

THE FIRST "OPEN MARKET" OPERATIONS

While they lasted, restrictions of this kind naturally pressed with peculiar severity upon the discount market, especially upon those houses which had turned to the dealing business; but they were really of only transitory importance. Of much greater significance were two other developments of the Bank's new attitude towards its responsibilities. The first development provided the earliest important example of what is now generally described as "open market" policy. Strictly, this term should be applied to any dealings by the Bank in the market, but as in recent years the authorities have rarely operated on any important scale except for the purpose of evening out the day-to-day flow of money,[1] "open market" policy has come to signify the Bank's stabilizing activities. Many post-war writers on the Money Market have regarded these activities and this particular technique as the successor to the earlier practice of the Bank of "borrowing" on Consols. This is hardly correct, for before the war the custom of selling stock for cash and buying it back forward was used much more generally as a means of making a Bank rate increase "effective" than as an equalizing device *independently* of Bank rate action. It resembled modern "open market" operations only in that these, too, are not infrequently employed to render Bank rate action more effective; but the true analogy with present stabilizing devices is to be found in practices which actually preceded by several years the "borrowing on Consols".

These practices originated directly from the Bank's new aloofness from the market after 1825. So long as Bank rate remained in touch with market rate, any money pressure, whether severe or not, would immediately be reflected in an increased demand for discount at the Bank. Provided, therefore, that the Bank was able and willing to meet such demands—as it was at all normal times—it was impossible for any violent stringency to develop. With Bank rate normally well above market rate, the position was very different. Any increasing pressure then would not produce a material increase in the demands on the Bank until the outside rate had risen to parity with, or even beyond,

[1] The recent activities of the Exchange Equalization Account, and operations required by the Bank's private business, by its capacity as agent for overseas central banks, or by sinking fund purchases, etc., are obvious exceptions.

Bank rate, and by that time considerable commercial inconvenience would have been caused. Such a rise in outside rates would, of course, be desirable and necessary if the originating cause of the pressure were an adverse trend of the exchanges and a consequent efflux of gold; but a tightening of money conditions from this, or similar causes, was infrequent in comparison with a tightening produced simply by a temporary immobilization of funds. Indeed, immobilization often produced really serious stringency, for the cheque habit was in its infancy, and the Treasury had yet to learn the value of an effective floating debt mechanism. Pressures of this type were naturally most acute in the few weeks before the dates on which large Government dividend disbursements were to be made, for in these periods money piled up in the hands of the tax-gatherers and on the Exchequer Account at the Bank. After the disbursements, with the Government balances more than usually depleted, the ease was generally as pronounced as had been the stringency, causing violent fluctuations in rates within a very short period. These difficulties were common even during the Restriction period,[1] but their accompanying rate fluctuations then were naturally much less noticeable than in the later period, when the Bank rate was normally ineffective.

This last circumstance, the greater fluctuation in market rates, which Horsley Palmer rightly held to be so harmful to trade, drew attention to the need for stabilizing action, and about 1829 [2] the Bank introduced a system of regular advances prior to the four big dividend dates of the year.[3] These facilities, generally called the "quarterly advances", but also described as "temporary loans" or "advances prior to the dividends", were available to all comers who offered the approved security and

[1] See *ante*, p. 14.

[2] A very crude form of stabilizing action before the dividend dates had, in fact, been employed during the Restriction period, for the Bank automatically supported the Exchequer Bill market whenever it showed any serious weakness; the purchases naturally recurred before each dividend date, and were generally most noticeable at such periods. In effect, therefore, these operations must have been somewhat similar to the quarterly advances, in that both tended to release notes before the dividends and to reduce them afterwards. The earlier practice, however, was designed entirely for the convenience of the Government and the Bank. See Thorton's evidence before 1819 Lords' Committee, Minutes, pp. 67, 76.

[3] See G. W. Norman before 1840 Committee, Minutes, p. 189; Horsley Palmer before 1832 Committee, Minutes, p. 21; Glyn before the same Committee (Q. 2907).

would take at least £2,000 for a minimum period of ten days. They were ordinarily obtainable at any time during the " shuttings ", that is, when the Bank's stock registers were closed for the preparation of interest warrants, normally for one month before the interest date, but the actual date on which they would first be available was announced by a public notice at the Bank. The maximum period of any loan was usually six or seven weeks, but the available period was naturally shortened as the interest date approached. The securities demanded as collateral were generally approved bills of exchange having not more than six months to run, Exchequer bills, India bonds, and other approved British securities,[1] so that the range of the assistance given was very wide, especially as the system was later also operated from the Bank's branches.[2] The collateral requirements, however, were occasionally made more stringent. In March and June, 1837, for example, the *échéance* of acceptable bills was reduced to 95 days, and in the crisis of 1839 the Bank took the extreme course (in the June " shutting ") of refusing to lend against Exchequer bills or stock, demanding good commercial bills.[3]

This system bears some superficial resemblance to the modern practice of discount market borrowing at the " turn " of each half-year, but actually there is a fundamental difference. These quarterly advances had to be made at such a rate as would induce the public to apply for them *before* any serious pressure developed. They were accordingly made at or near the outside market rate. Norman told the 1840 Committee that the Bank fixed the rate at what it " conceived to be the rate current out of doors ",[4] but S. J. Loyd held that the Bank often lent fractionally *under* the market rate, and agreed with the suggestion of the chairman of the Committee that if the Bank's rate were the " usual rate of discount on mercantile bills " the accommodation sought might in ordinary circumstances be smaller than was desirable.[5]

The new system naturally proved a great boon to the banks and the discount market and thus, indirectly, to the commercial world. Glyn, discussing in 1832 the evils produced by irregularities in the credit supply, declared that " at the end of the quarter, which is the period when the bankers used to feel the

[1] Norman, *loc. cit.*

[2] See evidence of J. Lister, Manager of the Union Bank of Liverpool, before 1848 Lords' Committee, Minutes, Q. 2459.

[3] See 1840 Committee, App. 19; 1841 Committee, App. 9; and 1848 Commons' Committee, App. 10.

[4] Norman, *loc. cit.* [5] 1840 Committee, Minutes, QQ. 2836–8.

greatest pressure on their deposits, the evil is now remedied ".[1] His experience of the benefits of the new scheme may be gathered from the following [2]:

> . . . before the Bank made this late regulation, had not your house sometimes before quarter-day been obliged to make sacrifices in order to raise money ?—Very frequently.
>
> Now that necessity is entirely done away. . . . The banks are enabled to be just as liberal a fortnight before quarter-day as at any other time. . . . I regard the regulation as highly beneficial.
>
> Do not the Bank by those means relieve those persons who otherwise would call upon the private bankers for assistance ?—
>
> Yes ; in part. They likewise, by relieving the circulation, generally enable the private bankers to do that with ease which they would otherwise have to do for their customers at the cost probably of raising money at a high rate of interest.[3]

Glyn affirmed that the money-dealers continued to complain at the irregularities of the credit supply, but Samuel Gurney [4] stated that he, and similar dealers, had found the new arrangements " a great convenience ". David Salomons, of the London and Westminster Bank, also agreed that the system was " of a very useful nature ", although he severely criticized other aspects of the Bank's credit policy.[5]

Salomons, however, wrote in 1837, and by that time there was good reason for criticism. After 1832 the Bank board had argued, with unimpeachable logic, that if it was so far to under-

[1] 1832 Committee, Minutes, Q. 2907.

[2] *Ibid.*, Q. 2987, *et seq.*

[3] At first sight this suggests that the London bankers were quite inordinately considerate of their customers' interests. Further light on the point is shed by the fact that in discounting *for customers*, they did not conform to market rates, but charged the higher Bank rate. In consideration for this, they did not usually feel themselves at liberty to refuse good bills for customers, so long as excessive accommodation were not demanded, and continued discounts for them through good times and bad. For bills bought as investments, however, they naturally had to give the market rate, and they would also charge market rate to " a man known well, though not a customer ", for he might otherwise take his business elsewhere. Thus it was only " private discounters' rates "—in effect, those of the bill market proper—which expressed the true value of money, and when the difference between Bank rate and market rate became very marked, the private banks lost some business to the discount market proper. Apparently, the brokers or dealers then proceeded to re-sell the same bills to the London banks at the true rate ! (See Glyn, QQ. 2926–33, and Loyd, QQ. 3319–26.)

[4] 1832 Committee, Minutes, p. 250.

[5] *A Defence of the Joint Stock Banks* (1837).

take the functions of a central bank as to assume responsibility for equalizing market conditions during the " shuttings ", it ought to follow a similar course with temporary immobilizations at other times. The principle was sound enough, but it was not easy to ensure that it was always applied with discretion: with the dividend immobilizations, the date, the duration and the extent of the pressure were always known more or less precisely, and some time in advance; other pressures were less readily appraised or diagnosed by a board unaccustomed to such delicate market operations. The Bank at such times was often over-liberal, and may have been influenced in its decisions by consideration for the needs of its proprietors, for rigid adherence to the new rule of aloofness from commercial discount business implied an appreciable reduction in potential earning power. Many private observers, indeed, did not scruple to assert that the dividend motive was the dominant one.[1]

At all events, special loan facilities were often available for a substantial part of each year. The dividend advances ordinarily became available early in March, June, September and December[2]; and accommodation thus granted could not normally be outstanding in the aggregate for much more than 168 days in each year—four periods of six weeks each. But, from 1834 to 1836, the periods for which temporary advances of one kind or another were outstanding were respectively 229, 237 and 280 days.[2] There were, indeed, special factors at work in the shape of large loan operations, but the fact remains that the Bank, though deeming competitive lending " so objectionable ", was operating on strictly competitive terms for seven, eight, or even nine months in the year. In 1834, when large special deposits were received from the East India Company, the Bank, having agreed to allow interest on the money, actually went out of its way to find employment for it.[3] It approached the bill " brokers "

[1] See William Leatham's Letters, published in 1841, and dated Dec. 23, 1840.

[2] 1840 Committee, App. 19, and 1841 Committee, App. 9.

[3] The East India Co. was liquidating its commercial assets, and sought remunerative employment for the proceeds while the liquidation was in progress. It therefore invited a " tender " from the Bank, which offered 2 per cent.; this rate was raised to 2½ per cent. in August, 1836, and to 3 per cent. in December, 1836. The rates charged by the Bank to the brokers varied from 2½ to 4 per cent. during the period. The accumulation reached its maximum of about £4,700,000 on January 3, 1837. A similar policy was adopted for an accumulation of Savings Bank monies between February and October, 1834. (See 1840 Committee, Minutes, QQ. 1155–61.)

—Horsley Palmer, who explained the transaction, presumably meant "dealers"—and offered them special advances at what it believed to be market rate.[1]

RE-DISCOUNT FACILITIES FOR THE BILL MARKET

Although the principle that the Bank should "equalize" the money supply was sometimes abused, its recognition implied a substantial advance towards true central bank control and regulation. The second step in this direction—the opening of accounts for the bill "brokers"—was of even greater importance. Actually, it was a logical consequence of the new resolve of the London private bankers to be independent of the Bank of England. In a period of genuine shortage of credit, the deficiency, then as now, had eventually to be supplied by the Bank. If the London banks were no longer to be the channel through which this new credit was made available, then some other channel had to be found. To have left the application solely to the public would have caused grave disturbance: in a pressure the private banks, even though they avoided infringement of their rule, would have been obliged to refuse discounts to their customers, and this refusal would only have intensified the discredit, and produced needless injury to the banks' reputations. In addition, application to the Bank would have been delayed for a longer period than was desirable, for the public would not quickly alter its normal course of business, and the delay would have tended to increase the ultimate demands. Moreover, the new credit would have been spread far less evenly or readily through the business world. And in an extreme pressure, involving withdrawals of deposits from the private banks, not even a refusal of all fresh loans would have saved them from being forced to abandon their rule.

The authorities had no desire to see a reversion to the unsound banking methods of the restriction period, and were ready to take any measures necessary to support the improved system. In the circumstances, the only satisfactory solution was to make the discount dealers the new channel for additional issues when these were required. As the private banks were beginning to keep their reserves in the bill market, it was the latter which felt the first impact of a pressure; thus it became clear that, so long as the bill dealers had the right to approach the Bank, a void in the credit supply would be almost automatically and

[1] 1840 Committee, Minutes, QQ. 1170, 1181–2.

smoothly filled by their action in applying for official accommodation. Indeed, credit thus made available would circulate even more rapidly through the whole commercial community than it did when the London banks re-discounted direct: the big discount dealers would not only supply the London banks with funds by repaying call loans, but, if necessary, would also employ new official credit in discounts for traders of every kind, whereas the private banks in a pressure always refused fresh accommodation to all but their own customers. And the dealers —always provided that the rates offered were sufficiently attractive—would perform similar services for the provincial banks, many of whom would be glad in an emergency to sell above Bank rate bills which would not have been eligible at the Bank.

It was such considerations as these, and not any special regard for the interests of the bill market, which led the Bank in November, 1830,[1] to sanction the opening of discount accounts by bill "brokers". It is doubtful whether at the time the authorities fully realized how important the new facilities were to the bill market, and they certainly did not foresee the consequences of their decision,[2] which was eventually to change the whole course of money market development. Had it not been taken then, or subsequently, the call loan market could never have become really extensive; thus it is virtually certain that the discount market, as a separate entity, would have disappeared with the end of the bill broker agency system, and the commercial banks would to this day be re-discounting with the Bank of England. Had the board perceived the impetus which it had unwittingly given to the new system of bill dealing, the change would probably not have been made, for in the ensuing quarter of a century the facilities offered by the rapidly growing discount houses were certainly a partial cause of the abuse of bill credit which became so pronounced an evil.

In the early years, however, not more than two or three

[1] Evidence of G. W. Norman before 1840 Committee, Minutes, p. 188; see also Gilbart, *Logic of Banking*, pp. 555, 556.

[2] Then, and for many years afterwards, the members of the Bank board could not see—or professed not to see—any fundamental difference between a bill broker and a bill dealer, and invariably referred to both as "brokers". The Governor, when taken to task in 1858 for his looseness of expression, and the looseness of reasoning which apparently resulted from it, defended himself by declaring that dealers really were brokers, because all they did was to take a difference between two rates "in lieu of commission"! (1858 Committee, Evidence of Neave, Minutes, Q. 718.)

houses besides Gurney's could derive any advantage from the Bank's action, for brokers proper had no use for re-discount facilities. But those who did open accounts came to rely upon the Bank, and based their whole business upon the assumption that in case of need they could always meet their obligations by borrowing there. The extent of this reliance is clearly shown by Tooke's remark in 1840 [1] that because " the Bank are looked to as a constant resource by the great discount brokers " any " forcible narrowing of the discounts " would have a " prodigious effect ". Chapman's experience in 1839 is even more illuminating.[2] Returning hurriedly to London during the crisis of that year, he found that Lombard Street " had a dark cloud hanging over it ". On inquiring the reason for the general apprehension, he was told that the Bank had intimated that it might not discount for the discount houses. In consequence, discount business had virtually stopped, and " Samuel Gurney's desk was piled with the finest bills which he dared not discount ". Chapman thereupon went to the Governor, Sir John Rae Reid, and explained that " if you, who have been in the habit of supplying us with money when we required it, will not do so now ", the firm could not continue to discount for the public. Reid then said that he would take in good bills, whereupon Gurney's discounted " everything " for their customers without going to the Bank " for a shilling ".

> When the Bank refused, the effect was to lock away millions immediately; for a large portion of the banking money deposited with us is in great masses, because the parties know that they can have it in a moment. If, in our arrangements between the Bank and ourselves, the Bank say " We will not do this," all that is stopped in a moment; and those millions, which would otherwise be of benefit to the public, under existing circumstances become immediately locked up; because people say, " We would rather have no interest at all, than have a doubt about our getting the money in case we require it."

These passages reveal clearly that in London, at least, the Bank was moving quickly to a position comparable to that which it occupies to-day. Its prestige was high, and in the commercial world it was already regarded as an ultimate resort in time of need, and as something more than a purely trading institution. In 1832 its standing and peculiar position were thus explained by George Grote, a London banker:

[1] 1840 Committee, Minutes, Q. 3796.
[2] 1857 Committee, Minutes, QQ. 5194, 5195

> . . . first, the commercial world has accustomed itself to the present routine of the Bank, and looks constantly to the Bank as the great centre of discount, especially in difficult times ; next, the Bank is a perfectly well-known place, accessible to those who may not know how or where to find an individual discounter. . . a man can get to the Bank without that special, permanent and exclusive connexion which he preserves with his own Banker, and which cuts him off from all other Bankers.[1]

The Bank's changing attitude towards its functions is also indicated by the greater consideration it showed for the convenience and needs of the market and the private banks. Whereas formerly the first impact of a drain had almost invariably fallen upon its discounts, after the late 'twenties, as Horsley Palmer explained,[2] its policy was always to realize its Exchequer bills first, and to curtail its discounts only in the last resort, and then only when the maximum legal rate had been reached. Another, though less important, innovation was made in the late 'thirties, when it was announced that London bills, which formerly had been discounted only on Thursdays, would in future be discountable on any day in the week.[3]

Abuse of Bill Credit in the 'Thirties

These various improvements in Bank of England policy and technique all made for the smoother and more efficient working of the bill market, and greatly aided its growth. But not even the Bank's better appreciation of its responsibilities, the opening of Bank Branches, the growth of joint-stock banking and the new reserve policy of the London private banks—the four great changes which were to have made impossible a repetition of the disaster of 1825—were able to prevent the germination of the seeds of a new crisis. Indeed, by the very fact that they stimulated the expansion of the bill market, these changes were the indirect cause of a new source of trouble—an unduly reckless use of " the extraordinary facilities " (the phrase is that of S. J. Loyd [4]) for re-discounting in London. Actually, the fault lay not in the new mechanism, but in the manner in which it was utilized ; nor could the blame for its misuse be laid solely either upon the discount houses or upon the banks who so

[1] 1832 Committee, Minutes, p. 379. [2] *Ibid.*, p. 16.
[3] 1840 Committee, Minutes, p. 189 ; see also 1810 Committee, Minutes, p. 97, and 1819 Committee, Minutes, p. 171.
[4] 1840 Committee, Minutes, Q. 3276.

liberally re-discounted with them. In a sense, ultimate responsibility lay with the Bank, for permitting, if not fostering, an easy credit position which favoured the growth of doubtful paper; while an additional influence was an increasingly adventurous spirit in the commercial world, whose appetite for high yields and quick profits was being whetted by the new railway and joint stock bank flotations, and a host of accompanying projects.

At the time, it was the joint stock banks which seemed to attract most of the blame, and the popular view was probably the right one. At all events, it is certain that the operations of many of them far surpassed the bounds of ordinary prudence. According to John Amery, manager of the Stourbridge and Kidderminster Bank,[1] it was not uncommon for banks with a paid-up capital of £50,000 to have *endorsed* re-discounts of £1,000,000 outstanding at one time, while he thought that, on the average, re-discounts amounted to six or eight times the paid-up capital. The latter ratio might have been reasonable if the banks' advances and discounts in portfolio were low, but in fact the reverse was more generally true. Re-discounting seemed to be regarded to a great extent as a means of enabling a bank to accept new business when its direct obligations (as opposed to contingent obligations on bills re-sold) had reached their limit. The practice of "re-discounting after endorsement, following a kind of mode, losing sight of caution and common rules, and consequently engaging in liabilities wholly unjustifiable by any means of meeting engagements" was thus described by a contemporary authority[2]:

> The practice [of the provincial joint stock banks] seems to be, to establish a Bank upon a nominal capital of £500,000 or a million, upon which a deposit of some £50,000 or £100,000 only (as a guarantee capital) is called up. Upon the strength, or rather weakness, of these inefficient means, the new Bank, by virtue of deposits entrusted to it, or notes issued, advances, by way of loans or discounts, say £400,000 or £500,000, which is of itself quite sufficient engagement in proportion to the paid-up capital; but in fact, too many of these institutions go far beyond this, because, whenever

[1] 1836 Committee, Minutes, p. 39.

[2] From an anonymous pamphlet, explaining the need for a properly conducted London joint stock bank—the London and Westminster Bank, whose prospectus and proposed board were detailed in an appendix.—*Hints by way of Encouraging the Formation of a Joint-Stock Banking Company in London, etc.* Second edition (Effingham Wilson, 1834), pp. 11 and 12.

> the bills offered to them exceed the amount of the available capital, of the deposits in hand, and of the notes issued, they still go on discounting all that is offered, relieving themselves by re-discounting the excess in London, and thus running into liabilities upon a scale more imprudent than any now practised by the private bankers, who, in consequence of severe and repeated losses, and moreover aware of the existing distrust, have certainly gained some useful experience.

Such practices led Simon Martin, of Gurneys' of Norwich, to declare[1] with scorn that " in truth, half the joint stock banks in the north of England are merely bill brokers "—unless they issued notes.

Excessive re-discounting was not, however, the only or even the main evil, for its effects might have been comparatively innocuous had the quality of the bills re-discounted been generally good. Joplin pointed out that the fact that a holder of a dishonoured bill could prove against the estates of all the parties to it concurrently, led bankers to prefer bills to any other form of security.[2] Owing to this preference, fostered also by the ease of re-discounting, " a temptation is held out to parties to create fictitious bills, which often proves too great for persons in want of capital to resist. They are thus led to a system of accommodation which terminates in consequences fatally injurious both to themselves and the public ; whilst the Banks, if they manage well, are kept harmless. . . . The Banks, as long as they are safe, frequently accommodate parties in this manner, who, they believe, must ultimately fail ; and when at last they will do so no longer, and the parties are obliged to stop, it is found that the banks are covered, but nothing is left

[1] 1836 Committee, Minutes, Q. 2436.

[2] *Examination of the Report of the Joint Stock Bank Committee*, second edition, pp. 17–19 (Ridgway, 1837). Joplin declared that " a holder of a bill of exchange can bring actions at one and the same time, against every party whose name is attached to it, and in the event of the failure of them all, can prove upon the estate of each for the full value of the bill. Thus if there be six parties on it, and he receives upon the average 3*s*. 4*d*. in the pound from each estate, he is paid his whole debt. He is in fact permitted to prove six hundred pounds, where other creditors can prove only one. . . . With a sufficient number of names upon it, a bill may therefore be a good security for money advanced upon it though all the parties to it may in reality be insolvent. . . . A system of bill accommodation can never be long pursued without the banker not only being aware of, but accessory to it, and thus the law in effect encourages a species of fraud between the banker and his customers, which there would be more propriety in its endeavour to prevent."

for the public." Martin declared [1] that the joint stock banks commonly took bills drawn against the deposit of goods or securities instead of against sales, and that renewals and long-dated paper were common.[2] Such a "ruinous system of bill accommodation" could not have failed to produce over-trading and the seeds of collapse even if the bills had not been re-discounted.

Samuel Gurney attempted to show that the bill market did not re-discount for the joint stock banks solely upon the strength of their capital—though he evaded a direct reply to the question [3]—and if this had been true, very little of the really objectionable paper could have been re-discounted at all. Gurney's themselves probably did refuse paper which was transparently undesirable, but there is no doubt that they and other dealers would rely upon the endorsement of the joint stock bank where the undesirable character of the bills was less apparent, although, had the same paper been tendered by others, they would have made inquiries before accepting it. In normal times, as has been shown,[4] it was desirable that the discount houses should place special reliance upon the joint stock endorsements, for otherwise many perfectly legitimate, though purely local, bills would not have been negotiable; but the existence of those endorsements ought not to have led the market to ignore the wholly disproportionate liabilities which were being assumed by particular acceptors. To that extent the discount market was largely to blame for the trouble which followed; but where the acceptors were substantial houses undoubtedly engaged in genuine trade, there was little to indicate that their bills represented gross overtrading, and, no less than pure accommodation paper, ought to have been rejected by the prudent discount house.

In the middle 'thirties excesses of this kind became most serious in the Anglo-American trade. Horsley Palmer [5] sought to throw the initial blame upon America, explaining that the determination of the American Government not to renew the charter of the Bank of America had thrown the deposits of that

[1] 1836 Committee, Minutes, QQ. 2326, 2415.

[2] Joplin explained that bills were frequently created for the "sole purpose of money being borrowed upon them", two houses each drawing fictitiously on the other, and both, therefore, discounting accommodation paper with their bankers. (*Currency Reform*, pp. 82–4, Richardson, 1844.)

[3] 1832 Committee, Minutes, Q. 3743.

[4] *Ante*, pp. 45–6.

[5] 1840 Committee, Minutes, Q. 1273.

institution into the hands of many private banks, causing considerable extension of credit and encouraging imports to an "enormous extent". These imports were financed by the big merchant houses in this country under acceptance credits, and there is no doubt that the boom in the Anglo-American trade was due largely to the readiness of the provincial joint stock banks to take the paper of these houses and to unload it, after endorsement, on the London discount market. But it was the almost unprecedented ease in the money market which made the absorption of so large a volume of paper possible, and for this the policy of the Bank of England was clearly responsible.[1] Actually, the Bank claimed that it never did more than return to the market the funds which special operations—notably the liquidation of the commercial assets of the East India Company [2]—had immobilized; but it is clear that if the East India Company had employed the funds itself, only a proportion of them would have remained in the short money market. It was probably a recognition of this that led the Bank after 1835 to accept stock, as well as commercial and Exchequer bills, as security for the funds it thus re-lent.[3] But as the Bank merely took the stock as collateral, and did not buy outright in the market, the innovation merely widened the scope of the growing speculation.[4]

William Leatham's letters [5] contain a graphic account of the combined effect of these various circumstances:

> Now what did I find to be the effect of these measures [he referred to, and blamed, the Bank's "temporary" loans], as a Banker,

---

[1] G. W. Norman admitted to the 1840 Committee that the Bank had been "much more accommodating than formerly" in its discounts for the public. (Minutes, p. 189.)

[2] See *ante*, p. 87 *n*.

[3] See 1840 Committee, Minutes, Q. 1202.

[4] The practice of making loans against stock was strongly criticized by a number of writers. Leatham, advocating the discontinuance of such loans, declared that they "are vicious in their tendency, connecting the first banking establishment in the kingdom, and which ought to be the *purest* in fame, with the Stock Exchange", which he regarded as the home of gamblers. They "have their origin *not* in times of difficulty and distress, but in periods of *low rates of interest*, as expedients to create *profit* by finding interest for money. As a regular system they are bad; because when money is abundant, loans become a dangerous stimulant, instead of a help in times of difficulty".—*Letter to William Raynor Wood*, January 26, 1841.

[5] *Letters to William Raynor Wood, On the Currency* (Second Series), 1841, p. 9.

on the money market, where, by the nature of my business, I am always a lender of cash?—that while the Banker was allowing 2½ per cent. on Deposits he could not make even that rate in London, for a time; and at last information came from the bill brokers, that cash could find no employment at all on bills. The bills of the old highly respectable American Houses in London, thus encouraged and created, were scrambled for by the bill brokers at that time . . . millions of money were lent on foreign securities with broad margins, and millions more were actually invested in them, especially Dutch and American. In proportion to the cheapness of money, made so by the Bank; and the length of time it operated, in the same degree was, and always has been, the intensity of reaction, when the exchanges came thus to be turned against us. . . .

The first sign of the reaction came in the autumn of 1836, when the enormous extent of the American credits began to attract attention. The Bank of England belatedly refused to take the paper of the Anglo-American houses as collateral from the bill brokers, and thereby at once rendered all such paper virtually undiscountable.[1] An acute discredit was the inevitable result, followed by a collapse of prices of securities and produce which threatened to engulf many of the joint stock banks, and to reveal the dangerous character of much of the paper which was afloat.[2] It quickly became known that the Anglo-American houses were in no position to take up their bills if their American clients defaulted, and wholesale failures therefore seemed inevitable, especially as the Agricultural Bank of Ireland had stopped in October and in the following month it was rumoured that the Northern and Central Bank of England had been forced to apply for assistance. The Bank of England, alarmed at the

[1] See 1840 Committee, Minutes, QQ. 1273–76.

[2] The most reliable estimates of the fluctuations in the bill currency at this period are afforded by the investigations of William Leatham. He gives the following figures of *drawings* in each year, based on the returns of bill stamps. The figures are apparently conservatively based, for Leatham explained that (*e.g.*) where a given stamp duty would cover a bill ranging from £100 to £200, the figure he had assumed was £150—

1824	£316,363,000	1835	£405,403,000
1825	354,405,000	1836	485,943,000
1826–7* . . .	282,222,000	1837	455,084,000
1832	356,153,000	1838	465,504,000
1833	383,660,000	1839	528,493,000
1834	379,155,000		

* From July 1, 1826, to June 30, 1827

—Leatham, *op. cit.*, pp. 13 and 14. Leatham presented his investigation in detail in a paper before the Statistical Section of the British Association.

consequences of its action, decided that it dare not allow the Anglo-American houses to fail, and therefore came to their assistance in order to make possible an orderly liquidation.[1]

Thereafter, the panic gradually subsided, and really serious distress was avoided. But the underlying causes were not removed, nor were the American commitments liquidated. Less than a year later it was said that three houses alone had £5,500,000 of acceptances on the market, most of which was American paper, and another £1,500,000 of American credits was attributed to Barings.[2] Yet throughout 1838 the Bank's circulation continued to rise, and by May of that year market discount rates had dropped to 2½ per cent. About the same time, the gold holding began to fall steadily, owing mainly to a drain to America. Meanwhile, the restrictive effect of the Corn Laws had produced a severe shortage of corn, and a failure of the domestic harvest necessitated foreign imports on an unprecedented scale, adding seriously to the already considerable pressure on the exchanges. In the summer of 1839, Continental fears that the Bank would not be able to maintain specie payments led to the immediate remittance of long sterling bills held abroad, precipitating the worst crisis since 1825. Once again the Bank was obliged to seek assistance in the Paris market in order to avoid a suspension, having in the meantime pursued a policy of stringent restriction of credit facilities.[3]

Advantages of the Re-discounting System

The precise course of the crisis need not be detailed here, but the resultant distress inevitably revived the controversy as to the correct method of note issue control, and raised fresh doubts as to the soundness of the commercial banking system. It is somewhat surprising that in the inquiries—both public and private—which followed, very little attention was paid to the discount market. The general view seems to have been that if the discount houses had acted unwisely in assisting the undue creation of bills, they had been accessories rather than principals, and had suffered from the imprudence of others. The question of the liberality of the Bank's credit policy was bound up with the problem of note issue control, and, apart from the attacks on the Bank, most criticism was directed against

[1] See 1840 Committee, Minutes, QQ. 1273–76.

[2] See *Journal of Thomas Raikes*, Vol. III, p. 157, cited by Powell, *op. cit.*; and Horsley Palmer before 1840 Committee (Q. 1362).

[3] See *ante*, p. 82.

the practice of bank re-discounting. But although the joint stock banks on this score were vigorously attacked by many witnesses, the only objection which could be raised to the practice in principle was that it tended to cause inelasticity in local credit conditions.[1] It was argued that when a bank re-discounted largely in London, the local supply of credit was made dependent upon conditions in the London market: if money in London was plentiful, the bank would seek to expand its local discounts and advances; if London conditions were stringent, local facilities would be abruptly curtailed. This was undeniable, but the only means of protecting the local credit supply from London-imposed fluctuations would have been for the banks to restrict local accommodation within the limits set by local deposits, and that would have been a step backwards in banking organization. It would have involved a great waste of credit facilities, and an inadequate accommodation in the very districts where liberal facilities were most necessary. Moreover, it was actually desirable that changes in the London market should produce their appropriate reactions over as wide an area as possible, for, as long as they did so, there was an automatic tendency at work to maintain the foreign exchanges in equilibrium with the domestic credit- and price-structure. And at a time when most provincial bankers had no conception of the mechanism of the foreign exchanges,[2] much less of the indications they might afford of approaching stringency and a need for a general shortening of sail, an automatic adjustment was peculiarly necessary.

This particular advantage of close contact with the London market was, needless to say, not generally appreciated at the time, but there was widespread realization of the value of the re-discounting system as a means of ensuring the most economic distribution of credit supplies.[3] And Joplin showed that

[1] See evidence of J. Gibbins, who was connected with joint stock banks at Birmingham and Gloucester, before 1836 Committee, Minutes, QQ. 997–1004.

[2] Vincent Stuckey was the only banker of his day who professed to regulate his issues and lending policy by reference to the exchanges. J. P. Wilkins, a private banker of Brecon and Merthyr Tydvil, and formerly manager of the Bank of England's Swansea Branch, declared that "exchange has no more to do with our circulation than the last year's snow". (1832 Committee, Minutes, p. 110.)

[3] See, for example, Joplin's *Money Pressure of 1836* (Ridgway, 1837): "It may be observed that discounting bills of exchange is with bankers a favourite mode of employing their deposits; and if we look to Scotland, to Ireland, and to every part of England, with the exception of the

even from the narrow standpoint of the short-period interest of traders, dependence on London was advantageous, as in times of stringency a pressure was mitigated by being widely diffused.[1] " Re-discounting," he declared, " when conducted with the prudence which is necessary to the safety of all Banking, is neither dangerous to the Banks nor the Public, and it is difficult to imagine how the Committee [of 1836] could have been led to entertain the opinions with which they seem to have been impressed on the subject." [2]

His approval was echoed by Paul Moon James, in a passage which so aptly describes the part played by the bill brokers that it deserves quotation in full [3]:

> . . . as far as I know the country bankers and the use they make of their deposits, they use those deposits with great caution and wisely. The money which is in the hands of the great bill-brokers in London is chiefly supplied from the bankers in the agricultural districts ; they have a surplus quantity of money raised, perhaps, upon their circulation, and they make use of that surplus by obtaining from the bill-brokers commercial bills of exchange, and of very great use it is. The money of the agricultural districts is used in supplying the wants of the manufacturing districts ; in that way the bills of the manufacturing districts are converted into money by means of the agricultural districts. . . . Manchester absorbs a great deal of the surplus capital which is raised in Norfolk, or in any other large agricultural district, by the bills of Manchester going up to the bill-broker in London, who receives money from the issuing banker.

---

manufacturing districts, we shall find that the deposits of the bankers much exceed their means of employing them ; and it is the result of experience that, with the exception of those periods, when the state of the exchanges and the operations of the Bank of England produce a sort of monetary derangement, the demand by Bankers for bills of exchange, on the average of the whole kingdom, much exceeds the supply. Hence the demand for money by the Joint Stock Banks on bills of exchange is convenient to the banking interest as well as beneficial to the country."

[1] " It must be remembered that in resorting to the London market, the Joint Stock Banks do not make the money they borrow, and if not lent to them, it would, directly or indirectly, be lent to private traders in London. When, therefore, a pressure came, if it did not fall upon the customers of the Joint Stock Banks it would fall upon some other customers, and whether it is most dangerous to have it fall with concentrated force upon one point, or to have it spread by the Joint Stock Banks over a very wide surface ? . . . It must be a great advantage for the pressure to be lightened by being more extensively diffused." —*Examination of the Report of the Joint Stock Bank Committee.*

[2] *Ibid.*, p. 17. [3] 1841 Committee, Minutes, QQ. 1525, 1527.

Gilbart was equally unstinting in his praise of the mechanism. "It is a most excellent system. We know of no better means of making the transfer of super-abundant capital from the agricultural to the manufacturing districts than by the re-discount of bills of exchange; and the bill brokers are the agents by whom these operations are effected."[1] In short, the whole weight of competent opinion favoured a retention of the re-discounting system, although all informed observers agreed that it had been grossly abused. In consequence, no restrictions were imposed on the freedom of the banks to re-discount as and when they chose, nor was any modification of bill market practice recommended. The bill brokers therefore continued to perform their distributive and equalizing functions as described by James, and this was to remain their principal activity for the greater part of the ensuing quarter of a century.

Unfortunately, no serious measures were taken to ensure that the machinery should not again be abused. In part, the abuses were due to the inexperience of bankers, for not only were the exceptional facilities offered by Lombard Street comparatively new, so that all bankers, in greater or smaller degree, had gradually to acquire a fresh technique, but the executives of many of the provincial joint stock banks lacked adequate experience of any class of banking. These were sources of trouble which time alone would remove; but history has shown repeatedly that not even the most highly trained banking community can be trusted to avoid credit excesses at all times; and if the Bank of England policy were not always above reproach, there was a special danger that the commercial banks would be trapped, unawares, into undue liberality. The real remedy, which was not perceived for many years, was the development of a qualitative as well as a quantitative control of credit by the central bank. Actually, the opportunities for the successful application of such a policy were exceptionally wide, for the Bank's resources, in comparison with those of the commercial banks, were vastly greater than they are to-day; and the discount market was more often, and proportionately more largely, indebted to the Bank. In theory, some attempt was made at qualitative control, for the Bank's rules as to discountable paper, as has been explained, were fairly stringent. But the excesses which occurred are a sufficient proof that the rules upon which the Bank professed

[1] *Logic of Banking*, p. 556. Gilbart's testimony is the more significant in that he wrote more than ten years later, after the re-discounting system had been subject to renewed grave abuses.

to act could not have been strictly applied in practice.[1] In all probability the authorities did not often intentionally ignore their rules, but were led by an inadequate grasp of theoretical principles to an unduly narrow interpretation of their scope. For example, a bill would be rejected if it were quite evidently " speculative ", but a bill drawn for merchandise sold at excessive prices would be approved, because it financed " genuine " trade. It is this absence of effective qualitative control, perhaps more than any other factor, which distinguishes the aim of Bank of England policy of that time from the policy of to-day.

[1] Some measure of qualitative control was apparently applied more or less successfully at the Bank's branches. P. M. James, though pointing out that their discount rules were not altogether adapted to the needs of trade, remarked " but they are always corrective, and the influence is beneficial ". He agreed that the rejection of a bill by a Branch Bank tended to discourage the circulation of bills of similar character; but this effect was probably of importance only in those districts which were served by banks having special discount arrangements with the Bank.—Evidence before 1841 Committee, Minutes, QQ. 1518, 1519.

CHAPTER IV

CONSEQUENCES OF THE ACT OF 1844—(1) THE BANK'S "NEW DISCOUNTING" POLICY

In less specialized histories of banking than the present inquiry, the year 1844 is rightly considered as marking the beginning of a new epoch: in many respects the banking structure after that date had to contend with, and was moulded by, forces completely different from those which had operated in earlier years. Bill market evolution, on the other hand, presents no real counterpart of this experience. With few exceptions, the factors which made for the steady growth in the importance and size of the various members of the market after 1844 had emerged before that date. If it were possible adequately to trace the growth of discount business *in vacuo*, so to speak, without detailing the many various (and obviously relevant) contemporary developments in the general banking sphere, there would be little justification for any break in the narrative from 1825 until about 1858. For over the whole of this period the major influences upon market technique and development were those, already fully discussed, which arose shortly after the crisis of 1825—the only difference was that in the later years their importance steadily increased. Nevertheless, the year 1844 brought so complete a change in the general background against which bill market trends must be viewed, that to treat this date as a landmark in market history is no mere subservience to the convention established by other writers.

Theory of the Act of 1844

The difficulties of 1836–9, as has been shown, had directed attention once again to two major problems—that of preventing banking excesses in general and the abuse of bill credit in particular, and that of ensuring a "sound" control of credit by the Bank of England. For the first of these problems no direct solution was proposed; but the question of credit control, in a quantitative sense, received serious and prolonged attention. Unfortunately, it was construed by most contemporary economists and bankers solely as a problem of *currency* control, the predominant opinion being that if only note issues (of the private issuers, as well as of the Bank) could be properly regulated, credit in the form of cheques and bills could be left to take care of itself. This, as events have subsequently proved repeatedly, was a vain hope.

To examine the course of the note-issue controversy, and detail the manner of its dénouement, would be to extend quite unreasonably the scope of the present work, although the temptation to do so is strong. It is sufficient to explain that the critics of Bank of England policy, generally grouped as the "Currency School", triumphed over the opposition "Banking School"; and that the "Currency" theory, that note issues should be controlled so as to ensure that their volume fluctuated automatically with the bullion holding, and, therefore, more or less automatically with the foreign exchanges, was embodied in the Bank Charter Act of 1844. Under the terms of this Act, the Bank's note issue was to be segregated from its other business; all Bank of England notes above a fiduciary £14,000,000 were to be backed by their equivalent in bullion [1]; existing private issues were to be limited; and new banks of issue absolutely prohibited.[2] This legislation thus finally and firmly consolidated the Bank's monopoly, and thereby laid the foundation of its evolution into the all-powerful central bank of modern times. The close connection between that evolution and the Act of 1844 is now universally recognized; yet, paradoxical as it must seem to-day, the first effect of the Act was to make the Bank less of a central bank than it had been previously.

In the light of contemporary theory there was no paradox. The question of the Bank's right to operate freely as a commercial bank and earn profits for its proprietors had always been one of acute controversy; but, even of those who recognized the special position of the Bank, few had ever suggested that its freedom as a trading bank was limited by anything more than its duty to preserve the safety and convertibility of its note issue. Actually,

[1] 7 and 8 Vict., c. 32, s. 1 and 2. Silver could be held as well as gold provided that it never exceeded one-quarter of the gold.

[2] *Ibid.*, s. 10, 11 and 13. The only other provision of the Act which need be noted here was that which required the Bank to publish a weekly return of its position. The form then prescribed is the basis of the present Bank Return, and was unaltered until the amalgamation of the Currency and Bank of England note issues in 1928.

as has been demonstrated, the board after the late 'twenties had professed to work within much narrower limits than this principle alone would have demanded. Its policy of aloofness from the discount market, and its laudable intention to refrain from " forcing " its issues, had, in their essentials, much in common with the central bank technique of far more enlightened times. These principles, however, were evolved more from a conviction, partly intuitive and partly reasoned, that some restraint in the Bank's " banking " business was necessary to ensure at all times the convertibility of the note issue, than from a recognition that there was anything inherently undesirable in active commercial banking by an institution which was the ultimate source of credit. And it has been seen that the board frequently failed to live up to the high canons by which it was avowedly guided.

The Act of 1844, by providing an apparently fool-proof mechanism for regulating the note issue, completely destroyed this theory of credit control. Power to manipulate the issue, or to vary its gold backing, was entirely lost to the directors, who in this respect became merely " mechanical instruments ".[1] " The issue department might be in Whitehall, and the banking department in Threadneedle Street," said the Governor in 1848.[2] In other words, the one circumstance which, according to the prevalent theory, had restricted the Bank as a trading bank had been removed. The Bank was therefore free to act in precisely the same fashion as any other privately-owned bank. " The functions of banking, as regards the Bank of England," said Newmarch, explaining the principle of the Act, " should be carried on by the directors precisely in the same way as the functions of banking are carried on by any of the large houses in Lombard-street ".[3] Sir Robert Peel himself had expounded this, the underlying theory of the Act, even more explicitly [4]:

[1] See Lord Overstone (S. J. Loyd) before 1857 Committee, Minutes, QQ. 4015–17.

[2] James Morris before 1848 Commons' Committee, Minutes, Q. 3007.

[3] 1857 Committee, Minutes, Q. 1359.

[4] In a speech in the House of Commons on May 6, 1844, when he introduced the Bill. (Hansard, Series 3, Vol. LXXIV, col. 743.) He opened his explanation of the proposed legislation as follows : " With respect to the banking business of the Bank, I propose that it should be governed on precisely the same principles as would regulate any other Body dealing with Bank of England notes." (Col. 742.) Overstone echoed this statement, and declared that " persons will never get a correct or simple view of these things until they accustom their minds to look at the Bank of England as they would look at the bank

> The principle of competition, though unsafe in our opinion when applied to issue, ought, we think, to govern the business of banking. After the issue of paper currency has once taken place, it is then important that the public should be enabled to obtain the use of that issue on as favourable terms as possible . . . banking business, as distinguished from Issue, is a matter in respect to which there cannot be too unlimited or unrestricted a competition. . . .

The only logical interpretation of these statements was that the Bank's only duty, so long as it maintained a reserve adequate for the repayment of deposits—the primary obligation of any banker—was to its proprietors.[1] Actually, the Governor and Deputy Governor admitted a duty also to the public, inasmuch as they felt bound " to take care . . . not to interfere generally with the monetary affairs of the country ".[2] But they also argued, in effect, that the change of viewpoint wrought by the Act was more apparent than real, in that the true interests of the proprietors of the Bank and of the public were identical. In this they were supported, and even complimented, by the Commons' Committee of 1848, which, while pointing out that the magnitude of the Bank's resources, its exclusive privileges, and peculiar relationship to the Government imposed upon it a duty to consider the public interest—a duty " which the Bank has never disclaimed " —declared that the identity of interests made it unnecessary to impose any obligation in law.[3] It is to the credit of the Lords' Committee that it was able to take a more detached view, noting that the principle of identity of interest, though possibly true,

of Messrs. Smith, Payne or Messrs. Jones, Loyd, or any other firm upon a large scale . . . the Bank of England is only an ordinary banking concern on a large scale ; its business must be conducted and regulated upon ordinary banking principles ". (1857 Committee, Minutes, Q. 4149.)

[1] Thomas Tooke declared that " it was the favourite boast of the advocates of this measure . . . that the issue of notes being placed under the new restrictions, the Bank was to be placed, with reference to all its other business, in a position as free as that of any other banking company ; the only responsibility of the Directors, thenceforward, being to the proprietors of bank stock ; and their only duty ' to make as much as they could ' of the capital at their command ".—(Tooke's *History of Prices*, Vol. IV, p. 62, 1848). Overstone thought that the principles upon which the banking and issue departments were to be conducted were not only " perfectly distinct ", but also " antagonistic to each other " (1857 Committee, Minutes, Q. 4017). See also 1848 Commons' Report, p. iv ; Sir Francis T. Baring from the Chair, Minutes, QQ. 5191, 2654 ; Loyd, QQ. 5261–6 ; and Lords' Report, p. iv.

[2] 1848 Commons' Committee, Minutes, QQ. 2653–6.

[3] 1848 Commons' Report, pp. iv–v.

" does not appear to have been practically recognized in all cases ".[1] In other words, the Lords' Committee was prepared to agree that the *ultimate* interest of Bank proprietors might be identical with the public interest; but was implying that the board had failed to recognize that a policy of maximum activity (and profits), though clearly beneficial to the proprietors in the short run, might be disadvantageous for them in the long run.

Competitive Discounting by the Bank

At all events, the Bank was not slow to utilize its newly gained freedom, and, immediately after the Act became operative, it began to compete for commercial business more aggressively than at any other time in its history. Indeed, there is evidence to show that the directors considered such competition not merely as their right, but also as their *public* duty.[2] Peel had declared that Bank of England notes, once created against gold, must be made available on terms as favourable as possible, which, as Tooke pointed out,[3] meant their issue at as low a rate of interest as possible. Thus the Bank directors argued that they were obliged " to look to the amount of our deposits, and the amount of the reserve that we have for meeting them ",[4] and that it was incumbent upon them immediately to employ all notes in reserve which were not required as normal backing for liabilities.[5] If

[1] 1848 Lords' Report, p. iv.

[2] " The effect of that doctrine [the principle of the Act] has been, that the Directors of the Bank of England have considered themselves not merely at liberty, but, to a certain degree, bound, to enter into competition in the way of discount, in times of cheap money, with the houses in Lombard Street." (Newmarch, 1857 Committee, Minutes, Q. 1366.)

[3] *Op. cit.*, p. 294.

[4] Evidence of Morris and Prescott before 1848 Commons' Committee, Minutes, Q. 2651.

[5] This argument was reinforced by a contention that, if the Bank held a large reserve, the circulation would be contracted, and money would be dearer than if " a large portion " of the reserve were employed; in that event, " the effect that ought to be produced by gold coming into the country is counteracted " and " gold will continue to come in ". (*Ibid.*, Q. 3009.) This was indisputable (indeed, the same principle forms a recognized part of central banking theory to-day); but the directors' ideas of what was an adequate reserve to retain would shock the modern banker. They were based not only on the belief that credit could not be unduly expanded so long as the note issue were controlled, but on the assumption that the Bank, as an " ordinary commercial bank ", would not (or at least, should not) be called upon for special assistance in time of crisis. See *post*, p. 109.

the directors were to pursue the same Bank rate policy as had been followed in the previous twenty years, there was only one means by which a surplus reserve could be employed—by purchases of Government or similar securities. This method was not favoured. "The practice of buying securities when money was abundant and the price high, and of selling securities when money was scarce and the price low," said Morris, explaining the procedure before 1844, "caused a loss to the Bank and inconvenience in the money-market which it was desirable to avoid." [1] The only alternative was investment in bills of exchange, involving a competitive discount rate; and the board, in deciding to adopt this course, then recalled [2] an advantage of bills which appeared to have been ignored by the Bank directorate for nearly a quarter of a century—the advantage that money employed in bills returned automatically to the lender at the end of a fixed and short period.

Thus arose what was termed the "new discounting" policy of the Bank. A special committee was appointed [3] to consider how Bank rate should be regulated in order to ensure a full employment of the banking department resources, and this committee recommended that "reference should be made" to the market rate. "The main recommendations," said Morris,[4] "were that it is advisable from Time to Time to advert to the State of Discounts out of Doors, for the Purpose of considering the Market Rate, in order that the Bank should assimilate its Rate to the Market Rate." Apart from this, no hard-and-fast rule was laid down: whether the Bank rate was to be below, above or equal to market rate was to depend upon the state of the reserve.[5]

The implementation of the new policy immediately upon the passage of the Act (it came into operation on September 2) required drastic action. From the end of 1841, market rate had fallen without interruption [6]: in 1843 it had never exceeded $2\frac{1}{2}$

[1] 1848 Commons' Committee, Minutes, Q. 2641.

[2] "It was considered advantageous that a portion of the Bank's deposits should be constantly employed in the discount of bills, and constantly, therefore, under control. It was in consequence determined that in fixing the Bank's rate of discount regard should be paid to the market rate." (*Ibid.*)

[3] See 1848 Lords' Committee, Minutes, Q. 488.

[4] *Ibid.*, Q. 490.

[5] This was styled "the Principle of the Management of the Bank" (*Ibid.*, QQ. 492, 493).

[6] See Tooke, *op. cit.*, pp. 47–63.

per cent., and in May and August, 1844, had dropped to the unprecedented level of $1\frac{3}{4}$ per cent., compelling the Bank to make the quarterly advances at $1\frac{3}{4}$ and $1\frac{7}{8}$ per cent. Thus, despite a reduction of Bank rate from 5 to 4 per cent. in April, 1842, the margin between the two rates had become very wide, and even an appreciable recovery in market rate at the end of August and early September, 1844, left a differential of $1\frac{1}{2}$ per cent. This did not deter the directors from acting in strict conformity with the new principle of competition. In the circumstances, and especially in view of the rising tendency of the outside market, it might have been expected that they would have been content to reduce their rate only slightly, and then to watch market reactions before making a further move. What they actually did was to bring Bank rate immediately into line with the market, by announcing on September 5 that they would discount first-class paper of not more than 95 days' currency at $2\frac{1}{2}$ per cent.—$1\frac{1}{2}$ per cent. under the lowest rate which had ever been charged previously. The natural effect of this step was to check the increase in the market rate,[1] and to bring the Bank into active competition with the discount houses and banks. Horsley Palmer stated [2] that "the consequence of that reduction was that the money-dealers in the public market brought down their rate below the Bank rate . . . it compelled the money-dealers to go down to 2, or even $1\frac{1}{2}$, per cent.".

That, despite this weakening of market rates, the directors over a period succeeded in maintaining an effective contact with the market is shown by the rapid increase in their discounts. The first Bank return giving effect to the Act (that dated September 7) showed that the Bank's London discounts had virtually ceased. They amounted to no more than £113,000,[3] and even the Branch discounts (the bulk of which were made in pursuance of the special arrangements with non-issuing bankers, at rates below Bank rate) were only £2,003,000. At the same time, the banking department reserve stood at £9,033,000. A year later,[4] the aggre-

[1] Tooke, *op. cit.*, p. 63.

[2] 1848 Commons' Committee, Minutes, Q. 2222.

[3] The figure was erroneously given as £1,113,000 by Morris in his evidence before the 1848 Commons' Committee (Q. 2641). For the actual Bank returns, both in the new form (showing the separation of the departments) and in the old form, but with a detailed analysis of deposits and securities, see 1848 Commons' Committee, Apps. 6 and 8.

[4] By the end of 1844, London discounts had risen to £1,148,000, while Branch discounts had fallen to £1,882,000. The former had touched £1,288,000 on November 30, 1844, but after that date they

gate discounts amounted to £6,526,000, of which £3,616,000, was made in London, while the reserve had fallen to £5,937,000.[1]

The whole theory of Bank rate had, indeed, been radically altered. Whereas before 1844,[2] the directors had deplored undue fluctuations in discount rates, and had contended that the Bank, as the ultimate source of credit, ought to be an important discounter only in times of stringency in the outside market, they now argued that "there is no reason why the Bank should not vary the rate of interest in the same way as any discount broker, or any other parties discounting would do." "The circumstances which ought to guide the Bank are fluctuating continually," said Morris, "if the Bank is to discount, it is necessary to follow the changes in the rate of interest, or if they do not do so, they had better relinquish discount business altogether." [3] In support of this policy, it was contended that the public attached too much importance to variations in Bank rate, and, with the object of correcting this "misapprehension", the Bank towards the end of 1844 actually suspended the regular issue of Bank rate notices.[4] Bank rate was no longer to be the "advertised" rate at which accommodation could be obtained at all times and by all comers against approved securities. As an ordinary commercial bank, it was said, the Bank ought no longer to be regarded as a lender from whom, in the last resort, holders of good securities could demand assistance, almost as of right. Morris held that the "public mind" should be disabused of this "error",[5] and he was supported by William Cotton,[6] Governor at the time of the passing of the Act, and by S. J. Loyd.[7]

The Principle of the "Minimum" Rate

In consequence of the new principle, Bank rate became not only a fluctuating rate (as opposed to one virtually stable), but a

steadily declined to a low point of £670,000 on February 1, 1845. Thereafter the trend was more rapidly upwards, and the high point for 1845 was reached on December 6, when the total was £5,781,000. Country discounts at that date totalled £3,622,000.

[1] See Appendix 5, 1848 Commons' Committee. [2] See *ante*, p. 78.

[3] 1848 Commons' Committee, Minutes, Q. 3421.

[4] See Morris before 1848 Lords' Committee, Minutes, Q. 484.

[5] 1848 Commons' Committee, Minutes, QQ. 3224, 3225. He also said that "Persons were absurd enough to suppose that the Bank was to assist any one who required it, provided the Securities offered were good". (1848 Lords' Committee, Minutes, Q. 308.)

[6] *Ibid.*, Q. 4566 (but *cf.* QQ. 4410–15).

[7] 1848 Commons' Committee, Minutes, Q. 5190.

" variable " rate (as opposed to a uniform one). Thus emerged the practice of the " minimum " rate, which has endured to the present day.[1] It was first adopted in March, 1845,[2] when the Bank intimated that the published rate would be applicable only to first-class bills of a given currency (at the time, 95 days or less). Previously, as has been explained,[3] all bills which were deemed acceptable had been taken at the same rate, irrespective of their currency, and regardless of whether they " were good or whether they were indifferent ". In future, the rate was to vary with the currency of the bills and with their quality,[4] and in one week in 1847 the range of rates at which bills were taken was actually from $5\frac{1}{4}$ per cent. (for very short bills) to $9\frac{1}{2}$ per cent. Thus the applicant for discount accommodation, unless he held absolutely first-class and short-dated paper (bearing at least two undoubted names, one of which had to be a *London* acceptor), could never know in advance precisely what rate he would be charged, for the Bank did not make a general practice of fixing and announcing differential rates for the various eligible usances.[5] In times of real ease, however, the new principle of adjusting the rate according to the life of the bills was a nominal change only, for in order to secure any business at all in London the Bank was obliged to apply the minimum rate to 95-day bills, and this was

[1] A brief, but very valuable, explanation of Bank rate policy before and after the Bank Act will be found in the Report of the Commons' Committee. Before, 1844, the Committee explained, " the practice of the Bank of England had been to discount at a rate nearly fixed and uniform . . . This system was abandoned in September, 1844. For the rate of discount already described, there has been substituted a rate which fluctuates from time to time ; a minimum rate has been substituted in the Bank notices, for a uniform one, and the practice has been introduced of discounting bills at the same time (even on the same day) at different rates ". (Report, pp. xxxiii, xxxiv.)

[2] March 13, 1845. The *Bankers' Magazine* commented : " in this respect the Bank, for the first time, we believe, assimilates its discount practice to that of other banking establishments . . . it appears pretty evident that the Directors are now anxious to push their business, as bankers, to an extent hitherto quite unknown to their system of management." (Vol. III, April, 1845, p. 53.)

[3] *Ante*, p. 81.

[4] Actually, the " variable rate " principle had been considered before 1844, and there is evidence to show that it would probably have been adopted even if the Bank Act had not been passed. See Lords' Committee, Minutes, Q. 483.

[5] 1848 Commons' Committee, Minutes, Q. 2769. No intimation whatever was ordinarily given of the possible or probable range between the minimum and maximum rates. (Lords' Committee, Minutes, Q. 486.)

the maximum eligible usance. In such cases, the "variable" principle applied only to differences in *quality*.

In many respects, as will be seen later, the Bank's competitive discounting was not in the best interests of the commercial world. But that general statement demands one important qualification. The practice of placing absolute restrictions upon discounts in times of pressure, which had caused so much distress in the past, was virtually abandoned.[1] Whenever it became necessary to check discount demands, this was done by the perfectly fair and legitimate method of increasing the cost of accommodation, instead of by imposing absolute limits [2] or by refusing assistance to particular classes of applicants. For the "*échéance* weapon", as formerly understood, there was substituted the "rate weapon", the principle of the latter being that if the published minimum rate were restricted to short bills, discounts of longer (eligible) bills should always be available at higher rates.[1] The recognition of this principle, even though in the early years it was not always applied discreetly, marked a great step forward, for it spread the burden of a pressure over a large part of the commercial world, instead of concentrating it mainly upon particular trades. In times of extreme pressure, the Bank did depart from its normal practice of not disclosing the differential rates,[3] as it was held that public disclosure might afford an additional protection, by acting as a deterrent to the drawing of long bills, and as a warning to the discount brokers of the danger of taking them. In any case, the fact that it was known to be the practice of the Bank to make differential charges exerted a useful influence upon the business world, by tending to promote greater liquidity in commercial contracts. Unfortunately, the degree of restraint which this practice could impose was quite inadequate to check a reckless growth of credit for which the Bank's competitive activities were to a large extent responsible.

Yet this principle of the minimum (or "variable") rate, evolved as an instrument of competitive commercial banking, was in later years to form an important part of true central banking technique. The Bank rate weapon of to-day—the central bank weapon *par excellence*—was in fact chiefly forged in

[1] See Morris before 1848 Commons' Committee, Minutes, QQ. 2766–72.

[2] See, however, *post*, p. 139, for a noteworthy exception to the new practice.

[3] See evidence of William Cotton, *ibid.*, QQ. 4431, 4432; and *post*, p. 141.

these years after 1844, when the Bank's aim was not a paternal control, but active competition. That is an interesting paradox; but the experience which the Bank gained from active contact with the discount market—indeed, as part of the discount market—proved invaluable, and it probably could not have been gained in any other manner. Thus when the Bank eventually resumed its earlier practice of standing aloof from commercial trading, as a central bank should do, and acted solely as a controller and regulator of the commercial world, it did so with the important difference that its regulations, instead of being burdensome and needlessly exacting, were attuned to business needs and practice. Arbitrary restrictions and limitations, so common in the period before 1844, were never restored as regular features of policy—they were superseded by an elastic rate of discount. The Bank rate weapon had been tempered in the only suitable furnace—in the discount market itself.

Steady Growth of the Bill Market

It might have been expected that the aggressive discounting policy of the Bank of England would have reacted adversely upon the discount market proper, and especially upon the discount houses as opposed to the bill brokers. The rapidly mounting discounts of the Bank, it might be argued, surely represented so much business appropriated from the private discounters, seriously damaging their connections and eating into their profits; and it might equally have been anticipated that if the Bank had long persisted in competition, its superiority of resources would ultimately have forced the private discount houses out of business. But in fact the discount market steadily grew and prospered.

To a great extent, this growth was undoubtedly due to the continued operation of the various forces already mentioned as major determinants of market expansion from about 1825 onwards. Most important of these influences, from a quantitative point of view, was the rapid expansion of the provincial joint stock banks, both in size and in number, side by side with the natural increase in trade, both domestic and overseas. The volume of commercial operations was vastly greater than in 1825; yet this larger commerce was still served by a "unit" banking system, for although branch banking had begun, the branches were generally few and were grouped round the parent institution, in districts having similar activities and needs. Thus this early branch banking did little to enable the provincial banks to "equalize" the borrowing and lending needs of different areas—the equalization function had still to be performed by the London money market, and especially by the bill brokers. Demand for the latter's services therefore grew with the growth of trade. Indeed, the increase in demand was more than proportionate, for the spread of the banking habit to the smaller trader and agriculturalist, and the provision of banking facilities in areas not previously "banked", brought demands upon the central money market which the mere increase in the scale of trade could never have done.

Such general factors as these explain the continued growth of the demand for discounts in London and the growth in the volume of funds which gravitated thither seeking employment. These influences benefited both the old style bill broker and the newer discount house. But they do not explain why the increasing discount activities of the Bank of England had no detrimental effect upon the private market. The business of the true bill broker, of course, was not in any event in danger of destruction by the Bank's new methods, for provincial clients were just as inclined—or nearly so—to employ a broker when the eventual discounter might be the Bank of England, as when it was almost certain that it would be a trading bank. In either case a London intermediary's services were required, and it mattered not at all to the bill broker whether his buyer were the Bank of England or the London and Westminster. And the position was almost the same even when the prospective provincial seller of bills was within reach of a branch of the Bank of England: for the Branch Banks invariably charged rates above the Bank's minimum London rate. Morris declared [1] that the general practice was to charge $\frac{1}{4}$ per cent. more, but he made it clear that the criterion in each case was the level of local commercial bank charges. These must frequently have justified a much wider differential; for even in such an important centre as Liverpool the rate charged by the Branch Bank to merchants was 1 per cent. above the Bank's London minimum,[2] while in Birmingham [3] the excess charge was $\frac{1}{2}$ per cent. for bank paper and 1 per cent. for general commercial paper.

[1] 1848 Commons' Committee, Minutes, QQ. 3574–8.

[2] Evidence of A. Hodgson, director of Bank of Liverpool, *ibid.*, Q. 155; and see Lords' Committee, QQ. 2082–3.

[3] Evidence of P. H. Muntz, a Birmingham merchant, *ibid.*, Q. 1265.

Thus even though the provincial trader wished to send his bills to the Bank of England in London, he could not utilize the Branch Banks, but was obliged to employ his own London agent. Having done so, it would be a matter of indifference to him whether the Bank, or a private discounter, bought the bills, so long as the cost to him was the same in either case.

The London discount houses were very differently placed. Their business as discounters, though not as recipients of deposits, was hardly distinguishable from the " new discounting " of the Bank. If, coincidently with the incursion of the Bank into the private market, there had not been a very marked expansion of discount demands, the turnover of the discount houses would inevitably have been substantially reduced. In competition with the Bank they laboured under one very serious disadvantage—they regularly re-discounted the bills which they bought, or at least pledged them as collateral for their borrowings, whereas the Bank of England, naturally, did neither. This was an important difference from the standpoint of the seller of bills, for many people, especially bankers, did not like their endorsements to be afloat in the money market, available to the curious, and perhaps suspicious, scrutiny of many expert eyes. The trader feared that the bills might reach his competitors, who might thereby glean valuable information; while the banker feared that the volume of his commitments might become too widely known, or that the mere fact of his re-discounting at all might arouse doubts about his stability. For these reasons, the Bank of England could secure *competitive* discounts even when its rate was a fraction above market rate; and when the two rates were identical, the Bank would generally secure preference.[1] This being so, it is of peculiar significance that in each of the years 1845, 1846 and 1847 the *average* Bank rate was actually *below* the average market rate. The excess market rate in 1847 was to be expected, for that was a year of acute crisis, but in 1846, when no such special factor was at work, the excess actually amounted to over $\frac{3}{8}$ per cent.

[1] The point was fully explained by Geo. Carr Glyn to the 1848 Lords' Committee, Minutes, Q. 1686; see also Prescott, " in order that the Bank should retain its discounts, it is quite sufficient for it to reduce its rate to the level of the market rate. There are many persons who prefer discounting at the Bank to discounting elsewhere, if it can be done on equal terms " (*ibid.*, Q. 508); and also Morris, *ibid.*, Q. 630.

—a striking contrast to the relationship between the rates in 1843 and in the first eight months of 1844.[1]

This differential makes the continued increase in the business of the outside market at this period seem the more remarkable. The bill dealers, however, not only shared with the brokers the advantages of the general increase in demands for discount accommodation, but benefited substantially from the growing popularity of call loans. The practice of lending money at call, as has been shown, had been known for some 20 years before the Bank Act; but not until the late 'thirties did it become sufficiently extensive to attract any great attention.[2] It was, in fact, in the 'forties that the system became really widespread.[3] This development was principally brought about by the narrowing of the market for Exchequer bills, formerly the favourite channel for the employment of surplus bank reserves. In the late 'thirties, and especially in the 'forties, the flood of railway company flotations, introducing to the Stock Exchange a vast mass of high-yielding railway debentures, greatly impaired the liquidity of the Exchequer bill market. The Exchequer bill ceased from that time onwards to be of interest to the general public; even the investor who sought security at all costs, and a steady return, turned instead to railway securities. In consequence, the Exchequer bill market became highly erratic: in times of pressure the bills became "almost inconvertible", and even at other times a substantial seller could never be sure that his approach would not turn the market very seriously against him. This change made the Exchequer bill completely unsuitable for the employment of bank resources, and the banks began to look instead to the call loan market.

[1] See *ante*, pp. 80, 108. The actual averages during the period were as follows:

	Bank Rate. %			Market Rate. %		
	£	s.	d.	£	s.	d.
1843	4	0	0	2	3	4
1844 (to end Aug.)	4	0	0	1	19	4
1845	2	13	8	3	0	0
1846	3	6	6	3	15	0
1847	5	3	6	5	17	6

[2] It did not figure at all prominently in the extensive evidence laid before the various Parliamentary inquiries until 1848.

[3] For a valuable description of call loans in the middle 'forties, see Sir Robert Peel's speech on the Loan (Discounts on Instalments) Bill, in the Commons, May 10, 1847. (Hansard, Third Series, Vol. XCII, Cols. 600–1.)

The Bank of England, indeed, had largely forsaken Exchequer bills as far back as 1833 or 1834,[1] substituting Government stock, because the directors held that the "Three per Cents." were more readily convertible. At that date, however, the Bank was concerned not only with the relative facility with which stock or Exchequer bills could be *sold*, but also with their relative merits as securities upon which money could be *borrowed* for short periods [2]—it was about this time that the practice of "borrowing on Consols" was first adopted. This facility for borrowing—actually, selling stock for cash, and buying it back for "time"—involved a degree of market organization which the Exchequer bill market had never attained. Thus the Bank's change of practice did not necessarily imply that the Exchequer bill market had even in the early 'thirties become seriously affected by the competition from new securities. The withdrawal of Bank of England support, however, must have been an important contributory cause of the decline of the Exchequer bill, and thus of the increase in the importance of the short loan market.

On the other hand, the practice of lending at call could never have assumed substantial proportions but for the availability of important and credit-worthy short-term borrowers—its growth was dependent upon the increase in the operations and standing of the discount houses themselves. It is not surprising, therefore, that some observers cited the growth of the bill market as a cause of the decay of the Exchequer bill. The following remarks by Morris, in 1848, are especially interesting:

> I have always considered that Railway Debentures interfere very much with Exchequer Bills, and also the Practice which has grown up within some few Years of Discount Brokers receiving from Bankers Money repayable at Call; the Bankers preferring to lend their Money in that way to investing it in Exchequer Bills.[3]

Actually, it was a clear case of action and reaction: there can be little doubt that the originating cause of the growth of the call loan market after 1832, or thereabouts, was the change in the Exchequer bill market, and that the expansion of the discount houses was a secondary cause, largely (but not wholly)

[1] See J. H. Palmer, 1848 Commons' Committee, Minutes, QQ. 2068–70. Palmer at the time disapproved of the change, holding that the risk of loss through depreciation was greater with stock than with Exchequer bills.

[2] 1848 Lords' Committee, Minutes, Q. 1041. [3] *Ibid.*, Q. 403.

attributable to the first. Another factor, which also operated to some extent before 1844, was the custom of the joint stock banks of allowing interest on deposits, thus compelling them to employ their reserves more closely than they might otherwise have done, or than many of the private banks actually did. This influence, however, did not assume very great importance until after the 1847 crisis.[1]

The Supremacy of Overend, Gurney

By far the largest share in the rapidly growing call and short-loan business was secured by Overend, Gurney & Co. Their key position in the whole financial structure, as custodians of a large part of the reserves of bankers throughout the country, will be readily appreciated. In Gilbart's phrase, they "became bankers of the London and of the country bankers"[2]; and in the words of *The Times* could "rightly claim to be the greatest instrument of credit in the Kingdom".[3] Yet in the 'forties, despite their great importance, they were still exclusively a discount house, though one which completely dwarfed its competitors. Samuel Gurney, asked in 1848 whether there were many others engaged in bill dealing (as distinct from broking), said that there were "not a great many"; and when the Chairman of the Lords' Committee suggested that the firm's business was "equal to all the rest put together", Gurney agreed that he had a "considerable proportion" of the total.[4] As the estimates given on a subsequent page reveal, the Chairman's suggestion was not far from the truth.

For practical purposes, there were only three other bill dealing houses—Alexander & Co., Bruce, Buxton & Co., and Sanderson & Co. The first of these, as the only bill market firm founded before the 'fifties which has retained its separate identity until the present time,[5] is of exceptional interest. It was established within a few years of the formation of Richardson & Co.,[6] and can thus claim to be the second of the original "true" broking firms. Throughout all the vicissitudes and crises of the century, its credit was never called in question. Like Gurney's, the firm was of Quaker origin, for its founder, William Alexander, a former clerk in the London banking house of

[1] See *post*, pp. 174, 175. [2] *Logic of Banking*, p. 555.
[3] *The Times*, May 11, 1866.
[4] 1848 Lords' Committee, Minutes, QQ. 1342, 1343.
[5] As Alexanders Discount Co., Ltd. [6] See *ante*, pp. 17–23.

Robarts, Curtis, Robarts & Curtis,[1] was a member of the Society of Friends. Technically, it dates from 1810, but at that date William Alexander had actually been in business as a bill broker for four years.[1] In 1806 he had joined one John Rickman, and a bill broking house was established at 11, Change Alley under the style of John Rickman & Co., which removed some two years later to 14, Birchin Lane.[2] In 1810 the partnership was dissolved,[3] and William Alexander set up an independent bill business at 33, Lombard Street, as Alexander & Co. A curious change of name occurred in 1819, when William Alexander died. His eldest son, George William Alexander, who had been with the firm as a clerk for several years, took over the management; but as he was then only seventeen years of age, his mother's name was incorporated in the firm-name, which became Ann Alexander & Co. The name was again changed in 1824, to A. & G. W. Alexander & Co., when the son became a partner on attaining his majority. From that date until 1864, the partners of the firm were exclusively members of the Alexander family. There is no positive evidence of the date at which the firm forsook the purely agency business, and began to take deposits as a bill dealer, but it is almost certain that it was one of the first to do so.[4] The change prob-

[1] See Gilbart, *op. cit.*, and Hilton Price, *op. cit.*, p. 2.

[2] This address, it will be noted, was the second address of Richardson: Rickman and Alexander must have moved to it almost immediately upon its vacation by Richardson, Overend & Co. (See *ante*, p. 21.)

[3] From the evidence of the *London Directories*, it seems clear that Rickman promptly took another partner, for the firm was continued at 14, Birchin Lane under the style of Rickman & Parry. It apparently disappeared about 1817.

[4] From figures courteously furnished by Alexanders Discount Co. from such early records as remain, it is clear that the firm took *some* deposits even in 1811. Their amount was then £27,329, but it seems probable that they were derived mainly from family and personal connections, and their existence hardly affords sufficient evidence to justify a conclusion that even then the firm was pursuing a dealing business of the type which Richardson, Overend & Co. developed after 1825. (See *ante*, pp. 64–9, both for the change in Richardson, Overend's practice, and for the reasons for the belief that no bill dealing, in the technical sense, was possible before about 1825.) Figures are also available to show that Alexanders' capital in 1811 was £4,937, and that its profits in that year amounted to £928—no mean return on the resources employed for a firm in its first year, even allowing for the experience of the bill market and the connection which William Alexander must have built up in his few years with Rickman & Co. If all the brokers' profits were on a like scale, the rapid growth in their activities in the ensuing decade becomes readily comprehensible!

ably occurred shortly after 1825, and from that time onwards the house played an increasingly important part in the bill market, for many years ranking in size and influence only after Gurney's, whose peculiar relationship with the Norwich banks gave them a special advantage.

Less precise data are obtainable about the origin of the other two bill dealing houses of the 'forties. Bruce, Buxton & Co. was apparently established in 1825, for the *London Directory* for that year lists one James Bruce [1] as a bill broker at 1, Popes Head Alley.[2] Buxton became a partner about 1837, but disappeared shortly after the 1847 crisis, and a few years later the firm became Bruce and Wilkinson. The new partner was apparently Joseph Wilkinson, a bill broker who had worked on his own account for at least twenty years. The only other bill dealing firm, Sanderson & Co., was older than Bruce & Co., and was certainly in existence for several years before the 1825 crisis. It was founded by Richard Sanderson, a clerk in Richardson, Overend & Co., who left to start in a " new line ", specializing in discounting the bills drawn by the Cheapside wholesale houses upon their customers in the provinces.[3] This business gave the firm an extensive commercial connection outside London, and, when it began to take deposits, it rapidly became an important factor in the market,[4] later developing a large business in grain bills and in Indian and Eastern paper.[5]

The relative size of these firms can be estimated with tolerable accuracy from material made available after the 1847 and 1857 crises, in both of which Sanderson's and Bruce's suspended payment, while the other houses had to lean heavily upon the Bank. To utilize this material involves, however, simultaneous estimates for the middle 'forties and 'fifties, and a good deal of detailed and close reasoning. The precise argu-

[1] This firm should not be confused with Bruce & Warren, which was founded about 1820 and certainly did a bill broking business at some period in the 'twenties (at Shorters Court and later at Copthall Chambers). In the 'thirties, however, it is listed simply as " brokers ".

[2] In 1840 the firm removed to 34, Abchurch Lane, which remained a famous bill market address for 45 years.

[3] The firm first appears in the *London Directory* in 1825, at 32, Lombard Street, and was for five years incorrectly described as " insurance brokers ". From 1845 onwards its address was 83, King William Street.

[4] In 1826 Sanderson became M.P. for Colchester, and later achieved a very successful marriage.

[5] See Gilbart, *op. cit.*, and *Bankers' Magazine*, 1856, pp. 545–8.

ment has been published elsewhere,[1] and need not be restated here, but the resultant estimates may be thus summarized:

BILL MARKET DEPOSITS

(Estimated)

	Middle 'Forties. £ (Mill.).	Middle 'Fifties. £ (Mill.).
Overend, Gurney	6·0	8·0 to 10·0[2]
Alexanders'	2·0	4·0
Sanderson's	2·0	3·5
Bruce	1·0	2·0 to 2·7
TOTAL	11·0	17·5 to 20·2[2]

The figure of £11,000,000 may be taken as a rough (and almost certainly a conservative) estimate of the extent of specialist bill dealing in the middle 'forties. It is therefore clear that the general impression that down to 1848 the Bank of England's London discounts were at least equal to those of private discounters is definitely incorrect. This impression derives from James Morris's evidence before the 1848 Lords' Committee,[3] upon which much reliance has been placed by Palgrave and by subsequent writers, nearly all of whom have accepted Palgrave's judgment. Actually, the Bank's London discounts in the middle 'forties never reached even £8,000,000, and were generally much below this figure (in 1846 they at one time dropped below £3,100,000); while even its total discounts never exceeded £13,137,000, and their maximum yearly average was no more than £9,616,000. As the discounts of the London commercial banks probably amounted to nearly £9,000,000, it is clear that London "private" discounters (banks and bill dealers) must have afforded at least £20,000,000 [4] of bill credit at normal times.

It is possible that, apart from the four houses already discussed, there were a few firms which also acted technically as dealers

[1] See the author's article in *Economica*, August, 1935.

[2] These estimates, though based on official statements, are probably unduly conservative, for at the time of the trial of the Overend, Gurney directors in 1869 (see *post*, pp. 255–6) it was revealed that the firm's deposits had amounted at end-1858 to £16 millions. It should also be noted that by the time of the 1857 crisis the newly-formed discount *companies* had deposits of between £2 and £3 millions. (See *post*, pp. 217–21.)

[3] QQ. 510, 511; but *cf.* Q. 625.

[4] Full details of the sources of these various figures will be found in the *Economica* article cited above.

rather than as brokers. It is certain, however, that none of them ran a " book " of any appreciable size. They may have secured small deposits from commercial sources, but most of their business must have consisted of a quick turnover of bills, differing from that of the strict broker only in that they made a profit from a " turn " in the rate instead of from a fixed brokerage. These quasi-dealer houses—representing a sort of mid-way point between " true " bill broking and " true " bill dealing—would naturally endorse the bills which they sold, but as they were usually firms of little substance, their technical liability on re-discounts in practice gave the purchaser no greater (and no less) protection than did the broker's " moral " guarantee. In both cases, the purchaser's real safeguard lay in the need for a bill market firm to preserve, at all costs, its reputation for infallibility in judging the paper which it transferred.

There is no means of assessing the extent of the business transacted by these smaller firms, but, from classified lists of financial agents included in the *London Directory* in the later 'forties, it is possible to form a reasonably accurate idea of their number. Bill market firms appear in the *Directory* of 1845 under three heads—" Bill Brokers ", " Discount Agents " and " Discount Brokers "—presumably for the simple reason that the firms thus described their business, and not because of any real distinction between the three types. Excluding the four bill dealing houses (three of which were listed as " bill brokers ", and the fourth—Sanderson's—as " discount brokers "), there were 16 firms in the first category, 6 in the second, and 3 in the third, a total of 25 firms.[1] Five of these were apparently established after 1840,[2] but 13 of them were at least ten years old. Comparison of the total in 1845 with that at earlier dates is difficult, if not impossible, not only because the earlier issues of the

[1] No exactitude can be claimed for this figure, for it is possible that then (as indeed now) the *Directory* descriptions of firms were inaccurate. In particular, " exchange " brokers still tend to be confused in such works of reference with bill brokers. One firm listed in 1845 as a " bill " broker is, indeed, described ten years earlier as an " exchange " broker. Again, the 1845 list of bill brokers included one firm—John Dew & Co.—trading at Pall Mall, which address hardly indicates the true " Lombard Street " house. Another firm is listed in 1845 both under " Bill Brokers " and " Discount Agents ". Allowance has been made for this in the figures above quoted.

[2] Six firms appeared in the 1845 list which were not trading as such in 1840, but one of these was apparently established by a partner who left an existing firm to set up on his own. Nine houses disappeared between 1840 and 1845.

Directory did not include the " Commercial " classifications, but because some bill market firms were apparently described simply as " brokers ", a term then used to embrace a multitude of widely different financial and commercial activities, of varying degrees of respectability. Nevertheless, an attempt to sort out the bill market firms suggests that in 1835 their number was not less than 16, and in 1840 not less than 28—again excluding in each case the " big four ".

The number given for 1835 should be treated with reserve. It represents simply the *minimum* number of firms which can with reasonable certainty be identified as members of the market; a good many others, whose activities cannot be definitely ascertained, probably were engaged in bill broking. Much greater accuracy can be claimed for the 1840 figure, so that it can be safely assumed that between 1840 and 1845, if not also between 1835 and 1845, there was a distinct contraction in the number of " true " bill brokers. This was probably a direct consequence of the growth of bill dealing. The dealers not only fulfilled the intermediary function of the true broker—both, for example, received bills from one part of the country and remitted them to other parts—but their activities actually reduced the relative number of bills re-sold to the banks, and consequently also the chances of employment for the broker agent. With few exceptions, an increase in the proportion of bank assets employed at call implied a corresponding reduction in the proportion of " broker's " bills (*i.e.*, bills bought as investments from the bill market, as opposed to those bought from customers). Moreover, when the banks did buy bills, they would naturally tend to go to the discount house to which they lent short money, instead of to the pure broker. In addition, the spread of the country connections of houses such as Overend's and Sanderson's must have made it much more difficult for the small broker to secure bills direct from the industrialist or trader, who would be only too glad to avoid the broker's commission.

In actual day-to-day routine, the business of the dealing houses did not differ greatly from present-day practice—on all essential points, the resemblances are certainly more marked than the differences. Samuel Gurney [1] thus described his operations:

> My business is usually denominated that of a Bill Broker, in fact a Dealer in Money, taking from those who have a surplus and distributing it to those who require it. . . .

[1] Before 1848 Lords' Committee, Minutes, QQ. 1094, 1338–41.

The practice of your business is to visit the different Bankers to take their superfluous capital beyond what they can employ, and then furnish aid to those who want it ?—That is the general Tenor of our daily Transactions.

So that in fact there centres in you, supposing you to be the only Party carrying on this Business, the whole Amount of disposable Capital at the Time ?—It is so in considerable Degree with ourselves, and others in the same Line of Business. The Stock Exchange also absorbs much of similar floating Money.

What is your business called ?—It is usually called Bill Brokers ; but that is not true, because we do not act as Brokers ; we act as Dealers.

Are your Transactions confined to the City, or do you do Business at the West End ?—We do Business with the West End bankers occasionally [1] to a large Extent, and transact Business with a large Proportion of the Country Banks.

But while the routine in the short loan market presented close parallels with modern practice, it is quite evident that the discount houses financed, and the banks accepted as collateral, many bills of a kind which would be rejected without hesitation to-day, or bills which, if discountable at all, would be taken only on onerous terms.

Long Usances and their Abuse

One important difference from modern experience was the much longer currencies at which bills were drawn. This was most noticeable in the import trades. For domestic trade, the usance was ordinarily three months, and in the export trades four months' drafts appeared to be the most common. In Lancashire, sales to the big Manchester manufacturers or wholesale houses were almost universally made at four months' credit : one month after delivery the buyer could either pay cash (securing a rebate on the invoiced price for 3 months at 5 per cent. per annum) or he could give a three months' bill. If discounts could be obtained in London at under 5 per cent., the buyer would pay cash.[2] Export trade was generally financed through accept-

[1] Horsley Palmer declared that the practice of lending at call to "brokers" had existed for "several years" with City bankers, but stated that West End bankers were more accustomed to hold Exchequer bills. (1848 Lords' Report, Minutes, QQ. 1048, 1049.) It is interesting to note that traces of this preference of the West End banks are still to be found to-day—bills and call money normally form a smaller proportion, and gilt-edged securities a larger proportion, of total assets of these banks than they do with the "Big Five".

[2] See 1848 Commons' Committee, Minutes, Q. 26; and *ante*, p. 58.

ance credits—by drawings on the big merchant houses of London or Liverpool. In the cotton trade, and Lancashire trade generally, the practice was for the manufacturer to draw at four months upon one of the Liverpool Anglo-American houses, which had close relationships with the overseas importers, and which financed the shipments.[1] The import trades were less highly organized, and in consequence import drafts were generally of much longer date, especially in trade with India, the East Indies and China. Here the usance was six months' sight or ten months' date, with drawings occasionally even at twelve months.[2]

Long drawings were, of course, inevitable in the absence of speedy communications, and while the longer life of bills naturally produced a lower degree of banking liquidity than is general to-day, it did not render "genuine" bills less legitimate objects of bank and money market finance.[3] Unfortunately, the need for very long drawings in some trades opened up avenues for abuse. One of the most serious abuses was fully described to the 1848 Commons' Committee[4] by C. Turner, a Liverpool East India merchant. When goods were sold in the East against the customary ten months' draft, the bills of lading were despatched separately, and usually reached the English importer in about ten weeks. For some eight months, therefore, before the goods arrived or the bill fell due for payment, the buyer was in possession of a security upon which he could raise money. He generally proceeded to do so by drawing bills against the bill of lading, discounting them in Lombard Street. This undesirable practice had apparently endured for many years, and was always "thought disreputable"; yet Turner declared that such bills constituted "one of the largest" classes which the bill brokers discounted. Probably this was an exaggeration, but there is no doubt that the device was widely adopted. Turner complained bitterly that the brokers "kept secret":

> The bill broker looks to the security, and he says "I am safe", and persons out of doors are not aware of what is going on; if we

[1] See A. H. Wylie, a Liverpool merchant, before 1848 Lords' Committee, QQ. 2096–100. These bills, and, indeed, cotton bills generally, were "favourites" with the discount brokers (*ibid.*).

[2] See 1848 Commons' Committee, Minutes, Q. 2349.

[3] Paul Moon James, a champion of the bill, and an excellent judge of the quality of bills, remarked in 1841 that "regular legitimate bills, whether they are drawn at 4 or 6 months, if the date is accounted for by the nature of the transactions for which they are drawn, are received by us"—the Birmingham Banking Co. (1841 Committee, Minutes, Q. 1509.)

[4] Minutes, QQ. 978–83.

had known . . . we should not have trusted them [the pledgors, not the brokers] a moment afterwards; we considered that the partners in those houses were men of undoubted property.

Another somewhat similar abuse arose from precisely the opposite cause—the fact that in some classes of distant import trade, especially that conducted through Liverpool, the bills drawn by the seller on the importing merchant often matured before the goods arrived, or at least before they could be sold. To secure funds with which to meet the bill, the merchant would pledge the produce "to arrive" with a produce broker, and draw upon the latter, subsequently discounting the bill. The bulk of these bills were taken by the provincial joint stock banks, and, with their endorsement, would be readily taken by the discount houses. Moreover, if the produce, on arrival, did not find a ready market, the drawer would arrange a renewal bill, and the operation would be repeated. According to one witness,[1] the discounting bank did not even then usually take a letter of lien on the goods in warehouse.[2]

That the discount market financed, or arranged for the finance of a large volume of these various types of undesirable bills is beyond question. But the real character of the paper was not always readily apparent, and there is evidence to show that the bill market, and certainly Overend, Gurney & Co., did profess to discourage such practices wherever possible. Overend, Gurney, for example, were said to have "set their faces" against renewal bills, and preferred not to take long bills. They generally refused what was known as "cross-paper"—bills drawn by one country tradesman on another—for this was still ineligible at the Bank of England, and was not liked by the firm's country bank clients.[3] The difficulty of placing this type of paper, however, could not have caused serious inconvenience to trade, for by far the greater part of the supply of bills, even of purely domestic bills, were drawn on London. In 1838, for example, London bills[4] were said to account for 90 per cent. of the discounts taken in Liverpool.[5]

[1] See 1848 Lords' Report, QQ. 2512–15.

[2] This practice, like that of pledging bills of lading, was not a new one. See Martin before 1836 Committee, Minutes, Q. 2326.

[3] This popularized the London acceptance credit for internal trade.

[4] See 1838 Committee, Minutes, Q. 275.

[5] It is interesting to note, however, that in trade with Ireland the preponderance of the London bill had become less marked. The change had been noticeable even by the late 'thirties. J. Marshall, secretary of the Provincial Bank of Ireland, describing the bills which

One interesting consequence of the bill market's reluctance to take " cross-paper ", and of its attempt to pursue purist principles so far as possible, was to encourage competition from a wholly unexpected quarter—from Scotland. The Scottish joint stock banks (as opposed to the older chartered banks, which preferred gilt-edged securities to bills) had for years been large buyers of bills in London, generally through the bill brokers ; and the fact that higher returns could be obtained on paper not readily rediscountable in London led them to establish connections in Liverpool, from which they obtained large quantities of local paper. They were also large buyers in London of bills at longer dates than those customarily taken by the discount brokers.[1] In this connection, it is worth noting that Irish bill brokers, who had existed in Dublin for some years, at times actually competed successfully with London brokers and local banks in Manchester and Liverpool.[2] Such competition, however, could occur only when the Bank of Ireland rate was below the London Bank rate—a very unusual feature.[3]

Bill Market Borrowing at the Bank

It might have been expected that the substantial growth of bill dealing in the 'forties would have led to more frequent

his bank discounted locally, declared that " London is not, as it once was . . . almost the representative of all the other parts by bills being made payable there . . . the custom now is much more that the bills are payable in those towns where the parties reside on whom they are drawn, though London, of course, still has the pre-eminence ". (1837 Committee, Minutes, Q. 4412.) In Ireland, however, the seller of an English provincial acceptance was not penalized ; other things being equal, such paper was discountable at the same rate as London paper commanded.

[1] 1848 Commons' Committee, Minutes, QQ. 6168–9.

[2] See P. Mahony, of the Agricultural and Commercial Bank of Ireland, before 1837 Committee, QQ. 4032–8.

[3] The Bank of Ireland regulated its rate " almost entirely " by the Bank of England rate, and fixed two rates ; the first, normally equal to the Bank of England minimum rate, was for English bills, usually export bills drawn from Ireland on an English provincial town ; the second rate, ½ per cent. above the first, was charged for Irish domestic paper, generally between one shopkeeper and another, or between a Dublin house and a country shopkeeper. The differential in favour of English bills was due, first, to the need for accumulating funds in London ; and, secondly, to the fact that English acceptors were usually more " solid " than Irish acceptors. (See evidence of J. McDonnell, Governor of the Bank of Ireland, before 1848 Lords' Committee.) Drafts from Dublin on London were generally at 60 days.

approaches by the discount houses to the Bank of England, especially as the persistent "effectiveness" of Bank rate removed the ordinary discouragement to such borrowings. But, in fact, there is no evidence to show that at this period the market relied unduly upon the facilities which it was afforded. During the quarterly "shuttings" the discount houses went to the Bank as a matter of course, either for the customary "temporary" advances or for re-discounts (much as they ordinarily do now in the last week of each year), but at other times their applications were infrequent. Overend, Gurney & Co. certainly never borrowed at the Bank unless absolutely forced to do so, and sought so to arrange their business that such borrowing would never be necessary, except at the Government dividend dates. Gurney's own evidence [1] is quite explicit on the point:

> You say that it is very seldom that you apply to the Bank?—We never apply to the Bank, unless the circulating Medium in the City is below the Requirements, then we become in large degree the Agents in getting it from the Bank. If the Supply of Circulating Medium is adequate we never go near them.

Again, when asked [2] whether a loan by the Bank to a bill market house was taken out in notes, he replied that eventually this was invariably so, and added:

> . . . It applies more particularly to ourselves and to Gentlemen in our Line of Business, because our House never does apply to the Bank for Money, except when Bank Notes are wanted in Lombard Street. While one Banker has a Surplus and another wants it, we adjust it between them. It is when there is a short Supply on the whole that we take Money [3] from the Bank, and it immediately becomes diffused in Bank Notes in Lombard Street.

This particular passage strongly suggests that the other discount houses ("Gentlemen in our line of business"), followed a similar

[1] 1848 Lords' Committee, Minutes, Q. 1344. [2] *Ibid.*, Q. 1140.

[3] Gurney presumably did not mean that he withdrew the actual cash from the Bank, but that when a commercial bank called money from Gurney's, it would be paid by a cheque on the Bank of England which it would subsequently "cash". All the bill "brokers" (presumably dealers) had accounts at the Bank. Incidentally, Gurney's reference to evening up the supply of floating money in the City suggests that his firm practised a sort of money "jobbing" in short loans, in addition to bill dealing, for none of the City banks, whether private or joint stock, ever re-discounted. Somewhat similar money operations are, of course, practised to-day, although no clearing bank would now *borrow* from a discount house. Lesser banks, however, have been known to do so within recent years.

policy, but it seems that with Overend, Gurney & Co. avoidance of Bank borrowing save at "the quarters" was regarded as a matter of prestige. Thus, when the chairman of the Committee suggested that the right to borrow at the Bank might induce a discount house to employ its resources too closely, Gurney neatly turned the question, and assumed that it meant a right to borrow during the "shuttings" or at times of emergency (a meaning which the chairman had evidently not intended to convey).[1]

This infrequency of bill market applications to the Bank was unquestionably largely due to the abundance of credit created by the Bank's vigorous commercial discounting policy. But it is also evidence that the discount houses, in their efforts to meet the Bank's competition, did not unduly or imprudently strain their resources, as the ease in money might well have led them to do. Bill market over-trading, had it occurred, would inevitably have produced at least short-period difficulties, with resultant borrowing at the Bank. Another indication that there was no undue rate-cutting by the market, despite its technical disadvantage in competition with the authorities, is afforded by the average rates, already quoted,[2] showing that the Bank rate in 1845, 1846 and 1847 was actually below the average market rate.

Several factors—the natural growth of banking resources and the spread of the call loan habit—have already been mentioned in explanation of the seeming paradox of continued market expansion in spite of Bank of England competition. These, however, were mainly long-term influences, and if the discount houses had had to rely upon them alone, it is tolerably certain that the three years after the Bank Act would have witnessed a substantial decline in market portfolios. But in fact the Bank's "new discounting" was directly and indirectly responsible for an increase in general demands for bill credit which far surpassed the volume of actual bills withdrawn from the outside market into the Bank's own portfolio. To appreciate this consequence demands an examination of the general credit situation and of the scale of business activity at the time.

[1] 1848 Lords' Committee, Minutes, Q. 1345. [2] *Ante*, p. 115.

CHAPTER V

CONSEQUENCES OF THE ACT OF 1844—(2) THE CRISIS OF 1847

THE year 1839, as has been noted, was one of crisis and acute depression, whose effects endured until well into 1842, with prices of all commodities steadily falling. They " touched bottom " about July, 1842, when a general improvement set in, aided by the satisfactory settlement of the Chinese War, foreshadowing the opening up of new and substantial markets for English products. This led to speculation in colonial produce, the prices of which rose appreciably. Various factors, including the expiration of a commercial treaty with Brazil, improved relationships with the United States, and a contemporary trade revival on the Continent, reawakened the export trades ; by early 1844 the country was enjoying a substantial measure of prosperity. According to Tooke,[1]

> . . . there was a brisk and increasing demand for manufactured produce, at home and abroad ; and the prevalence of full employment in every branch of industry, with moderate prices for all the principal articles of food, increased very considerably the demand for consumable articles of every description.

Only in agriculture, owing mainly to the reduction in tariffs in 1842, was there any lingering distress, but the burden of this was being rapidly alleviated by the increasing opportunities for the absorption of surplus agricultural labour.

THE RAILWAY " MANIA "

Meanwhile, there had arisen a new interest in railway enterprise, which, following the rapid building of the 'thirties and the collapse of share prices in 1839, had been under a cloud. Railway securities had stood at substantial discounts, but by 1842 the

[1] *History of Prices*, Vol. IV, p. 54.

stocks of the leading lines had climbed back to a premium. As the year 1844 progressed, public attention was increasingly drawn to the favourable results which these lines had achieved; and railway securities gained a new attractiveness after the conversion of the "Three and a Half per Cents" and a rise in Consols to par. Money was almost phenomenally cheap, materials—especially iron—were almost equally so, with the inevitable consequence that extensions to existing systems were planned on a large scale. Many new railway projects naturally followed, and by September over ninety prospectuses were almost simultaneously before the public, avowedly foreshadowing an aggregate outlay of nearly £100,000,000. Such a situation clearly contained all the germs of dangerous speculation in many branches of trade; especially as the measure which was to make the currency system secure for all time, which was to ensure maximum abundance of cheap credit, and to obviate recurrence of the crises of the past, had just been placed on the Statute Book.

This was the atmosphere into which the Bank launched its aggressive lending policy, with an energy which took the commercial world completely unawares. The theory behind the Bank Act had been well recognized; yet the City had not envisaged any step so drastic as the immediate cut in Bank rate to 2½ per cent., more particularly as the outside rate had at last begun to respond to the general increase in business activity.[1] The immediate result was to arrest the natural rise in the outside rate (which, if continued, might have afforded some check to the speculations which followed), and to force the discount houses to maintain lower rates throughout the autumn than they otherwise would have done. The Bank's action naturally aroused much criticism and many bitter complaints from the bill market, for though the volume of its business was not adversely affected, there is no doubt that its profit-margin suffered perceptibly. But worse was to come, for the Bank followed up its competitive discounting with equally competitive short-term lending.

The actual notice appeared on January 15, 1845, and read as follows[2]:

[1] See, for example, the following comment by the *Bankers' Magazine*: "Notwithstanding the well-founded predictions of many, that the Bank would adopt this course of action [that of immediate and active competition with the discount houses], directly she was relieved from the responsibility of managing the circulation, her recent proceedings have taken the monetary world entirely by surprize." (*Bankers' Magazine*, October, 1844, p. 57.)

[2] See 1848 Commons' Committee, App. 10.

> The Governor & Company of the Bank of England are ready from the present time, and until further notice, to receive Applications for Advances on the security of Bills of Exchange not having more than six months to run, Exchequer Bills, East India Bonds and other approved Securities ; such Loans to bear Interest at the rate of 2½ per cent. per annum, and to be repaid at periods to be fixed at the time of Advance ; but such repayment not to be later than the 11th of April next, and the Loans to be for not less than 2,000 *l.* each.

In its general form, this announcement resembled the notices which the Bank had issued regularly before the quarterly dividend dates, but in scope it was wider and more liberal than any previous offer. In the first place, the quarterly notices had invariably fixed a date, generally about ten days after the actual dividend date, beyond which fresh advances would not be made (sometimes modified later by special renewal notices if money continued to be scarce)—never before had the Bank offered " temporary " advances " until further notice ". Moreover, the securities acceptable as collateral included those formerly accepted only in times of special pressure or difficulty. Normally, they were limited to *three* months' bills, although sometimes six months' bills were accepted : Exchequer bills and East India Bonds were only exceptionally included.[1]

In the outside market situation there was nothing to suggest any need for this liberality. The dividend date was long past, and the normal advances of the previous quarter-end were being repaid, although the repayments had occasioned momentary increases in short loan rates. But there was no sign of any lasting pressure. In the circumstances, the news caused real excitement in Lombard Street, where it was rightly interpreted as an indication that the Bank intended to use its newly-gained freedom to the utmost—that loans against collateral at competitive rates would in future be a regular feature. *The Times* regarded the Bank's action as " a more complete departure than any of their former acts, from their previous character of the

[1] In one respect, it might appear that the offer was less liberal than the usual quarterly offers. The latter, before 1844, were always made at market rate, or what the Bank deemed to be market rate (see *ante*, p. 85), whereas the offer of January 15, 1845, was made at Bank rate (2½ per cent.). At the time, however, the two rates were virtually at a parity, so that to offer money at Bank rate was not less liberal ; indeed, the experience of the ensuing three years shows that, on the average, loans at market rate would have been more costly to the public than loans at Bank rate.

'Regulators of the Currency'", while the *Bankers' Magazine* was convinced that "if this line of conduct continues, a monetary crisis will become inevitable".[1]

The Bank did continue "this line of conduct". Temporary loans, as well as discounts, remained constantly available at low rates, and the prediction of the *Bankers' Magazine* proved disastrously accurate. The free lending policy fanned the stirring embers of railway (and other) speculation, which rapidly became a veritable blaze. The first projects were mainly for lines in districts genuinely in need of railway facilities, although for each of these routes there were quickly three, four, five, or even more, competitive schemes; but it was not long before plans were launched for even the most remote and sparsely peopled areas.

> Norfolk and Suffolk were presently cut-up into mince meat (on paper) by rival projectors, whose terror of being too late in the field left them very little either of time or wit to render their proposals remarkable for judgment or completeness . . . every nook and avenue of England which, with any shew of decency, could be described in a public print as "an important district, abounding in traffic of a certain description", etc., was forthwith occupied by an incipient railway company.[2]

Many of these schemes collapsed even before they had been formally listed for the consideration of Parliament, but by the opening of the Parliamentary session of 1845–6, no less than 1,428 new schemes were afoot, requiring an aggregate capital stated in the prospectuses at £701,243,000, and aggregate deposits of £49,592,816 before their claims could be heard.[3] Many projects, too, were entirely fictitious; but the fiction served to enable fraudulent promoters to benefit handsomely from the public mania for share market profits—some of which must have been enormous. Even the shares of the old-established trunk lines rose between 75 per cent. and 90 per cent. in the first half of the year (Great Western £100 shares commanded £228 in July), while the market values of the securities of some of the new companies of real merit multiplied themselves seven or even ten times in as many months.[4] By the middle of 1845, it was estimated that £500,000,000 of securities were selling in the

[1] *Bankers' Magazine*, Feb. 1845, Vol. II, p. 310.

[2] *Ibid.*, May, 1845, Vol. III, p. 75.

[3] See *The Times*, Nov. 17, 1845.

[4] See paper before the Royal Statistical Society in Jan., 1847, cited by Tooke, *op. cit.*, p. 299. The £40 shares (£4 paid) of the Bolton, Wigan and Liverpool Railway stood at £4 10*s*. in Jan., and at £42 15*s*. in Sept., 1845.

market at a premium—many in the form of allotment letters—and the uncertainty of the Parliamentary sanction merely added piquancy to the speculations.

Such a boom was bound to collapse, as it did with disastrous consequences in the closing months of the year, when the market values of even " respectable " railway securities were decimated. The bursting of the share market bubble did not, however, terminate the stimulating effects of this railway " mania " upon speculative activity in other fields. In the first place, many people who had heeded the warnings [1] of the time had reaped substantial gains while the boom lasted, and the public appetite for speculative profits had been whetted. There is abundant evidence to show that this general speculation had assumed substantial proportions even before the railway boom reached its zenith [2]; and one of the most remarkable features of the period is the fact that this activity suffered hardly more than a temporary rebuff from the violent break in the railway market. Secondly, while the collapse of that market eliminated hundreds of bubble schemes, the boom in railway building, as opposed to speculation in railway shares, went on. In the calendar year 1845, Parliament had authorized the raising of £60,266,228 of new railway capital, and in the following year the figure was £130,176,374. The sums actually raised by the companies in the two years were £16,457,094 and £38,678,680 respectively.[3] Railway spending on this scale involved a substantial demand for goods of all kinds,[4] and an all-round increase in employment which provided an apparent justification for the ancillary and other speculations.

[1] See, for example, the *Bankers' Magazine*, July, 1845, p. 250, and *Bankers' Almanack*, 1849, p. 45.

[2] " The railway speculation went at that time [1845] to such an extent as to occupy the attention of the public almost exclusively. But it is evident . . . that a good deal of what now appears to have been improvident outlay in fixed capital abroad, including foreign railways, was also then in progress, and was, no doubt, encouraged by the advances which were so liberally and so largely afforded upon distant forthcoming returns. Investments, too, in mills and mines, and various projects of internal improvement, besides railways, entailing the conversion of circulating into fixed capital, were going forward on a scale sufficiently extensive to have attracted public notice, but for the all-absorbing topic of the railway mania. This was surely not a time during which it was desirable or (looking to probable, if not inevitable results) safe, to aid the continuance of so low a rate of interest."—Tooke, writing in 1847, *op. cit.*, p. 295.

[3] See 1848 Lords' Committee, App. D.

[4] The price of bar iron, for example, was doubled even by March, 1845; it then stood at £10 10*s*. per ton, compared with £5 7*s*. 6*d*. per ton only six months' earlier.

Bank's Competition Stimulates Credit Abuses

The railway share market might conceivably have got out of hand even if monetary factors had been comparatively unfavourable; but there is no doubt that the "secondary" speculation, and the actual railway building, were very largely fostered, if not literally created, by the ease with which accommodation could be obtained at the Bank and in Lombard Street. The frantic railway speculations did not, apparently, raise even the faintest doubt in the minds of the Bank directors as to the expediency of their free policy, far less any suspicion that it might be the actual cause of the prevalent excesses. Throughout the summer of 1845 the Bank's rate, both for advances and discounts, remained at 2½ per cent., and its security portfolio [1] steadily expanded. Not until October, when the railway collapse was imminent, and when the immobilization of railway parliamentary deposits, railway calls, and seasonal demands had combined to raise the market rate to 3½ per cent. and over, did the Bank increase its rate—by a mere ½ per cent. And in the following year, after a further increase, the Bank reduced the rate immediately market rate began to fall towards its own. Thus over the whole twenty-eight months from the passing of the Bank Act to the end of 1846, market rate averaged only 3·24 per cent. and Bank rate only 2·93 per cent.

With so many speculations in progress, these abnormally low rates naturally stimulated over-trading and a revival of serious abuse of bill credit. The discount houses, although their rate was frequently somewhat above the Bank's, undoubtedly secured a very large business. Many of the bills sent for discount in London were accommodation paper, especially those sent from Liverpool for the colonial and East Indian trades. The accommodation bill system, indeed, seems to have been more extensive at this period than at any earlier date. It was even *organized*: there were a number of financial agents, sometimes styling themselves "bill brokers", and trading from such addresses as the Old Kent Road, who gained a livelihood solely by furnishing specially manufactured bills to needy traders or private individuals,

[1] At times after 1844, the Bank actually invested in railway debentures (holding roughly £2,500,000 at one time), as an alternative to Government stock. (See 1848 Lords' Committee, Minutes, Q. 397.) The practice was strongly condemned by the Lords' Committee, as "giving a high sanction and an effective stimulus" to the railway speculations "augmented" by the Bank's rate policy. (Report, p. xxxvi.)

in return for a small commission, and who secured a clientèle by circularization. In some cases, they procured drafts by and upon more or less respectable houses, but in other cases the bills " advanced " to the borrowers were fraudulent or fictitious. But even the worst types of this manufactured paper got into circulation, and were often so drawn as to deceive even the most wary discounter.[1]

The London discount houses probably escaped any serious victimization by such methods—the chief victims seem to have been the country banks—but there is no doubt that the London market (and possibly also the Bank of England) discounted large quantities of finance bills created in much more reputable quarters. Accommodation paper was not always readily detected (especially when produce had actually been shipped, but had been made the subject of *two* drawings by different parties), and even where its nature was known, the parties were often of such standing that their bills dare not be rejected. The following passage,[2] from the *Manchester Guardian*, reveals very graphically the technique adopted, and also throws additional light on the practice of drawings against bills of lading in the import trades, already noted [3] :

> The India trade has been one huge system of credit. If goods were bought in Manchester, by a house in London, they were paid for by bills at six months' date ; and, as soon as shipped, an advance was obtained again by a bill at six months for a large part of the first cost, by the consignee, who, again, in his turn, not infrequently drew upon the house in India, against the bills of lading when transmitted. The shipper and the consignee were thus both put in possession of funds, months before they actually paid for the goods ; and, very commonly, these bills were renewed at maturity, on pretence of affording time for the returns in a " long trade ". Moreover, losses by such a trade, instead of leading to its contraction, led directly to its increase. The poorer men became, the greater need they had to purchase, in order to make up, by new advances, the capital they had lost on the past adventures. Purchases thus became, not a question of supply and demand, but the

---

[1] See " Accommodation Bill Swindling ", in the *Bankers' Magazine*, April, 1845 (Vol. III, p. 1) and correspondence and notes in that journal during the subsequent months of the year. A common trick of the worst type of bill " manufacturer ", if indeed he shrank from actual forgery, was to seek out a person with a name identical (or nearly so) with that of a well-known house, and induce him to " accept " bills in a handwriting resembling that of his namesake.

[2] *Manchester Guardian*, Nov. 24, 1847.

[3] See *ante*, p. 124.

most important part of the finance operations of a firm labouring under difficulties.

But this is only one side of the picture. What took place in reference to the export of goods at home, was taking place in the purchase and shipment of produce abroad. Houses in India, who had credit to pass their bills, were purchasers of sugar, indigo, silk, or cotton,—not because the prices advised from London by the last overland mail promised a profit on the prices current in India, but because former drafts upon the London house would soon fall due, and must be provided for. What way so simple as to purchase a cargo of sugar, pay for it in bills upon the London house at ten months' date, transmit the shipping documents by the overland mail; and, in less than two months, the goods on the high seas, or perhaps not yet passed the mouth of the Hoogly, were pawned in Lombard Street,—putting the London house in funds *eight* months before the drafts against those goods fell due.

The parties to such bills were frequently old-established Manchester, Liverpool or London merchant houses, or Mincing Lane firms, whose paper had been taken without question for many years. Few even of those who were aware of what was going on suspected that the accommodation thereby afforded was anything more than a matter of convenience. In fact, it was often one of dire necessity; the accountants who dealt with the liquidation of many of the firms which eventually crashed revealed that most of the failures were those of houses which had once been wealthy, but had long ceased to be so.[1] They were kept alive solely by a complex series of cleverly devised accommodation bills; in effect, the bill market—from funds repayable at call—was making good the inroads into working capital which past losses had effected. Any serious weakening of general confidence, much less any rumour that these houses were not as secure as they were thought to be, could not fail to wreck them beyond any possibility of reconstruction.

Without doubt, excesses of this type, and many of the more legitimate speculations, were directly traceable to the abnormal facilities obtainable in Lombard Street, and to the unduly low rates at which accommodation was afforded,[2] thanks to the policy pursued by the Bank. The Bank directors, however, were merely acting in accordance with the spirit of the Bank Act, in a placid faith that they had no greater power for good or evil

[1] See 1858 Committee, Report, Sections 35, 36, and evidence of Coleman and Ball.

[2] That rates *were* unduly low is shown by the tendency of market rate to rise above Bank rate.

than any "other" commercial bank. As Tooke pointed out, no blame whatever could attach to them, or "at all events, they are not open to reproach from the promoters and admirers of the Act".[1] They had full justification for looking to their own interests and in working to achieve a maximum profit (Bank dividends rose after 1844). Moreover, it is questionable whether at the time any of them realized the direction in which their activities were leading. It was apparent to all that trade was running at an unusually high level, and that many speculations were afoot. But the supporters of the Bank Act and the Bank board were not looking for signs of over-expansion of trade; the Bank Act had imposed a new discipline upon note issues, and the opponents of the new system had urged that it would fetter and restrict trade. Hence the authorities, both in Westminster and in Threadneedle Street, were concerned to satisfy themselves simply that there was no unnatural *contraction* of trade and speculation. As may be imagined, that satisfaction was readily obtained, and the buoyancy of economic and financial activity was actually cited as proof of the success of the new system. Sir Robert Peel himself declared that "our experience . . . has been decidedly in favour of the policy and justice of the measures sanctioned by this House. . . ."

> Since these measures were adopted, we have had in this country a period of extraordinary commercial activity; we have had a great demand for the application of new capital to manufactures, and other branches of the public industry; and we have had a very unusual degree of speculation connected with the internal improvement of the country. I refer particularly to the projects for the extension of locomotion by means of railways. But I cannot find that the restrictions imposed . . . have, in the slightest degree, cramped or fettered the commercial energies of the country.[2]

That this "very unusual degree of speculation" might be dangerous, simply did not occur either to Peel or to any other whole-hearted supporters of the Act. They had effectively stopped the over-issue of bank notes, and were convinced that so long as the legal restrictions remained, there could be no possibility of credit excesses.[3] Speculation and overtrading

[1] Tooke, *op. cit.*, p. 295.

✓ [2] Debate on Scotch and Irish Banking, April 25, 1845. (Hansard, Series 3, Vol. LXXIX, Col. 1324.)

[3] A modern counterpart of this fallacy might be found in the popular belief, especially current in 1932, that the high level of the Bank of England's gold holding, and consequently also of the banking depart-

were therefore allowed free rein, and liberal credit facilities were afforded, at low rates, right up to the time when a rapid diminution of the Bank's reserve made an immediate change of policy imperative. According to the Chancellor of the Exchequer, until February or March, 1847, no one had anticipated any serious trouble,[1] and the Bank directors appeared to have no misgivings until early April.

Reckless Lending—and Its Sequel

Actually, the storm-clouds had begun to gather in the previous autumn, when a short wheat harvest and an almost complete failure of the potato crop, necessitating heavy imports, led to a severe drain on the Bank's gold holding. The Bank, however, continued to lend freely, with Bank rate at 3 per cent. In early January, difficulties in Paris drew funds from the London market, which was then faced with almost simultaneous calls on railway shares, both home and foreign, to the amount of at least £6,000,000. The unaccustomed stringency thus produced, coupled with the prospect of further heavy wheat imports—a hard winter suggested another short crop in 1847—aroused public apprehension, and led to reflections that the lavish outlay on fixed capital might have unduly strained national resources. On January 14 a belated increase in Bank rate to 3½ per cent. drew attention to the state of the bullion reserve (which stood at rather under £13,000,000, compared with £16,400,000 in the previous September), and, when Bank rate was raised to 4 per cent. a week later, the public showed definite signs of alarm. But, despite the severity of the pressure in Lombard Street and the many disquietening features of the situation, this increase in Bank rate marked the limit of the Bank's precautionary measures. The drain of gold continued, and the market and the banks waited daily for the expected penal increase in Bank rate.[2] For three months, market rate stood appreciably above Bank rate; but

ment reserve, was conclusive evidence of the absence of any credit inflation in Great Britain at the time. It was largely forgotten that, with sterling divorced from gold, purchases of gold merely became one means of credit expansion—a convenient alternative to the usual purchases of securities.

[1] Debate on Loan Discount Bill, May 14, 1847. (Hansard, Series 3, Vol. XCII, Col. 870.)

[2] See S. J. Loyd, before 1848 Commons' Committee, Minutes, Q. 5133.

the Bank of England continued to discount freely,[1] taking bills up to 95 days, and met all applications for advances before the April dividends.

Not until April 8, when the bullion had fallen to £9,870,000, and the Banking Department reserve to £3,460,000 [2] (against £8,920,000 on January 2), did the directors realize the danger of their position. Bank rate was raised to 5 per cent., but proved insufficient to check the demands, and a week later the usual "no change" notice omitted any reference to the currency of bills to which the minimum rate was applicable. To the dismay of Lombard Street, and of the commercial world, it was found that only bills with a few days to run were discountable at the published rate, "much higher rates" [3] being charged even for 10 or 14 day bills. In addition, the outstanding quarterly advances were called in, and the usual option to renew for a short period was withheld. These, moreover, were not the most onerous restrictions. Following the precedent set up in 1795,[4] the Bank simultaneously placed a limit upon the *amount* of bills which it would discount, regardless of the quality of the paper offered or the standing of the applicants.[5] Finally, it borrowed heavily on Consols, raising £1,275,000 in this way between April 6 and April 23.[6]

The effects of so drastic a reversal of policy may readily be imagined. For a short period, it was literally impossible to discount bills in Lombard Street, or to raise money upon even first-class securities; and when discounting was resumed, it was at rates "hitherto unknown in this country" [7]—the finest six months' paper sold at 12 or 13 per cent. A virtual paralysis—the word is used by at least three authoritative contemporary commentators—of trade resulted. According to Lord Ashburton [8]:

[1] Between January 9 and April 3 the Bank's London discounts rose from £4,953,000 to £6,861,000 and its total discounts rose from £7,490,000 to £11,146,000.

[2] Figures shown in the Bank return of April 10. (Returns were then made up on Saturdays.)

[3] Tooke, *op. cit.*, p. 304.

[4] See *ante*, p. 71.

[5] It was proposed at a meeting of the Court that instead the rate might be raised to 7 per cent., but this was over-ruled by a majority vote. (See 1848 Commons' Committee, Minutes, Q. 2461.)

[6] 1848 Commons' Committee, *ibid.*

[7] See Petition of the Merchants, Bankers and Traders of London, against the Bank Charter Act: July 13, 1847. (This petition is reproduced in full in Professor T. E. Gregory's *British Banking Statutes and Reports*, Vol. II, p. 4; see also *Economist*, 1847, pp. 749, 760.)

[8] *Financial or Commercial Crisis Considered* (1847), pp. 18–19.

> . . . this fright of the Bank . . . of violating this parliamentary restraint, has driven her into proceedings which have depreciated, to a very great extent, every description of property, food only for evident reasons excepted. It would not be easy to estimate this depreciation, extending over all merchandise, stocks, railroad shares, etc.; it probably would not have been over-stated at 10 to 20 per cent.; but, what is worse, it has paralysed this property in the hands of the possessors, rendered it unavailable towards meeting their engagements, and thus produced, in many cases, pecuniary sacrifices, much beyond the mere depreciation of the property itself. It has further occasioned the suspension of the execution of orders from our customers in every quarter, thus distressing manufacturers, and impeding those very operations which would have corrected the tendency to an unfavourable balance of trade, and given safety to the circulation of the Bank.

These difficulties and this distress did not, however, mark the climax of the crisis, for at this stage there were no outstanding commercial or banking failures. The rise in the market rate, together with the news that the Russian Government intended to employ certain resources in the purchase of British funds,[1] had a salutary effect on the exchanges, thus reversing the gold drain and inducing the Bank to moderate its restrictions.[2]

Some measure of confidence was thereby restored, but the fundamental sources of disequilibrium remained. The constant succession of railway calls kept rates in the outside market very firm and prevented any rapid replenishment of the Bank's reserve; while in July the payment of the dividends and a renewed export of gold to America combined to produce another serious drain—in the six weeks to July 31 the reserve fell by £2,100,000 to £4,440,000. Another source of trouble then began to compel attention—the highly vulnerable position in the grain market.

Adverse seasonal conditions throughout the winter and early spring had threatened a short wheat crop, both in England and on the Continent. This prospect, following the shortage of the season 1845–6 (in the autumn of 1846 the French, Dutch and Belgian Governments had taken the abnormal step of throwing open their ports to grain imports, duty-free), led to heavy "bull" speculation in wheat, and the price rose from 45*s*. 1*d*. per quarter

[1] The object was to employ in interest-earning assets part of the gold behind the Government note issue. (See Tooke, *op. cit.*, pp. 73, 74.)

[2] It lent fairly freely during May on stock and Exchequer bills, and discounted fine 95-day paper at 5½ per cent.

in August, 1846, to 79*s.* 6*d.* per quarter in April, 1847. In May the excitement was intensified by the receipt of substantial buying orders from the Continent, and by the end of the month, despite the extreme stringency in Lombard Street, the price reached 102*s.* 5*d.* (it momentarily touched 124*s.*). As events proved, this alarm was largely misplaced ; in June foreign supplies were offered freely, and, in addition, it became evident that the domestic harvest would be less deficient than had been feared. By the beginning of August, therefore, speculators were already facing heavy losses, with the price down to 75*s.*

It was at this point that the Bank realized—again belatedly—the severity of the threat to its reserve, though it was probably unaware of the dangerous position in the grain trade. On Monday, August 2, without waiting for the usual Thursday meeting of Court, it intimated that its current minimum of 5 per cent. would apply only to one month bills—those at two months would be charged $5\frac{1}{2}$ per cent., and those at 95 days, 6 per cent. On the ensuing Court-day, the differential scale was confirmed, and the *minimum* raised to $5\frac{1}{2}$ per cent. These measures greatly intensified the commercial distress, for although in the previous few months confidence had been partially restored, the restoration had been based entirely on hopes that the worst of the crisis had passed. The mercantile difficulties of the spring remained, and it was realized that they could be satisfactorily resolved only with the aid of a continued fall in discount charges. Hence the Bank's restrictions, with their accompanying movement in Lombard Street (to fully 1 per cent. above Bank rate), produced extreme alarm, whose intensity was accentuated by painful recollections of the severity of the April panic.[1]

In Mark Lane, the effect was immediate. From August 6 [2]

[1] The Bank's measures were whole-heartedly approved by the *Economist*, which, for weeks before the April crisis, had regularly called upon the Bank board to raise its rate. The August restrictions were therefore hailed as an indication that the Bank intended to take precautions in good time. This, however, was an obvious attempt to minimize the danger of the situation and thus to allay public fears. The paper, having remarked that the news had " produced more alarm and excitement than are warranted ", went on to explain the reasons for the Bank's step, and produced so formidable an array of adverse features that its laudable intention must have been sadly frustrated ! (See *Economist*, 1847, p. 889.)

[2] On that day Douglass & Son failed with liabilities of about £300,000 followed three days later by the important house of Lesley, Alexander & Co., with liabilities of £500,000. An especially severe blow to confidence was the failure, on August 21, of W. & H. Robinson & Co.,

onwards, there was a constant succession of failures in the grain trade, and each fresh suspension, by further depressing the price of wheat,[1] made additional suspensions the more probable. In the last week of the month came the first important failures in general commerce. "These *mercantile* failures," says Tooke,[2] "in number, and in the amount of property involved in them, were beyond all precedent in the commercial history of the country." They naturally placed an acute strain upon the discount houses, and on September 14, Sanderson's, which had carried a large amount of corn bills, was obliged to suspend payment.[3] This suspension, together with that of Bruce & Co., induced an extreme caution on the part of the other discount houses and the London banks, and discounts in the outside market became obtainable only with extreme difficulty.

Meanwhile, on September 2, the Bank had intimated that advances in anticipation of the October dividends would be obtainable for periods (not less than 14 days) up to October 14 at 5 per cent.[4] As the published minimum was still $5\frac{1}{2}$ per cent.,

whose senior partner was the Governor of the Bank, who was thereupon obliged to resign. The firm's difficulties were attributed to speculations in rye-meal.

[1] It had dropped to under 50*s*. per quarter by mid-September. The August grain failures were estimated by the *Mark Lane Express* at £5,000,000.

[2] *Op. cit.*, p. 316.

[3] No suggestion was raised, either then or subsequently, that the firm's difficulties were in any way due to its own misconduct or to overtrading. It had, however, been handicapped by the sudden retirement, a few years previously, of a wealthy partner, named Gard, and, later, by the death of the third partner, Morris, which had left Sanderson in sole charge of the business. In consequence, its turnover had shrunk to some extent in the period before the crisis. (See *Economist*, 1847, p. 1089.) Despite these handicaps, the firm was quite solvent, and a meeting of creditors held a week after the suspension passed a resolution, signed by S. J. Loyd, declaring that "Sanderson's own conduct has been correct and highly satisfactory in all respects". (See Morier Evans, *The Commercial Crisis, 1847–8*, App. p. xlii.) After the crisis had subsided, the firm re-opened for business, with an additional partner, Sandeman, a former stockbroker. Its new title was Sanderson, Sandeman & Co.

[4] From January 15, 1845 (see *ante*, pp. 130, 131), when the Bank invited applications for temporary advances "until further notice", the issue of regular quarterly notices was suspended: the advances were available at the published minimum rate at any time. A special notice was issued on September 2, 1847, simply because the Bank then offered loans *below* Bank rate. Before this date, loans had been granted at less than Bank rate only when they were for exceptionally short periods, each application being considered on its merits. (See *Bankers' Magazine*, Vol. VII, p. 393.)

this announcement evoked much surprise and not a little criticism.[1] Whether in fact the board was actuated partly by motives of private profit, as was freely alleged at the time, will probably never be determined ; but the Governor later claimed that the step was intended as a precautionary measure. He explained that as discounts might overrun the dividend date, the board sought to encourage the public and market to apply for loans rather than discounts.[2] For a time, this greater liberality relieved the worst pressure on the outside market,[3] though it failed to diminish public alarm or to prevent fresh mercantile suspensions. These included the famous merchant house of Reid, Irving & Co.,[4] whose stoppage on September 18 created " a very profound impression ", and Cockerell, Larpent & Co with liabilities (including acceptances against bills of lading from India) of £600,000.

[1] The *Bankers' Magazine* referred to this as " unnecessary censure ", and reminded its readers that the Bank had no longer any special responsibilities. " Bearing in mind, as it is most essential that it should always be borne in mind, that the directors have been explicitly released from the guardianship of any interests beyond those of their immediate constituents, there can be little doubt that the posture of their accounts at the time [the reserve stood at £4,752,022 on Sept. 4] left them at full liberty to seek with safety more business, by affording additional advantages. Whether or not the actual value of money . . . was or was not more than 5 per cent., is a subject more debatable . . ." (*Bankers' Magazine*, Vol. VII, p. 520 ; and see p. 322.)

[2] See Morris before 1848 Commons' Committee, Minutes, Q. 2642.

[3] The difficulties of the outside market were temporarily accentuated by a report in the *Observer* of Sunday, September 19, that Overend, Gurney & Co. had been " indebted to their friends " for assistance after the suspension of Sanderson & Co. This report was wholly unfounded, and elicited the following response from the firm : " We feel it incumbent on us to state that it is a *gross falsehood* throughout, and to add, in justice to ourselves, and for the satisfaction of our friends, that up to this moment, notwithstanding the demands which the extraordinary state of the times has generated, they have been met by us with perfect ease, out of our own natural resources, without so much as even a loan, or the discount of a bill at the Bank of England." (See *Economist*, 1847, p. 1114.) Gurney afterwards explained that his house had foreseen the crisis, and had " dressed themselves " accordingly.

[4] The senior partner was the eminent Sir John Rae Reid, a director (and former Governor) of the Bank. The firm had become heavily involved in advances on sugar estates and other immobilizable investments. Of assets totalling £1,121,000, over £800,000 consisted of debtors, advances, etc., in the West Indies.

Another firm whose failure involved a Bank director (A. A. Gower) was Gower, Nephews & Co. which failed on September 11. This house, whose liabilities were £450,000, was also heavily committed in Mauritius sugar estates. Its advances to one planter exceeded £250,000.

First Suspension of the Bank Act

The climax came after October 1, when the imminence of the dividend payments, and a further fall in the reserve, forced the Bank to renewed restrictions. (The Governor explained subsequently that by September 30 the directors had " accomplished their object " of lending out for terms before October 14 the bulk of the Government dividend monies.[1]) The restrictions took the form of a complete refusal to make *any* advances on stock or Exchequer bills, and an application of the published minimum discount rate to bills falling due before October 15 —*i.e.*, all bills maturing on or after that date were to be taken only at rates above 5½ per cent., the actual charge to be decided at the time of the application. In the circumstances, the first measure, though in reality a reversion to the normal practice before 1844, precipitated a severe panic on the Stock Exchange, which was inundated by a flood of selling orders from the banks, both in the City and in the provinces. Most of the pressure was upon Consols and Exchequer bills, and in every case the holders sought to sell for cash. At one time, the price of Consols for " time " commanded a premium of a full point over the " money " price, this differential being equivalent, from the point of view of the seller for cash, to a loan at 50 per cent. per annum for nine days (the unexpired period of the " account "). Exchequer bills, which had stood at par before the restriction against them, went to so heavy a discount that on October 6 the Bank deemed it prudent to relax its rule to some extent, and offered to lend on these bills " to a limited amount ".[2]

In Lombard Street, where rates were already high, the immediate effect of the Bank's curtailment of facilities was less spectacular. The discount houses, naturally, were not *directly* hit by the refusal to lend on Government securities ; and, on second thoughts, they were probably relieved to find that the Bank had not repeated its April step of placing an absolute

[1] 1848 Commons' Committee, *loc. cit.* On September 30 demands for advances totalled no less than £362,600, despite the fact that the rate was raised, without announcement, to 5½ per cent. The reduction in the reserve on that day alone amounted to £450,000, and the Governors decided " that they could not with prudence make further advances beyond such as the public might call for in the way of discount ".

[2] See *Economist*, Oct. 9, 1847, and *Bankers' Magazine*, Vol. VII, p. 585.

restriction on discounts. There was nothing in the announcement of October 1 to imply that discounts would not be obtainable *at a rate*; nor, indeed, did the Bank refuse then, or subsequently, any discount applicants in London who were willing to pay the rates demanded.[1] The Stock Exchange panic, however, greatly added to the alarm throughout the country, precipitating heavy demands on a number of provincial banks, whose troubles were intensified by the difficulty of securing re-discounts in London. On October 13 came the first important bank failure, that of the Abingdon Old Bank (Knapp & Co.), followed five days later by the Royal Bank of Liverpool, with a paid-up capital of £646,000.[2] The latter failure, which completely paralysed Liverpool trade, sent Consols down by fully 2 points, and led to heavy calling of funds by the London banks. From that time on, private discounts in London, whether by the banks or the discount houses, virtually ceased. Even Overend, Gurney & Co., who on October 5, despite the general pressure, had been so "full of money" that they had offered "a very large sum indeed" to the Bank for the "general good",[3] were obliged to refuse fresh business. They first applied to the Bank on October 19, and recalled that on October 5, when the special deposit was made, the Governor had declared that "any money we can give you, you shall have, in case of your requiring it". In spite of that assurance, the house was charged 9 per cent. for the discount of £80,000 of prime short bills.[4] Under such conditions, discounts

[1] See Morris before 1848 Lords' Committee, Minutes, QQ. 536, 537. One application was refused because it was not made through the regular channel, and because the applicant "did not seem in real need". There were, however, refusals by the Bank's branches: "where we employ Agents, we are not able to allow them the same discretion as we can exercise in London."

[2] The difficulties of this bank, whose proprietary was believed to be the most wealthy of all the joint stock banks, and whose "connexions were well known to be of the first class", were largely due to heavy advances to a small number of Liverpool firms, including the large Colonial brokers, Littledale & Co. (This house gave a certain amount of discount accommodation in Liverpool, and was frequently, though quite erroneously, described as a discount house.) The Royal Bank reopened for business later in the year. (See *Bankers' Magazine, loc. cit.*, pp. 541–2, 569–70.)

[3] 1857 Committee, Evidence of D. B. Chapman, Minutes, QQ. 5244, 5245.

[4] See Chapman before 1857 Committee, Minutes, Q. 5107. On the morning of Saturday, October 23, Gurney applied for a further £200,000, and although he met the Bank's demands as to the quality of the bills "in every respect", the Bank declared its intention of charging 10 per

in the open market became entirely a matter of negotiation, and some fantastic rates were charged. Tooke states definitely that on October 21, after two more bank failures,[1] a parcel of £10,000 of City bankers' acceptances, all having not more than seven days to run, was discounted at 13 per cent.[2]

Practically the whole demand for accommodation was therefore thrown upon the Bank of England,[3] which discounted freely so long as the securities offered were good.[4] It is evident, however, that the directors did not so far relax their rules as to render discountable the many bills which, though normally ineligible at the Bank, were nevertheless taken by the discount houses. Thus " the large mass of bills which under ordinary circumstances are discounted by bill-brokers, could not be negotiated ".[5] Despite the Bank's caution in this respect, the reserve by Friday, October 22, had dropped to £2,376,472 (of which only £1,600,025 was in London), and the directors realized that, if the Bank Act were not to be infringed, they would be obliged to refuse further assistance.[6] On the following morning, a deputation of ten City bankers and merchants (including Samuel Gurney) waited upon the Chancellor of the Exchequer, and implored him to take steps to remove the legal restriction

cent., and refused to decide before 2 o'clock whether it would lend or not. Ultimately, the advance was made at 9 per cent., after Gurney had pointed out that if it were known in Lombard Street that his house had been charged 10 per cent. a serious panic might have resulted. (*Ibid.*, QQ. 5407–9.)

[1] The Liverpool Banking Co., and the Newcastle, Shields and Sunderland Union Joint Stock Bank. Scholes & Co., of Manchester, the North and South Wales Bank, and Brodie & Co. of Salisbury, suspended payment subsequently.

[2] Tooke, *op. cit.*, p. 318, and *Bankers' Magazine*, *loc. cit.*, p. 587. At no time during the week ended on October 23 were the finest short bills discountable under 8 per cent. ; the general rates were 9 and 10 per cent.

[3] See 1848 Lords' Report, p. v., and speech by the Chancellor of the Exchequer (Sir Charles Wood) in the House of Commons on Nov. 30, 1847. (Hansard, Third Series, Vol. XCV, Col. 399.)

[4] The rates charged, however, were very high. Of the total amount discounted or lent during the week to Oct. 23 (£971,083) only £7,178 was at the published minimum of 5½ per cent., and only £133,096 (13·7 per cent. of the total) was granted at rates under 7½ per cent. Discounts and advances at the higher rates were as follows : 7½ per cent., £144,266 ; 7¾ per cent., £265,541 ; 8¼ per cent., £3,092 ; 8½ per cent., £108,980 ; 8¾ per cent., £1,825 ; 9 per cent., £314,283.

[5] Sir Charles Wood, *loc. cit.*

[6] See 1848 Commons' Committee, Minutes, QQ. 2642–5.

on the Bank's issues.[1] The Ministers, while not informing the deputation that they would do so, acceded to the request, and on Monday, October 25, the first of the famous "Treasury Letters" was issued, recommending the directors of the Bank—

> . . . to enlarge the amount of their discounts and advances, upon approved security; but that, in order to retain this operation within reasonable limits, a higher rate of interest should be charged. In present circumstances, they would suggest that the rate of interest should be not less than 8 per cent.
>
> If this course should lead to any infringement of the existing law, her Majesty's Government will propose to Parliament, on its meeting, a bill of indemnity.[2]

The purport of this letter was communicated to the Bank on the Saturday, and the directors immediately began to lend more liberally, with the result that the reserve at one time dropped to £1,194,000. This low figure, however, never appeared in the Bank return,[3] for immediately it became generally known that the Bank was no longer bound by the Act of 1844, the panic subsided.

Gurney related [4] how, on the Monday morning, there was "the same cloud" over the City, and how bankers in Town and out of Town, and "gentlemen in the country" were desperately calling in funds or seeking to convert securities and bills into cash. He himself was obliged to go to the Bank and seek a second £200,000, which was "urgently required in Lombard Street". The Governor told him to return at two o'clock; but at one o'clock the Treasury letter was received, and at once many of those who had called funds declared that they no longer

[1] See Tooke, *op. cit.*, p. 319, and *Bankers' Magazine*, *loc. cit.*, pp. 533–4. A similar deputation of Liverpool merchants on Oct. 19 had been dismissed without the slightest hint that the Government would contemplate interference.

[2] The letter concluded with the following significant passage: "Her Majesty's Government are not insensible to the evil of any departure from the law which has placed the currency of this country upon a sound basis; but they feel confident that in the present circumstances, the measure which they have proposed may be safely adopted; and that, at the same time, the main provisions of that law, and the vital principle of preserving the convertibility of the bank note, may be firmly maintained." (See 1848 Lords' Report, p. x.)

[3] The lowest point shown in the weekly returns was £1,606,124, on Oct. 30. The figures for Oct. 16 and 23 were £3,071,215 and £1,994,516 respectively.

[4] See 1848 Lords' Committee, Minutes, QQ. 1120, 1122, and 1848 Commons' Committee, Minutes, Q. 1600.

required their money. Later in the day the London banks were offering call money to the discount market,[1] and Gurney's eventually borrowed only a further £100,000 at the Bank. Panic demands on the banks ceased, hoarded notes and gold reappeared, and, within a week, Gurney's were begging the Bank, " as a favour ", to sanction the repayment of their accommodation before its due date. Rates in the outside market eased immediately, and were shortly below the Bank's rate of 8 per cent.[2]

In consequence, the Bank's security portfolio declined rapidly,[3] and four weeks after the Treasury letter, when the reserve stood at £4,719,207, the directors—on a Monday—sought Treasury permission to reduce the minimum rate to 7 per cent. By the end of the year it had been reduced to 5 per cent. The crisis was over.

Was the Bank to Blame ?

By its action in authorizing a temporary " suspension " of the Bank Charter Act, the Government had undoubtedly saved the commercial world from complete paralysis.[4] It did not thereby escape bitter criticism. But the controversy centred around the Treasury Letter was insignificant in comparison with the acrimonious and wordy battle fought on the merits of the Bank's conduct and upon the principle of the Bank Act, as all who study the evidence taken by the 1848 Commons' and Lords' Committees will readily agree. To enter fully into the interminable debates which followed is far beyond the scope of this work. Briefly, it may be said that most of the contestants fell into one of two camps : those who attacked both the Bank and

[1] " There was at once a great and instantaneous restoration of confidence and consequent liberation of funds previously withheld, and the same phenomena have become more decided with the lapse of every day." (*Bankers' Magazine*, Vol. VII, p. 714.)

[2] In early November, fine short bills were being taken by discount houses at 7½ per cent., and bills were being " enquired for " at higher rates. After Nov. 5, the market was refusing call money at over 5 per cent., and was " eagerly seeking " good bills at 7 per cent. First-class three months' paper commanded as favourable a rate as short paper. From that time onwards, rates fell rapidly, call money being 3½ per cent. in Jan. 1848, and discounts, 4 per cent.

[3] On Oct. 30 the Bank's discounts touched their highest point for the year at £12,738,000, of which £7,844,000 was made in London. By the year-end, the figures were £8,541,000 and £4,340,000 respectively.

[4] Chapman declared that a temporary return to barter would have been inevitable had the letter not been issued, or even if it had been delayed. There would have been " one universal convulsion ". (1857 Committee, Minutes, QQ. 5220–3.)

the Bank Act, affirming that the system as it had operated had literally created the greater part of the excesses that occurred; and those staunch supporters of the Act who obstinately declared that the whole blame was upon the commercial world, for its reckless overtrading, its foolish speculations and its irrational exuberance. So far as the authorities were concerned, the controversy was never clearly decided, except in a negative sense. Neither of the Committees recommended abandonment of the system of 1844: the Commons, indeed, found that it was not expedient to make *any* alteration in the Act, while the Lords' strong recommendation of a "relaxing power" was unobtrusively shelved.

Except in its refusal to provide for greater elasticity in the currency mechanism, the Government's inaction was, indeed, well-advised. On all other points, the Act of 1844, as such, was satisfactory enough; its faults, if faults there were, were those of omission and not of commission. They involved such thorny problems as the legal control of bank deposits as well as notes, and the formulation of a legal central banking code—problems which have puzzled many later generations, and whose final solution has hardly been achieved to-day. The statesmen of the 'forties preferred a sure foothold on firm ground to the treacherous territory of this most difficult province of monetary theory; and they were prudent in their choice. But to argue that there was no fundamental flaw in the Bank Act is by no means to lay the whole blame upon the commercial world. To do so would indeed be a counsel of despair; for, given the appropriate credit background, among other things, the commercial world and the general public of all ages since capitalism began have been prone to overreach themselves by an irrational and cumulative optimism which must ultimately bring its own corrective in the shape of a more or less sharp recession, both of confidence and economic activity.

Factors such as these were certainly at work in the three years after 1844, as they have been, in greater or less degree, on many occasions subsequently, and doubtless will be in the future. But they were not the only, and probably not even the major, causes of the troubles of 1847. The fundamental cause, which acted and reacted upon all others, was the so-called "principle of the Bank Act". This principle—that so long as the note issue was legally regulated, and placed beyond the Bank's control, the Bank was free to act as any other bank would do—was not embodied in the Act of 1844 or in any other statute. It represented simply the logical and practical expression of the Currency theory from which the Act was evolved. If the two things—the theory behind the law, and the law itself—be considered as one, then the Bank Act was indeed to blame for much of the distress which followed its passage. Fortunately, the two were quite distinct, and were easily separable.

The distinction was not explicitly recognized at the time, but it was implicit in many of the most potent arguments employed by the Bank's critics. The Bank was strongly attacked, even by those who supported the Bank Act, for its reckless lending policy, which, it was said, had furnished the cheap credit upon which the commercial excesses were based. To this the Bank management (which approved both the " principle " and the Act) replied with a flat negative, arguing (in effect) that it was absurd to suppose that the actual increase in the Bank's discounts and advances could have supported the colossal speculations which were afloat. That was undeniable, but it begged the question. The real issue was whether or not the Bank had power to control the *market* rate. If it had, then clearly the directors were largely to blame for the speculations directly engendered by the abnormal and liberal facilities afforded by the discount market. If it had not, then either the market or the commercial world (or both) was to blame. This problem, which clearly afforded unusual scope for variations of opinion, occupies a very large part of the minutes taken by the Committees. In view of the light it throws, not only upon the contemporary workings of the discount market, but upon the fundamental theoretical principles involved, the discussion deserves examination in some detail.

The Governors of the Bank, quite naturally, took their stand by the Bank Act and the famous " principle ". They justified the reduction in Bank rate, and their vigorous commercial lending, by Peel's own dictum that, within the only sphere in which they had discretionary power, they were as free as any other bank. And, for the same reason, they contended that they had no more power to regulate, fix or control the market rate than had the London and Westminster or Jones, Loyd & Co. Their duty, as Peel had explained,[1] was to make notes available at the most favourable terms possible. James Morris thus explained his belief to the Lords' Committee [2]:

[1] *Ante*, p. 105.

[2] 1848 Lords' Committee, Minutes, Q. 495; and see Commons' Committee, Minutes, Q. 3420.

> The Bank can only lower the Rate [market rate] for a limited period. The Bank may raise the Rate of Interest by withdrawing its Notes, but the Bank cannot lower the Rate beyond a certain period. If the Bank was to go into the Market and make Money cheap, when the Means of doing so by the Bank were exhausted, those who might have Notes out-of-doors would be able to discount at a higher Rate.

Prescott, the Deputy-Governor, wholly agreed with the Governor, and lamely sought to support the argument by declaring it proved by the fact that, before the " new system of discounting ", when Bank rate was above market rate, the Bank " did not hold above £200,000 or £300,000 of discounts in London " ![1] This theory was strenuously attacked by the Chairman of the Committee, but the most that Morris (and the echoing Prescott) would concede was that in some cases the Bank might temporarily have checked the rise in market rate, and that the Bank rate " affected " the value of securities and money out-of-doors. S. J. Loyd endorsed the Governor's main thesis in almost identical terms, declaring that the Bank could not regulate the rate of interest for any length of time : " the Bank rate can only be below the market rate for that period which shall enable the public, by taking the cheaper article, to exhaust the supply of the Bank ".[2]

On the other hand, the Chairman of the Lords' Committee and Horsley Palmer, J. A. Anderson (Manager of the Union Bank of Scotland) and Samuel Gurney—to mention the most important witnesses—were firmly convinced not only that the Bank had the power of controlling market rate, but that it had exercised it most imprudently. Gurney[3] affirmed that—

> The Bank in a very material Degree does, in our Market, govern the Rate of Interest. I would not say that nothing else operates upon the Rate of Interest, but we inevitably fluctuate as the Bank fluctuates . . . whether the Exchanges are for us or against us.

He agreed, however, that there were periods (principally after the dividends, should the exchanges be favourable) " when we fall very considerably below the Bank Rate, in which we are

[1] *Ibid.*, Q. 512. The Chairman immediately exposed the fallacy of this reasoning, by remarking that in such a case the Bank obviously left the market to itself, except in so far as it acted upon it by buying Government securities or by employing its capital " in some way or other ".

[2] 1848 Commons' Committee, Minutes, Q. 5260.

[3] 1848 Lords' Committee, Minutes, QQ. 1107–9.

not entirely governed by the Bank Rate ". He thus described what he regarded as the normal relationship:

> At a time of gradual reduction in the Stock of Bullion in the Bank, or of an adverse Exchange, the Market Rate of Money is invariably somewhat beyond that of the Bank of England; and I might state the reverse in the reverse State of Things. In a favourable State of the Exchanges, when there is a gradual Accumulation of Bullion, we are necessarily and inevitably a little below the Bank.

Very similar evidence was given by Horsley Palmer,[1] who also blamed the Bank for the unduly low rates which had ruled in Lombard Street. " If the Bank reduce their rate of interest," he said, " the rate of interest in the London market falls below it, and when the Bank raise their rate, the market rate immediately advances."

Bank's Special Power to Influence Rates

Each of these two opposing views, considered separately, was apparently convincing. In fact, neither was correct, but each contained an element of truth. Except in a " closed " system, with an inconvertible currency unrelated to any international standard of value, no institution or Government could control the rate of interest[2]; under a gold standard, or any other international standard, the rate- and price-structure had eventually to conform more or less exactly to an international equilibrium. This was the fundamental truth which the Governor of the Bank (and the others who thought with him) had perceived. But, so precarious was his grasp of the principle, that he relied upon it to the point of asserting that the Bank had not even the power to *influence* the rate, except in the very short period. In that he believed (or at least asserted) that the Bank in its banking department was no different from any other commercial bank, there was some justification for this theory. He could plead in support of it that although the average commercial bank, by drastically reducing its lending rates, might influence the

[1] Commons' Committee, Minutes, Q. 2224.

[2] There are, of course, certain ultimate limits to this control even in a " closed system "; they are roughly coincident with the limits (set by public confidence on the one hand and by the needs of business on the other) to the power indefinitely to expand or contract an inconvertible currency.

general market rate, its power to do so was clearly both very small and ephemeral.

Several witnesses, therefore, realizing the basic truth of the Governor's main thesis, concentrated their attack on the Bank in a demonstration of the fact that its position was in reality very different from that of other banks, however true it might be that its banking business was (and possibly even should be) conducted on similar principles. Most of these critics dwelt mainly upon the superior resources of the Bank rather than upon its other peculiar characteristics, as by so doing they could prove its power considerably to *influence* the rate, without the prior need (or perhaps even the desire) to attack one of the major bases of the Bank Act. This angle of attack is implicit in the following question [1] by the Chairman of the Lords' Committee:

> Will you state, as a Person of Experience in business, as well as the Governor of the Bank, whether you do not conceive that a body like the Bank of England, with a large Capital, with the Power of issuing £20,000,000 or more of Notes, and holding twelve or fifteen millions of Deposits, coming into the Market of any Country in the World where it is established, does, in point of fact, command the Rate of Interest in the Country; and that when you speak of the Market Rate of Interest, it is not really the small retail Dealers (if we may so call them, as compared with the great dealings of the Bank of England) which, in point of fact, command the Rate of Interest, nor can the Bank of England, in many cases at least, be said to follow the Market rate of Interest?

To this involved question Morris replied by asserting that in the ordinary course the Bank's bill portfolio was not unduly large.[2]

A similar line was taken by J. A. Anderson, whose evidence shows an especially sound grasp of the issues involved. Asked before the Commons' Committee why there was a disadvantage in the Bank's open market competition with private discounters, he declared [3]:

> Chiefly upon the great extent of their operations, and their influence upon the whole money market; it is not fitting for them to go up and down with every $\frac{1}{2}$ per cent. rise and fall of interest; it is more their duty to be the regulators of the general transactions of the country, and to follow the rise and fall in the rate of interest than to lead.

[1] 1848 Lords' Committee, Minutes, Q. 510.

[2] See *ante*, p. 120.

[3] 1848 Commons' Committee, Minutes, QQ. 6357, 6358.

For the same reason, " as long as the Bank continues in its present position ", he strongly opposed the principle that the Bank should regulate its business on the same lines as any other bank did : " . . . if all the banks in London were upon a par, and also all private and joint stock banks throughout the Kingdom, they might safely follow that course ; but in the position which the Bank of England occupies, I do not think it ought to do so." Tooke amplified this argument, citing [1] eight distinguishing characteristics of the Bank, almost all of which gave it a greater power than that possessed by any other Bank. The special characteristics were as follows : (1) its size ; (2) its management of Government transactions ; (3) the *weekly* publication of its accounts (in what was then considered " minuteness of detail ") ; (4) its traditional position as a resort for " loans and discounts, wholly distinct from other banking business ", and as a refuge in time of emergency, when other channels of assistance were closed ; (5) its function as a general settling-house for debts not only of the United Kingdom, but of the " commercial world " ; (6) its special *moral* influence, and the fact that a change in Bank rate had a vastly greater psychological effect than the change in the rate quoted by any other lender ; (7) the special susceptibility of its reserve to an import or export of gold, and the consequent influence of its policy upon the foreign exchanges ; and (8) the fact that any other bank could stop payments without necessarily endangering " the convertibility of the Note Circulation or the maintenance of cash payments ", whereas a stoppage by the *banking* department of the Bank would gravely endanger both.

The arguments of these various witnesses may be regarded as a representative selection of the different views current at the time. The essentials of the problem can be briefly stated. No bank had the power to *control* the rate of discount, even in the short run ; but any bank, if it so desired, could temporarily *influence* the rate in greater or less degree (roughly proportionately to the scale upon which it could and did in fact operate). In all cases, the power to *depress* the rate was greater than the power to *raise* it. The Bank of England, for reasons noted above, had this power of temporarily influencing the rate to an exceptional degree ; so great, in fact, was its power in contrast with the very small influence which could be exerted by any other bank individually, that it was no unreasonable distortion to say that *in the short run* it could actually *control* the rate.

[1] Tooke and Newmarch's *History of Prices*, Vol. V (1857), pp. 543–5.

Indeed, there is one factor, omitted by Tooke, which is more important than all others. To the extent that the commercial banks were beginning to regard the Bank of England as a repository for their reserves, and thus to treat deposits with the Bank as equivalent to cash in hand; and to the extent that the cheque system had developed, a new investment or purchase of bills by the Bank of England *created*, as it does now, additional *bank cash*. To that extent (admittedly far smaller than it now is), the direct effect of an increase in the Bank's security portfolio was far less important than its secondary effect: so long as the proceeds of a new Bank of England loan were ultimately deposited with another bank which regarded Bank of England deposits as cash, the capacity of that bank to lend or to buy additional bills was increased by a multiple of the amount of the deposit, and the additional accommodation could be granted without any impairment whatever of the bank's technical liquidity and (probably) without any early depletion of the Bank of England's reserve.

These principles are as true to-day as they were in the 'forties. Any bank, by vigorous lending (*i.e.*, by reducing its cash ratio), can depress the rate in the market below what may be described as the natural or " equilibrium " rate. That depression and that lending will eventually set in motion an increased volume of trade commitments and speculative transactions. Various factors may delay the natural reactions, but ultimately the excessive activity will impose a strain upon bank reserves and render inevitable a reversal of bank lending policy. The greater the initial depression of the rate and the greater the consequent unnatural expansion of trade and speculation, the greater will be the eventual strain and the severity of the measures necessary to meet it. In other words, there must eventually be a rise in rates *above* the original equilibrium level to an extent which will be more or less commensurate to the unnatural depression of the rate. If the adjustment proceeds smoothly, without any violent blow to confidence, it is theoretically possible that the *average* rate over a period will roughly equal the equilibrium rate. To that extent, but to that extent only, the argument that the Bank has no power whatever to control the rate may be literally true. But, in fact, if the artificial depression of the rate be severe and long-sustained, the ultimate correctives may have to be concentrated within so short a space of time that the ultimate rise in the rate may be out of all proportion to the earlier depression.

That is precisely what happened in 1847 and in the three preceding years. The Bank had not only depressed the market rate below its natural level (mainly by preventing a necessary and wholesome rise), but, on each occasion when difficulties threatened, it had maintained its liberal rate and its extended portfolio until the very last moment.[1] Its ultimate restrictions had therefore to be both harsh and violent.

Bank Act Controversy Obscures the Real Issues

The most obvious sign of the disequilibrium created by the Bank's conduct was the wholly unprecedented degree of fluctuations in market rates (quite apart from Bank rate), which in the three years had ranged from under 2 per cent. to 10 per cent. and over. These highly disturbing variations [2] were seized upon by a number of witnesses (notably by Tooke, Gurney, and Bevan [3]), and made the spear-head of their attack upon the Bank. But in nearly all these discussions the vital issues were hopelessly confused with the problem of the merits or demerits of the machinery of the Bank Act. On the one hand, the sup-

[1] One example of these last-minute attempts at lending, in addition to those already quoted, was afforded by the Bank's announcement on Sept. 23, 1847 (a week before its stringent restrictions), that it would lend against *2 months*' bills at 5½ per cent., loans having been previously restricted to periods before the dividends. This action, together with the offering of short loans at 5 per cent., was vigorously attacked by the *Economist*. (See 1847, p. 1155.)

[2] There can be no doubt that the effect of violent fluctuations in discount rates upon commercial, and even social, conditions was much more direct and severe than similar fluctuations could be to-day. Nevertheless, it is difficult to take very seriously the evidence of A. Allison, for thirteen years Sheriff of the County of Lanark, who solemnly affirmed that in the whole of his experience he had found that " any rise in the rate of discount of the Bank of England has been immediately, or at least shortly, followed by an increase both of crime and of civil suits, and if it continues long, of mortality and Typhus fever. So much so, that, as I am an official member of the prison board and of most of the charities, I have always made it a rule to say to the gentlemen of those boards when a rise in the rate of discounts takes place, ' Gentlemen, the Bank of England have raised their discounts, you had better immediately take measures for enlarging the Prison accommodation, and for extending the infirmaries and poor-houses '; and they have since admitted to me that my Prognostications were too well-founded, for we have been obliged to make a proportionate increase a year or two after the Bank of England have raised their rates of discount ". (1848 Lords' Committee, Minutes, Q. 3844.)

[3] See 1848 Commons' Committee, QQ. 5417, 1575, 2275.

porters of the Act sought to minimize the evident evils of the Bank's complete freedom because they believed that to admit them would imperil the Act; on the other hand, those who stressed, and stressed rightly, these evils, regarded them as proof of the failure of the Act. Even Gurney, who on the whole took a well-balanced view, declared that the discount market had been " under the bondage of this Act ",[1] when what he really meant was that it had suffered sorely from the Bank's indiscreet use of the freedom which the Act (or, rather, its sponsors' interpretation of it) had bestowed. Some witnesses had evidently a sort of instinctive grip of the real problem, but in no case within the knowledge of the present writer was it expressly stated. One group saw no reason for altering the Bank Act because it believed that the sources of disturbance lay outside the banking sphere, and the other group, equally convinced that the banking system was largely to blame, cried incessantly for the scrapping of the Act. There was no one, then, to point out that what needed scrapping was not the Act, but the so-called " principle " that the Bank was as free as any other bank. It is to the credit of S. J. Loyd, who was guilty of much bigotry in many of these discussions, that he came near to stating this, the real need. For example, he was " sure that the recent tendency of the Bank to become a more active and competing body " was a " tendency in the wrong direction ". He even admitted that the " magnitude of the Bank's resources " made it desirable that it should be " more subject to fixed rules " [2] —more fixed, presumably, than other banks.

It is perhaps not surprising that the witness who most nearly

[1] 1848 Commons' Committee, Minutes, Q. 1575. He complained bitterly that because of the Bank's previous sustained lending, it was obliged to compress within a few days a contraction which it formerly would (and should) have spread over months, " to the serious derangement of the money market, and to much alarming disaster ". (1848 Lords' Committee, Minutes, Q. 1098.)

[2] 1848 Commons' Committee, Minutes, QQ. 5190, 5191. His evidence at other points, however, was at variance with this standpoint. For example, one of his reasons for disapproving of the Bank's competitive methods was that he thought that such activities tended " to foment that unfortunate feeling on the part of the public, that they are entitled when there is a pressure on the commercial world, to look to the Bank of England for all the support they may require ". Again, in one passage he excused the Bank's competitive methods by affirming that they were due to an unduly liberal attention " to what they [the Bank] conceived to be the public interest . . . they yielded to the pressure of the time, and were not firm enough in maintaining their position ". (See *ibid.*, QQ. 5261–6.)

stated the real issue was a Scottish banker, removed from the intensity of the controversy which surrounded the Act. Anderson declared that—

> The practice of the Bank in former times was to keep their rate generally above the market rate in London, and I think that that was a sound practice for a bank in the position of the Bank of England, which must have a great influence upon all commercial transactions of the Kingdom; and I think that they must revert to the idea of regulating the money market generally, and act upon that, and not so much with a view to their dividend.[1]

That was, indeed, the fundamental solution: that the Bank should act as a regulator of the market, and not as a competitive part of it. Regulation, however, implied a reasonably close contact with the market, and, therefore, a reasonably effective Bank rate at most times. A reversion to the practice of a Bank rate "virtually fixed and uniform" would have been a retrogressive step, for under that system (to mention only one disadvantage) the Bank for months together lost all contact with the market and all knowledge of the types of bills in circulation, and yet at other times was called upon to meet practically the whole demand for discount accommodation and to lend upon bills whose parties it did not know. It was therefore desirable that the rate should be more elastic than it had been before 1844; but it was at least as important that the motive in its determination should not be, as it was between 1844 and 1847, the attraction of discount business in competition with private discounters.

Morris attempted to prove that this had, in fact, been the policy of the Bank, declaring [2] that it was bound to take care not to interfere with the monetary affairs of the country, and sought to disturb the "natural condition of the market" as little as possible [3]; it tried to avoid producing any "extraordinary effect".[4] He then affirmed, as he was bound to do to support these assertions, that he did "not think it desirable that the Bank should run into competition with other parties with regard to

[1] 1848 Commons' Committee, Minutes, Q. 6357. Horsley Palmer also had doubts about the wisdom of the Bank's competitive activities: "Such was the operation of that measure [the competitive reduction of Bank rate], which tended very much to increase the speculative feeling in the country; it is a question whether it is not exceedingly prejudicial to attempt at all times to govern the Bank rate of discount by the public market." (*Ibid.*, Q. 2222.)

[2] *Ibid.*, Q. 2654.

[3] 1848 Lords' Committee, Minutes, Q. 628. [4] *Ibid.*, Q. 630.

the rate of interest ".[1] These statements could not, of course, be substantiated, for in view of the Bank's special advantages (already discussed) it was bound to compete with and disturb the market unless its rate were somewhat *above* market rate. And Morris was compelled to agree that even an equal rate must have that " extra effect on the market " which he had declared the Bank sought to avoid. Yet he virtually denied that the Bank aimed at maintaining the higher rate; and, after agreeing that the Bank's policy would not be to " remain quiet and passive ",[2] argued with little logic that—

> . . . if we were to put our rate intentionally above the market rate it would be tantamount to preventing parties coming to us; it would be tantamount to keeping out of the market altogether.[3]

These conflicting statements serve to show that the Bank directors had only the most confused view of what their functions should be. If the evidence be interpreted in the light most favourable to the directors, it might be said that they realized in a general way that the Bank's special position gave it special responsibilities, and that those responsibilities might be abused by an aggressive interference with the market; but that they had no clear idea of how that realization should be translated into practice and day-to-day policy. And they were undoubtedly confused and misled by Peel's assertion that they, as the controllers of an ordinary trading bank, should lend liberally on competitive terms. But for that assertion, they might have acted far more prudently. As it was, at times they were even less restrained than an ordinary commercial bank should have been. Moreover, although they had doubts as to the expediency of Peel's advice upon lending policy, they strenuously denied that there was any special obligation upon the Bank to provide assistance, in time of crisis, to all who had good security to offer. That is yet another proof of the confusion of thought at the time.

There were, in fact, two problems so far as the Bank was concerned, and both of these resolved themselves into the need for a clear appreciation of its special responsibilities and the evolution of a practical policy appropriate to those responsibilities. The first problem was the achievement of a Bank rate technique which would neither arbitrarily interfere with the discount market nor entirely divorce the Bank from it. The second

[1] *Ibid.*, Q. 625.
[2] 1848 Commons' Committee, Minutes, Q. 3008.
[3] 1848 Lords' Committee, Minutes, Q. 629.

problem was that of ensuring that the Bank, although admittedly impotent to create unlimited supplies of notes and to give unlimited assistance, should at all times so govern its position that it would be able to afford such assistance as was required. To the solution of both problems the experience gained in the 1847 crisis, and the vital period which preceded it, made a very important contribution. On neither point was there any specific recommendation made by either of the Committees. Both Committees, and especially the Lords', realized the harm which had been wrought by the undue reduction of the rate, but the Bank sought shelter from criticism of this kind by pleading the principle of " identity of interest ". Here again, the trouble was that the principle which the Bank admitted in theory was not that by which it was primarily guided in practice. But the Lords' Committee, while refraining from laying down any precise Bank rate policy, did remark pointedly on this difference between theory and practice.

Whether this hint had any important influence upon the Bank board it is impossible to say, but it is certain that the full ventilation of the various problems before the Committees had revealed more clearly than the directors would then admit the policy which should be followed in the future. Thus, despite the absence in 1848 of clear-cut proposals on Bank rate technique, after the crisis the Bank did gradually effect an important modification of its practice. Once again, bitter experience had afforded a valuable lesson, whose benefits were to be felt for many years to come.

Upon the second problem—that of the Bank's duty to assist the commercial world in time of crisis—no apparent advance had been made. This problem, however, could safely be left to solve itself; for, no matter what the views of the directors, the habit of regarding the Bank as a last resource in emergency had become so deeply impressed on the public that it could not be eradicated. The Bank was gradually forced to realize this, and as it did so the responsibilities which the public attitude implied became more and more important determinants of policy and technique. In spite of the extreme confusion of thought at the time, and in spite of the unsatisfactory and inconclusive results of the Parliamentary inquiries, it can be said that the crisis of 1847 did produce a vital contribution—perhaps even *the most* vital contribution—to the theory and practice of central banking.

Bank Rate Technique after 1847

The modification of the Bank of England's practice after the 1847 crisis was not, then, forced upon it by any change in the law or by any definite recommendation of a Parliamentary committee; and it was not even announced by a statement in Parliament or by any public notice from the board. Many expert contemporary observers would certainly have strenuously denied that any noteworthy change took place at all. Possibly their perception of facts was dulled by a continued preoccupation with the still furious Bank Act controversy. At all events, he who bases his judgment of this period upon the evidence tendered to the 1857 or 1858 Parliamentary inquiries into the Bank Acts, without due reference to the course of rates and banking figures, will almost certainly conclude that Bank of England policy was still dominated by that aggressive and narrow self-interest which produced such disastrous results in 1847. The statements of the Bank witnesses in 1857 and 1858 do, indeed, exhibit some important contrasts with those made a decade earlier; but, with the experience of the contradictory evidence of the Bank governors in 1848 in mind, the serious student would hesitate to take their statements at face-value in the absence of supporting facts. Without corroboration, the assertions by the Governor in 1857 that the Bank could not control the market rate and never attempted to do so, that it merely followed the market, and that it avoided active competition,[1] would seem but empty echoes of the statements of his predecessor in 1847. And no such corroboration was afforded by the remaining evidence, considered as a whole. The opponents of the Bank Act, one and all, appeared to assume that because the Act itself had been left unaltered, the famous principle of competition must have remained equally intact. The evidence of these witnesses in 1857 and 1858 on the question of Bank competition might, indeed, have been tendered, almost without verbal alteration, in 1847. But, in fact, their attacks on the Bank Act, *via* the principle of competition, were based almost exclusively on the legitimate criticisms of Bank policy in 1844–7, and only to a negligible extent upon its actions between 1848 and 1857. The result was a wholly misleading impression of Bank policy during this period—and the impression has been perpetuated by some subsequent writers.

[1] See evidence of T. M. Weguelin before 1857 Committee, Minutes, QQ. 250–70, 477–9.

Consider, for example, the following statement [1] by Chapman, the managing partner of Overend, Gurney :

> . . . I think that the Bank of England do not cease their competition for bills one moment earlier than they can help. They say, we have to make a profit for our proprietors, the same as any other concern, and we must have our bills ; and it is not until they are driven to it, and they see their till sinking too fast, that they take those defensive measures.

and also this statement [2] by Newmarch :

> . . . whenever there has been . . . an accumulation of reserve in the banking department, the Directors of the Bank of England, acting, as they considered, in strict conformity, or rather, it may be said, in necessary obedience to the principle of the Act of 1844, have endeavoured to turn their reserve to profitable advantage by reducing their rate of interest.

Newmarch affirmed that the Bank was " bound " by the Act to compete with the discount houses,[3] and attributed the violent fluctuations in rates which occurred between 1848 and 1857 " distinctly to the operation of the Act of 1844 and distinctly to the working out by the banking department of the Bank of England of the principle upon which the Act was formed and defended ".[2]

Such statements as these, coming from such witnesses, might well excuse an assumption that the Bank had done little to mend its ways since 1847, even if it be noted that the evidence of these same witnesses was at some points in conflict with the passages above quoted. Actually, to take the Bank evidence on this point at face-value would afford a tolerably accurate view ; whereas to do the same for the opposition witnesses would produce grave distortion of perspective. That is not to say that Bank policy after 1847 was immaculate ; nor does it imply that the change of practice was a consequence of any sudden decision. The change came gradually, and it is quite possible that the Bank board in 1857 would have been surprised to realize how far it had moved from its theory and practice of 1844–7. But there is positive proof that a change did occur : after the 1847 crisis the Bank's open market activities definitely ceased to have any quality which could possibly be described as " aggressive ". Whereas in the earlier period its competition with the discount market

[1] 1857 Committee, Minutes, Q. 4935.
[2] *Ibid.*, Q. 1359. [3] *Ibid.*, Q. 1366.

had been free to the point of recklessness, after 1847 it became decidedly more restrained, and within a short period its discount business could hardly be deemed competitive at all—it was competitive only when there was a definite shortage of discount facilities elsewhere.

The first and most obvious proof of the change is afforded by the relative levels of the Bank's minimum rate and market rate. As has been noted,[1] in each of the three years from 1845 to 1847, as well as in the latter part of 1844, the average Bank rate was below the average market rate. But, except in 1851 (when the averages were equal), in every year from 1848 to 1856 the Bank *minimum* was above market rate. The actual averages during the two periods are shown in the following table:

Year.	Average Bank Rate. (a) % £	s.	d.	Average Market Rate. (b) % £	s.	d.	Average Excess of (a) over (b) % s.	d.
1845	2	13	8	3	0	0	*−6*	*4*
1846	3	6	6	3	15	0	*−8*	*6*
1847	5	3	6	5	17	6	*−14*	*0*
1848	3	14	5	3	5	0	9	5
1849	2	18	7	2	5	0	13	7
1850	2	10	1	2	5	0	5	1
1851	3	0	0	3	0	0	Nil	
1852	2	3	0	1	17	6	5	6
1853	3	13	10	3	10	0	3	10
1854	5	2	3	4	17	6	4	9
1855	4	17	10	4	10	0	7	10
1856	6	1	2	5	10	0	11	2

The contrast here revealed is striking. In the first period, market rate exceeded Bank rate on the average by no less than 9*s.* 7*d.* per cent., while in the second period Bank rate exceeded market rate on the average (ignoring 1851) by virtually 8*s.* per cent. That is a substantial excess, and one which must have been fully sufficient to put the Bank beyond the range of true competitive discounting. Nevertheless, it might be argued on three grounds that these figures alone are not conclusive proof of the Bank's altered attitude. First, it might be pointed out that in four years in the second period the Bank rate excess on the average was in the neighbourhood of 5*s.* per cent., which in those days was a much less important differential than it is in the post-war market, even at times of high rates. Secondly, it is

[1] See *ante*, p. 115.

possible to argue that the Bank, in view of its special advantages,[1] was able to achieve *competitive* discounting with its rate above market rate, and had aimed at preserving the appropriate differential and no more. (Even this argument, had it been sound, would have presupposed an important advance in the Bank's practice.) Finally, and this is quite the most important objection which could be raised, it could be said that *averages* distorted the facts: that on the figures given it was theoretically possible that a very large differential against the Bank for comparatively short periods of extreme ease in the outside market might have obscured a reasonably close competitive contact with market rate over much longer periods.

Against these possible objections it may be urged that the Bank's standard of eligible bills was definitely higher than the market's: in normal times, many bills which the Bank would take only at rates above the minimum were discountable in the outside market at the "fine" rate, while very large numbers of bills not discountable at the Bank at all could nevertheless be placed outside at rates appropriately above the prime rate. But the conclusive proof of the cessation of Bank aggression is afforded by the trend of its bill portfolio. Unfortunately, separate figures for the Bank's London and country discounts are not obtainable after 1847. It is therefore necessary to consider its total discounts, which were still segregated from other securities and from "temporary" advances. From its peak level of £12,738,000 on October 30, 1847, this total fell steadily week by week, until by June 24 of the following year it had reached £3,636,000, falling below £3,000,000 early in 1849. In no week after that date until November, 1850, did it rise to £3,000,000, and was generally below £2,500,000. Thereafter the figures were somewhat higher, but until 1853 they were very rarely above £5,000,000. The following table, giving the range of variation and the average in each year, affords an adequate picture of the position:

[1] Chapman remarked that, other things being equal, the public preferred "the courtesies of the Bank, which everybody knows". (1857 Committee, Minutes, Q. 4864.)

BANK'S TOTAL DISCOUNTS.*

Year.	Minimum.	Maximum.	Average.
	£	£	£
1845	2,030,000†	9,561,000	4,680,000
1846	5,568,000	13,137,000	9,030,000
1847	7,490,000	12,738,000	9,616,000
1848	3,182,000	8,100,000‡	4,289,000
1849	2,284,000	3,287,000	2,590,000
1850	2,207,000	4,231,000	2,660,000
1851	3,571,000	5,883,000	4,544,000
1852	2,674,000	3,654,000	3,020,000
1853	4,158,000	9,116,000	6,137,000
1854	4,575,000	7,488,000	6,086,000
1855	3,604,000	9,054,000	6,004,000
1856	3,761,000	9,780,000	6,700,000

* Compiled from the detailed weekly returns given in App. 6 to the 1848 Commons' Report and App. 13 to the 1857 Report. The averages are taken from Palgrave, *op. cit.*, p. 14.

† The minimum in the *second* half of the year, after the "new discounting" policy had become fully operative, was £3,760,000.

‡ The maximum after July 1, *i.e.*, after the effects of the crisis had dispersed and the special assistance had been repaid, was only £3,790,000.

The testimony of the Bank returns, therefore, as well as of the actual rates charged, shows that Weguelin's description in 1857 of the Bank's practice was fully justified. He stated [1] that the Bank never "led the way in the rate of interest", and, when it was suggested that the Bank had competed with the market, declared that—

> . . . that competition has not been to any very great extent. The rule that has been adopted in such cases [of abundant money] by the Bank of England is *in some degree* to follow the market rate of interest. If, for example, the market rate was $2\frac{1}{2}$ per cent., the Bank would reduce its minimum rate to 3 per cent. It does not lead the way in reductions of the rate of interest; it has only followed the previous state of the market.[2]

J. G. Hubbard, a former Governor, gave similar evidence, declaring that the Bank of England "never goes quite as low as its competitors, and when the rate is highest it is never quite as high".[3] Even Chapman, who had so strongly attacked the Bank for competing, agreed that market rate was more frequently below than above the Bank rate,[4] and remarked that "practically,

[1] 1857 Committee, Minutes, Q. 270.
[2] *Ibid.*, Q. 250. [3] *Ibid.*, Q. 2844. [4] *Ibid.*, Q. 4865.

the Bank of England rate operates as a sort of maximum to private discount ".[1]

The relationship of Bank rate to market rate after 1847 can, in fact, be quite shortly stated. At all normal times, and in times of abnormal ease in the outside market, Bank rate was invariably above market rate; but in times of stringency, when the contracted resources of the outside market were inadequate to meet the demands (which were often unusually large at such times), and increasing applications were made to the Bank to meet the deficiency, Bank rate was frequently below the market rate. Even on these occasions, however, the excess market rate was never as great as appeared from the published figures, for during periods of pressure the Bank usually shortened the eligible currency of bills to 65 days (and sometimes less), charging for 95-day bills more than the minimum published rate. No details of these higher rates were obtainable,[2] but, for a proper comparison, it was the rate charged by the Bank for 95-day paper which should have been compared with market rate, for the latter invariably applied to such bills; shorter bills, save in the most extreme crisis, were generally taken in the market at rates below that described as " market " rate.

An Unconscious Advance towards Modern Practice

On a superficial view, it might seem that the Bank after 1847 had simply reverted to the practice it had followed before the Bank Act.[3] In a sense, this was true, but there was one vital difference between Bank rate policy after 1847 and before 1844: in the earlier period the rate had been rigid, and the Bank made no attempt to follow downward movements of market rate, whereas after 1847 the rate was an elastic one, maintained always in reasonable contact with market rate. This, together with the principle of the minimum rate, represented a fundamental difference of technique. Step by step the Bank was almost unwittingly equipping itself for the performance of central banking functions which in principle differed but little from the central banking practice of much later years, and even of to-day. It had evolved a technique which would enable it to play the

[1] 1857 Committee, Minutes, Q. 4860.

[2] Details of differential rates are in fact given in the appendices to the various Committees' Reports, but the returns do not show the types of bills to which the various rates were applied.

[3] See *ante*, pp. 78–81.

rôle of impartial regulator and disciplinarian of a market which was moving rapidly towards a high degree of organization, cohesion and centralization.

The achievement of this new technique may be further illustrated by the relationship between the two rates in a further decade:

Year.	Average Bank Rate. (a) % £ s. d.	Average Market Rate. (b) % £ s. d.	Average Excess of (a) over (b) % s. d.
1857	6 13 3	6 15 0	− 1 9
1858	3 4 7	2 15 0	9 7
1859	2 14 7	2 10 0	4 7
1860	4 3 7	4 0 0	3 7
1861	5 5 4	5 0 0	5 4
1862	2 10 7	2 5 0	5 7
1863	4 8 2	4 5 0	3 2
1864	7 8 0	7 0 0	8 0
1865	4 15 4	5 6 7	−11 3 [1]
1866	6 19 0	6 8 2	10 10 [1]

These figures plainly indicate a continuance of the policy which has been outlined: except in times of crisis, as in 1857, when a drying-up of discount facilities outside the Bank forced market rates above Bank rate, the Bank's rate remained a little above market rate, but was always within reasonable touch with it. In normal times, therefore, the relationship between Bank rate and market rate between 1848 and 1864 was not greatly different from the normal relationship in the twentieth century. But, *prima facie*, the motives which governed this similar adjustment of Bank rate in the two periods present marked contrasts. After 1847 the Bank began to realize the practical implications of the principle of "identity of interests", and grasped the essential fact that aggressive competition and attempts to maximize its own profits in the short period were not to its own ultimate advantage. Its rate policy, therefore, became governed by two leading considerations: first, that the Bank must avoid undue interference with the outside market; and, secondly, that at all costs it must preserve an adequate reserve. Subject to these considerations, it felt itself free to earn the maximum profit for

[1] The latter part of 1865 was marked by a feverish state of the market, severe stringency, and fears of impending trouble, which forced rates above Bank rate, and maintained them above it until after the crisis of May, 1866. The quiet which followed the crisis sent rates well below Bank rate in the second half of the year.

its proprietors. From these considerations there was evolved the practice of regulating Bank rate almost solely according to movements in the Bank's reserve.

In modern times, on the other hand, Bank rate technique is part of a complex central bank control whose ultimate aim is to maintain an approximate equilibrium between the internal price- and rate-structure and the price- and rate-structures of the world markets. Such a policy is determined and influenced by a complicated array of internal and international factors far beyond the conception of the bankers of the 'forties, 'fifties and 'sixties. Superficially, the two aims of policy appear to have little or nothing in common. Yet it is no unreasonable distortion of facts to say that most of the numerous factors which now determine rate policy are considered because in the last resort they may affect the Bank's reserve. In a sense, it might be said that the Bank management now does scientifically what its predecessors of the 'fifties and 'sixties were beginning to do empirically. The fundamental principle of both policies is the same: the practice of to-day has evolved directly from, and is a perfection and refinement of, the earlier practice. In that evolution the Bank has learnt that an exclusive attention to the reserve, and an inadequate attention to the many factors which influence it, is likely to necessitate unnecessarily violent and sudden changes in rates, and correspondingly marked oscillations between ease and stringency in the outside market, to the great detriment of the commercial world. While still governed by the same general principle, it has therefore perfected a technique for counteracting in advance influences which would otherwise affect the reserve and thus compel similar action at a later date. The Bank of to-day aims at producing a natural stability in the outside market; the Bank of yesterday sought to avoid producing an unnatural instability.

One other modification of rate practice after 1847 remains to be noted, and this change also marked a step towards modern conceptions of central banking. The Bank not only dropped its aggressive discounting policy, but it ceased to grant temporary loans on competitive terms. The change in temporary lending policy represented a sort of compromise between, or rather a fusion of, the two different practices which had been followed in the past. Before 1844, it will be recalled, the practice had been to offer temporary loans at market rate during the quarterly shuttings, and at such other times as the Bank deemed advisable. Between 1844 and 1847, since Bank rate was maintained in competitive contact with market rate, the loans were offered at Bank rate, but were obtainable at all times of the year. This rule was maintained intact after the crisis: short-term loans, as well as discounts, were obtainable against approved securities at all times at the Bank's published minimum, thereby establishing the principle that accommodation could always be obtained at the Bank at a price. But as the minimum rate was generally above market rate, this rule would have pressed harshly upon the discount market and the public generally during the shuttings. Thus at the regular quarterly periods the Bank reverted to its pre-1844 practice of lending below Bank rate. The reversion was not, however, complete: the Bank no longer offered to lend at what it deemed market rate, but at such periods fixed a uniform rate of ½ per cent. below the published minimum. In exceptional cases, and for short periods, the rules were occasionally altered. In January, 1856, for example, loans against bills were made, in accordance with the rule, at ½ per cent. below Bank rate, but loans against Government stock were charged the full rate. Normally, however, loans against stock or bills, and discounts of first-class bills, were all obtainable at the same rate.

These rules accord closely in principle with the best central bank practice to-day. Owing to the much greater degree of centralization and cohesion of the market, periods of immobilization of funds occur less frequently and with less severity than they did a half-century or so ago; but the principle is well recognized that at such times the Bank should ease the strain upon the outside market, and save it from the expense of borrowing at the normal (costly) terms. At such times the Bank appears in the open market as a buyer of bills from those who are hardest-pressed, quoting rates which, though generally slightly more expensive to the seller than market rate, are nevertheless below Bank rate. The more prolonged and regular immobilizations of earlier years necessitated a more formal practice, but the net result of the rule which operated during the shuttings was the same as that of the modern practice, except that the terms, in relation to market rate, were probably slightly more liberal.

CHAPTER VI

THE BANK AND THE MARKET: WITHDRAWAL OF RE-DISCOUNT FACILITIES

It has been shown that after 1847 the Bank ceased actively or aggressively to compete for discount business with the outside market. The important change in Bank discount policy which has been described did not, however, dispose of the difficult problem of the proper relationship between the Bank and the discount market. This question was destined to recur in various guises many times before the modern relationship and technique were evolved as the most practicable solution. Indeed, in less than a decade it had re-emerged in so acute a form as to provide the most important single topic of discussion before a Parliamentary inquiry—the 1858 Select Committee on the Bank Acts. Explanation and discussion of the issues involved demand, once again, a brief review of the general trend of current economic development.

Rapid Growth of Trade and of Banking

Economic activity engendered in the middle 'forties by the railway mania had seemed, to observers at the time, phenomenally rapid; but the expansion at that period was slow in comparison with the growth in the following decade. In that period, industry and commerce, shipping and agriculture, reaped the first fruits of the final abandonment of the old protectionism; as the period advanced, the transition to free trade (including abandonment of the Navigation Laws) was made complete, and the movement made important headway on the Continent. Secondly, the country began to feel the permanent benefits of the new railway system and of improved shipping, which began greatly to outweigh, as they had not done in the 'forties, the effects of the strain imposed by new construction. New building did, indeed, proceed on an important scale—expenditure averaged twenty to thirty millions yearly [1]—but this expansion, thanks to the general growth of trade and of the national income, no longer absorbed a disproportionate part of available capital resources. Thirdly—and this was the factor whose effects were most spectacular—the period witnessed the important gold discoveries in California and Australia.

These various influences combined to produce a vast expansion in every sphere of economic activity. Until the early 'fifties, the improvement was unostentatious, and was mainly traceable to the continuing railway expenditure and the cheapness of food and raw materials; but a rapid fall in interest rates,[2] and retrenchment in private finance, necessitated by the earlier recklessness in railway investment, were providing a sound basis for revival of confidence. News of the Californian gold discoveries reached London early in 1849, and might have produced a new and rapid movement towards boom conditions but for political difficulties and the disclosure of serious railway frauds—followed by a violent break in share prices—later in the year.

The boom actually began three years later. In September, 1851, it was learned that gold had been found (in the previous May) at Bathurst, New South Wales, and in the spring of 1852 there began a frenzied rush of prospectors, engineers, labourers and adventurers to Australia. This was the signal for an all-round increase in activity. Supplies, machinery and manufactured goods of all kinds were required for the development of the new area. Ships were needed for their conveyance; yet, for a time, accommodation could not be found even for all the would-be emigrants themselves. Feverish activity was induced in shipbuilding, and raw materials such as iron were almost doubled in price.

Meanwhile, the first gold arrivals from both California and Australia were beginning to have their effect on money rates. Bank rate was reduced to the unprecedented level of 2 per cent. in April, and remained at that figure for the remainder of the year—although, in fact, only a *rise* in rates could in such conditions have prevented a dangerous boom. Abundant supplies of credit were thus made available on cheap terms to finance the many developments in progress. Once again, an unnatural depression of interest rates brought in its train a host of new speculative ventures. From July onwards there was a new mania for public

[1] Tooke, *op. cit.*, Vol. V, p. 229 and pp. 348–90.

[2] Bank rate had dropped to 2½ per cent. by Nov., 1849, while outside rates were substantially lower.

companies, especially those for railway, mining and emigration development. In early November, the *Morning Chronicle* drew attention to the fact that 153 " bubble companies " had been formed in the preceding four months, and remarked that a considerable part of their capital would never be called up because " the weakness or absurdity of the schemes will ensure their failure ".

A blithe confidence made this fresh speculation peculiarly dangerous. It was widely believed that in some mysterious way the gold discoveries and the adoption of free trade had suspended or rendered obsolete the fundamental principles the neglect of which had taught so bitter a lesson in 1847. " In all shapes, on all sides, among all classes," says Tooke,[1] " engagements were made and enterprises were started, implying sooner or later the employment of more capital. There was every apparent inducement for embarking in such adventures ; for the common topic of conversation was the boundless prospect of wealth opened up to us by the Australian Discoveries and the Australian Markets, and the utter hopelessness of ever seeing again a High Rate of Interest in this country."

Such beliefs sufficiently explain why the painful memories of 1847 provided no check to the new speculation, which continued, and even increased, in 1853. There seemed, indeed, real justification for optimism. Almost every branch of trade was prosperous ; unemployment was at a low ebb, and poor rates were falling ; wages were rising ; and exports were increasing by leaps and bounds—they were more than doubled in the decade.[2]

Side by side with this development, partly as a cause, partly as an effect, there occurred a marked growth of banking resources. Throughout the country a better understanding of the facilities offered by the banks, the general growth of private incomes, and, above all, the allowance of interest on deposits, brought in millions of new funds from persons who previously had not kept banking accounts at all. For example, the Chairman of the Association of Private Country Bankers estimated that in the few years before 1858 the banking habit had increased four-fold in the Ipswich district, and remarked that " almost every farmer, even those paying only £50 per annum rent, now keeps deposits with bankers ".[3]

[1] Tooke, *op. cit.*, p. 288.

[2] Their total in 1857, despite the crisis, was £122,155,000, whereas before 1848 they had never exceeded £60,110,000 (touched in 1845). See 1858 Report, p. i.

[3] 1858 Report, p. v.

In London the movement proceeded at an amazing rate, for intense competition between the nine joint stock banks forced deposit rates to much higher levels than obtained in the country, where the general practice was to allow a flat rate of 2½ per cent.[1] David Salomons, of the London and Westminster, explained in 1858 that in its early years his bank allowed 2 per cent. for sums below £1,000 and specially agreed rates for larger sums.[2] In the 'thirties there was no uniformity, and rates varied between different banks according to whether notice of withdrawal was required, and according to the period of the notice; but, in general, the allowances were never above 3 per cent. About the middle 'forties, however, competition, reinforced later by the general rise in interest rates and the attractiveness of alternative means of investment, led to a marked rise in the allowances. The natural limit to the rates which the banks could afford to allow was, of course, set by the rates they could themselves earn, and deposit allowances, therefore, came to be regulated by Bank rate. Thus, by the 'fifties, the London joint stock banks were offering 1 per cent. below Bank rate.[3] This practice committed the banks at times to very generous allowances, and it was only when, in 1857, Bank rate threatened to rise to 9 per cent., that the expediency of modifying the rule was considered. Attempts to secure general agreement upon a maximum of 7 per cent. failed, with the result that allowances subsequently rose to 8 per cent., but when Bank rate was raised to 10 per cent., the London and Westminster refused to make any further alteration.[4] Some

[1] See 1858 Committee, Minutes, Q. 1536. This, indeed, was the country practice until quite recently.

[2] 1858 Committee, Minutes, Q. 1131.

[3] The London and Westminster—by far the largest of the London banks—restricted this rate to deposits above £500, and increased the margin below Bank rate to 2 per cent. for smaller sums. (*Ibid.*, Q. 1132.)

[4] Salomons' explanation of his bank's decision on this occasion has been much quoted, and frequently misinterpreted, notably by Palgrave and by the *Economist*. Salomons, speaking of the increase in Bank rate to 10 per cent., declared, " we at that time altered our system. We do not now follow so closely the Bank rate ; we have, as far as we can, broken from it, adopting what may be called an expedient rate, not following the Bank as closely as we have done." (See 1858 Committee, Minutes, Q. 1145, and also QQ. 1164–5.) Palgrave regarded this as conclusive proof of the waning financial (as opposed to moral) power of the Bank, and of the fact that Bank rate had ceased to be a reliable guide to the value of money. His conclusion was quite unwarrantable ; the step resulted simply from the prudence of bankers in times of " crisis " rates, and the rule of " one per cent. under " remained operative, for all normal times, for many years after 1857.

of the younger joint stock banks were less cautious, for not only did they allow interest on the minimum monthly balance on current account, but on deposit account several of them were obliged by the terms of their prospectuses to pay at least 1 per cent. under Bank rate.[1]

With such attractive rates obtainable, the keeping of a banking account became, for many people, simply a peculiarly convenient (and apparently risk-free) method of investment. This system, and the simultaneous expansion of trade, multiplied the deposits of the London joint stock banks nearly five times in the decade. In 1847, their total was £8,850,774; by 1857, it was £43,100,724.[2] Yet only a small part of the increase in London deposits was attributable to expansion of the balances maintained by the country bankers.[3]

Expansion of the Call Loan System

So vast a growth of trade and of banking inevitably had important reactions on the discount market. The increase in trade, with its accompanying expansion of the bill currency and of demands for discount, on the one hand, and the increase in the banking resources seeking employment, on the other, would in any event have expanded greatly the volume of bill market operations. But, as on former occasions, the bill dealers gained more than proportionately. Banking expansion was greatest among precisely those banks which most favoured the call loan system—the joint stock banks—while the call loan habit also grew in popularity with the country private banks. Hardly less important than the increase in bank resources, however, was the fact that the high rates allowed on deposits had the effect of increasing the *proportion* of them which was re-lent at call. Sheffield Neave's evidence makes the point very clearly[4]:

> It has been of late years a growing practice on the part of bankers to employ an increasing portion of their reserve at call, not in direct discounts themselves, but with bill brokers, whom they have used as agents for that purpose?—Yes; I think that the joint stock banks especially, who give interest for money forced upon them by depositors, which they are obliged to employ immediately and

---

[1] 1858 Committee, Minutes, Q. 1133.

[2] 1858 Report, p. v. Salomons declared emphatically that of the increase only " a very inconsiderable part represents persons who have left other bankers ". (1858 Committee, Minutes, Q. 1138.)

[3] 1858 Committee, Minutes, Q. 1135.

[4] *Ibid.*, Q. 616.

quickly; therefore being unable to find discounts enough for themselves for short periods, so as to make that money available to them, they have put it in the hands of the brokers, with the option of having it back at any moment; and that has brought, of course, a greater sum of money into that category.[1]

The discount houses thus found a very large increase both in the London banks' offerings of short money and in their demands for "brokers' bills" for investment purposes. In consequence, the old-style "true" bill broking virtually disappeared, for although few of the remaining brokers had sufficient credit to enable them to attract really large call loans, they were able to profit by the banks' desire for a full employment of resources, and readily secured sufficient funds to finance a "quick turn" in-and-out bill dealing business. Thus although before 1856 the houses taking really large deposits were still identical with those of 1847,[2] by the later date the bill market, broadly speaking, had become a market of bill dealers, and not of brokers.[3]

Nevertheless, the discount houses retained, almost undiminished, their ancient function of acting as an intermediary between the borrowing and the lending country districts. The country banks, despite their growth, were rarely large enough geographically to enable them to achieve a balance between deposits and trade demands. Nor, to any important extent, did they utilize their London bankers as the equalizing agents: surplus deposits were rarely accumulated on London clearing agents'[4] accounts, nor were bills generally sent direct to them for re-discount. This vital function of equalizing the needs of different districts was still performed almost exclusively by the discount market. Proof of this, and of the fact that in its essentials the system was identical with that practised by the earliest bill brokers, is afforded by the following extract from Neave's evidence in 1858[5]:

. . . the bill brokers in London are the . . . medium through which the spare capital of one class of the community is employed usefully by another class of the community where it is required? . . . The capital which is not required in particular districts of

---

[1] See also, *ibid.*, Q. 926.

[2] *Cf.* Gilbart's *Logic of Banking*, pp. 554–5.

[3] *Cf.* Neave, 1858 Committee, Minutes, QQ. 717–19.

[4] The London joint stock banks were admitted to the clearing house, established by the London private banks and jealously guarded by them, on June 8, 1854. Shortly afterwards the final clearing began to be adjusted through the Bank of England.

[5] 1858 Committee, Minutes, QQ. 627–33.

the country is sent up to London to the bill brokers, and money which is to spare in the hands of bankers in London is also placed in their hands for use ?—Yes.

Through those bill brokers the commercial trade of London is supplied with money to which it would not otherwise have direct access ?—Partly so.

And the manufacturing and mining districts draw large sums of money from the bill brokers, which have been sent up to them from the rural districts when it has not been required ?—I suppose that it so operates ; what is not wanted in one place reaches another.

Therefore these bill brokers are . . . the channel through which the spare capital of one part of the country finds its way to and is utilized in another part of the country where it is required ?—Yes ; that is the nature of the operation.[1]

In consequence of the continuance of this system, the bill market felt the full impact not only of the growth of trade and banking in the metropolis, but also of the similar growth in the country. Its operations therefore expanded enormously. The larger discount houses, moreover, not content with the automatic increase in their turnover with the country banks, greatly enlarged their own private connections in the country districts, both with lenders and with borrowers. Chapman declared that his firm's depositors were so numerous that it was impossible to classify them, but added that deposits from " private parties " had " very much increased " in the few years before 1857.[2] His firm's direct connections with the manufacturing districts, from which the industrialist himself remitted bills for discount, were also " very large ".[3] Indeed, both Gurney's and several other discount houses took very active steps to cultivate these direct provincial contacts. Neave thought that " a good many " traders and industrialists in the manufacturing districts, especially in Lancashire and Yorkshire, were in direct correspondence with London bill dealers. He had also observed that the discount houses frequently had agents, living in towns where money was in demand, who sought out the traders with bills to sell ; and that in times of abundant money in London this force of outside representatives was augmented.[4]

One other factor making for bill market expansion may be noted—the spread of the system of acceptance credits. The system was not, of course, new, and was very widespread in the

[1] Very similar evidence was given by Chapman to the 1857 Committee, Minutes, QQ. 5098–101.

[2] 1857 Committee, Minutes, QQ. 4947–8. [3] *Ibid.*, Q. 5325.

[4] 1858 Committee, Minutes, QQ. 636–9.

'forties [1]; but in the succeeding decade it was practised on a much larger scale than ever before, and was extended to trades and areas in which it had previously been only exceptionally used. It was especially important in all classes of trade with America, Scandinavia, China and the East, and in the colonial trades. Partly as a result of this development, from about 1850 onwards, bills drawn to finance overseas trade, as opposed to purely domestic paper, came to play an increasingly important part in bill market and bank portfolios.

Even in the absence of aggravating circumstances, the outstanding growth in bill market facilities, and the increase in the prestige and importance of the discount houses, could scarcely have failed to produce a fresh crop of bill credit abuses. But the reckless and widespread optimism engendered by the gold discoveries and the general prosperity provided an aggravating factor of the most serious kind. The period was, in fact, marked by one of the most grave cycles of credit abuse which are to be found in the entire history of the market. The abuses took three distinct forms—excessive re-discounting, undue reliance upon loans repayable at call, and the imprudent extension of acceptance credits. Increased re-discounting by country banks was, of course, the natural and necessary accompaniment of the expansion of industry and trade in the provinces; provided that the bills concerned were good, this development could be only beneficial. It was not always possible, nor is it now, for the discount houses to be sure that all the paper which they took was "good",[2] but so long as they adhered to sound rules, the proportion of bad paper capable of defying scrutiny would generally be comparatively small. Broadly speaking, it seems that when money was abundant, and bills therefore relatively scarce, the discount houses were inclined to relax their rules, but at the first sign of approaching stringency all paper would be rigorously scrutinized. Normally, therefore, the mere increase in the volume of bills provided a reasonably sure protection against their reckless

[1] See *ante*, p. 124. On all essential points, the practice was identical with that followed to-day. Commissions, however, were somewhat higher than is the rule now.

[2] Neave, for example, remarked that it was impossible to detect accommodation paper "except by knowing the transactions of the parties, and using your best discretion in deciding whether the bill is legitimately drawn by one in such a trade upon another; you only form the best opinion you can; you cannot actually fathom or discover that it is or is not an accommodation bill". (1858 Committee, Minutes, Q. 303.)

creation and re-discount. But in the early 'fifties the force of this "automatic" corrective, reinforcing the primary check imposed by a rising discount rate, was greatly weakened by the arbitrary expansion of the credit supply occasioned by the Australian and Californian gold influx.

"One-Name" Re-discounts

A pronounced ease in money, especially the pressure of funds furnished by the London joint stock banks, thus led the bill market into indiscretions which would scarcely have occurred in other circumstances. In particular, the discount houses came, more freely than ever before, to take country paper solely on the strength of the endorsement of the bank which remitted it.[1] They argued that they could run no risk in so doing, if the bank itself were sound. As has been noted, where purely local paper was concerned, the London discounter often had no means of knowing the standing of the immediate parties,[2] and was justified in assuming that if such bills bore the endorsement of a reputable bank, they must in fact be good bills. But the prudent dealer would confine his discounts of such "unknown" paper within narrow limits. Unfortunately, it is certain that neglect of this precaution was not the only reason for the excessive reliance on provincial bank endorsements. In some instances, bill dealers relied upon the bank's signature and bought its bills even though they were fully aware that the paper was in other respects undesirable. The effect of such methods was to afford the banks concerned almost unlimited credit; all that a provincial bank had to do to obtain funds from London was to procure a new supply of accommodation bills, and remit them, duly endorsed, to a London discount house.[3] Such a system inevitably fostered

[1] See 1858 Report, p. xlix, and Minutes, QQ. 1885, 4353, 4364 and 1965. Dixon, of the Borough Bank of Liverpool, the most notorious of the reckless re-discounters, stated that the brokers discounted parcels of their bills "as a whole", and hardly ever returned individual bills after the parcels had been examined.

[2] 1858 Committee, Minutes, Q. 1886.

[3] In 1857, for example, the Borough Bank of Liverpool had £3,500,000 (nearly three times its deposits) under re-discount, and of these bills from £700,000 to £1,000,000 had "no negotiable validity" except the bank's endorsement. The case of the Western Bank of Scotland was even worse. This bank at one time had re-discounts of £5,400,000, and took many bills (its portfolio reached £20,691,000 by the date of its failure) which its correspondents had reported to be "unsatisfactory or positively bad". (See 1858 Report, Sections 45, 49, and *post*, p. 198.)

over-trading both by the banks and by their customers, and afforded insolvent or fraudulent firms with handsome opportunities for postponing their bankruptcies and/or prosecutions.

In a few isolated cases, bill dealers even relied upon a bank endorsement when they had reason to believe that the bank itself was insolvent, counting upon the known (or fancied) wealth of the bank proprietory (and its " unlimited " liability) to save them in the event of a collapse.[1] J. Dixon, a shareholder and director (and, later, managing director) of the Borough Bank of Liverpool, which failed in 1857, related how, in conversation with a bill broker about the failure, he remarked, " If I had only known half as much of the proceedings of the Borough Bank while I was a director, as you must have known, by seeing a great many of the bills of the bank discounted, you would never have caught me being a shareholder." The broker's retort was significant: " Nor would you have caught me being a shareholder; it was very well for me to discount the bills, but I would not have been a shareholder either." [2] It is as well to emphasize that this conversation occurred *after* the failure; but if the broker's was no idle boast, his conduct bordered upon the criminal, and was at best a " legal " fraud upon the bank's shareholders. Such conduct, happily, was certainly not general in the discount market. The testimony of J. Ball,[3] the accountant who dealt with many of the subsequent liquidations, and an austere critic where criticism was merited, strongly suggests that the market generally acted in more or less complete ignorance of the extent of the abuses which occurred. Gurney's too, then at the zenith of their career, seem usually to have adhered closely to sound principles. There is no reason to doubt D. B. Chapman's honesty when he asserted that his firm " would not countenance " renewal bills, that it never lent on any speculative securities (he actually declared that this was true of " Lombard Street " as a whole), and never held Consols or Exchequer bills.[4] On this last point, he remarked that some houses did hold such securities, but added, " It would be a very unpleasant thing for us to hold any fluctuating property whatever . . . there is not much pleasure in holding Exchequer bills; I could not sleep if that were the case."

To apportion equitably between the bill market and the country banks the blame for imprudent re-discounting is therefore virtually

[1] *Cf. ante*, p. 46. [2] 1858 Report, p. xlix.
[3] See 1858 Committee, Minutes, Q. 1886.
[4] It did, however, accept them as collateral. (*Cf. post*, p. 189.)

impossible. But both came in for strong criticism by many of the witnesses before the subsequent banking inquiries. In 1858 the re-discounting practice as a whole was in very bad odour, and the country banks who adopted it were contrasted in scathing terms with the big London banks.[1] No critic was more severe than the Governor of the Bank, Sheffield Neave, but even he had finally to concede that the practice was not intrinsically objectionable. Under cross-examination before the 1858 Committee, he suggested that the even " distribution of capital " could be effected equally well if the brokers relied entirely upon the direct discount of country bills, but the Chairman pointed out that the collection and original purchase of local paper was clearly better left to the resident banker with special knowledge of local conditions and names.[2] Then followed this illuminating evidence :

> Do you see any objection to a banker in Leeds or in Manchester acting as the agent through whom those bills are collected in those districts, for the purpose of being discounted with the spare capital which is accumulated in London ?—Certainly not, if confined to that ; but the effect has been most imprudent advances on their part, re-discounting very largely on account of their keeping money at call [this referred to the granting of interest on current accounts, or on " deposits " withdrawable without notice], and being obliged to make a gain out of the difference of the rate of interest.
>
> That is to say, that it has given rise to a great number of bad bills ?—Yes.
>
> But the fault is the quality of the bills rather than the system ?—Certainly.
>
> Then it is only the abuse of the system of re-discounting, and not the act of re-discounting, to which you object ?—Yes.[3]

The Chairman had, in fact, put his finger upon the root cause of the trouble—the recklessness of business houses in creating accommodation paper, and bills for fictitious values, made doubly so by the constant stream of new finance paper. This reckless-

[1] Chapman, in 1857, argued that the London joint stock banks, by granting interest on deposits, had " run into " the business of bill-dealing as practised by Gurney's, but was forced to admit that their refusal to re-discount presented a vital difference. He had " never heard " of re-discounts by the principal London banks, and had never seen a bill bearing the endorsement of any one of them. (See 1857 Committee, Minutes, QQ. 5210–16.) *Cf.* also 1858 Committee, Minutes, Q. 2245, evidence of G. H. Foster, a director of the London Joint Stock Bank, and evidence of Salomons, QQ. 1169–78, 1225, 1226.

[2] 1858 Committee, Minutes, QQ. 634–5, 640.

[3] *Ibid.*, QQ. 641–4.

ness, of course, was made possible by the willingness of the provincial banks to negotiate the bills; and there is no doubt that in the first instance the blame must lie with the banks for their improvident preoccupation with immediate profits and their insane competition for (expensive) deposits. Had they not encouraged bad bills, the bill market would not have had the chance of re-discounting them. That does not exonerate the bill dealers, nor does it presuppose that no other parties were guilty of recklessness. In a sense, the worst offenders of all were the acceptance houses, generally also merchant and importing firms. Prevalent abuses were thus described by the Committee:

> . . . another class of failures is disclosed. The nature of these transactions was the system of open credits which were granted; that is, by granting to persons abroad liberty to draw upon the house in England . . . those drafts . . . then found their way to England, with the understanding that they were to be provided for at maturity. They were principally provided for, not by staple commodities, but by other bills. . . . There was no real basis to the transaction, but the whole affair was a means of raising a temporary command of capital for the convenience of the individuals concerned, merely a bare commission hanging upon it; a banker's commission was all that the houses in England got upon those transactions, with the exception of receiving the consignments probably of goods . . . which brought them a merchant's commission . . . but they formed a very small amount in comparison with the amount of credits which were granted. One house at the time of its suspension was under obligation to the world to the extent of about £900,000, its capital . . . was under £10,000. . . . In these cases the inducement to give the acceptance is a commission varying from ½ to 1½ per cent.[1]

There was, indeed, a well-recognized "technique" of raising funds by the creation of fictitious bills. One house, the notorious Macdonald & Co., of Glasgow and London, originally a reputable muslin manufacturing business with a large American and home market, actually employed 75 agents in London and elsewhere for the sole purpose of accepting its fictitious drafts for subsequent discount! Some may derive amusement from the fact that a "large proportion" of these drafts was placed in Glasgow.[2]

[1] 1858 Report, Section 38. See also evidence of Ball, Minutes, QQ. 1671–91. He stated that the *usual* commissions ranged from ¼ to 1 per cent.

[2] 1858 Report, Section 30, and Morier Evans, *The History of the Commercial Crisis, 1857–8*, p. 50.

When the firm failed, it was indebted to the Western Bank of Scotland to the extent of £422,000.[1]

Market Call Loans and Reserve Policy

These various abuses—the excessive re-discounting, incautious granting of acceptance credits, and reckless creation of accommodation bills—were probably the principal causes of the crisis which followed. But there was another type of abuse, which arose from increasing reliance by the bill market upon the Bank. Inevitably, the rapid growth of business had raised new problems, both of principle and organization, for the bill dealing houses. The smaller ones, formerly conducting only a rapid turnover business with responsibilities hardly greater in practice than those of the " true " brokers, found themselves more and more in the position of " true " dealers and borrowers of money. The big dealers, accustomed previously to carrying only a small proportion of their deposits repayable at call, found this proportion steadily increasing to a point of definite preponderance. Neither type of house probably desired to check these tendencies; but it would not have been easy to do so even had they wished. The banks had big funds to employ, and for a market house to refuse employment to a portion of them would be to endanger its whole valuable connection. Increasing call liabilities really demanded increased reserves in the form of highly liquid bills of very short date, and even a reserve of actual cash. That solution to the problem of the instability produced by the call loan system did not, apparently, occur to the bill dealers at the time; but, in any case, it was not one which could have been readily adopted.

Generally speaking, very high rates were " allowed " [2] by the discount houses on the deposits they received at call. The relationship of their published allowances to Bank rate was not entirely constant, but in general the margin under Bank rate was either 1 per cent. or $\frac{3}{4}$ per cent. In such circumstances, with the market discount rate frequently appreciably under Bank rate,[3]

[1] The Western Bank failed on Nov. 9, 1857. It had also lent £537,000 to Monteith & Co., and £227,000 to Wallace & Co., two other houses which had created accommodation bills on a vast scale, and which collapsed with the Macdonald failure.

[2] The practice of referring to the rates " allowed " by brokers to bankers for call money, and not to rates *charged* by the bankers, is a significant indication of the standing and importance of the discount houses at that time.

[3] See *ante*, p. 163.

the gross profit on financing bills was clearly too small to allow any latitude for the maintenance of more than a fractional balance of idle cash. The consequence was that the discount houses kept no reserve at all, although houses with relatively large capital resources naturally maintained a bigger cash balance than did those with a small capital. Even Gurney's, however, did not reckon to keep any appreciable reserve. D. B. Chapman's evidence [1] on this point deserves detailed quotation:

> You are aware that it is the habit of the Bank of England, as well as, I believe, of other bankers, to keep a certain amount of their deposits in Bank notes in reserve ?—Certainly.
>
> Do the money-dealing houses in Lombard Street [the discount houses] act on the same principle with regard to that money which is left in their hands at call ?—They could not afford to do it; it is not the nature of their business, except under circumstances of danger as to the currency. They could not afford to pay interest for money and not to use it; it is the nature of their business to bring into action and useful employment the banking money of the country; it is their business to use it.
>
> Do you think then that they may safely use all the money which they borrow, in lending it out at interest, provided it is on safe security ?—Assuming that they employ it on bills of exchange falling due *de die in diem*, then experience shows that they may do it safely, without any hazard.
>
> Without keeping any reserve beyond a banking balance ?—Certainly. How could I afford to pay 5 or 6 per cent. for money if I did not use it ? It would certainly be the road to ruin.

There was much to be said for Chapman's argument. Then, as now, the call loan system rested upon the fundamental assumption that if one London banker were calling in loans, another banker would shortly receive a roughly equivalent amount, which he would seek to re-lend. In normal times, that was, and is, a warrantable assumption, and is the basic principle of deposit banking, as well as of bill dealing. It is manifestly impossible for either the banker or the bill dealer, apart altogether from the question of deposit allowances, to maintain such a cash reserve as would suffice to meet a real "run" by depositors. In the event of widespread panic withdrawals, neither the banker nor the bill dealer could hope to avoid a temporary suspension of payments unless new credit were made available (directly or indirectly) by the Bank of England. The banker's duty, apart from that of holding virtually all his assets in liquid form, and

[1] 1857 Committee, Minutes, QQ. 5205–9.

part of them in highly liquid form, is therefore to maintain such a balance of idle cash as will at all *normal* times exceed the foreseeable margin of public cash withdrawals over public cash deposits. In principle, the duty of the discount dealer is precisely similar. First, he must eschew all but readily realizable assets; and, secondly, he must maintain an idle balance proportioned to the probable normal discrepancy between the demands from bankers for repayment of short loans and the supply furnished by the recipient bankers who are re-lending. Neither he nor the banker can hope to legislate for the day when all or many of his creditors may call in their funds simultaneously.

There is, however, one vital practical difference. In the ordinary course, both the time and the extent of the probable net cash demands of bank customers can be foreseen with a high degree of accuracy. They are mainly seasonal, and can be reduced almost to a "rule of thumb". Demands substantially above the average are therefore very infrequent. The probable net demands upon the discount houses for repayment of call loans, however, are much more variable both in point of volume and in point of time. The *average* net demands are small in proportion to the total volume of call loans, but demands far above the average occur comparatively frequently, and occasionally do so without any previous warning. Theoretically, by refusing to work save at a wide margin between their "deposit" allowances and discount charges, the discount houses could maintain an idle cash holding determined by the probable *maximum* demands upon them in normal times. Such a practice might go far to stabilize conditions in the short loan market, but its adoption would not be really desirable, for it would involve both an unnecessarily high charge for discount accommodation (with some repercussion upon bank charges and/or allowances) and a needless waste of available credit resources—a waste inseparable from the fact that *both* the banks *and* the discount houses (despite the latter's intermediary position) would be carrying large idle reserves. Yet this system of maintaining reserves sufficient for all probable needs would have been unavoidable unless the discount market relied upon the Bank of England for assistance in meeting all demands appreciably above the average.

Such were the problems raised for the discount houses by the rapid transition to a large-scale call loan system. It seems safe to assert that their implications were not fully grasped at the time, for the discount dealers, even if they sought to find the best solution, never really had a free choice in the formulation of their practice. They were squeezed between two opposing forces: on the one hand, the avidity of the banks for a large return on call money, wherewith to recoup the cost of their expensive competition for deposits; and, on the other, the anxiety of those same banks to employ their growing deposits in the purchase of bills. Such competition depressed the yield obtainable on bills, but even if it had not, there was a definite (and not much more liberal) limit to discount market charges set by the published rate of the Bank of England. Forces beyond their control, therefore, compelled the discount houses to follow the line of least resistance in adjusting their practice to the changing conditions. They had not the opportunity of establishing reserves based on probable maximum demands, and therefore made no attempt to do so. Their reserves, where determined by policy at all, thus came to be based upon average demands—in effect, upon day-to-day experience.

Reliance upon the Bank—and Over-Trading

Whenever, therefore, there was a more than usual pressure for money, the discount houses were obliged to seek assistance at the Bank of England.[1] This system was not of itself objectionable, and is, indeed, not greatly different from the system adopted to-day. So long as the discount houses took steps to ensure that their applications to the Bank were as infrequent as possible, and so long as their demands were not out of reasonable proportion to their capital, it was quite the most appropriate arrangement, making both for the most economical use of available credit, and for the maximum degree of central bank control over the whole money market and banking situation. The mere fact, which Neave deplored in the strongest terms, that in the early 'fifties the discount market made more frequent applications to the Bank than it had ever done previously, was no proof that it was abusing the re-discounting privileges afforded to it. More frequent borrowings were the unavoidable accompaniment of the new dependence on call loans and of the growing sensitiveness of the London market to international influences. To appreciate this, it is necessary to remember that, despite the surprising spread of the banking habit, cash payments were still extensively employed in commercial transactions; that communications, despite their rapid progress, were still much slower and less

[1] See evidence of Neave before 1858 Committee, Minutes, Q. 400, and also QQ. 399, 925.

dependable than they are to-day; and that the short loan market itself, despite its expansion, lacked the extreme fluidity which is now its most remarkable characteristic. For these and similar reasons, short-term immobilizations—temporary stoppages in the even circulation of funds round the market—were bound to be comparatively frequent. Each one of these immobilizations, some of them arising from the most trivial of causes, might force one or more discount houses "into" the Bank.

More numerous re-discount applications, therefore, did not necessarily imply either any fundamental change in the system followed by the market, or any deterioration in its methods of doing business. Indeed, Gurney's, and possibly certain other houses, still aimed at avoiding recourse to the Bank at all other periods than the quarterly "shuttings", when they deemed it both a necessity and a public duty to re-discount. Borrowings at other times (when loans were available only at Bank rate) were held to be unprofitable for the discount market. Chapman thus explained his policy:

> If we find that the demand for money is so considerable as to drive us to take money of the Bank, we dislike it; we do not want to get a profit by our transactions with the Bank in the ordinary course of things. We think that it is our natural business to go to the Bank during the quarters when the public money goes into the Bank; somebody must supply that vacuum, and it is our natural business to do it; but we should not like to carry on our ordinary business with the money of the Bank of England. Indeed, it would not pay us; the public would not pay us for first-class bills, which we alone deal in, a rate higher than the Bank rate, because they would rather go to the Bank themselves; we therefore should not be very long in that state which would enable us to carry on our business with the money of the Bank of England, because we should charge a higher rate than the Bank of England, which would have the effect of throwing off a great number of bills on the Bank or other channels. . . . If . . . we find the necessity of frequently going to the Bank for discount, we check it by charging a higher rate.[1]

This standpoint was doubtless common to the discount market as a whole, for in ordinary times no dealer could hope to make a profit by financing his bills on money borrowed from the Bank. But Chapman's argument did not dispose of the whole problem. There was another way in which ability to borrow at the Bank

[1] 1857 Committee, Minutes, Q. 4684; and see also QQ. 4930–1, 5189, 5196. (*Cf. ante*, pp. 127–8.)

could be turned to profitable account. Unscrupulous dealers in times of easy money could confidently take all the business offered to them, and could pile up liabilities on call loans and re-discounts out of all proportion to the extent of their capital, with the certain knowledge that in a moment of pressure they could unload a substantial part of their portfolio upon the Bank. The only check to such activities was imposed by the fact that if rates should rise suddenly, the bills would have to be re-sold to the Bank at a loss. Some dealers certainly did not count this a serious risk, for except in the most extreme panic there was a reasonable chance that the handsome profits from over-trading, especially if second-grade bills were at all largely discounted, would much more than offset the ultimate loss on re-discounts at the Bank. And if the dealer were shrewd (and fortunate) he might escape loss altogether. In short, it was a " fair " gamble. Gurney's, at this stage in their career, seem to have avoided any serious excesses of this type, if only because their world-wide prestige, and the known vast resources of their partners, made them feel that it was beneath their dignity to go to the Bank if this could possibly be avoided. Other houses had no such scruples, as the commitments of Sanderson's and of Bruce & Co. at the time of their suspension in 1857 plainly revealed.

Bill market over-trading therefore began to be a serious abuse, and with it there came a noteworthy increase not merely in the frequency of applications to the Bank, but also in the actual amounts demanded. It is unfair, however, to single out the bill market for special censure, as was done by the Committees of 1857 and 1858 : excesses in Lombard Street were one result of the whole wave of reckless optimism and speculation which swept the entire country. " It was, perhaps, inevitable that false appearances should present themselves," says Tooke,[1] writing of the Australian gold arrivals. " The Public saw the rapid elevation of the Bullion Reserves of the Bank—they heard of the untold treasures of the land from which those reserves were derived—and they knew that almost every day brought into our harbours ships laden with further additions to a stock of gold already without precedent. It was not unnatural that such a state of things should foster unduly sanguine anticipations." The bill market developments of the period were neither wholly a cause, nor wholly an effect, of this optimism. The point of view of the discount dealer was simply this : he had large sums offered to him by the banks, and he not only saw no legitimate reason

[1] *Op. cit.*, p. 280.

for refusing them, but knew that if he did so he would actually damage his existing business. In seeking to employ these resources he thus provided a channel for the excessive re-discounts by the provincial banks.

Neave claimed, and with justification, that this system encouraged the creation of doubtful paper:

> I made no objection to their [the brokers] taking in money at call, but I called the attention of the Committee to the effect of large sums being accumulated in few hands when accumulated there through the means of depositors at call. I wished to state that the system of money at call necessarily compels the broker, as well as the banker who takes it, to make immediate use of it, because he could not afford to allow interest if it was not employed at the same instant at a better rate of interest, for the sake of his profit; it therefore occasions the party who takes the money at call to look out for securities wherever he can find them; and not to be very chary in the selection of them, when there is no difficulty in getting them. It leads therefore to the encouragement of an inferior class of bills, and is in some degree instrumental in giving currency to bills that probably ought not to be discounted.[1]

These were valid criticisms; but while Neave roundly asserted that the reason for bill market over-trading, and for the stimulus which this gave to bad bills, was the market's undue reliance upon the Bank, he seemed completely to have overlooked the fact that this reliance could never have produced the creation of any very large volume of doubtful bills unless the Bank itself were willing to re-discount them.

The Bank's rules as to the eligibility of re-discountable paper did, in fact, definitely foster the growth of undesirable paper. In theory, its rules were beyond reproach: like other banks, it would discount only for those customers who had opened approved "discount accounts", and it invariably insisted on "two-name" paper. But the discount account had in practice become "a nominal thing". Whereas the Bank formerly demanded a deposit of at least £500, by the 'fifties much smaller sums sufficed, especially for discounts made at the Branches. One witness suggested in 1857 that a deposit of £5 or £10 was often sufficient, and pointed out that in any case the discount applicant would retain his requisite "account" even though he withdrew his balance on the day after it was deposited.[2] But a

[1] 1858 Committee, Minutes, Q. 924.

[2] See evidence of Twells, a partner in Spooner, Atwoods & Co., before 1857 Committee, Minutes, QQ. 4820–30.

much more serious source of slackness arose from the practice of looking solely to the " security " which the bills offered. " Security ", in this context, meant security for the Bank, and not security for the public. Unhappily, the two are not necessarily coincident. Weguelin admitted quite frankly that the Bank took no account of the purpose for which bills were drawn, and had no objection to speculative paper unless its speculative element impaired the Bank's security. In other words, a house whose resources were believed to be large could engage in almost unlimited speculations without affecting the negotiability of its paper at the Bank.

That the bill market over-reached itself is not, therefore, very surprising. Discount houses, paying high rates for their deposits, could scarcely be expected to refuse paper which the Bank of England, whose deposits cost nothing, thought fit to accept. It is easy to see that, once the dangerous practice of taking " secure " finance paper were admitted, some houses were bound to carry it to extreme lengths. And if the traditional rules of prudent finance could be relaxed for bills, there seemed no harm in relaxations for other securities. In 1852, especially, when the first really large Australian gold arrivals [1] produced a plethora of funds, anxiety to employ them remuneratively led many houses into securities other than bills. Loans to stock market dealers against gilt-edged collateral were then, as now, a recognized and legitimate part of the large bill dealer's business,[2] but as the pressure of resources on the lender increased, so were his requirements as to collateral broadened. Gurney's, for example, admitted railway debentures, and even lent money direct to the companies upon them. Chapman, however, did not like the innovation, and remarked that " nothing except our being excessively full of money would induce us to do it." [3]

Another practice which became popular in Lombard Street was that of lending money on dock warrants and upon produce in warehouse. Coleman told the 1858 Committee that this had

[1] Gold imports from Australia totalled £7·28 millions in 1852 and £14·97 millions in 1853. (See Tooke, *op. cit.*, p. 302, quoting the *Morning Chronicle.*)

[2] The regular system was to lend on Consols from one "account" to another. In times of pressure very high rates could be obtained by such methods. Chapman told how, in the spring of 1857, he lent over £200,000 in one morning to the same stock market dealer. The loans were made in three separate amounts, at 7, 7½ and 8 per cent. Bank rate then was 6½ per cent.

[3] 1857 Committee, Minutes, Q. 4953.

been "largely" adopted, and that, despite the very high prices which obtained for produce, the margins demanded were often inadequate.[1] It is probable, however, that Coleman based his evidence mainly upon his personal investigation of the position of the two discount houses which later failed, for Chapman, while admitting that securities other than bills were sometimes taken in the market, vigorously denied that warrants and similar securities were ever extensively accepted—"that was the exception and not the rule". He himself would "to a certain extent" take dock warrants of goods "either sold or in the course of sales"; and, so long as the transaction would be liquidated in two months, he thought it legitimate. But he would confine such operations to the firm's own capital, and would never adventure call money in them. Thus he thought that "no man could advance more than a very limited amount on such security".[2]

Were the Discount Houses Mis-Judged?

If Chapman's evidence be taken literally, then it appears that no dealers could have conducted their business more circumspectly than did the bill market; reliance upon the evidence of Neave and several of the other Bank witnesses implies that the discount houses were the most reckless over-traders in the whole financial machine. The truth clearly lay between these two extremes. Gilbart, writing in 1859,[3] after a careful study of the reports of the Committees, and of the evidence which they took, definitely exonerated the bill market as a whole from the charges made against it. Examination of the position of Sanderson's, and of Bruce & Co., he said, would certainly have substantiated those charges, but "it would have been gratifying to the existing bill brokers to know that the failure of two of their body arose only from their own misconduct and not from any defect in the principles on which their business is generally conducted". In sum, it is reasonable to conclude that, in greater or less degree, all the discount houses were guilty of some over-trading and of the acceptance of speculative bills, and that they all took some securities which were not strictly "money market" securities; but that there was no really gross recklessness or dangerous excess, except on the part of the houses which failed.

On the whole, the market at the time was misjudged. The

[1] 1858 Committee, Minutes, QQ. 2000–3.
[2] 1857 Committee, Minutes, QQ. 5200–3.
[3] *Logic of Banking*, p. 556.

extent of its dependence upon the Bank was made the test of its guilt, and the figures produced by the Governor certainly made a deep impression on the Committee of 1858. But it was never pointed out that the greater dependence was due only partly to market over-trading. Chapman was the only bill market witness called, and his house, except in the crisis itself, relied least upon " official " assistance, both in the number of its applications and in their amount. Other members of the market, had they been asked, would certainly have explained not only that the growth of large-scale call loans increased, inevitably, the *frequency* of market applications, but that the larger *amount* of these was primarily a function of the general growth of trade and of banking, and only secondarily a result of market over-trading.

One reason why these considerations were overlooked by the Governor was probably the fact that, owing to the comparative stability of the Bank's resources, *any* increase in bill market borrowings was bound to increase the relative, as well as the absolute, strain on the reserve. Despite the very rapid growth of joint stock and private bank resources, and some increase also in the bankers' balances with the Bank, the Bank's total deposits had shown little, if any, increase. Their annual average had, it is true, risen from £15,963,000 in 1848 to £20,149,000 in 1852, but dropped back to £15,740,000 in 1854; and it was not until four years later that the record of £20,262,000, touched in 1846, was exceeded. The average reserve, similarly, while it rose very sharply after the 1847 crisis, reaching £12,764,000 in 1852, thereafter fell abruptly to average levels below those of the middle 'forties.[1] The Bank had lost for ever its *quantitative* supremacy in the London market. Its deposits still exceeded those of any other bank,[2] but by 1856 were rather under one-fifth of the total for the other London banks, whose aggregate resources were estimated by Newmarch at £110 millions.

Its proportion of the resources actually employed in the London money market was even smaller. Even in 1850 these resources were believed to aggregate £116 millions,[3] employed either in or through London in commercial discounts and advances and bank reserves. Newmarch computed that of this total the London banks contributed £64 millions; private lenders (especially

[1] See Palgrave, *Bank Rate and the Money Market*, pp. 11–15.

[2] Deposits of the London and Westminster Bank, the largest commercial bank, were £3·59 millions in 1845, £6·26 millions in 1853, £11·17 millions in 1856, and £13·89 millions in 1857.

[3] See Newmarch's famous bill " survey ", published as Appendix XI to Tooke and Newmarch's *History of Prices*, Vol. VI.

insurance companies) to the bill market, £10 millions; country bankers (in call loans to or bill purchases from London), £30 millions; and the Bank of England a mere £12 millions.[1] For the same year, the aggregate amount of bills under discount at one time, in or through the London market, was estimated at £78 millions,[2] and of this the Bank was assumed to have financed £5 millions,[3] in contrast with £43 millions financed by other London sources and £30 millions by the country banks (in or through London). From every standpoint, therefore, the Bank's share in the business of the market had greatly diminished.[4]

Consequently, even if there had been no bill market over-trading, the market's re-discount applications would inevitably have placed a growing strain upon the Bank's resources. As it was, the Bank found that the bulk of its bill portfolio invariably consisted of bills re-discounted for the discount houses.[5] The increasing strain was no fault of the bill market, but it explains why the Bank, in judging the conduct of the market, considered only the *absolute* increase in market demands, and not their increase *relative* to the growth of market turnover, of commercial bank deposits, and of trade. The Bank was, in fact, at one of the great turning-points in its history: it was preoccupied with the problem of reconciling a vast increase in its actual and potential responsibilities with a trifling increase in its resources. It had, as has been shown, gradually assumed most of the vital functions of a central bank, and had ceased actively to participate in the competitive race for commercial banking. But it had been accustomed, where necessary, to control the outside market

[1] This was taken to be the amount employed by the Bank in *commercial* accommodation.

[2] *Local* discounts by country banks were put at £22 millions (£10 millions in Scotland, whose bills were rarely made payable in London, and thus were largely discounted north of the Tweed, and £12 millions for England), making an aggregate under discount at one time of £100 millions. Newmarch estimated the total bill *circulation* (for 1843–6) at £116 millions, consisting of £16 millions of foreign bills, £18 millions in Scotland, £12 millions in Lancashire, and £70 millions in the rest of England. He believed that £13 millions of the foreign bills and £87 millions of the domestic would be under discount.

[3] The Bank's *actual* average discounts in 1850 were £2,660,000; its temporary advances averaged £1,848,000. (Palgrave, *op. cit.*)

[4] It was, however, widely believed that the Bank was still the largest dealer in discounts, and this opinion was clearly held by the chairman of the 1857 Committee. Chapman thought that the Bank had a "very considerable proportion", but declared that others held "considerably more". (See 1857 Committee, Minutes, QQ. 4841–61.)

[5] See 1857 Committee, Minutes, Q. 315.

almost entirely through sheer preponderance of resources; it was now confronted with the problem of disciplining an organism whose resources completely dwarfed its own. In the circumstances, it could not be expected to be over-nice in apportioning the blame for the discomfiture which these changes implied.

The Crisis of 1857

The magnitude of the Bank's task, but dimly recognized by the directorate in the early 'fifties, was brought home to it by the crisis of 1857. Had there been no crisis, it seems probable that the Bank would have moved gradually to a real solution of its problem; that it would have admitted the inevitability of the new tendencies in the money market; would have accepted the new responsibilities which these tendencies involved; and would have sought the means of substituting a qualitative or "moral" control for its lost quantitative control. Such an approach might have altered the whole course of money market history for a generation. As it was, the crisis forced the Bank to act, and act quickly. It therefore attacked those houses which seemed most directly to menace its own security—the discount houses who had been its largest debtors. Its action, by imposing a salutary check upon the bill market, seemed to some at the time to be a solution of the problem: in fact, it was no solution, but was a shirking of Bank responsibilities by an effort to restrain the fundamental and inevitable banking tendencies of the period.

The course of the crisis itself can be briefly traced. Its broad antecedents have already been indicated—they lay in the feverish speculation produced both at home and in the colonial markets by the gold discoveries. The first signs of trouble appeared as early as the middle of 1853, when Bank rate, following two increases in the previous January, was raised to 3½ per cent. This was not a high rate, but it indicated that the vast number of new flotations was beginning to absorb an appreciable part of the available capital supply. In addition, domestic trade and spending power had advanced at such a pace, owing partly to a sharp rise in wages,[1] as to lead to an expansion of imports which more than balanced the growth of exports. Despite the large arrivals of new gold, there had begun a steady net drain upon the Bank's gold reserves. Yet, at the very time when natural

[1] The increase in the first half of 1853 alone was estimated at 15 to 20 per cent., and at 20 to 25 per cent. in some trades. (See Tooke, *op. cit.*, Vol. V, p. 282.)

influences were producing a hardening of money rates, the Government launched a scheme for the gradual conversion of Consols to a $2\frac{1}{2}$ per cent. basis,[1] and to facilitate this reduced the rate on Exchequer bills to 1*d.* per day ($1\frac{1}{2}$ per cent. per annum), thereby materially weakening the moral effect of the rising tendency of Bank rate. Speculative formations therefore continued unabated.

New difficulties then arose in the shape of labour disputes and strikes for higher wages ; in a rise in corn prices to their highest since 1847 ; and in a consequent drain of gold to America to pay for grain imports.[2] In the autumn came the first rumblings of war with Russia ; indications that the Australian markets, which had been inundated with export produce of all kinds, were nearing saturation point ; and an increase in Bank rate by $1\frac{1}{2}$ per cent. to 5 per cent. in four weeks.[3] Meanwhile, there had been a considerable recession in important branches of trade. Factory Inspectors reported that a number of factories had been obliged to institute short-time working, and that depression was marked in the cotton trade. This was partly attributable to the political tension on the Continent and in the East, and to the rise in food prices, but a major cause was undoubtedly the undue expansion of productive equipment. The Inspector for Lancashire, for example, ascribed the difficulties to " the very great increase in the number of Mills, causing production to go far beyond the demands of existing markets, numerous and extensive though they may be ".[4] These troubles merely aggravated the labour problem, and in October there began at Preston a strike which involved 17,000 workers, and ended only when trade union funds were exhausted, seven months later.

The year 1854 therefore opened ominously. Conditions in Australia grew steadily worse, and the markets there became completely glutted with unsaleable British products, causing serious failures among the export houses in London and the

[1] The project was outlined in Gladstone's Financial Statement of April 18, 1853, which also provided for the first issue of Exchequer Bonds.

[2] Previously there had been a net *inflow* of gold from America, in consequence of the vast demands for British manufactures caused by the boom in California and the general speculation which it engendered. (See Tooke, *op. cit.*, p. 311.)

[3] Between Sept. 1 and Sept. 29. On the latter date the Bank's reserve stood at only £6,840,000, in contrast with £10,400,000 in the preceding January, when the first upward move (to $2\frac{1}{2}$ per cent.) was made.

[4] Quoted by Tooke, *op. cit.*, p. 291.

provinces. In March, the commencement of the Crimean War produced a sudden rise in raw material prices, and, despite the war demands, wages and prices in the textile industries began to fall.[1] The boom in shipping, which had raised the value of tonnage by 50 per cent. and had trebled many freight rates in a few months, was temporarily enhanced by Government demands, only to collapse violently when, in the autumn, the pressure of these demands slackened.[2] This, too, brought a wave of failures, with repercussions in the timber and other trades which had prospered from the reckless building of new vessels. Timber importers, in particular, suffered heavy losses.

In America, an even more dangerous speculative position had been built up. The intensive Californian developments had been in progress for over four years, and had been made the basis of a gross over-investment in land, railways, and supposed mining ventures, not only in California, but in most of the leading cities of the whole continent. Speculative company formations of every kind, and a dangerous "trust company" movement, had been carried to absurd lengths, while the actual seat of the gold operations was flooded with surplus supplies. Many consignments ultimately failed to realize even the agents' commissions charged upon them.[3]

Both in London and New York, therefore, there were in 1854 all the ingredients of a violent crisis.[4] That the storm did not burst for another three years must be ascribed to the continuing Australian gold arrivals. In the latter part of 1854 and the first half of 1855, these more than made good the inroads into the Bank's reserve caused by the export of gold for the maintenance of the army in the East, and by foreign loans floated for War purposes. In consequence, the Bank imprudently followed the market rate downwards, reducing its minimum rate gradually to $3\frac{1}{2}$ per cent. by June 14, 1855. These reductions gave to the commercial world a false sense of security, which, together with activity in certain trades directly affected by demands for military supplies, served to maintain the rage for speculation. This must

[1] By Oct., 1854, production at Bradford had fallen to one-third of its "normal rate". (West Riding Inspector's Report, Oct. 31, 1854.)

[2] Activity in building of *steam* ships, however, continued.

[3] See Morier Evans, *op. cit.*, pp. 102–3.

[4] Considerable discredit was caused in June, 1854, by the disclosure of the notorious frauds by Davidson and Gordon and by Cole Bros., Colonial and Metal Brokers, who had raised large sums on fictitious warrants. Overend, Gurney & Co. were heavily involved, and it is from these revelations that their decline is generally dated.

explain, what otherwise seems inexplicable, the fact that the stream of new enterprises continued in the very trades where depression was causing constant retirements. One example must suffice. In Lancashire, 71 new cotton mills, with an aggregate power of 1877 " horses ", were set up in the year to October 31, 1855; while in the same period 38 mills, of 835 h.p., were closed down, and no power extensions were notified by existing factories.[1] The same period also witnessed a minor boom in flotations of banks and financial companies. The Bank of London, the City Bank, and the Western Bank of London, to mention the more important, all began operations in 1855–6; while among formations of ancillary banking companies there must be noted that of the National Discount Company, the first joint stock discount house, in early 1856.[2]

This sustained speculative activity could not fail to impose a strain on the money market, and the period from the autumn of 1855 until the actual crisis was one of high rates and frequent spasms of stringency. In September and October, 1855, a sudden Commissariat demand for gold so weakened the Bank's position that Bank rate was rushed up from 3½ to 6 per cent. in six weeks, and the minimum rate restricted to 60-day paper. But the arrival of new gold averted the expected panic, and after the cessation of hostilities the rate declined to 4½ per cent. Fluctuations of this order recurred several times; and it was in one of these sudden pressures (shortly after the collapse of the Royal British Bank) that the Bank first discriminated against the bill market—by restricting its re-discounts for " brokers " to bills of 30 days or less.[3] Despite the severity of this measure, the influx of Australian bullion prevented, as it did on a number of occasions subsequently, that extreme stringency which would have precipitated a collapse. " We have looked to the arrival of those steamers from Australia," said Chapman, " as much almost as to anything else, to know whether we were safe in going on

[1] Lancashire Inspector's Report for the year. (Tooke, *op. cit.*, p. 327.)

[2] The origin and early history of this house are fully discussed in the succeeding section. (See *post*, p. 217, *et seq.*)

[3] The restriction was imposed on Nov. 11, 1856. It caused " much derangement " of the money market and a marked reluctance on the part of the brokers to discount at all, even though the usual monthly advances were still obtainable on bills of longer date. (See *Economist*, 1856, p. 1269, and 1857 Committee, Minutes, Q. 34.) The new rule was dropped in Jan., 1857, but was reimposed on April 7, when the Bank also refused to advance for brokers for more than a fortnight on bills over 30 days. (See *Economist*, 1857, pp. 390, 404, and *The Times*, April 8, 1857.)

with our business." [1] Thus was speculation kept alive until the eleventh hour: as late as August, 1857, even the Governor of the Bank had no fears that trade was " otherwise than sound ",[2] and calmly arranged for the shipment of £1,000,000 of bullion to the East. Nor had the outbreak of the Indian Mutiny in June, and the general uneasiness which it created, prevented the Bank from reducing its rate from 6½ to 5½ per cent.

Thereafter events moved swiftly to a climax. In mid-September, uncertainty caused by adverse Indian news, a drain of bullion to the East, and rising Continental discount rates,[3] quickly became a general alarm upon receipt of news of a violent break in American security prices and of the disgraceful failure, on August 27, of the Ohio Life & Trust Co., with liabilities of $7,000,000. Advices in the next three weeks revealed wholesale bank suspensions (in New York sixty-two out of sixty-three banks stopped [4]), menacing unemployment, and discount rates of 18 to 24 per cent.[5] The repercussions in this country may well be imagined, for some £80,000,000 of American securities were estimated to be held by " English capitalists ", apart from the heavy commitments upon acceptance credits. Panic in Glasgow and Liverpool, severe pressure in London, and a drain of gold to America, forced three increases in Bank rate, to 8 per cent., in eleven days, two changes being made on " non-Court days ". Upon the increase to 7 per cent. (on October 12) no terms were announced for bill brokers' facilities, and the discount houses were obliged " to make arrangements from day to day ". This was a salutary check, for many houses had already been refusing even first-class bills at Bank rate, except when offered by clients whom they dared not offend; and even then they had carried the paper direct to the Bank for re-sale at the same rate.[6] One minor, but old-established, market firm failed two days afterwards.[7]

Mercantile failures then followed in quick succession,[8] beginning with the notorious Glasgow firms already mentioned.[9]

[1] 1857 Committee, Minutes, Q. 5310. [2] 1858 Report, Section 14.

[3] *Bankers' Magazine*, 1858, pp. 99–102.

[4] 1858 Report, Sections 15–16, 19.

[5] Total failures were put at 5,123, with liabilities of $299,801,000. Discounts at times reached 50 per cent. (See *Bankers' Magazine*, 1858, p. 103, and Morier Evans, *op. cit.*, pp. 92–147.)

[6] *Bankers' Magazine*, 1857, pp. 794–5, 848.

[7] S. F. Stephens, established before 1835.

[8] The course of the crisis is graphically described in the 1858 Report (Sections 18–34).

[9] *Ante*, p. 181, 182 *n*.

The Borough Bank of Liverpool, with deposits of £1,200,000 but £3,500,000 of London re-discounts, stopped on October 27, and on the following day Gurney's sought an assurance from the Bank that they would receive any loans they might require. The Bank directors, urgently pressed for assistance from all sides, from banks, bill brokers and commercial houses, and faced with a rapid drain of gold to Ireland and Scotland, raised their rate to 9 per cent. on November 5, and to 10 per cent. on November 9, when the reserve had dropped to £2,834,000. On the latter date, two days after the failure of the famous house of Dennistoun & Co., American bankers and exchange brokers (with liabilities of £2,142,701),[1] the Western Bank of Scotland failed. This produced the wildest panic in Glasgow, necessitating the calling out of troops, and culminating in the stoppage of the City of Glasgow Bank on Wednesday, November 11, and demands on the Bank for a further £1,000,000 of gold. Meanwhile, in London, urgent calling in of call loans had paralysed the bill market and driven all the brokers to the Bank, which was required to meet virtually the whole demand for discounts. On the Tuesday alone it had lent £1,126,000, of which £400,000 was for one "leading" discount house, and on the following day, when Sanderson's [2] failed, the amount was even larger. Despite a large increase in deposits from the London bankers, the reserve was reduced to £1,462,000; and the shock caused by Sanderson's suspension, bringing enormous demands upon Gurney's (they actually paid out £800,000 in one day),[3] made it plain that a suspension of the Act of 1844 would be inevitable. This was authorized on Thursday, November 12, on which day Gurney's did, in fact, receive £700,000 from the Bank.

[1] The partners in this house, which had branches in London, Liverpool, New York and New Orleans, besides its headquarters at Glasgow and an Australian associated house, held £208,873 shares in the Borough Bank. Its balance sheet at the date of failure, together with those of many of the other firms which failed, is given by Morier Evans.

[2] Sanderson's held £3,283,413 of bills at the date of failure, and had re-discounted a further £2,015,585. The bills included £132,000 from the Borough Bank, and £52,848 on other firms which had failed, while sundry loans and debtors of £287,566 were expected to realize £162,026 at the date of the first statement to creditors (Dec. 10). The estate was wound up under inspection and by 1859 had paid 11*s.* in the £. (See Morier Evans, *op. cit.*, pp. cxliv–cxlv.)

[3] Speech by Chancellor of Exchequer in debate on Bank Indemnity Bill (Hansard, Series 3, Vol. CXLVIII, Dec. 4). The speech contains an excellent account of the crisis, and especially of the effect of Sanderson's failure.

While the issue of the Government letter [1] led to some abatement of the panic, and certainly marked the turning-point in the crisis, it did not, as in 1847, immediately reduce the strain on the Bank. On the very day it was issued the directors lent £2,373,000, reducing the reserve to only £581,000; and the maximum "excess" issue of notes was not reached until November 20, when the figure was £928,000. Discounts, too, which on November 11 had stood at £15,900,000, continued to rise until November 21, when they touched £21,600,000, or more than the Bank's aggregate deposits.[2] Thereafter, the crisis gradually subsided. At one period, it had been virtually impossible to discount in the open market at all, "the charge under the most favourable circumstances being 12 to 15 per cent."; but towards the end of the month the leading houses became willing to work at fractionally under 10 per cent.[3] Just before Christmas, large arrivals of Australian and American gold, and a reflux from the country, enabled the Bank to reduce its rate to 8 per cent. Not for many months, however, did the trade of the country recover from the blow. No fewer than 85 important firms, involving a capital of £42,000,000,[4] apart from the banking suspensions, had collapsed in the two months before November 12, and at least fifty further failures occurred in the last seven weeks of the year, causing grave dislocation in every branch of commerce. So violent a purge [5] was inevitably followed by a period of extreme quiescence, which carried Bank rate down very rapidly in the opening weeks of 1858.[6]

The Bank Closes Market "Discount" Accounts

It was in this period of quiet that the Bank directors faced up to their problem. They had borne an unprecedented strain, and were determined to devise means of preventing its recurrence before the credit position could again get out of hand. Confronted daily by fresh revelations of the disgraceful methods of speculators, they might have been expected to seek, above all, a way to curb the more glaring mercantile abuses of the financial

[1] For the text of the letter, see 1858 Report, Section 24.

[2] *Ibid.*, Sections 25, 34.

[3] Morier Evans, *op. cit.*, p. 181.

[4] Disraeli in Indemnity Bill Debate, *loc. cit.*

[5] *The Times* (of Jan. 1, 1858) remarked that "of the 'disasters' just witnessed two-thirds at least are now admitted to have been palpable blessings, purging commerce from the most pestilent beings that ever disgraced its name".

[6] By February 11 it had reached 3 per cent.

machine. This was the obvious and, indeed, the only ultimate solution. Possibly it was considered by the board, and abandoned because of the extreme difficulty of devising adequate checks. At all events, what seemed to be an alternative solution was certainly much easier to apply in practice. It could be plausibly argued that if there had been no opportunities for bill market over-trading, then the serious abuse of bill credit would have been difficult or even impossible; and, accordingly, that one effective remedy would be to keep bill market activity within narrower limits. Such a restraint could readily be imposed by the simple expedient of withdrawing re-discount facilities from the market. That was, in fact, the "remedy" adopted; but it is open to doubt whether the Bank, in taking this step, was guided by even as broad a view of its functions, or of the whole problem, as that just indicated. What is more probable is that the directors, stunned by the extent of the crisis demands upon their reserve, thought only in terms of the Bank's own safety, quite narrowly interpreted.[1]

Neave, who was plainly obsessed by the problem of the bill market's reliance upon the Bank, declared that half of the Bank's loans and discounts during the crisis had been made to the bill brokers, "partly upon securities which, under other circumstances, the Bank would have been unwilling to accept".[2] This was an exaggeration, for the actual proportion was 26 per cent. of total advances, or 36 per cent. of London advances (including those made in London to Scottish banks)[3]; but the ratios were clearly large enough to substantiate Neave's plea that it was the bill market borrowings which were the direct cause of the Bank's exhaustion. These borrowings, he argued, were in turn produced by the call loan system. Thus he believed that a check to the bill market, which would automatically impose a check upon the practice of lending at call, would greatly reduce the potential strain upon the Bank. In deciding upon this course, he must also have been influenced by the fact that, under stress of emergency, when it really had no choice, the Bank had already taken a decision upon the most vital question of principle which was involved—the question of whether it ought to discriminate

[1] This view derives strong support from the Governors' own explanations to the 1858 Committee (see especially QQ. 397–719, 924–6).

[2] 1858 Committee, Minutes, Q. 526.

[3] Appendix 13 of the 1858 Report gives classified details for Oct., Nov. and Dec., 1857. The aggregate was £35,802,000 and the London total was £26,269,000, of which £9,456,000 was for bill brokers and discount houses. London merchant houses received £14,440,000.

against particular classes of the community on the sole basis of the trade which they happened to follow.[1]

Without waiting, therefore, for the verdict of the 1858 Committee,[2] or even for the conclusion of the Governors' evidence before it, the Bank elected to apply its own remedy. On March 13, 1858, it announced that in future the bill brokers and discount houses would be debarred altogether from the right to take bills to the Bank for discount, and that they would also be refused temporary advances, save only during the shuttings, when "quarterly" advances (but not discounts) would be open to them on the same terms as other applicants. Three days later[3] Neave thus explained the new rule:

> Hitherto the discount brokers have had access to the Bank at all times for discounts; the change made now is to decline giving them discounts any longer, but to make the transactions with the Bank confined entirely to advances. Those advances will be the usual quarterly advances, and if they apply for advances at any other times, they will be considered special, and dealt with accordingly. . . .
>
> The object is to keep the resources of the Bank more within her own compass, and not to give the opportunity to the discount brokers, who accumulate such very large sums in their hands, to rely entirely and totally for cashing their bills upon the Bank of England. When those who have deposited money with them want it, the discount brokers have been in the habit of considering that they could repay their loans at an hour's notice by merely coming over to the Bank, and asking for the cash to do it with. The immense drain upon the Bank in the last panic has shown that that power is an inconvenient one.

The announcement was received with open hostility in the bill market, and with criticism or qualified approval in the

[1] See *ante*, p. 196.

[2] The Report was issued in the following July. While it deplored in the strongest terms the reckless use of bills, accommodation paper and open credits, and criticized the bill brokers for accepting paper "upon the credit of the bank alone, without reference to the quality of the bills or otherwise", it offered no suggestions for the prevention of these abuses, possibly because the problem was not strictly within the Committee's terms of reference. Nor did it approve or comment upon the Bank's discrimination. On the central question entrusted to it, the question of the Bank Act, it gave no decisive answer, although it impliedly supported the Act in its entirety. "This is rather a verdict of 'not proven' than 'not guilty'," one contemporary aptly commented, "leaving the same question again to be tried on the next recurrence of a similar financial convulsion" (*Bankers' Magazine*, 1858, p. 657).

[3] 1858 Committee, Minutes, QQ. 397, 399.

technical press. The *Bankers' Magazine*, in its first comment,[1] asserted that " it is plain that the practice of the Bank of England in re-discounting for the bill brokers was just as inherently vicious as that of the bill brokers re-discounting for the joint stock banks ", and added that it was to be hoped that the rule of refusing advances as well as discounts would be " rigorously adhered to ". The argument was unfortunate, for joint stock re-discounting was demonstrably not *inherently* vicious, and a month later the journal radically altered its attitude. While it defended the Bank board against charges of having acted from ulterior motives, or personal " pique ", it described the step as " essentially arbitrary and exclusive " and thought that it might " even aggravate the derangement of the money market in critical times ".[2] To the extent that the change discouraged the abuse of re-discounting by provincial banks, checked imprudent bank competition for deposits, and compelled both banks and discount houses to " look farther forward " in engaging to repay deposits, the paper agreed that " the real interests of the community will be promoted ". But it " confessed to an apprehension that too much good must not be expected " from the new rule [3]:

> . . . Let us suppose a pressure to arise . . . that a great discount firm applies to the Bank for accommodation . . . upon unexceptionable securities. In numerous similar cases the Bank have readily extended assistance to establishments really solvent but temporarily embarrassed. Could they refuse to do so in the case supposed, knowing that the mere suspension of the house would involve the fall of hundreds of others, and infallibly precipitate a general crash ? If the new rule is not to hold good in such a case—and the Bank would not venture to uphold it—its assumed beneficial influence must be proportionately diminished.

---

[1] *Bankers' Magazine*, 1858, pp. 290–91. [2] *Ibid.*, 1858, pp. 340–2.

[3] Incidentally, the *Bankers' Magazine* considered that the Bank's shaft was " virtually aimed " at Overend, Gurney & Co., " the old established and eminent firm who monopolize the great bulk of the Lombard-street discount business ". It declared that it " would be difficult to exaggerate the importance of the functions discharged by these establishments " [the discount houses], which were " really bankers and dealers in money upon a collossal scale ", but remarked that the crisis had reduced their number to " less than half-a-dozen " discount houses, " properly so called ". " Of these only two carry on transactions upon an important scale." The paper thought that some merchants who had discounted solely with Gurney's " so long as they knew that their resources were practically inexhaustible ", would in future also open a discount account at the Bank, " whose position is thus rendered more elevated than ever ". But " those who see in the alteration at the Bank a fatal blow to the firm, labour under a great mistake "

The *Economist* made up its mind immediately, and argued on similar lines. While it supported any measure which would compel the brokers to establish reserves, which it considered even more necessary to the broker than to the banker (since the broker's call money represented bank reserves), it nevertheless regarded the Bank's discrimination against one class " without regard to the character of the house, its known capital, or the quality of the bills it may offer ", as a step " which every sound principle of business would point to as being as doubtful in its policy as it is novel in itself ".[1]

After eulogizing the distributive functions of the bill market, it pointed out that the new problem had arisen because the change from broker to dealer had concentrated within a narrow circle the responsibility which formerly was spread among all the various bankers in London and the country for whom the broker agents had acted. One apparent solution, failing a reversion to pure broking, was the establishment of " fair " market reserves ; but the *Economist* was doubtful whether this was practicable, pointing out that it would be costly to depositors and bankers (who would receive smaller allowances), and would necessitate a wider dealing margin, adding that " amid great competition it is difficult to maintain a rule the beneficial consequences of which come into operation only occasionally ". Moreover, the paper contended, even though the brokers *did* maintain larger reserves, the benefits would be negatived if the money were employed by the bankers to whom the reserves were entrusted ; and if these bankers did not employ the money, then the Bank of England, in its turn, might do so. It was upon the Bank itself, therefore, that the ultimate responsibility devolved :

> . . . It is, therefore, to the directors [of the Bank] that we must really look to maintain permanently, and at all times, a larger unemployed reserve than hitherto to meet the pressure of a crisis. . . . And when it is considered that the Bank pays no interest for the large deposits with which it is entrusted, there can be no excuse for a neglect of a precaution, to the necessity of which they now appear to be so much alive.[2]

---

[1] *Economist*, 1858, pp. 305–6.

[2] This was possibly a reference to the Governor's speech at the previous meeting of the Court, when Neave had defended the Old Lady against the taunt that her dividend was smaller than that of the " young ladies " by explaining that " in our position " it was necessary to maintain a much larger reserve than did the private banks. He also drew attention to the Bank's public duty. (See *Bankers' Magazine*, 1857, p. 820.)

Neave's rigorous cross-examination before the Committee [1] led to an almost identical conclusion : that while the rule was designed to protect the Bank in times of crisis, it was precisely at such a time that the directors would be least able to enforce it.[2] At other times the discount houses' demands had rarely been important, but the Governor agreed that in " moments of extreme difficulty when we have to step in to be useful, I do not know but what we should assist them ".[3] That did not, of course, prove that the rule was useless, for if it succeeded in keeping the *normal* market activities within reasonable bounds, then it was possible that the extent of mercantile over-trading before a crisis would also be limited, reducing proportionately the ultimate stress on the Bank. But it was also possible that if, for fear of over-trading, the brokers refused bills, the banks would take them direct. Neave would not, however, agree that the rule would discourage bill dealing, or in any way reduce the facilities afforded by the market, which (together even with the system of provincial re-discounts) he admitted to be enormously valuable. He thought that it would reduce the volume of market call money, and then was driven to concede that, in consequence, the bill market would afford a less safe medium for bank investment. He agreed that the market existed as much for the convenience of the banks—to keep their resources highly liquid—as for the public, and argued strongly that " money dealing " was " still virtually bill broking, because it is receiving the difference between the rate of interest in lieu of commission, and having no reserve ". But he thereby played into the hands of the questioner, who showed that just because the discount houses were in principle intermediaries, they gave security for all their borrowings, and could not, therefore, pursue the same reserve policy

[1] See 1858 Committee, Minutes, QQ. 397–403, 616–721, 924–31.

[2] Salomons, arguing that all good bills should *always* be discountable at the Bank, remarked that " the Bank of England will have great difficulty in getting rid of that inconvenient idea which is in the mind of the public, that the Bank of England is something more than an ordinary joint stock bank. I think it must depend very much upon the circumstances whether you can or cannot refuse the discounting of good bills which are offered to you." (1858 Committee, Minutes, Q. 1195.)

[3] On the question of advances, as opposed to discounts, the Bank would still be open to receive " special applications ", but would feel " more at liberty " to refuse them than it had previously felt. Its rule was to be a " wholesome method " of counteracting an " inconvenient impression "—the impression that the brokers " had only to ask for money to receive it ".

as a bank, implying that if they did so they could not as satisfactorily fulfil their true functions.[1]

In sum, Neave's examination not only destroyed a large part of his case, but proved conclusively, by its volley of well-reasoned questions from the Chairman, Sir Edward Cardwell, strongly backed by George Carr Glyn and several other members, that the Committee was highly sceptical of, if not actually opposed to, the Bank's " remedy ". The attitude of the Committee did not, however, shake Neave's belief in the soundness of the measure he had adopted, and not for many years was its modification contemplated.

The Practice of " Keeping Strong "

Fortunately for the bill market, what might otherwise have proved an almost crushing blow was greatly softened by the continuance of trade depression. Throughout 1858 there was an acute dearth of trade credit demands. " Deposits ", said the *Bankers' Magazine*, " are crowding in upon the banks daily, only to remain locked up in their strong-rooms, or to be sent for greater security to swell the practically useless hoards in the Threadneedle Street cellars." [2] The consequent plethora of

[1] Chapman's evidence on the same problem was given before the crisis, which, in a sense, makes it the more valuable. He thought that if ever the Bank were unable to discount for the brokers, then that would be an occasion for the suspension of the Bank Act, provided that the bills offered " were all representing the true commerce of the country, and all of undoubted security ". If " we stopped our discounts ", he declared prophetically, " the increase of discounts at the Bank would be quite frightful . . . it would create very great injury indeed ". The money dealers, he argued, merely represented the public, and were " only the medium by which the facilities in the banking world are managed ". If they did not go to the Bank, the public would have to do so direct. " But inasmuch as it is infinitely better done through the money dealer, who has all the sympathies of the market with him, and if there is £10,000 in Lombard-street he can find it, and bring it forth so long as there is no panic, it is a relief to all parties to do it quietly through the money dealer." He thought that " every person of proper delicacy " would abstain from unnecessary re-discounting, but if an approach once made were refused, it would be the public alone which would suffer. " A money dealer, if his affairs were in proper order, would soon rectify himself, assuming that there was no malicious feeling on the part of the Bank, which it is difficult to imagine . . . give us two or three days and we will never ask the Bank for a shilling." (See 1857 Committee, Minutes, QQ. 5190–3.)

[2] 1858, pp. 513–14. The year's average Bank rate, though only £3 4*s*. 7*d*. per cent., was over 9*s*. 6*d*. per cent. above average market rate.

funds saved the discount houses from the sudden spasms which formerly had sent them in haste to the Bank. They thus secured a convenient breathing-space in which to re-adjust their practice, and the larger houses, at least, made good use of it. Few could afford to hold large cash balances, but they did provide themselves with " reserves " in Exchequer bills and Consols sufficient to meet " an ordinary emergency should it arise ".[1] Secondly, they endeavoured, so far as possible, to reduce the proportion of deposits repayable at call, offering attractive differential rates for money repayable at notice.[2] Finally—and this applied also to the smaller firms—they sought to develop their " turnover " business by larger and more rapid re-sales to the banks. These changes were precisely those for which Neave had hoped; but any gratification they may have given him must have been much diminished by the further effects which shortly made themselves felt.

The first real test came at Easter, 1859, when fears that the country might be drawn into the Franco-Austrian war, crystallizing at a time when stock dealers were heavily " over-bought ", brought a violent Stock Exchange crisis, and upwards of 50 stock market suspensions, over 20 of which occurred on one day.[3] As the dividend date had been passed, the discount houses knew that they could not count upon Bank assistance, and therefore took extreme—even unnecessary—precautions. " The great bill brokers ", remarked the *Economist*,[4] " provided themselves with enormous reserves." At the first suspicion of trouble, they raised their rates even for the finest paper to Bank rate ($2\frac{1}{2}$ per cent.), and exacted much higher rates for second-grade bills. The result was an abnormal commercial demand on the Bank, which almost at once raised its rate to $3\frac{1}{2}$ per cent. Immediately, the London banks, fearing a " freezing " of their market loans, began to restrict facilities to the bill market, and refused to

[1] See letter from " *R. S. T.*" to a " daily paper " on Feb. 6, 1860, quoted by *Bankers' Magazine*, 1860, p. 158. Securities of this kind were apparently not ordinarily accepted as collateral, so that they could not be held extensively except by houses with large capital and some proportion of unsecured deposits.

[2] Separate rates were advertised for 3, 7 and 14 days, and special terms offered for long fixed deposits.

[3] It is noteworthy that two of the " first houses " in the Stock market would have failed but for assistance—one by Gurney's, and the other by Rothschild's. Gurney's were said to have been " among those most forward to render the necessary aid " wherever good securities could be offered. (See Morier Evans, *op. cit.*, pp. 151, 167.)

[4] 1859, p. 342.

discount save for their own customers. Discount houses, in their turn, were compelled to check demands upon themselves. No rates were quoted for six months' paper, 60-day bills were refused at anything less than Bank rate, and 4 per cent. was charged for three months' bills. Three days later the minimum market terms were $3\frac{3}{4}$ per cent. for 60 days, 4 per cent. for three months, $4\frac{1}{2}$ per cent. for four months, and $5\frac{1}{2}$ per cent. for five months. "Exceedingly numerous" mercantile demands were then made on the Bank, whose rate was raised to $4\frac{1}{2}$ per cent. on the following Court day.

That increase marked the climax of a pressure which, though short-lived and purely local in origin, had repercussions throughout the country. "The absence of assistance to the brokers and others", declared the *Times*,[1] "is producing an interruption to the general progress of the country; since the refusal to discount for them is preventing the negotiation of four months' and longer dated paper, which otherwise would be dealt with if the discount houses could secure partial facilities when they require them." Three months' bills, of course, could be taken direct to the Bank, but as longer acceptances were still essential in many trades, their loss of negotiability was a serious hardship. But, besides causing needless expense and inconvenience to traders, the Bank's rule was at least partially defeating its own object. The mere knowledge that the banks and discount houses were restricting facilities—almost wholly in consequence of the rule—was sufficient to produce a discount demand on the Bank out of all proportion to the volume of business rejected outside; and, through its reactions upon public sentiment, the effect was bound to be cumulative. But for these special factors, it seems probable that the "panic" of 1859, apart from a possible precautionary increase in Bank rate, would have been purely a stock market affair. As it was, the flurry caused general disturbance, and left its mark on discount rates for three months.

Nine months later an even greater pressure was produced by a less serious originating cause. In January, 1860, a "rage" for investment in India, which had been growing steadily from the time of the Mutiny,[2] led to a drain of gold to the Continent to pay for silver required for shipment to the East. This coincided with a weakening of the reserve by the payment of the dividends, and on January 19 the Bank unexpectedly raised its rate from

[1] May 6, 1859.

[2] See *The Times*, Jan. 20 and Feb. 1, 1860, and also the paper's review of the year 1857.

$2\frac{1}{2}$ to 3 per cent., reinforcing the rise by sales of stock. The very abruptness of the movement, coming upon a quiet money position, caused general uneasiness, and the bill market took immediate steps to " keep strong ". As before, this intensified the alarm, and sales of securities by the Bank, the London banks, and the discount houses led to such a fall in Exchequer bills that for a time they " could scarcely be considered saleable ".[1] Thereupon, the discount houses, finding that the very reserves they had provided to meet such an emergency could not be liquidated except at a heavy loss, " would hardly . . . discount for anybody ; and it need hardly be added that a step so unusual on their part caused immediately a good deal of public apprehension ".[2] Abnormal demands were therefore thrown on the Bank, and on January 31, without waiting for the weekly Court, the directors raised their rate to 4 per cent. That sufficed to diminish the external drain, and public excitement abated ; but continued caution on the part of the bill market and banks in carrying large reserves prevented any important easing of money rates.

From first to last, the spasm lasted barely a fortnight ; yet at one time it had produced " a degree of apprehension resembling, though by no means equalling, that felt in the panic of 1857 ". The *Economist* [2] quite openly blamed the Bank :

> The rise from $2\frac{1}{2}$ to 4 per cent. . . . would not, however, have of itself caused any such feeling as we have seen during this week in the City . . . it would have been easily borne when trade was acknowledged to be sound, when there was no rumour of speculation, when every one had long been complaining of quiescence, and when especially the resources of the Bank of England and of the discount houses were known to be ample. . . . The immediate cause of this remarkable state of feeling is the rule adopted by the Bank of England.

The whole problem, thus widely advertised, then became a topic of heated public controversy, for it had been realized that what at first appeared to be the private concern of the discount market and the Bank did, in fact, closely touch the interests of every trader and industrialist.

Discount Houses *versus* The Bank

Lombard Street itself became the scene of wordy battles ; long articles appeared in the daily as well as the technical papers ;

[1] *Bankers' Magazine*, 1860, p. 134. [2] *Economist*, 1860, p. 109.

letters were sent to the press ; and rival pamphlets were published in quick succession. Several of the latter merit detailed examination, especially as, in the opinion of the *Bankers' Magazine*,[1] they were singularly fair and temperate in tone—" a qualification rarely earned by writings on day-to-day finance " ! The first,[2] published in February in support of the discount houses, pointed out that—

> Since the new rule came into practice, the whole machinery of the money market has been subject to a succession of jerks never before experienced ; reaching such a dangerous pitch in April, 1859, and January of this year, that men found themselves abruptly encountered by actual panic, at periods when they were congratulating themselves on the almost unparalleled soundness of trade. . . . All, at length, were induced to suspect that the cause lay in the newly organised crusade of the Bank against the money dealers.

The writer, under the description of " *A.B.C.*", then contended that the rule was not only bound to have serious reactions upon the public—for short-term irregularities in the money flow were unavoidable—but that it could not achieve the ends for which it was applied. In particular, he argued that in the last resort, whatever the conduct of the market, the quality of bills created depended upon the rules enforced by the Bank and the banks for discounts and collateral, and that it was with them that the ultimate remedy for speculation lay ; that if, as some contended, the Bank sought to increase its own business, its attack was misdirected, for its real rivals were the joint stock banks, " into whose hands the present system is daily putting fresh power ". Yet " their managers and directors, almost without exception, are liberal enough to overlook their own interests, and advocate a relaxation of the objectionable restrictions now in force ".

A.B.C.'s own solution, since the Bank clearly could not afford *unlimited* facilities to the market, was that it should treat the discount houses much as it treated banks which had relinquished their issues in favour of Bank of England notes : that it should make them regular customers with a *minimum* as well as a maximum discount limit, any further assistance to be entirely within the discretion of the Bank. This, he believed, would solve the market's problem, would afford the Bank a regular and facile business, and would reassure that " very large portion of the

[1] *Bankers' Magazine*, 1860, p. 208.

[2] *The Bank of England and the Discount Brokers*, by *A. B. C.* (Richardson Brothers, Cornhill.)

public " which was totally excluded from the Bank because they found it inconvenient to keep direct accounts there. Somewhat similar views were expressed by another contestant,[1] who emphasized that not even severe sacrifices by some houses, in selling stock to aid their customers, had prevented a panic; and that a " middle course " would be to afford moderate assistance, proportioned to the capital of the applicants, in case of need.

These arguments provoked a vigorous rejoinder from a writer styled " *X* ",[2] who attacked *A.B.C.* for referring to the dealers as " brokers ", and virtually repeated Neave's denunciation of the call loan system, which he thought could not fail " to lead to constant apprehension, sudden contraction of facilities, shocks to credit, and disarrangement of the circulation ". He therefore " warmly applauded " the Bank's rule, on the ground that " casual relief is the worst mode of dealing with mendicants "! As the *Bankers' Magazine* pointed out,[3] *X* showed a " direct leaning " towards the Bank; that journal refused to accept his leading arguments, and, while refraining from advancing its own solution (*X* sought a reversion to " true " broking), hoped that the rule would be " in some degree modified ".

X's attack, however, had raised high indignation in Lombard Street, and shortly afterwards there appeared a considered " *Reply to X* ", by an anonymous writer believed at the time to be inspired by the discount houses, but who was not, apparently, the original *A.B.C.* At all events, this pamphlet was by far the best-informed of the three. The writer began by explaining that the change from broker to dealer had been necessitated by the mere increase in the scale and speed of mercantile transactions, and by the growth of deposit banking, which had led bankers generally to confine themselves to shorter bills than formerly. He then roundly attacked *X*'s assumption that the discount houses' practice was the same as had been condemned by the 1858 Committee:

> They do *not* conduct their business in the same way, neither will they revert to their old system, even if the Bank directors think fit to relax the regulation now in force. They admit that their former practice had a mischievous tendency, and have, as a body, refused to continue to take those unlimited amounts of call money, which they themselves acknowledge to be a most likely source of danger in times of pressure. The practice survives, from want of information, only in the imagination of *X*.

[1] Letter to *The Times* from *R. S. T.*, *loc. cit.*
[2] *The Grievance of the Discount Houses*, by *X* (Effingham Wilson).
[3] *Loc. cit.*, p. 213.

> Every dealer . . . is ready to admit that were he to return to old practices [taking excessive call money], he would have himself alone to blame for any ruinous consequences which might ensue from his misconduct. He would then be, what he can now only be wrongly accused of being, a banker without a reserve. Convinced of this, he has ceased to conduct his business on such a false basis, and moreover does all in his power to avoid very short notice of repayment of loans. If inquiry were made amongst the discount houses, it would be found that with the majority of them, the plan is pursued of re-discounting with bankers a large proportion of the bills received from their clients, thereby following up, as far as altered circumstances will permit, the method of the original brokers. And, as the next best alternative, they take loans at from 3 to 14 days' notice, and for fixed periods of from one to three months, offering in all instances the highest rates they can afford, to secure the advantage of the longer notice.

To judge from the comments of the financial press, there is no reason to doubt the accuracy of these assertions, which certainly did much to gain support for the discount houses' case.

The *Bankers' Magazine*,[1] advocating a relaxation, and arguing that in any case much distress had been caused by the failure to impose the rule gradually, supported *A.B.C*'s contention that it would not check speculation—

> . . . any measures tending to check undue speculation are deserving of approbation; and if the action of the Bank had this effect, it would doubtless receive general concurrence. But, in the first place, we hold that the alleged proofs that it would exercise such an influence, are by no means conclusive. Secondly, supposing them to be so, there can be pointed out many steps that would be equally obstructive, but would at the same time inflict much general injury. . . . That it will tend to check a headlong burst of speculation, which many persons appear fondly to expect it will do, seems so contrary to reason and precedent that it would be waste of time to discuss the point.[2]

The *Economist*, which in the early stages of the controversy had merely attacked the supposed claim of the market for *unlimited* emergency advances, and had stressed the dangers of excessive

[1] 1860, p. 278.

[2] Objective proof of the soundness of this argument was afforded only two months later. At the very time that the controversy was at its height, a wholly unsuspected, but amazingly complex, fabric of fictitious credits was being built up in the leather trade, this time without any sort of connivance from the legitimate discount houses or banks. (See *post*, p. 225.) (See *Bankers' Magazine*, 1860, pp. 529–32, 621–5.)

call loans,[1] now tackled the whole problem, virtually admitting the false perspective of its first article by referring to market practice as "*formerly* unsound ".[2] It still opposed any market dependence upon the Bank, but thought that absolute exclusion was dangerous. The inconvenience it caused to the public was "undeniably great ", while enforced refusals of discounts by the discount houses would not only damage their business, to the ultimate detriment of trade, but would always intensify any public discredit. " In the next panic ", the paper argued, " the credit of the bill broking firms cannot be as good as it was in the last ", when it had been known that the Bank would stand by them. " Sanderson's failed simply because they had no more good bills to offer." It then advocated a solution closely resembling that proposed by *A.B.C.*:

> Why should not the bill brokers become regular customers of the Bank ? The bill brokers, it is evident, must now keep some reserve . . . why should they not keep it at the Bank of England ? If the bill brokers habitually kept a large balance to their credit at the Bank of England, they would be good customers of the Bank, and would have a right to be treated as other good customers are.

This suggestion, like several others which have been mentioned, was both practicable and reasonable ; but the Bank stood its ground.[3]

" Intimidation " by Gurney's

Indeed, there is reason to believe that the board's policy was not wholly free from spite against the discount houses. If this be true, the defence would doubtless have been that the bill

[1] It had pointed out that if the rule were ever to be enforced, Jan., 1860, was a proper occasion for enforcing it—otherwise it would have become a dead letter. A banker, it was argued, had no obligations save to his customers ; the bill broker was not a customer of the Bank, but was actually its rival, ordinarily desiring neither to borrow from nor deposit with the Bank. At other times, he sought and expected advances which, in similar circumstances, " other bankers would not think it wise to make ", and which the Bank of England, more than any other bank, ought to be chary of granting. The Bank had a special duty to guard against " excessive and injudicious advances ". (*See Economist*, Feb. 4, 1860, p. 109.)

[2] 1860, p. 362.

[3] At the Bank Court on March 15, in reply to a request for exclusion of 30-day bills from the rule, the new Governor (Bonamy Dobree) did, however, concede that the rule would be " re-considered " if its continuance " would be adverse to the interest of the commercial community ".

market appeared to be the aggressor. Although, in February, reaction from the "panic" stringency brought an easing of market rates, the discount houses remained cautious; and, as soon as the quarterly advances became available, they made strong demands upon the Bank. This, as market interests contended, may have been due solely to fears of a recurrence of the January difficulties, but elsewhere it was freely stated that the market was acting maliciously. At all events, on March 29 the Bank unexpectedly raised its rate to 4½ per cent., thereby infringing the generally understood principle that it would never, except in emergency, raise the rate during the shuttings. Accordingly, the move was interpreted as an attack on the bill market, and even *The Times*, which had never shown any love for the discount houses, greeted it with strong criticism.[1]

Overend, Gurney & Co. thereupon determined to bring matters to a head. As their aim was to focus public attention upon the problem, they chose the most spectacular method open to them. On a single day in early April, on the eve of the dividend date, they withdrew from their account at the Bank no less than £1,650,000, all in £1,000 notes. The effect was an immediate rise in Bank rate to 5 per cent., followed by intense excitement in the City, which, being at first in ignorance of the cause, feared a repetition of the earlier squeeze. A few days later the matter was raised in the House of Commons, by a question to the Chancellor of the Exchequer. Gladstone's lengthy reply could have afforded little satisfaction to the Bank: while refusing to pre-judge the issue, he showed, by an insistence on Gurney's right to raise it in this fashion, that his sympathies were chiefly with the market:

> It is within the knowledge of all that whatever has been done in this case has been done, not so much as a private transaction, but rather in the exercise of a power which every mercantile house may think itself entitled to put into operation, in order to expose what it may think wrong in the existing state of the law, so as to bring into view what may be considered a public evil and thereby to produce and promote a disposition to apply a remedy. . . . The parties who are affected by this rule think it is a very bad and injurious rule—that it tends not only greatly to their own inconvenience, but to that of everybody else; but they likewise think it will tend to throw what they consider their own legitimate business into the hands of the Bank. These undoubtedly are very grave matters for consideration on both sides, and they well deserve

[1] *The Times*, March 30, 1860.

> deliberate investigation. . . . All these are matters lying far above the region of the mere selfish or personal interests of any mercantile establishment; they, in fact, cut deeply into the whole question of the policy of the present law.[1]

Ordinarily, no doubt, support from such a quarter, for a case already widely canvassed, would have made a strong impression on the Bank; but Gurney's action, which certainly was lacking in tact, had so embittered the controversy that an amicable settlement was no longer possible.[2] Although all the notes were returned within a fortnight, Gurney's were openly accused of intimidation, and even the *Economist* considered that they had succeeded only in showing their power.

Gurney's themselves argued[3] that, since their exclusion from the Bank, they always required, prior to the payment of the dividends, a cash reserve of between £1,000,000 and £1,500,000, because the interest of their depositors and customers " demands prudence and circumspection ". What, they asked, would be the result if other bankers and brokers followed their example, " to be prepared for any adverse contingency " ? The remedy which they sought was thus summarized[4]:

> The discount houses . . . fully recognise the right of the Bank to protect themselves, and to have a proper control over their own resources. They express themselves perfectly willing and even anxious to come to a business-like arrangement with the national establishment. They say, " Place us on the footing of your ordinary customers. Do not refuse to take from us bills of a character which you are prepared to take from other mercantile houses. Place, if you like, a limit upon the amount of accommodation which we may ask of you. Limit also, if you please, to 30 or 40 days the duration of the bills you will discount for us. Take from us no bills of the soundness of which you are not perfectly satisfied. In order that the arrangement may not be one-sided, we will agree, if you consider it requisite to your position as bankers, to have always a *minimum* amount under discount with you, no matter if the rate of discount elsewhere is lower. We are likewise willing to lodge a considerable *minimum* drawing balance permanently in your hands. Finally, we are prepared to discuss with you, in a dispassionate spirit, any proposition, as between one moneylender and another, that you may think reasonable."

The *Bankers' Magazine*, supporting this proposal, argued that if the Bank had any reason to complain of the withdrawal,

[1] Hansard, Third Series, Vol. CLVII, Cols. 2002–7.
[2] *Cf. Bankers' Magazine*, 1860, p. 280.
[3] *Ibid.*, pp. 361–2. [4] *Ibid.*

"they ought to remember that the graceful submission of their opponents has placed them in the apparent situation of victors . . . it would be a corresponding act of courtesy for the Bank to modify their rule".

But the dispute had passed beyond the stage at which "graceful courtesies" could be expected, and it is not surprising, though regrettable, that the Bank refused to listen to the arguments raised by its critics. Had it done so, it would have perceived that the controversy had revealed not only the essential weakness of its policy, but also the real solution of the whole problem raised in 1857. That solution lay in the assumption by the Bank of a direct *qualitative* control of credit. To restrict its own facilities quantitatively, in the hope that thereby others would be impelled to improve the quality of their commitments, was inadequate, if not actually useless; while at times it could be positively dangerous. Direct qualitative control demanded that the Bank, by exercising a rigorous discrimination against speculative bills or accommodation paper, should itself set an example to the other banks and the market; that this discrimination should be applied with especial care to re-discounts for the discount houses, and that, as an additional precaution, such re-discounts should be confined where possible to bills of shorter currency than the Bank held itself open to discount for its private customers; finally, that every market house should be given clearly to understand that, while the Bank would always re-discount legitimate short bills, the total accommodation to be afforded, even on such security, would always be considered strictly in relation to the capital and private resources of each applicant. By such means, any discount house which was guilty of over-trading or of knowingly taking bad bills would immediately be penalized, and would run grave risk. The banks, lest they should be involved with a house which might be debarred from re-discount facilities, would scrutinize closely all bills received from the market, whether for outright purchase or as collateral. Discount houses, in their turn, would be compelled to demand a high standard of paper from the banks and traders for whom they re-discounted, and thus would the example set in Threadneedle Street exert a powerful influence upon the quality of bill credit throughout the country.

Such principles were eventually to become the corner-stone of the Bank's market and credit policy, but their complete adoption did not occur for several decades after 1860. The 'sixties, therefore, were marked by a pronounced lack of co-operation between the Bank and the bill market; and the friction was increased, rather than lessened, by the decision of the larger houses virtually to ignore the Bank, and to refrain from borrowing even during the shuttings.[1] These special sources of disturbance, unfortunately coinciding with a rapid increase in the sensitiveness of the market to external influences, resulted in constant derangement of the credit position, and extreme instability of rates. Such instability was accentuated by the fact that the Bank, deprived of the steady supply of bills previously furnished by the market, found it necessary to follow market rate rather more closely than it had done in the 'fifties, and the average differential between the two rates was perceptibly narrowed.[2] The net result of these various influences was a surprising increase in the number of Bank rate changes—in the sixteen years from 1860 to 1875 there was an average of 11 changes yearly (24 occurred in 1873), in contrast with 4 changes yearly in 1845–59.

So variable a policy naturally aroused much criticism, especially when, to retain contact with the market, the Bank reduced its rate, only to find that the movement had to be reversed in a week or so. On one such occasion in the spring of 1863 it was remarked [3] that if the Bank directors did not retrace their steps, they became " the laughing-stock of Lombard Street, and of the body of brokers, who, ever since their exclusion from re-discount at that establishment, have not neglected to bring the directors and their guiding policy into ridicule ". Similar tactics were apparently adopted by the Bank's supporters, among whom was *The Times*, of which it was said that it " omits no labour of love in giving the discount houses in general, and Messrs. Overend, Gurney & Co. particularly, a malicious dig ".[4] It would be difficult to find more striking illustrations of the disharmony of the period—a disharmony which was scarcely conducive to the smooth working of the credit machine, and which frequently had unfortunate repercussions upon the commercial world.

[1] See *Money Market Review*, June, 1860.

[2] In 1852–6 Bank rate on the average exceeded market rate by 6*s*. 8*d*. per cent.; in 1858–64 the similar excess was 5*s*. 8*d*. per cent.

[3] By the *Bankers' Magazine*, 1863, p. 472.

[4] Reply to *The Times* by another " leading daily " in Sept., 1860, cited and supported by the *Bankers' Magazine*, 1860, pp. 710–12.

CHAPTER VII

THE RISE OF THE DISCOUNT COMPANIES [1]

It is an interesting paradox that the decade from 1856, probably the most troubled in the whole history of the market, witnessed more important discount formations than any other. Two factors gave the movement its initial impetus—contemporary banking development and the introduction into the joint stock legal code of the principle of limited liability. Banking expansion in the early 'fifties, accompanied by rapid increases in bank profits and dividends and a boom in bank shares, had not only vindicated the joint stock principle, but had drawn attention to the very large profits which could be won from financial business in general, and from discounting in particular. This led to reflections upon the great prosperity and power enjoyed by the bigger discount houses, and upon the "almost fabulous fortunes" [2] amassed by their partners, notably by Samuel Gurney. The rapid growth of bill dealing on the one hand, and the public appetite for new investments on the other, suggested that there was ample scope for a discount *company*; and that such a concern, with ability to attract a larger capital than all but the most wealthy private houses could hope to achieve, could be even more successful than the joint stock banks, especially as it could be formed, as a bank then could not, upon the new principle of limited liability.

[1] The material contained in this section, especially the figures of the various companies, has been gathered from so wide a range of sources that the system of detailed references, followed elsewhere, has not been found practicable in this case. The principal sources, however, were the *Bankers' Magazine*, *Bankers' Almanac*, and the *Economist*, all of which often reproduced the actual accounts of the companies concerned, and gave full reports of their meetings. To facilitate reference, and to clarify the text, the salient facts about the companies mentioned have been tabulated in a chronological table according to dates of formation. This will be found in App. I, *post*, p. 324.

[2] See *Bankers' Magazine*, 1859, p. 149; and *post*, p. 246.

Such considerations prompted the formation of the National Discount Company, Ltd., the first joint stock discount house and one of the first limited companies, in conditions which could hardly have been less propitious. It was launched at a time of almost crisis money rates, and when " the whole energies of the country "[1] were diverted by the Crimean War. The prospectus appeared in February, 1856 (when Bank rate stood at 6 per cent.—for 60-day bills), and invited public subscriptions for £1,000,000 in £25 shares, upon which only £5 was to be called up. It declared that the company was to carry on a " general discount business ", and was " not to act in any respect as a bank ".[2] The project was strongly backed, and the personnel of its board of twelve, under the chairmanship of Francis W. Russell, M.P., led the *Economist* to remark [3] that " the high respectability of the names put forth is a guarantee of good faith, and we have no doubt that the projected institution will be of immense value to the mercantile body ". This backing, together with the fact that the management was entrusted to men of experience—William Shipman,[4] from Gurney's, and R. P. Webber, from the London Joint Stock Bank —must explain what in the circumstances was an amazingly successful flotation. Although the company did not begin operations until June 2, by July, before any results had been submitted to the proprietors, it was convening a special meeting to sanction a doubling of the capital, explaining that the original amount had been restricted " partly because " of the stringency current in February.[5] By the date of this meeting —July 15—39,252 of the initial 40,000 shares had been taken up, and a further 40,000 were thereupon offered to existing shareholders at 10*s*. premium.

This spectacular beginning, and the reputed progress of the business, indicated by the premium on its shares, speedily brought a rival into the field. In the autumn it was announced that the London Discount Company, Ltd., was to be formed with an even larger initial capital—£1,000,000 in £20 shares, to be £5 paid-up. This company also procured an M.P.—

[1] See *Bankers' Magazine*, 1859, p. 149.

[2] A copy of the prospectus, reproduced by courtesy of the company, will be found in App. II, *post*, p. 325 ; see also *The Times*, Feb. 9, 1856, p. 7.

[3] 1856, p. 178.

[4] See *post*, p. 258.

[5] Bank rate was reduced to $4\frac{1}{2}$ per cent. by the end of June.

William Scholefield—for its chairman, and derived its joint managers from Gurney's (G. Brightwen) and Sanderson's (A. Kelly, formerly chief clerk). But although the National model had been closely followed, the reception was less friendly, for the early stages of the flotation unfortunately coincided with the failure of the Royal British Bank, involving alarming disclosures which brought great discredit upon all joint stock financial institutions. The Press, too, adopted a cautious attitude, the *Bankers' Magazine* remarking [1] that, " as the sum introduced into this branch of business will, with the addition now proposed, be fully adequate to all the requirements of the time, it may be hoped that no further attempts at rivalry will be encouraged until ample experience shall have demonstrated a necessity for them ".[2] For these reasons, applications lagged, and only 35,647 of the 50,000 shares were taken up. Nevertheless, the company opened for business on December 18.

The first report of the National seemed to justify the high hopes which had been entertained. In the seven months to the end of 1856 it had discounted £5,926,414 of bills, had opened 845 accounts, and was able to show a net profit of £7,767 (nearly 7 per cent. per annum on the capital actually employed). Of this, it distributed £6,376 in a dividend representing just over 5 per cent. per annum for seven months. So sanguine a policy was inevitably misplaced. Only a fortnight after the dividend was declared, £11,801 of bills were returned through a failure in the Levant trade,[3] which eventually involved the company in a loss of £5,800. Other bad debts followed,[4] adverse rumours were circulated, and the shares dropped sharply. In July, 1857, when an extraordinary meeting was called to elect a new auditor (the original auditor having been appointed to the board), it was reported that the half-year's losses (estimated at £16,000) had exceeded the net profits, including the carry-forward. This experience, it was explained,[5] had " brought home " to the directors the need for " more active supervision, which they believe to have been secured by the appointment

[1] 1856, p. 774.

[2] The *Daily News*, however, supported the new concerns, remarking in its annual review for 1856 that there was " no reason why discount business should not be successfully carried on by companies, as well as by private firms and joint stock banks ".

[3] Franghiadi & Sons, who failed on Feb. 20, 1857.

[4] Notably £9,600 in two timber failures in April and May.

[5] See report of the meeting in *Bankers' Magazine*, 1857, p. 764 *et seq.*

of a permanent committee of three of their number to be in constant daily communication with your managers, and to aid them with their counsel and advice ". The board pointed with pride to the fact that in its first complete year the company had discounted £10,441,067 (£4,984,652 in the first half-year, and £5,456,415 in the second), and recalled that conditions had been unfavourable. Despite these explanations, the meeting proved stormy, especially when the temporary auditor—the eminent J. E. Coleman—complained that the information given was inadequate; that at least £18,000 would be required for bad debts; that the purchase of premises was injudicious and their price excessive [1]; and that preliminary expenses ought to have been written-down before a dividend was paid. From the nature of the chairman's reply, it is apparent that some shareholders then proposed that the company should be wound up while their capital was still virtually intact.

Owing possibly to the difficulties of the National, and to the rumours current about it, the board of the London Discount pursued a conservative policy from the start, emphasizing the need for establishing a reserve before dividends could be paid. The first—and very detailed—accounts, covering 6½ months, showed a net profit of £11,276, of which £3,948 was reserved for rebate (at 6 per cent.), £3,495 for bad debts, and £3,833 was carried forward, this last item more than balancing the preliminary expenses. The company was, of course, much smaller than the National, and the difference at this stage was accentuated by the decision of the board, in view of the difficulties of the time, including " recent disclosures affecting some joint stock companies ", to limit discounts in the initial period to the " moderate sum of £2,500,000 ". Nevertheless, the deposits (which both companies merged with re-discounts in their published accounts) had at times reached £1,500,000, connections had been established with over 40 banks, and between 400 and 500 discount accounts had been opened. The relative position of the two companies at June 30, 1857, is shown by the following table [2]:

[1] The company had begun at temporary offices at 25, Birchin Lane, but almost immediately negotiated for a substantial site at 33, Cornhill, securing a lease at £6,000 per annum (plus £1,100 ground rent) on payment of £13,000 to outgoing tenants. At June 30, 1857, £18,495 had been spent, and the total cost was estimated at £30,000. It actually exceeded £44,000.

[2] Compiled from the accounts and reports of the meetings of the two companies.

	London Discount.	National Discount.
At June 30, 1857 :	£	£
Paid-up capital	178,235	386,605
Cash	16,208	19,324
Discounts and securities	1,157,291	2,397,652
Preliminary expenses	3,381	5,615
Balance sheet total	1,178,992	2,441,265
Half-year to June* 30, 1857 :		
Turnover	2,500,000	5,456,415
Bills returned unpaid	6,991	29,100
Profit before bad debts	7,328	15,362
Bad debts	3,495	16,000

* Initial 6½ months' trading for London Discount.

Such a comparison, which some shareholders of the London Discount evidently made, was definitely adverse to the National, despite its six months' " start ", and one shareholder of the smaller company, in congratulating the board, remarked that " our condition contrasts well with a neighbouring institution, which is supposed to be doing everything ".[1]

Taunts such as these doubtless served to force home to the National board the lesson of the first year's trading—a lesson which otherwise must have been learnt, at infinitely greater cost, in the 1857 crisis. As it was, the company took in sail just in time, and came through the crowded half-year which followed with a loss of only £11,000, which was comfortably covered by a net profit (after £18,400 for rebate) of £15,921. This was a surprising tribute to the new policy, which was reflected in the end-1857 accounts by a contraction of the balance sheet total from £2,441,265 to £1,946,536 and in a decline in the half-year's turnover to some £5,110,000.[2] The new report was, indeed, a model of conservatism—the rate taken for rebate, previously none too generous, was now disclosed, and was maintained at the 6½ per cent. ruling at the date of the accounts, despite a subsequent decline in market rates to half that figure ; a first step was made to reduce preliminary expenses ; and a balance of £3,127 was carried forward. The London Discount followed a similar policy of contraction—its turnover was reduced to £2,372,000 and its balance sheet total to £1,035,119—and in this was almost

[1] Nevertheless, another shareholder argued that discount business was too inherently risky, and, while admitting that the board had exercised " every possible care ", advocated winding-up—a proposal which evoked some support and much heated discussion, but which was finally lost by a " triumphant majority ".

[2] This figure is based on some percentage changes disclosed at a subsequent meeting.

equally successful, for expected bad debts were no more than £5,500, compared with net profits of £6,296.

For two companies in a business so sensitive to credit disturbances, and contending with the special prejudices against limited liability,[1] to face in their first year difficulties as extreme as those of 1857, and yet to emerge with credit unshaken and capital intact, is an achievement whose equal would be hard to find. But it failed to satisfy some of their proprietors, and at both meetings resolutions were again advanced for voluntary winding-up, one shareholder of the London Discount moving an alternative proposal that steps be taken to amalgamate with the National.[2] Both companies did, in fact, benefit from the crisis, not only through the improved credit which sprang from their success, but, as the London chairman remarked (with his eyes on Bruce's and Sanderson's connections), also through the " narrowing of the extent of competition ". In the following half-year, despite post-crisis depression, dividend payments were resumed by the National and initiated by the London, both paying 5 per cent. per annum (tax free) out of profits of more than 10 per cent.; while over the whole of 1858 the balance sheet totals of both companies were more than doubled.[3] Part of this additional business was apparently obtained at the expense of the private houses,[4] for by early 1859 the *Bankers' Magazine* was asserting [5] that " the discount companies are absorbing a considerable amount of the business that previously found its way to the private

[1] See chairman's speech at National Discount (first annual) meeting on February 6, 1857.

[2] The chairman's retort—that theirs was no " bubble scheme " and that the board would do nothing to " compromise the interests " of the company—is amusing in the light of subsequent developments.

[3] In the first half of 1858 the National's *turnover* was £6,130,000, but for later periods no indication of turnover was afforded.

[4] At this stage, at all events, the companies almost certainly gained from the fact that their position was apparently revealed to all the world in their published accounts, whereas the 1857 crisis had shown that private firms could for long retain first-class credit though their portfolios included many unrealizable or even fictitious securities. The public had yet to learn how much a balance sheet could *hide*! It may also be noted that the joint stock principle gained rapidly in public favour after the discussions in 1858 which culminated in the extension (in July) of the limited liability device to banking companies, should they wish to adopt it. A powerful argument in support of this change had been that the discount companies, which in some respects were rivals of the banks, could and did register with limited liability. (See *Bankers' Magazine*, 1858, pp. 209–13, 443–6.)

[5] 1859, p. 140.

bankers and private firms. Even some of the large provincial banks now make them depositories of funds which used to be employed in other channels." Their success was also beginning to attract attention, and the same journal, after listing the enormous difficulties which had confronted " this novel experiment " and declaring that failure would have been excusable, confessed to astonishment that, " in so short a period, the prosperity of these establishments has been made certain ".[1]

Discount Companies in the Leather Crisis

It was at this stage, before the adverse effects of the Bank's rule had made themselves felt, that the bill market first became the medium for undesirable flotations.[2] In the spring of 1859, one Albert Gottheimer, a former wine merchant and unknown in Lombard Street, put forth a prospectus for the Mercantile Discount Company, Ltd., which was to have a capital of £200,000 in £50 shares, £25 paid, and was to establish agencies in Liverpool, Manchester and other centres. The high-sounding character of the scheme, or the undoubted astuteness of its founder, convinced the *Bankers' Magazine*, which, in an obvious " puff ",[3] referred to the need for discount facilities " on reasonable and equitable terms ", and affirmed that the private houses " were not exactly the places where the general public could find accommodation " ! This, the paper argued, explained the formation of the National and the London, whose business was " quite sufficient to justify the formation of others ". The new concern, thus graciously introduced, promised 10 or 12 per cent. dividend in its first year, despite low money rates, and, in the view of the *Bankers' Magazine*, " very fairly argued " that the " slightest advance " in rates would augment its dividends. Its flotation coincided with the Stock Exchange " panic ", and only the strenuous efforts of the managing director—Gottheimer—and his friends, who certainly included several thoroughly discreditable " financiers ", procured

[1] *Ibid.*, p. 565.

[2] A third company—the General Discount Co., Ltd., with a paid-up capital of £11,543—had, in fact, started in Nov., 1857, almost in the throes of the crisis. There is no indication that it was a " ramp ", but its business was conducted on unsound principles. With a view to attracting *trade* deposits, it offered a *fixed* rate for all amounts up to a certain limit, and guaranteed repayment on demand. It collapsed in 1860, when, incidentally, its liabilities included £5,000 to two other discount houses.

[3] 1859, p. 349.

subscription for 1,720 of the 4,000 shares offered. Operations were nevertheless begun on May 16, 1859. They were said to have been hampered by the "not too favourable position" of the other two companies, but in the first 7½ months the turnover amounted to no less than £3,031,355—more than the London Discount had transacted with four times as much capital. A 10 per cent. (tax-free) dividend was thereupon paid, and was ostensibly fully earned. This brought great credit upon Gottheimer, who was warmly applauded [1] by both board and shareholders for the substantial business he had introduced. Just how he succeeded in doing so is best indicated by the following incident related by one of the company's clients:

> . . . Mr. Henry John Barker introduced me to Mr. Albert Gottheimer, who . . . was at that time studying closely the LIMITED SYSTEM. Mr. Gottheimer was willing to discount my promissory note of £3,000 for one week for the premium of £100, provided I gave him as collateral security a bill of mortgage on one of my small steamers, which he pledged his word of honour not to register in the Custom-House until the promissory note came to maturity. He further kindly promised that, should it not be convenient to me to take up the *petit billet* at the expiration of the time, he would renew on the same terms, and continue to do so, provided I invested £1,000 or £1,200 in the shares of the Mercantile Discount Company, Ltd., which was paying, he said, 15 per cent. per annum. . . . I took the shares to oblige him, and they soon burned my fingers.[2]

In January, 1860, the board had the effrontery to offer 1,280 shares at £2 10*s.* premium (10 per cent.), and apparently secured subscription for them; but whether they were ever paid up was never disclosed in the published reports.

Unfortunately for Gottheimer, the dangerous career of this concern was abruptly checked by difficulties which affected even the strongest of the new companies. In 1859, the first real impact of the Bank's rule upon the market had led both the London and the National to take steps to strengthen their position, notably by contracting their operations and establishing larger independent reserves. The National, indeed, accumulated £450,000 in Government securities, very little of which was apparently pledged as collateral against deposits. This policy

[1] At the meeting held on Jan. 18, 1860. It was evident that the board as a whole was ignorant of discount business, and unaware of Gottheimer's methods.

[2] Stefanos Xenos, *Depredations; or Overend, Gurney & Co., and the Greek and Oriental Steam Navigation Company* (1869), pp. 56, 57.

enabled both companies to withstand the recurrent shocks caused by the current disharmony in the market, but it did not save them from losses in a fresh accommodation bill scandal.

In the early months of 1860 it was freely rumoured that several small concerns in the leather trade were in difficulties, but as the trouble was believed to be confined to these firms, the rumours raised no alarm among the discount houses, although leather discounts were very large. At the end of June, however, the failure of one of the small firms suddenly revealed that Streatfeild, Laurence & Mortimore, the largest concern in the trade, was heavily involved, on what looked suspiciously like accommodation paper. These suspicions were quickly confirmed, for Streatfeild's failed three days later, with liabilities totalling £982,656, almost immediately bringing down their associated Liverpool house (Laurence, Mortimore & Schrader), with liabilities of £329,701. Within three weeks no fewer than thirty leather firms collapsed, with liabilities aggregating close upon £3,000,000.[1] The bankruptcy proceedings disclosed, what had been hidden from even the shrewdest bankers and bill dealers, that a large part of the whole trade had been conducted upon a vast system of fictitious credits, of which Streatfeild's had been the centre. This firm, until within a few days of its failure, had enjoyed first-class credit, and its partners possessed large estates. These proved to be fully encumbered, and letters were produced at the examination to show that for years the firm had maintained a regiment of agents for the purpose of drawing or accepting fictitious bills. These had been circulated both by the firm itself and by its many embarrassed debtors, to whom it had " advanced " manufactured paper for a commission.[2]

So unsuspected a collapse inevitably brought heavy losses to the banks and the bill market. Overend, Gurney & Co. were

[1] Many details of the failures will be found in the *Bankers' Magazine*. (See 1860, pp. 529–32, 542–4, 621–5, 710–12, etc.)

[2] The system had actually existed before the 1857 crisis, in which Streatfeild's had been assisted by the Bank of England. Accommodation drawings apparently originated with the renewal of debts due to the firm ; but the indebtedness, instead of being gradually liquidated, steadily increased, and the resultant bad debts became the basis of accommodation bills. To prevent detection through repeated renewals, inter-debtor drawings were arranged. Specific instances were exposed where Streatfeild's instructed debtors to send goods to factors for the sole purpose of drawing against them, and where, when one acceptor's name had been too freely used, satellite firms were told to draw on others specified by Streatfeild's. (See examination of W. G. Gibson, *Bankers' Magazine*, 1860, pp. 827–33.)

the most heavily involved, with over £150,000 of Streatfeild's acceptances alone, a fact which aroused a good deal of criticism. This was increased when, in the bankruptcy proceedings, it was revealed that D. Ward Chapman (D. Barclay Chapman's son) had exclaimed, on hearing of the firm's difficulties, " Oh ! You must not stop "—and had promptly lent another £20,000 on " lock-up " securities.[1] Censure on this point was possibly rather overdone, for Chapman had been deliberately misled by the debtors ; but the incident brought considerable discredit upon other discount houses involved in the failures. So exaggerated were the rumours about the losses of the London and the National that both companies promptly announced their position. That of the National was, indeed, comparatively satisfactory, for the company held only £46,831 of the bills of the failed firms, and put the final loss at £23,000 ; while, thanks to a substantial rise in profits, it was able to maintain its 5 per cent. dividend and yet raise its reserve (and carry-forward) to £31,003. The London Discount, however, held £52,000 of dishonoured bills, and expected a loss of about £21,000, which, in proportion to its resources, was double that of the National. Even so, this was not really a crippling loss, for, by passing its dividend, the company was able to raise its reserves to £19,513.

Nevertheless, the experience created widespread alarm among the shareholders. Although the half-yearly meeting, held in August, evoked no strong comments, it was later disclosed that the board had already reached an understanding with prominent shareholders that it would at once consider the expediency of winding-up. The chairman, and three other directors, who had been seeking to safeguard the company by strengthening its management, strongly opposed the proposal, and promptly resigned when outvoted. In November, 1860, therefore, a meeting was called and presented at once with the board's proposal for immediate liquidation.[2] The board argued that although the capital was still practically intact—total losses were estimated at £25,000, against undivided profits aggregating £22,173—experience had shown that the probable return was much less than commensurate with the risks involved. Over the four years of the company's trading, it was said, net profits had totalled £60,000, of which £47,000 had been swallowed up by bad debts ; while, on the assumption that no dividend could be paid for the

[1] *Bankers' Magazine*, 1860, pp. 725–8 (Examination of Streatfeild, Laurence and Mortimore).

[2] See report in *Bankers' Magazine*, 1860, pp. 898–905.

fifth year, the average return over five years would be only 1½ per cent. " Discount business," said the (temporary) chairman, " is inherently very hazardous, and calls for a very large profit indeed." Streatfeild's case, he contended, was not exceptional, and against such methods he saw no possible protection :

> If this company, in discounting bills of that firm, were not satisfied with public rumour as to their credit, and went into the bills themselves, what would they have found ? Why, that the bills themselves were drawn upon different tanners and leather factors in various parts of the country ; that they would bear the strictest examination, and carried upon their face the appearance of bona-fidedness. It would have been explained that Streatfeild & Laurence supplied these persons with the hides that they were to tan, and afterwards sold their leather for them. . . . The whole transaction would carry upon it that which was most to be desired—namely, value received.

To these arguments was added the fact that the Bank's rule had increased the risk " most frightfully ", and it was said that a discount house needed a reserve double that of a bank—£100,000 for the London Discount. Another shareholder affirmed that discount companies tended to get " more of the rough, and less of the smooth " than private houses. These arguments, together with the fact that the board, in publishing the resolution, had virtually pre-judged the issue, overwhelmed a strong opposition, and the liquidation began.[1]

It naturally aroused much surprise, for the company's *total* bad debts, compared with its aggregate turnover (£33,000,000), had amounted to no more than 1·4 per mille, which did not seem to suggest enormous hazards ; and it was recognized on all sides that the board, " including some of the best known and most favoured names in the City ",[2] had been both cautious and competent. Two principal explanations of the winding-up were stressed by the financial press. First, that the Bank's rule, necessitating larger capital, had pressed especially heavily upon the companies, whose capital was virtually fixed and had been determined before the rule was made. " The change," said the

[1] Two houses well-known in the market of to-day arose out of the ruins of the London Discount, for G. Brightwen, one of its joint managers, set up on his own account as Brightwen & Co., at 8, Finch Lane. This firm became Brightwen, Gillett & Co., but in 1867 Gillett separated from Brightwen, and established Gillett Bros. & Co., at 72, Lombard Street. In 1919 the firm was converted into the present private company of Gillett Bros. Discount Co., Ltd.

[2] *Bankers' Magazine*, 1860, pp. 861–5.

Bankers' Magazine, " was felt by every establishment. . . . Private establishments might meet the pinch by special resources and the profits of former years; but . . . a company is proverbially inelastic in all that relates to capital. . . . And what hope was there that the shareholders of a young company, whose average dividend had not exceeded $1\frac{1}{2}$ per cent., would agree to double its capital?" Secondly, it was argued that companies, whether limited or not, were peculiarly unsuited to discount business. Bill dealing, said the *Economist*,[1] was an exceptionally difficult trade: unlike an ordinary trader, the dealer could not afford bad debts, and unlike a banker, who had the evidence of his ledger to guide him, the dealer had no special aids to the discovery of who was sound and who was not. To avoid bad debts demanded long experience of the business and unremitting care, neither of which could readily be secured from a paid manager, however conscientious. The *Bankers' Magazine* argued similarly, adding that the belief that the companies were less vigilant than the private firms made them a prey to unscrupulous traders. " To that class who abound in all trading communities, whose needs, difficulties, recklessness and unscrupulousness shade down so finely through all the gradations from embarrassment to downright roguery, a discount company is their very city of refuge. . . . They swarm to it in shoals." [2]

The explanations, however, were not entirely convincing, for the opposition could point to the success of the National. General preoccupation with this controversy apparently explains why the scandal of the Mercantile Discount passed almost unnoticed. The *Bankers' Magazine*, in an oblique reference to the Mercantile, had indeed remarked [3] that one " minor " establishment had " adventured out of their depth in paper they should not have touched ", adding that " some very questionable operations have been brought to light in connection with the mode of dealing pursued "; but the paper refrained from comment upon the

[1] *Economist*, 1860, pp. 1392–3.

[2] The *Economist* laid down what it called the " true rules of bill-broking " for the avoidance of losses: (1) Insistence on two-name paper and self-liquidating transactions; (2) Knowledge of an applicant's discounts *elsewhere*, and of his advances and acceptances; (3) Demand for as many names as possible, but in domestic trade, where multi-name paper was becoming scarce (owing to the extended use of cheques), *re-discounts* should be preferred to discounts; (4) Realization that *bank* paper had no special virtue, and must comply with normal rules. (See 1860, p. 979.)

[3] 1860, p. 694.

company's grossly reckless dividend policy, possibly because it feared to name the delinquents. The report dated June 30, 1860, presented towards the end of July, congratulated shareholders upon the " prosperity " of the company, and after " good round provision " for bad debts (the phrase was Gottheimer's) showed profits equal to 20 per cent. on the increased capital, upon which 10 per cent. was paid. Grateful shareholders, especially those who already were heavy " bad " debtors to the company, duly applauded the managing director. Yet within a few weeks the concern was obliged to liquidate its commitments, and when, six months later, the inevitable winding-up began, the board " hoped " eventually to return £15 on every £25 paid-up. Even then Gottheimer escaped censure, and departed with several thousand pounds' compensation for cancellation of his contract,[1] blithely talking of a new formation.

These two retirements left the National Discount in sole possession of the joint stock discount field, and certainly helped to consolidate the position of the company. Its leather losses actually proved to be slightly larger than had first been expected—they were £26,336—but the following half-year's profit, after providing for them, sufficed to meet the usual dividend and still to leave a reserve of over £8,000. Shareholders continued to plead for winding-up, citing the London Discount; but the pessimists were finally silenced when, at the end of 1861, a further increase in profits led the board to raise the dividend to 6 per cent.

Boom in " Financial " Flotations

After the liquidation of the London Discount—which had certainly made a deep impression upon the investing public, and some impression also upon professional company promoters—it was freely predicted that no new companies would venture into the discount field. For two years that prophecy proved correct.[2] But those years witnessed great activity in other fields. A steady trickle of banking formations, which had its source in the limited liability statute of 1858, became by 1862 a rushing torrent. In the early months of that year three prospectuses for new and substantial London banks were before the public almost simul-

[1] See Xenos, *op. cit.*

[2] One small company—the London and Provincial Discount Co., Ltd.—was in fact formed in 1861, but collapsed, " hopelessly insolvent," within a few months.

taneously, and various projects were afoot for provincial banks. The domestic field becoming congested, promoters bestowed their favours upon the colonies, the Continent and the East, and by June there were schemes—many of them competitive—for "almost every clime and country ".[1] Fifteen new banks actually opened for business in the eighteen months to end-1862, while by the end of 1863 the list of bank shares quoted by the *Bankers' Magazine* had been swollen to 62, in contrast with 22 at the end of 1860. Meanwhile, the " limited liability mania " for general flotations had been fairly started by the middle of 1862. Company promoting had become a crowded profession, and appeared the one certain way to easy riches. While any scheme, however flimsy, could be distorted into plausibility and made to " go " provided that the capital asked were large enough and the board sufficiently decorative, for legitimate projects there was intense competition. In consequence, another increase in the National Discount dividend (from 6 to 8 per cent., against earnings of 15½ per cent.[2]) was the signal for a rush to the bill market.

Two discount prospectuses appeared in the first few weeks of 1863—those of the City Discount Co., Ltd., and the Joint Stock Discount Co., Ltd.—and almost immediately it was reported that some five other companies [3] were in course of formation. Competent authorities agreed that there was probably room for one or two new concerns, but for six or seven, as the financial press pointed out, there was clearly no justification. Fortunately, nothing more was heard of the five embryo schemes—some were possibly transformed into " credit " companies—nor did a project for the resuscitation of the London Discount materialize. The City and the Joint Stock companies showed more promise of success, for both sought connections with existing private discount businesses. The City prospectus appeared first, and revealed that T. Fraser Sandeman, of the firm of Sandeman & Co. (which had been created out of the ruins of Sanderson, Sandeman & Co.), was to be managing director, at £2,500 per annum, plus commission. Unfortunately, the contract had not been signed; and Sandeman, affected by the threatened competition, " bolted, like the favourite on a Derby Day, frightened at his own shadow ".[4]

[1] For details of the banking " mania ", see *Bankers' Magazine*, 1862, pp. 337, 770; and *Economist*, 1862, pp. 1373–4.

[2] For the half-year to Dec., 1862.

[3] The London, Liverpool and Manchester; General; Imperial; Universal; and Phœnix.

[4] See *Bankers' Magazine*, 1863, pp. 154–7.

The scheme thereupon collapsed, and application monies were returned, after fruitless efforts to find a more courageous member of the market. The Joint Stock Discount was more successful, for this company had arranged to buy an existing business, as well as to secure the services of its owner—James Freeling Wilkinson, a former partner in the ill-fated (and ultimately mismanaged) Bruce & Wilkinson, who had since " carried out important operations on his own account ".[1] Criticism that the purchase price was too high—it was £25,000, plus £3,000 per annum salary to Wilkinson, with a share in profits—was silenced by the evident strength of the board and the fact that the firm was said to have been making £8,000 per annum. The flotation was, indeed, hardly less successful than the National's had been seven years before, for within a few months the initial capital of £1,000,000 in £25 shares, £5 paid, was doubled by an issue at a premium.

Meanwhile, the weakness of several of the new banks, difficulties in meeting calls, and the still-birth of so many discount projects, had temporarily cooled the ardour of promoters for this type of flotation. But the financial field still held possibilities, and in May, 1863, there was launched the first important batch of " credit " companies, with professed functions so vague or so embracing as to defy description, but most closely resembling those of a modern " finance " company and mortgage bank rolled into one. These companies would build railways in any part of the world, finance every sort of public works (land development, sewerage, irrigation, road-making, swamp drainage, or even the building of museums), assist a Government, float loans, or make advances on fixed or floating property. They were, in fact, a belated imitation of the " Crédit Mobilier " companies which had aroused so much interest, and done so much damage, in France in the 'fifties. Some were from the start, and others quickly became, concerns which hid under high-sounding titles every sort of " shady " or even fraudulent business, but a few were legitimate and substantial. One of the latter type demands detailed attention, for it has been perpetuated in the largest discount house in the modern market. The new concern, one of the first of the " financial " companies, was the General Credit and Finance Company of London, Ltd.,[2] floated under the highest auspices (including the leading London and Paris banks), with a capital of £2,500,000 in £20 shares, £4 paid. On its

[1] *Ibid.*

[2] See especially *Bankers' Magazine*, 1863, pp. 476–7.

London board were Samuel Laing, P. W. Andrew, Samuel Beale, M.P., J. T. Mackenzie, Bramley Moore, M.P., Alderman Salomons and Samuel Leo Schuster, while there was a separate French board representing such houses as Devaux & Co., Bischoffsheim, Goldschmidt & Co., Edward Blount & Co., Hentsch, Lutscher & Co. Before any public announcement was made, the company had established connections in most of the big Continental centres, and all but £700,000 of its capital had been subscribed. It is a strange commentary upon the views of the time that, while the articles prohibited every species of "speculative" business, the functions most stressed were the "negotiation of loans and concessions, rendering assistance to industrial enterprise, public works and railway undertakings" and a general "commission" business. For a time, the business proved extremely lucrative, fully justifying the confidence of the board, which had agreed to take no fees until shareholders had received 5 per cent., and then to be remunerated solely by a share in profits. Before any accounts had been published, the company raised another £500,000 at 25 per cent. premium, and in its first year earned 17½ per cent.

The initial success of this company naturally gave additional standing to other financial flotations, and the boom gathered momentum. It was at this stage that Albert Gottheimer, after two years of apparent retirement from the City, reappeared—as Albert Grant, M.P.[1]—to float the imposing Crédit Foncier and Mobilier of England, a concern which eventually achieved a paid-up (or more correctly, *called*-up) capital of £1,000,000. About the same time there appeared a company called the Mercantile Credit Association,[2] whose promoter (another former wine-merchant, who also had found it convenient to change his name) had been associated with Gottheimer in the Mercantile Discount Company "deal". Its manager, significantly, was Henry John Barker, another of Gottheimer's associates, and one who, in 1860, had used a so-called discount business of his own (in Abchurch Lane) to supply the Mercantile Discount Co. with the bills which forced it into liquidation. There were in fact many similar flotations, neither more nor less respectable, in

[1] Sometimes styled "Baron" Grant.

[2] In May, 1864, the company amalgamated with the Imperial Financial Co., which had been joined by T. Fraser Sandeman a few months earlier. The name was then changed to the Imperial Mercantile Credit Association, Ltd. Its capital was £5,000,000, with £500,000 paid. Barker and Sandeman became joint managers.

1863 and 1864: but these two attained a special importance for the part they played in bringing about the Overend, Gurney crash.

The second wave of discount formations began in the autumn of 1863, after the further share issue by the Joint Stock Discount. Following the example of this company, the promoters in every case arranged to acquire private businesses. The first company, the Discount Corporation, Ltd., formed in October, was indeed in its early stages little more than a re-financing of the business of Bruce & Co., which had failed in 1857, but out of which a new partnership had arisen. Two partners, James Bruce and H. S. Coulson, became managers and directors of the new company; and when, a few months later, the firm of Weston & Laurie was also taken over, they were joined by R. Laurie. The price of the two businesses was £70,000, payable over a period, and based on three years' purchase of estimated profits, while the capital of the company was £1,000,000, in £100 shares, upon which not more than £20 was to be called. From the outset, the scheme was approved by the financial press, and by January, 1864, the shares (then £7 10*s*. paid) stood at 50 per cent. premium.[1] This success, in turn, prepared the way for another formation, that of the Consolidated Discount Company, Ltd., whose prospectus was published in December, 1863, inviting initial subscriptions of £2 on 10,000 shares of £50 each. The nucleus in this case was the business of Fraser Sandeman & Co. (of Threadneedle Street), which was taken over for £19,500, payable to H. Fraser Sandeman, who, with R. M. Sanderson and Samuel Baker, constituted the committee of management. These terms (£11,000 of the price was payable in shares) were expected to assure an initial dividend of 10 per cent. Actually, no dividend was ever paid, and Sandeman was later obliged to return £5,620 of his vendor's shares for cancellation.

Two other flotations must be noted—those of the London Mercantile Discount Company, Ltd., and the Financial Discount Company, Ltd. Both were small concerns, and both appeared in March, 1864. The London Mercantile, whose paid-up capital was eventually £50,000, took over the private business of Womersley & Burt (these gentlemen becoming managing directors) and also that of the British Reversionary Co., for a total cost of £26,000; but in this case, too, the vendors' estimates proved unduly sanguine, and £11,000 of the price was returned in the

[1] The company began business on Nov. 16, trading at 34, Abchurch Lane—the traditional address of Bruce & Co., see *ante*, p. 119 *n*.

first year. The other concern, the Financial Discount, with an initial capital of £150,000 in £50 shares, upon which £10 was to be paid, also acquired a private business, at a cost (including preliminary expenses) of £19,675. Its chairman, G. P. Lascaridi, a Greek merchant, was closely associated with H. J. Barker, but the concern was much more prudently managed than others of the "Gottheimer-Barker" group, although its dividend policy was dangerously reckless.

The National's New Capital

All this additional competition might have been expected to have had adverse reactions upon the National Discount. But in fact the business of this company continued to expand, and in the middle of 1863 the balance sheet total touched a new peak at £4,542,813, compared with £4,230,504 a year earlier and only £3,313,128 in June, 1861. Nevertheless, it was clear that the board would have to take special steps if continued supremacy was to be assured. It did so in a novel way. Under its articles, the company was obliged to distribute the whole of its profits when, and so long as, the reserve fund was equal to half the paid-up capital. Down to the end of 1863 the policy of the board had been to place, on the average, about one-half of the profits to reserve, which by this means had been raised to £98,500, compared with a capital of £400,000.[1] At that date, too, the dividend was raised to 10 per cent., against profits of 17½ per cent. If, therefore, the fresh capital could be raised at such a premium as would increase the reserve to one-half the capital (as increased), the company would secure its finance on very favourable terms, and the shareholders would benefit from an automatic and substantial increase in their dividend. To achieve this necessitated an increase in the subscribed capital from £2,000,000 to £3,000,000, and an issue of £1,000,000, or 40,000 shares (£5 paid) at £10 per share—100 per cent. premium. As this price was appreciably above the market price of the old shares, many shareholders declared that the plan would not work. But it did, and very successfully. Before the meeting to confirm the initial resolution had been held, the price of the old shares had risen to 10⅞, or 117½ per cent. premium! Eventually, the

[1] In the first half of 1863 the board had issued the balance of the authorized capital (not taken up in 1856)—2,931 shares, £5 paid, at £8 10*s*. The reserve was thereby increased by £10,112.

issue[1] was largely oversubscribed; and six months later, when the dividend, on the enlarged capital, was raised to 16 per cent. (2 per cent. more than had been promised), the shares were quoted at £15. The policy of the board was indeed justified in every respect, for, despite the growth of competition, the company's business (as measured by its balance sheet total) expanded by 50 per cent. within eighteen months, and the distribution, further increased to 20 per cent. at the end of 1864, was maintained at that generous level throughout 1865 and 1866.

Meanwhile, Alexander's—apart from Gurney's, the only important and old-established house which remained a private firm—also sought to strengthen their position. On Christmas Eve, 1863, the market was surprised by an announcement that, as from January 1, 1864, the firm was to amalgamate with Cunliffes & Co., and that a new partnership, Alexanders, Cunliffes & Co., comprising the partners of both firms, would operate from 24, Lombard Street.[2] This partnership, which endured for thirteen

[1] The following summary of profits was presented in connection with the issue:

	Net Profit. £	Net Profit. % p.a.	Dividend. % p.a.	Reserve Appropn. £	Amt. of Reserve.* £
Half-year to—					
June 30, 1861 . .	17,459	9	5	7,825	16,115
Dec. 31, 1861 . .	22,640	11½	6	11,079	27,437
June 30, 1862 . .	26,626	14	6	15,066	42,915
Dec. 31, 1862 . .	29,599	15½	8	14,185	57,744
June 30, 1863 . .	29,457	14¾	8	13,457	82,180
Dec. 31, 1863 . .	35,087	17½	10	15,087	98,500

* Amount shown in balance sheet *plus* current allocation.

[2] The address of Cunliffes & Co. This firm should be distinguished from Roger Cunliffe, Sons & Co. (a bill market house which endures to-day), although both firms had a common origin. About 1815 a member of the Manchester manufacturing and merchant firm of Cunliffe, Brooks & Co., one Roger Cunliffe, opened a London branch, and became listed as a London "banker" in 1821, as "Roger Cunliffe, jun., & Co.", at 33 (later, 24), Bucklersbury. In 1827 the firm became Cunliffes, Brooks, Cunliffe & Co., but was split into two firms in 1836, Roger Cunliffe continuing to trade under his own name at the same address, while Cunliffes, Brooks, Cunliffe & Co. removed to 29, Lombard Street (and to 24, Lombard Street in 1844). The Brooks partners disappeared in 1855, when the firm became Cunliffes & Co., and was unchanged until the amalgamation with Alexanders. It was never included in the lists of bill market firms; nor, until the early 'sixties, was Roger Cunliffe, Sons & Co. so included. (See Hilton Price, *op. cit.*, but note that he incorrectly states the date of the Alexanders amalgamation as 1862.) Alexanders, Cunliffes & Co. moved to 30, Lombard Street in 1866, and, on the retirement of the Cunliffe partners in 1877, to 9, Birchin Lane. Another change, back to 24, Lombard Street (the present address), occurred in 1880.

years (the Cunliffe partners retired in 1877), was designed to afford assistance, both of personnel and finance, to the members of both houses. Commenting upon the amalgamation, the *Bankers' Magazine* [1] remarked that, except for Gurney's, " who still stand a tower of strength in themselves, . . . most of the old discount firms have all very recently gone one way, and now shine out reflected lights through associated undertakings ".

This buttressing of two of the largest and most respected houses—the National and Alexander's—must certainly have hampered the rise of the new concerns, but the questionable progress which most of these made must be attributed very largely to their own lack of caution or to their inadequate standing. The Joint Stock Discount, it is true, started with a flourish. In its first ten months, the company amortized the whole of its goodwill out of share premiums, paid a dividend of 5 per cent., and, according to its chairman, T. W. Henderson, had already established its credit—thanks to the board's determination to profit by the experience of 1847 and 1857, by keeping the whole capital in Consols, working solely with deposits.[2] Henderson, however, was at that time unaware of the ways of the managing director, J. Freeling Wilkinson; and resigned when, a few months later, he learned that advances had been made on second mortgage to railways, and that a £5 call would be required.[3] Officially, the call was described simply as a precautionary measure,[4] following the failure of the Leeds Banking Co.; and the dividend was increased.

The failure of the Leeds Bank also involved the Consolidated Discount, which had clearly been guilty of over-trading. But while this company incurred heavy bad debts in its first year, there is no evidence to show that it departed openly from legitimate discount business. The careers of the two small companies were even less satisfactory: the London Mercantile got into difficulties at the very start, and collapsed in 1865 [5]; while the Financial Discount, although paying large dividends and presenting apparently reassuring accounts, failed to prevent its shares from dropping to a very heavy discount, and to zero in early 1866. Of the five new companies, only one—the Dis-

[1] 1864, p. 57.

[2] See Annual Meeting held on Jan. 25, 1864.

[3] See *post*, p. 241.

[4] Raising the called-up capital to £800,000, or £200,000 more than that of the National Discount.

[5] Some of the board were charged with " crass negligence ", amounting to fraud, in negotiating the purchase of the business absorbed.

count Corporation—appears to have been managed with even reasonable prudence. The dividend policy was somewhat over-generous, but the board did show signs of appreciating the peculiar dangers which faced a discount house—and especially a new discount company—at this period; and sought to meet them by restricting the scale of operations, by holding only short-dated securities (none was more than six months), and by keeping a large cash reserve.

The early record even of this company was not free from serious blemishes; but had the management of other concerns been even equally conservative, it is certain that much of the subsequent distress would have been avoided. As it was, the managements, broadly speaking, were either incompetent, reckless, or actually fraudulent; and vast quantities of bad paper endorsed and even accepted by the new banks readily found a home in Lombard Street.[1] Part of the blame for mismanagement, no doubt, lay with the public, whose clamour for dividends almost unknown in the past had forced the boards of new companies into high-yielding, and therefore questionable, securities.[2] The finance companies, necessarily, were the worst offenders, for their very *raison d'être* was to deal in securities which were beyond the legitimate scope of the banks and the discount market. Such long-term financing might have been conducted with reasonable safety in certain circumstances; but in the fever of competition and anxiety for high returns, not only was the quality of investments lowered, but the cardinal principle that to lend "long" one must also borrow "long" was quickly forgotten, if indeed it was ever fully understood, by the many newly-fledged and salaried financiers. To cheapen costs, deposits at short notice, even at call, became the order of the day[3]; everywhere were the dictates of experience and commonsense subordinated to the need for generous dividends. Such policies often sprang from nothing more culpable than a reckless optimism, or a pathetic faith in the magic of "limited liability"; but all too frequently their determinants were the interests of promoters and market-manipulators, whose capacity to bring forth yet another competitive concern depended upon the dividend record of its predecessor.

In such circumstances, it is hardly surprising that the new

[1] See, for example, *Bankers' Magazine*, 1866, p. 511.

[2] A vivid discussion of this aspect of the problem will be found in *The Times* of May 10, 1866.

[3] See *The Times*, May 12, 1866.

discount companies, finding bill dealing less readily profitable than they had supposed it to be, should have begun to mix high-yielding "finance" business with sober discounting; for where was the harm in doing what others, outside the bill market, did with such apparent success? Companies of this type, both within and without the discount market, became the obvious prey of every needy merchant or unscrupulous financier. Others, run by astute rogues, who profited by the opportunities which current practices afforded, became part of a systematic and fraudulent collusion whereby shareholders' funds were steadily drained into the pockets of "customers" and of the agents who introduced them. In these various ways there grew up in the early 'sixties, and especially after 1862, financial abuses which, for sheer recklessness and audacity, have hardly been surpassed by the worst scandals of more recent years.

The "Triumph" of Limited Liability

The worst abuses and frauds were not, of course, immediately apparent; but there were many who gave warnings that the insensate financial competition, built on foundations so precarious, could have but one result. Indeed, a general collapse was only narrowly averted in the autumn of 1864, when months of penal money rates, caused partly by the company activity, and partly by a prolonged gold drain consequent upon the cotton famine produced by the American Civil War,[1] precipitated many failures. But still the boom, and the dividend race, went on. It reached its climax in July, 1865, when the world was surprised by what the *Bankers' Magazine*[2] called the "greatest triumph of limited liability". In that month it was announced that Overend, Gurney & Co., whose name had long been uttered "with that curious solemnity, almost under the breath"; which in the minds of old men was the "best that could be thought of"; that this great house was to be transformed into "the worst they could think of"—a limited company. Surprise, however, quickly gave place to satisfaction, and a sort of wonder that a benevolent deity should have decreed that even the humblest might share in the great riches and power of so mighty an institution. Traces of this reverential

[1] See, for example, Goschen, *Essays and Addresses on Economic Questions, 1865–1893*. (First essay, "Seven per Cent.", reprinted from the *Edinburgh Review* of Jan., 1865.)

[2] *Bankers' Magazine*, 1865, p. 905, *et seq.*

atmosphere will be found even in the pages of the *Bankers' Magazine*,[1] which defended the price to be paid for goodwill by declaring that the wealth of the Gurneys was almost proverbial, and by the remark that, in any case, it was a question of detail for prospective shareholders to settle! The *Economist* knew better, as did many in the City who had learned the difference between good bills and bad. This paper, too, welcomed the change, but for the significant reason that it would compel the house to publish accounts. At last, it was said, there would be revealed what the discerning City man most wanted to know—the proportion which the firm's "extra" business bore to its legitimate bill dealing business; for it was a "matter of public notoriety" that for some time the house had transacted "business not at all in general of an illegitimate or unprofitable character, but still of a sort different from those conducted by bill brokers 'pure and simple'".[2]

The *Economist*, clearly, had a suspicion of the truth, which was that the house was encumbered by "lock-up" business, and was arranging the flotation to provide finance which would enable it to turn over a new leaf. But, save to the initiated, the prospectus afforded no sign that the business was not all that the world believed it to be.[3] All that was revealed was that the company would take over for £500,000 (of which £250,000 would be payable in cash, and the rest in shares) Gurney's "long established business as bill brokers and money dealers . . . the vendors guaranteeing the company against any loss on the assets and liabilities transferred"; that of the nine proprietors, three—John Henry Gurney, Henry Edmund Gurney and Robert Birkbeck—would retain "a large pecuniary interest" in the business and would join the board, which would also include Henry Ford Barclay, Thomas A. Gibbs (of T. A. Gibbs & Co.), Harry G. Gordon (chairman of the Oriental Bank) and William Rennie (of Cavan, Lubbock & Co.), all famous banking names; that the directors would "give their zealous attention to the cultivation of business of a first-class character only, it being their conviction that they will thus most effectually promote the prosperity of the company and the permanent interests of the shareholders"; and that H. E. Gurney and Birkbeck would be managing directors. The capital was to be £5,000,000 in £50 shares, upon which £15 was to be paid; but no details were given either of past profits or of the amount

[1] *Ibid.* [2] *Economist*, 1865, pp. 845–6.
[3] A copy of the prospectus will be found in App. III, *post*, p. 328.

of assets and liabilities to be transferred,[1] nor were these figures available in the deed of purchase which was open to inspection. This other document, however, did contain several clauses of significance to those whose suspicions had already been aroused, for it provided that the company should carry on all existing accounts "*except such accounts as the directors . . . shall require to be reserved or excepted to be wound up and closed by Overend, Gurney & Co.*", and that the vendors were to continue to act for the "winding-up, closing or settling" of any such accounts. Moreover, the board was empowered in this deed to demand that part or all of the goodwill moneys should be "applied and made available by way of material guarantee in aid of the covenants", *i.e.*, the vendors' guarantee against loss.

Needless to say, the general public did not look beyond the prospectus, and in consequence the issue was a great success. By the following October, despite a spectacular rise in money rates in that month, the shares (then £11 paid) had risen to a premium of virtually 100 per cent.; and for the first five months both the discounts and the deposits of the house continued to expand. But in this same period events were moving swiftly to a crisis. Although between June and October the Bank's gold stock rose appreciably, its banking reserve declined steadily, accompanied by an increase in Bank rate from 3 to 7 per cent., 3 per cent. of this rise being compressed within no more than nine days. So unusual a movement, at a time when the exchanges were favourable and foreign rates low, and when the only immediate sources of disturbance were a drain of funds to Ireland for cattle purchases, a reckless cotton speculation in Liverpool, and rumours of Fenian agitation, ought to have revealed that it required but one noteworthy failure to bring the whole precarious credit superstructure crashing down.

The first serious shock came in January, 1866, when it became known that Watson, Overend & Co., a firm of railway contractors, with liabilities of about £1,500,000, was in difficulties. This firm, and the Contract Corporation, with which it was closely associated, had placed large quantities of railway paper with the finance and pseudo-discount companies, notably with the Joint Stock Discount.[2] The two contracting firms and

[1] The balance sheet total at July 31, 1865, the date of transfer, was actually £15,552,003, exclusive of £8,808,699 of "contra" items for re-discounts, acceptances and guarantees.

[2] One such transaction was a "sale" by the Joint Stock Co., in Aug., 1865, of £267,000 of bonds and other "rubbish" to the Contract

the Joint Stock Discount had, indeed, been kept alive solely by a series of cross-drawings, and this paper had been liberally re-sold by the Joint Stock Discount to other discount houses, including the National and Gurney's. Watson, Overend & Co.'s default, following quickly upon an increase in Bank rate to 8 per cent. in consequence partly of a bullion drain to the East, therefore affected the credit of all discount and finance companies. In February, public disclosures [1] of the rottenness of the Joint Stock Co., and of the concerns with which it was connected, greatly intensified the alarm, which, among holders of " miscellaneous " securities, amounted almost to panic. Despite an easing of the general money position,[2] the Consols market had to be strongly supported by the Government broker, while the market for " financial " securities broke badly, and many bubble companies (including the Peninsular, West India & Southern Bank) collapsed. By March it was remarked that " company winding-up seems likely to become one of our national institutions ".

Corporation for £200,000, no payment to be made for 2 years. The Contract Corporation gave its acceptances, which the Joint Stock Co. undertook to meet at maturity, and these bills were then placed in the market, some with the National Discount. It was the default of the Joint Stock Co. on its undertaking which later caused the collapse of the Contract Co.

[1] At a meeting on Jan. 31, when a report by special investigators revealed that, unknown to the board, and despite its censure of certain transactions, the managing director, J. F. Wilkinson, had tied up the bulk of the funds in illiquid or actually fictitious securities. A few weeks' later, a shareholders' committee disclosed that entanglements in railway securities had been the real reason for the 1864 call, and that on the very day on which he was reproved, Wilkinson had lent from the new resources a further £240,000 to the same company. The committee then sought a fresh board, but the new directors discovered within a day of their appointment that actually while the investigations had been in progress—from Jan. 1 to March 1—Wilkinson had lent another £154,000 without security, except £50,000 of overdue bills accepted by the directors of the beneficiary companies! The company was thereupon put into liquidation, when it was revealed that, in addition, Wilkinson had gambled in the company's shares with the company's money, ingeniously showing all his payments to brokers as normal loans to them. The sentence was five years' penal servitude.

[2] It is worth noting that one reason for the easing of money was the fact that the National Provincial Bank, previously exclusively a provincial bank, had opened an office in London in January. It was therefore compelled to relinquish its note issue, and the Bank of England in February exercised its right under the Act of 1844 to increase its fiduciary issue by two-thirds of the private issue withdrawn. The fiduciary issue was thereupon raised by £350,000 to £15,000,000.

COLLAPSE OF THE "CORNER HOUSE"

Gurney's was especially affected by this general discredit, for the unfortunate resemblance of the name to that of Watson, Overend & Co. (actually, there was no *personal* connection) started withdrawals of deposits by the general public. By themselves, these withdrawals might not have proved fatal; but in January it became known in the City that the partners of the old firm were quietly realizing their securities. This precipitated withdrawals by much more influential quarters, who recalled the vendors' guarantee. The extent of the drain was not generally known, but it amounted to roughly £2,500,000 in two months, while heavy commitments piled up on account of the numerous "financial" suspensions. Even this did not mark the peak of the demands, which occurred after the collapse on April 7 of Pinto, Perez & Co., Spanish merchants, in which Gurney's was known to be largely committed. This failure, together with a "bear" attack on the company's shares (these had already fallen from a premium of 50 per cent. to only a shade over par), added greatly to the difficulties, but down to the end of April the directors believed that they would weather the storm.

Early in May, however, an outflow of gold, an increase in Bank rate, disclosure of the fact that Pinto, Perez & Co. had been guilty of serious frauds, and the knowledge that the Imperial Mercantile Credit Association was tottering, gave fresh opportunities to the bears, whose short selling precipitated a panic on the Stock Exchange and a violent collapse in quotations for financial companies and foreign bonds. Depression of Gurney's shares to a heavy discount led to a frenzied "run" by depositors. The directors, taken unawares by the magnitude of the demands, met hurriedly to consider the question of a call. But it was too late. New shareholders' resources, even if paid immediately, would have been swallowed up by the increased demands which the call itself would have engendered. Finally, on May 9, the status of the company's many railway securities was jeopardized by a Court ruling that acceptances of the Mid-Wales Railway were *ultra vires*, and therefore unenforceable. Application was thereupon made to the Bank; but the Governor took the view that the Bank could not assist one concern unless it was prepared also to assist the many others which were known to be in similar plight.[1] Frantic applications to other bankers were

[1] See *The Times*, May 11, 1866, and *Bankers' Magazine*, 1887, p. 232. Assistance was refused after a confidential report by G. G. Glyn

equally fruitless—all were intent upon saving themselves, and had no spare funds for any purpose, certainly not for loans on "lock-up" securities. The crash came on Thursday, May 10. At about 3.30 p.m. on that day, a bewildered world learnt that the famous "Corner House" had suspended payment.

There followed the wildest panic, and scenes in Lombard Street unknown since 1825. The effect, says one contemporary, was "as the shock of an earthquake. It is impossible to describe the terror and anxiety which took possession of men's minds for the remainder of that and the whole of the succeeding day. No man felt safe. A run immediately commenced upon all the banks, the magnitude of which can hardly be conceived".[1] As the panic spread, provincial bankers sent urgent demands for cash to their agents, and from the Bank of England notes and bullion were despatched hastily to all parts of the country. "It cannot be denied," said *The Times*, describing the Friday, "that about mid-day the tumult became a rout. The doors of the most respectable Banking Houses were besieged . . . and throngs heaving and tumbling about Lombard-street made that narrow thoroughfare impassable."[2] The Bank Court met, and raised its rate to 9 per cent.; but until that announcement, which was coupled with an intimation that loans on Government securities would be available at 10 per cent., it was impossible to sell either Consols or Exchequer bills, while jobbers in most other securities refused to deal throughout the day. The English Joint Stock Bank, of London, and two large contracting firms stopped payment, and there were signs that the Consolidated Discount and the Imperial Mercantile were on the point of doing so. Open market discounts were unobtainable, but the Bank met all "legitimate" demands. It lent over £4,000,000 in the one day, at the cost of a reduction of its reserve from £5,727,000 to under £3,000,000. But the panic remained unallayed, and in the evening the Governors, faced with the prospect of similar demands on the Saturday, sought and obtained permission to infringe the Bank Act. Treasury sanction was conceded on the usual terms, so that Bank rate was raised on the following morning to 10 per cent.

As in 1847 and 1857, the "suspension" of the Act sufficed

(son of G. Carr Glyn), R. C. L. Bevan and J. K. Hodgson, who had been deputed by the Bank to examine the books and decide whether assistance from the Bank, or from the London commercial banks, was merited.

[1] *Bankers' Magazine*, 1866, p. 639. [2] *The Times*, May 12, 1866.

to calm the more unreasoning fears,[1] but it did not mark the end of the failures. The Imperial Mercantile closed its doors on Saturday afternoon, and a petition was presented against the Consolidated Discount, but was withdrawn after a meeting of shareholders. In the following few weeks no less than ten banks suspended payment; only three ever resumed business. The most serious of these suspensions was that of the Agra & Masterman's Bank, on June 6, with liabilities of £19,000,000. This failure, of a reputable concern, whose shares had formerly stood at 150 per cent. premium, was almost wholly due to a bear raid on its shares, culminating in the despatch of false telegrams to the East reporting the bank's collapse.[2] Fortunately, the crisis remained chiefly "financial" in character; and despite the ruinous rates of interest (Bank rate remained at 10 per cent. for over three months), the appalling discredit in the security markets, and the special distress among Gurney's clients, mercantile failures were surprisingly few. They included, however, several disastrous suspensions at Liverpool, and in the shipping, colonial, Indian and Spanish trades. After the month of July, in which three more banks stopped, the storm dispersed, and discount rates for a few first-class names dropped well below Bank rate, which in the second half of August was reduced by three successive steps to 6 per cent. There then ensued a period of prolonged quietude and "sobering disipline", which carried Bank rate down to 2 per cent. by July 25, 1867, at which level it remained for nearly sixteen months.

It is surprising—and to the student regrettable—that there was never any official inquiry into the causes of a crisis which was as unique in character as it was unprecedented in magnitude. There were indeed many demands for an investigation, and one was tacitly promised. But the surfeit of unproductive inquiries in the 'forties and 'fifties apparently discouraged further efforts. Possibly, too, it was realized that the remedy for such troubles as those of 1866, even more than for those of earlier crises, lay not so much with the legislature as with the public. *The Times* cynically remarked that the public would never learn

[1] Demands at the Bank, however, remained very heavy, and in the ensuing four days it lent another £8,250,000. The total of "Other Securities" did not begin to decline (from a peak of £33,447,000) until early June.

[2] An excellent account of the disgraceful tactics of bear speculators against the finance companies and banks at this period will be found in *The Times* of May 26, 1866, and the *Bankers' Magazine*, 1866, pp. 790–2.

by experience, that every so often it would pursue a new craze —public works and social improvements, foreign loans, railways, commercial over-trading, or mere money-lending by means of companies—and that "every delusion is monstrous when it is found out, and, until then, a marvellous discovery ".[1] But the lesson of 1866 was driven home relentlessly by the enormous liabilities which had to be met on partly-paid shares; and the excesses of the period have never been repeated on any comparable scale.

Why did Gurney's Fail?

The general causes of the crisis were, indeed, apparent to all. Once the speculative bubble had been pricked by the collapse of such concerns as the Joint Stock Discount and the contracting companies, there was general wonder that they could have been floated at all. One question alone seemed unanswerable: how was it possible that a house whose business dwarfed that of all competitors, whose credit had for decades been unsurpassed, whose reputation was world-wide, and whose partners were men of undoubted probity and wealth—how was it possible that such a house could fail? The answer was supplied only gradually, as the liquidators' reports and protracted litigation slowly unfolded their tragic tale. It is possibly for that reason that the full story has never been told.

Records of failures are strewn, and doubtless ever will be, with examples of splendid businesses wrecked by over-confident, incompetent or dishonest sons of brilliant and industrious founders; but there can be no more tragic instance than that of Overend, Gurney. The Gurneys, as has been indicated, were men of the highest capacity and moral rectitude, and, until the early 'fifties, while Samuel Gurney was at the helm, their house grew rapidly in resources and reputation. David Barclay Chapman—also a Quaker—was of almost equal calibre, but it was he who, in 1853, made the first serious blunder. Discovering that metal warrants, pledged against advances of £200,000, were fictitious, he took fresh security where he should have taken proceedings. The fraudulent pledgors—Davidson, Gordon and Cole—were enabled, by trading on their connection with Gurney's, to perpetrate fresh frauds on others. They later failed with enormous liabilities. Chapman was ignorant of these subsequent frauds, but at the trial, where it was affirmed without

[1] *The Times*, May 14, 1866.

contradiction that he had asked the swindlers to keep the first frauds secret, his conduct was severely censured. The shock of these disclosures undoubtedly hastened the death of Samuel Gurney, an old and ailing man, and he died in Paris on June 5, 1856, in his seventy-first year.[1] Chapman remained to manage the house (then as senior partner), and, despite his folly in this instance, there is little doubt that he could have steered a safe course. But the widespread prejudice against him proved too great a handicap, and at the end of 1857 he retired, on payment to him of at least £250,000 by the remaining partners.

The chief acting partners then became Henry Edmund Gurney and D. Ward Chapman, for John Henry Gurney (the other principal partner) had ceased active management. For a time all went well,[2] although several retirements depleted the working capital, and profits were more fully divided. There were many, however, who knew all too well how to impose upon the credulity and weaknesses of the inexperienced. H. E. Gurney, though a man of true Gurney cast, was ambitious, and coveted the sense of power which, besides the prospect of easy wealth, the fashionable " financing " afforded. When money was cheap, he was ready to take business which Samuel Gurney would never have countenanced, and which he himself was ill-qualified to judge. Moreover, sheer pressure of work and responsibilities compelled him to delegate to D. W. Chapman the vital task of examining securities. So exacting a function was distasteful to Chapman, a handsome, pleasure-loving gallant who, like his brother and others of the junior partners, delighted in flattery, which a crowd of wily sycophants was curiously ready to supply. One of these attendants, at what Xenos calls the " miniature Court of Louis XIV ", was Henry John Barker. Another was one Edward Watkin Edwards, whose career as

[1] He left personal property valued at £800,000, and it was estimated that his real property, together with family settlements effected during his lifetime, would amount to another £800,000, despite the great philanthropy which he had shown for many years. (See *Bankers' Magazine*, 1856, p. 434.)

[2] The profits of the firm rose in 1858 from £144,460 to £293,628, and again to £442,074 in 1859 ; in these two years £600,000 was distributed. From 1851 to 1856 the extreme range of profits was from £148,617 to £212,977, and the aggregate was £1,013,442, of which £652,000 was distributed. These figures, however, do not include provision for the special loss of £219,377 from the metal frauds in 1853, when no dividend was paid. At least up to the end of 1857, in which year also no profits were divided, other bad debts were fully provided for.

partner in an eminent firm of accountants (Turquand, Youngs & Co.), and subsequently as official assignee of the Bankruptcy Court, had given him a peculiarly detailed knowledge of the underworld of finance. Edwards quickly became confidential adviser to Chapman, and when, in 1859, Chapman's extravagance—he kept ten horses and entertained lavishly at Princes Gate, Hyde Park—brought him into difficulties which he preferred not to meet by fresh drafts on the firm, his subjugation to the will of the assignee became complete. Edwards, according to his own evidence, was thereupon appointed as adviser to the *firm*, at a salary of £5,000 per annum. The first £5,000, paid in advance, was at once transferred to Chapman.

It was then there began those depredations which brought the firm to its downfall. Edwards did not wait for his advice to be sought, but, with Barker and his other associates, he appears systematically to have introduced one bad transaction after another. Within a few months, Gurney's became grain traders and speculators, iron-masters, shipbuilders, shipowners, large-scale railway financiers, and partners in almost every kind of speculative and lock-up business, much of which had only the flimsiest prospect of even ultimate success. "They covered the seas with their ships, ploughed up the land with their iron roads," declared the prosecutor at the famous trial of the directors in 1869. Chapman, however, was probably not fully aware of the nature of the worst business, for (as he later stated in a letter transmitted by his father to *The Times*) it was to Edwards that the examination of securities and management of the "financing" business were entrusted. Nevertheless, personal friends of Chapman, as well as Edwards' friends, were appointed to remunerative positions in the enterprises with which the firm became saddled. On such appointments, Edwards apparently secured handsome commissions. Commissions, indeed, seem to have been his primary concern, for there is unimpeachable evidence that he secured them from the various *borrowers*, as well as from Gurney's, in addition to his salary. Apart from this, his main aim was apparently to ensure means of procuring sufficient accommodation paper to finance the undertakings for which he was responsible. To him, the real worth of the security behind an advance was unimportant, and there are cases on record in which he, though acting as sole manager for Gurney's, took no serious steps even to check the debtor's valuations or to examine the property. Indeed, in some instances, bankrupt assets (of concerns with which Edwards was in touch in his official capacity) were taken up and made the basis of transactions whose sole object could have been only that of providing new accommodation paper—and of affording a double commission to the "introducer".[1]

The tangle of financial intrigue and almost unbelievable graft is so complex that complete unravelling will probably never be possible. A few transactions can, however, be detailed here to indicate the way in which the worst commitments occurred. The first bad business was apparently introduced by Barker, who early in 1859 was inducing the firm, through Chapman, to lend money to Xenos, of the Greek & Oriental Steam Navigation Co., against mortgages on steamers, charging 10 to 25 per cent. per annum in acceptance commissions alone.[2] It was Barker, too, who "arranged" finance for the notorious Galway Line, which involved Gurney's in a published loss of £1,417,346—the real loss was certainly greater. The promoter drew upon one G. P. Lascaridi, a Greek merchant connected with Barker (also an Anglo-Greek) and evidently already indebted to Gurney's. Lascaridi could not meet the bills, and Gurney's, presumably to avoid loss through his failure, took them up, becoming mortgagees of the vessels by which they were secured. Meanwhile, the Galway Line had been induced to buy seven further steamers which, having brought bankruptcy on two previous owners, had been advertised for sale by Edwards, as official assignee. Here, too, the finance was by pure accommodation bills, which Gurney's discounted to the extent of £175,000, against mortgage collateral. Both projects collapsed, and Gurney's thus became owners of two miniature fleets. On the advice of Edwards, the second of these was shortly formed into a subsidiary limited company, the East India & London Shipping Co., but the original fleet was for a time directly managed (at great running loss) by Gurney's, and was financed by renewal accommodation bills which the firm endorsed and re-sold whenever necessary. Ultimately, Edwards arranged for the flota-

[1] That this is, in substance, the real story of Gurney's losses can be ascertained by all who read the Law Reports of the period and who also accept (where his statements of fact are thus corroborated) the "background" furnished by Xenos, one of Gurney's largest debtors. Xenos was an aggrieved party, and as such was strongly biassed; but his statements have been drawn upon only where much careful consideration, and cross-checking upon "key" points, suggest that they may be relied upon.

[2] The actual letter announcing the terms of the accommodation is reproduced by Xenos, *op. cit.*, p. 59.

tion of these vessels as the Atlantic & Royal Mail Steam Packet Co., and devised an extravagant project involving the building of five large steamers at a cost of over £500,000, financing the business through Barker and Gottheimer. These companies made losses from the outset, and their early liquidation left Gurney's with deficits of £578,000 and £839,346 respectively.

Other transactions are no less illuminating. Early in 1860, Xenos, whose credit had suffered from Lascaridi's default, approached H. E. Gurney for £80,000 against steamers for six months.[1] The transaction was handled by Chapman and Edwards who, according to Xenos, charged a "bonus" of £30,000, plus 5 per cent. interest. This may have been an exaggeration (though the first quotation is given as £40,000, plus 10 per cent. !), but there is no reason to doubt Xenos's incidental details. The money, he affirms, quoting Chapman, was never to be paid to him direct, but only by cheques in favour of Barker's firm (Barker Bros., of 4, Abchurch Lane), as "we do not wish the name of the Greek & Oriental to appear in our books". Later, when Gurney's virtually took control of the business, all its receipts were paid to Barker for account of Gurney's, and Gurney's in turn met all its payments by cheques issued to, and in favour of, Barker, whose discharge was to be sufficient for all purposes.[2] Edwards, who acted as supervisor throughout, compelled Xenos to pay him £500 per annum before he would agree to complete the original loan, and admitted the payment in later cross-examination. Similar methods were certainly adopted for other transactions, for several debtors, figuring in the ultimate liquidation for large amounts, were actually only the "managers" of the transactions on which money had been lent. One such debtor was J. E. C. Koch, through whom £335,000 was advanced for the making of two railways, one of which was the Portadown & Omagh.

With reckless financing pursued on such a scale, it is not surprising that as early as the autumn of 1860 the house, despite the continuance of its thoroughly sound discounting business, was sufficiently hard pressed to resort to extensive accommodation finance. At that time, the Greek trade was severely affected by the collapse of the accommodation bill system by which Turkey had been surreptitiously financed during the Crimean War. The resultant failures, following closely upon the Leather

[1] See Xenos, *op. cit.*, pp. 73–8, for text of the letter.

[2] Xenos declares that Barker "licked up a little honey out of these transactions".

Crisis, put a heavy strain upon Gurney's, which also found that the Greek & Oriental acceptances could no longer be placed. Efforts to introduce new capital into the shipping firm, or to convert it into a public company, having failed, Edwards and Barker came to the rescue by arranging to sell several vessels to one Zachariah Pearson, Mayor of Hull and a successful tramp owner. Pearson was dubious of his capacity to employ the vessels, but the offer of £500 in cash from Gurney's and an undertaking to renew his acceptances for two years proved irresistible. By such methods, Gurney's secured credit-worthy acceptances in place of bad ones, and Edwards a " commission " of £2,000 from Pearson—in payment for services which brought the worthy Mayor to bankruptcy within twelve months, when the vessels once more reverted to Gurney's.[1] About the same time, too, the house began to relieve itself by the well-tried method of drawing against pledged bills of lading, received for account of the Greek firm's shipments of Danube grain, while there is also evidence of forced sales of grain.[2]

These transactions, at the end of 1860 and early 1861, mark the beginning of really serious difficulties. From that time onwards, the problem of sustaining a vast " lock-up " business by money market deposits became steadily greater, and as each venture collapsed or as spasmodic pressures caused withdrawals of deposits, the house was driven deeper and deeper into accommodation paper. In 1861 and 1862, steamers and other assets were mortgaged to London banks (notably Masterman's and the Bank of London) to secure accommodation acceptance credits,[2] and from time to time thereafter efforts were made to dispose of assets by their re-sale to public companies created for the purpose. This was done on a large scale in 1864, when Barker and Gottheimer, through the Imperial Mercantile and the Crédit Foncier, performed valuable services. One such flotation was the Millwall Iron Works Co., which took over the bankrupt property of C. J. Mare, and left Gurney's ultimately with a loss of £566,000 on its liquidation some months' later.

There seems no reason to doubt the later assertions of J. H. and H. E. Gurney that they were throughout unaware of anything more than that the house had made imprudent advances; for

[1] Details of these transactions emerged in Pearson's bankruptcy proceedings in 1864.

[2] Definite proof of these various transactions is afforded by Xenos, who quotes in his Appendices the actual instructions which Gurney's sent to him in connection with their efforts to procure finance.

several years they certainly did not realize that the firm was on the verge of collapse. Apart from Chapman (who professed ignorance of the double commission system), it was apparently Robert Birkbeck who first sensed Edwards' treachery, for in 1864 he accused Edwards of responsibility for the worst losses and terminated his contract, paying £20,000 compensation.[1] Strenuous efforts were then made to retrieve the position of the house, by refusing all fresh "financing" and endeavouring to liquidate the old commitments. The task was, however, well-nigh impossible, for although the discount business was estimated to be producing nearly £200,000 annually, from the end of 1860 the firm incurred *net* losses of some £500,000 a year. In 1865 the partners called in conference several of those who later became "outside" directors of the company, and together discussed schemes of reorganization. Introduction of capital from friends, admission of new partners, and even amalgamation with the National Discount (unhesitatingly refused by that concern[2]) were all considered and rejected in turn. There seemed but one remaining alternative to liquidation—the formation of a company.

Liquidation of Overend, Gurney & Co., Limited

This project was not, as it at first may seem to be, an open fraud on the public. It was an honest attempt to segregate the valuable discount business from the rotten financing commitments, and to provide for the gradual liquidation of the latter. D. W. Chapman retired (to become himself a promoter and, very shortly, also a bankrupt), and J. H. and H. E. Gurney, with Birkbeck, put the position of the firm squarely before the new directors.[3] In brief, these were told that unsound business had

[1] From Jan. 1, 1863, Edwards had secured from Chapman a five-year contract (produced at the Guildhall trial of the directors). Chapman, defending himself, later declared that Edwards "had become possessed of sufficient knowledge to have forced us to put up our shutters within 24 hours"; he accordingly "smoothed him down in the best way" he could.

[2] The chairman of the National later stated that they had said that they "would not give a halfpenny for Gurney's goodwill"; though, in fact, on this occasion Gurney's had not proposed any payment for goodwill. (See *Bankers' Magazine*, 1869, p. 202.)

[3] See Rennie's statement to the meeting held on June 11, 1866 (*Bankers' Magazine*, 1866, pp. 848–63.) It was later revealed that J. H. Gurney took a very cautious view and actually "toned down" the more colourful statements in the first draft of the prospectus.

resulted in a "lock-up" in bad assets (mainly claims on failed estates) which figured in the books at £4,213,896,[1] and which were being "carried" by unsecured deposits amounting to some £5,400,000 [2] and by £1,125,000 of partners' balances. No accountant was asked to value these assets (for to employ one at that time would have meant "utter destruction"), but investigation suggested that they would ultimately realize £1,300,000. Allowance for the partners' balances, cash in hand (£120,000), premises, and goodwill of the discount business (£500,000 on 2½ years' purchase [3]), reduced the deficiency to some £1,200,000, which was to be guaranteed jointly and severally by the vendors, whose separate estates were valued at £1,948,281, exclusive of £300,000 for goodwill of the Norwich bank. This guarantee was embodied in a special deed of arrangement—the "secret" deed—which provided that a "Suspense and Guarantee Account" in the new company's books (in effect, the account of the vendors with the company) was to be debited with the amount of the lock-up, and with all payments subsequently made by the company in connection with any of the lock-up accounts. Any such payments were to be refunded by the vendors within two months. On the other hand, the vendors were to be credited with the amount of partners' balances, the value of premises, the cash portion of the goodwill purchase price (and the proceeds of the share portion, as and when the shares were realized for account of the vendors), and with all receipts from the lock-up assets. The balance of this account on December 31, 1868, was then to be paid to or by the vendors.

Unfortunately, the hopes that the lock-up would be thus satisfactorily liquidated on behalf of the vendors proved unduly sanguine. Not only did the rapid rise in money rates cause a capital loss even on the discount business, but fresh failures necessitated heavy payments on the lock-up accounts.[4] The vendors were called upon under their guarantee, thus forcing them to that realization of their property which so disastrously attracted public attention. By this means, no less than £650,000 was paid to the company in the few months of its existence; yet

[1] This figure was computed after writing-off at least £310,000 out of partners' resources.

[2] The *total* deposits amounted to £14,425,678.

[3] Based on average profits over a decade, after eliminating both profits and losses from all extraneous business.

[4] Gross payments during the nine months amounted to £908,338 (exclusive of £131,000 due to the company for interest); net payments were £615,000.

at the date of suspension there was the enormous debit balance of £2,970,168 on the Suspense and Guarantee Account, and throughout the period the debit was never less than £2,500,000. As, in the meantime, the account had been credited with the partners' balances of £1,126,325, with £500,000 for goodwill, and with the £650,000 paid in, the total loss on the liquidation of the financing business up to May 10, 1866, was £5,246,493—a staggering figure even if judged by modern standards.

The first report [1] of the liquidators, presented at a meeting on June 11, revealed that the company's gross external liabilities amounted to £18,727,915, despite a decline in deposits over the nine months by £4,587,994. The salient figures, together with those for the old firm at the date of transfer, were as follows :

	Overend, Gurney & Co. Ltd. May 10, 1866.	Overend, Gurney & Co. July 31, 1865.
	£	£
Liabilities :		
Secured deposits	6,018,835	9,006,422
Unsecured deposits	3,818,849	5,419,256
Re-discounts	8,266,049	7,177,280
Acceptances	624,182	665,919
Guarantees*	—	965,500
Assets :		
Cash	63,621	120,395
Portfolio †	7,533,959	10,302,362
Debtors	461,696	915,142
Suspense account	2,970,168	4,213,896

* Not taken over from old firm.
† Excluding bills re-discounted.

The liquidators estimated that even after realizing the residue of the guarantors' estates (put at £1,250,000) the suspense account would yield a loss of £720,000. This, together with certain other known losses and the amount paid for goodwill, implied an immediately visible deficiency of £1,340,000, before taking account of heavy prospective losses on bills, re-discounts, etc. Upon this revelation, efforts at reconstruction—made because country banks had declared Gurney's to be " absolutely necessary to them, as to the public generally "—were abandoned, and a resolution for voluntary winding-up was unanimously passed.

By mid-August it was clear that creditors for £5,228,000 would rank for a first dividend, whereas only £660,000 of cash was in sight.[2] A call of £10 was therefore proposed.[3] It was the

[1] Full details will be found in the *Bankers' Magazine*, 1866, pp. 848–63.
[2] *Ibid.*, pp. 1106–9.
[3] The shares were £50 each, £15 paid. (*Ante*, p. 239).

signal for a legal battle which lasted for three years. A "Defence Association" sought the release of shareholders from further liability, on the grounds that the board had acted fraudulently in not disclosing the "second" deed[1] which revealed the insolvency of the old firm. The judge, while admitting that the directors could not "on principles of morality and justice" justify concealment of the lock-up, held that there had been no misstatement of fact and no fraudulent intent; nevertheless, "if the public by this prospectus had been told what those who issued it knew, no one share would have been taken". Hence shareholders could be released from claims by the board, but not from those by the public.[2] This ruling was upheld by the Lord Chancellor in the House of Lords, when he declared the share-contracts voidable and not void, and pointed out that in ten months there had been no disclaimers.[2] Shareholders therefore had to pay. They had, in fact, aggravated their losses, for the delay had forced the liquidators to realize under highly adverse conditions, and had also made creditors restive. When a second £10 call (secured by creditors' application to the Court) proved insufficient to meet the immediate claims, threats to enforce payment of the full £15 outstanding compelled the issue of interest-bearing certificates of indebtedness. These were eventually discharged in the autumn of 1869, after a further £5 call, making the shares £40 paid. Creditors had then received 20*s.* in the £, plus interest, while the shareholders had paid up substantially more than £2,000,000 in calls, bringing their total loss, including the original capital, up to over £3,500,000,[3] despite the simultaneous sale of the Gurney family estates and properties.

Even before the end of 1867 the calls were producing widespread distress, and the Shareholders' Committee begged incessantly for mercy.[4] They declared, "with how much truth only too many can testify from personal observation, that if the creditors knew how many homes have been broken up and how many well-to-do people ruined by the calls already made, they would forbear to

[1] The first deed, which alone was open to inspection, contained no reference to the "secret" deed or to its contents, save such reference as was implicit in the statement about "excepted accounts". (See *ante*, p. 240.)

[2] See *Bankers' Magazine*, 1867, pp. 100–5, 239–44, 894–9, etc., for full reports of proceedings.

[3] Over twenty years later, shareholders received the last instalment of a total return of £7 18*s.* 2*d.* per share. (See *Economist*, 1893, p. 1382.)

[4] See *Bankers' Magazine*, 1867, pp. 364–6, 1069–73, etc.

press ". But they did press, and thereby stimulated a great and bitter public controversy, out of which arose criminal proceedings. In January, 1869, amid great excitement [1] the famous Gurney directors (all but Gibbs, who had died) were charged with wilful conspiracy to defraud. The proceedings need not be detailed,[2] for their disclosures of the rottenness of the old firm and its methods, of the constituents of the lock-up, and of the operations of the official assignee, have been freely drawn upon already. But it may be noted that counsel for the " old " directors, referring to Edwards, who " landed Overend, Gurney & Co. in a debt of £4,000,000, and went off with the nice little sum of £20,000 ", declared that " it is difficult to believe that the old firm could have been dragged from one difficulty into another unless, in addition to an outsider who was betraying them, there had also been a traitor in the camp ".

On the other hand, prosecuting counsel, dealing with the " secret " deed, disclosed that some of the Gurneys had shown real alarm at the prospect of the guarantee. Family letters written in the spring of 1865 showed that J. H. Gurney had " great objection " to being a director and giving a joint guarantee ; he apparently favoured immediate liquidation, for in a letter to him his uncle, Daniel Gurney, wrote, " You appear to have done the right thing in negativing the proposal of continuing O., G. & Co.'s business, and I trust there will be no sidewind attempt to frustrate negotiations with the National Discount Co. . . . I regret very much that you think you have overrated the excess ". Later, when the flotation proposals had been adopted, Daniel was alarmed that marriage settlements on his family might be reached by the guarantee, and wrote that, " in the case of a real catastrophe all my family and myself would be in total destitution or almost so, and I do not see how these settlements would be protected ". Such statements suggested a *prima facie* case against the directors, and they were committed for trial. Nevertheless, they left the Court without any sort of molestation, whereas Edwards " was followed through the streets by a crowd of 200 or 300 persons, yelling and hooting, and had to take refuge in a cab in Basinghall-street ".

The actual trial,[3] one of the most famous in financial history, began on December 13, 1869, and was staged at Westminster,

[1] The crowd was so great that, after the first day, the proceedings had to be transferred from the Mansion House to the Guildhall.

[2] See *Bankers' Magazine*, 1869, pp. 120–42.

[3] See special supplement to the *Bankers' Magazine*, Jan., 1870.

to avoid the disturbance caused by the City proceedings. It lasted nine days, but although a dissection of the firm's operations from as far back as 1851 [1] provided the prosecutor with material for many vitriolic accusations, the judge's summing-up was wholly favourable to the defendants. The verdict of "not guilty", reached in less than ten minutes, was received with "wildest excitement and enthusiasm", both within the Court and among "the vast crowd without". The moral character of the Gurneys had been vindicated.

Supremacy of the National Discount

With public interest so largely centred on the Overend, Gurney affair, it is not surprising that the difficulties of the other discount companies after the crisis passed largely unnoticed.[2] Except in the liquidation of the Joint Stock Discount there were, it is true, no revelations at all comparable with those of the "Corner House" scandals, but of the five companies existing at the opening of 1866 only the National avoided serious loss. The Joint Stock Co. had gone into liquidation before the crisis, while the other three companies were forced to reconstruct. In September, 1866, the Consolidated Discount, after writing-off 50 per cent. of its capital, became the New Consolidated Discount Co., but despite successive calls went into voluntary liquidation in May, 1869. The Financial Discount, which on reorganization had significantly changed its name to

[1] The following figures of annual turnover and discounts were cited:

	Discounts.	Turnover.
1859	£62,000,000	£150,000,000
1860	62,000,000	170,000,000
1861	53,643,000	138,000,000
1862	64,314,000	167,000,000
1863	66,370,000	177,000,000
1864	74,984,000	198,000,000
1865 (to July 31)	41,388,000	117,000,000
1865–6	56,000,000	160,000,000

[2] It is worth noting that when, on the post-crisis reconstruction of the Crédit Foncier and Mobilier of England, Albert Grant was forced to resign from the managership, his successor was—H. J. Barker! Grant, together with other retiring officials, was held personally responsible for some of the worst commitments, and was compelled to pay large sums to the company to avoid legal proceedings. To do so he had to mortgage his properties heavily, but he did so because he was "still solicitous" for the company. Even this new burden did not prove crushing, for a few years later he was figuring largely in the new mania for foreign loan flotations.

"City" Discount, disappeared about the same time. The Discount Corporation was more successful, despite the fact that its position had necessitated arrangements for reorganization even in 1865. The scheme never materialized, and the company narrowly averted collapse in the following May. It sought reorganization by combination with "certain gentlemen from Overend, Gurney & Co.", but these plans also failed, and the final reconstruction fell far short of the original hopes. Early in 1867 the business was sold to a new company, the United Discount Corporation, on terms which represented a writing-off of a third of the capital. Efforts to introduce new resources and directors were unsuccessful—"first-class gentlemen are rather shy"—but the basic business was sound, and the board, by prudent management and adherence to short-dated paper, succeeded in nursing it in spite of shortage of capital.

Of the boom discount flotations, therefore, only one survived for more than a few years after the crisis, and in 1866 the virtual paralysis of all of them increased the great void created in market facilities by Gurney's collapse. Efforts to fill the gap came from an unexpected quarter—from the influential General Credit & Finance Co. of London. During the panic, this company's shares had dropped to a discount of 90 per cent, and only a call of £2 per share (raising the paid-up capital to £1,500,000) had averted its suspension. Actually, the reserve was expected to cover all losses, but the board had learnt its lesson, and in November, 1866, announced that it would abandon all "financing" and concentrate instead upon normal bill market operations. To make possible a reduction of the unpaid liability on the shares, the company went into liquidation, and as from January 1, 1867, transferred its business to the General Credit and Discount Co. of London. The subscribed capital of the new company was £2,000,000 in £10 shares, £7 10*s.* paid. This was an unprecedented amount for a discount company, but a large part was locked-up in illiquid—chiefly railway—securities, which probably explains why the company, despite the excellent banking connections of its board and the considerable expansion in deposits which it achieved, did not secure more than a fraction of the business relinquished by Gurney's. The *Economist*, indeed, while remarking that there was room for a third "good discount house", declared categorically that the General Credit could not be that house, because of its "other" securities.[1] "A discount company," it declared,

[1] 1866, p. 1336; and see *Bankers' Magazine*, pp. 1369–72.

"must be able to say to depositors 'We have no *back shop*; we have no hidden securities; we take bills for discount and we will leave you bills as security; this and this wholly is our business.'"

From the time of the metamorphosis of the General Credit to the present day, no entirely new discount company has ever been formed. But in 1866, 1867 and 1868 many new private firms arose out of the ruins of "boom" companies. From Gurney's came R. M. Sanderson (later joined by one of the younger Gurneys) [1]; Butcher, Haws & Co.; and T. A. Holmes & Rees Wood. From other concerns came W. Shipman & Co. (Shipman had previously resigned from the National Discount to join the unfortunate Agra & Masterman's Bank) [2]; H. D. Anderson; Spencer, Hobbs & Co.; John Green, Tomkinson & Co. Other formations in 1866 were White & Shaxson, Baker, Duncombe & Co., and Lyon & Tucker, all of which still exist, but none of them appeared in the contemporary lists of "discount brokers". In 1867 Gillett separated from Brightwen,[3] so that in these few years at least eleven new private firms came into being.

The new competition did not, however, prevent the National Discount from achieving a very marked increase in its business. Thanks to the extraordinary foresight of its board, the company had weathered the storm almost without damage. It had been aware of Gurney's plight for months before the collapse, and held none of their paper, and had also avoided most of the names which later became notorious, although all of them "endeavoured to get into our books as well as Gurney's".[4] It was, however, involved in the Joint Stock Discount failure, which may have dictated the decision in January, 1866, to raise new capital—£1,000,000 in £25 shares, £5 to be called, issued at £5 premium, with payments spread up to March, 1867. The new resources enabled the company to carry the lock-up without embarrassment, and in 1866 it actually paid its usual 20 per cent. dividend on the larger capital, although post-crisis quietude necessitated a reduction in 1867. Losses in the crisis (excluding the Joint Stock bills, eventually paid in full) averaged $4\frac{3}{4}$*d.* per £100, and were met without any depletion of pub-

[1] This firm was heavily involved in the famous Collie accommodation bill scandals of 1875, and collapsed in that year.

[2] Shipman collapsed in 1869, and was then sentenced for speculation with the bank's funds.

[3] See *ante*, p. 227 *n*.

[4] Half-yearly meeting on Jan. 20, 1869.

lished reserves.[1] The company was, therefore, particularly well equipped to profit from the new openings created by the failures. It did so, and in the six years to 1872 its operations expanded very rapidly, exceeding those of the General Credit and the United Discount combined.

Its only other important rival—Alexander's—also came through the crisis with reputation and resources unimpaired. No figures were ever published, but it is probable that until the National's increase in capital in 1864 Alexander's business was at least of equal size. One incident in the crisis plainly indicates the standing and strength of the firm. At the height of the panic, a banker and old Quaker friend of G. W. Alexander on his own initiative transferred £100,000 of 3 per cent. Annuities to the partners of the firm, remarking that he was glad to have the opportunity of showing his entire confidence in the firm. Actually, the assistance was unnecessary, and the Consols were never used; nor were they transferred out of the names of the partners until their return to the lender after the panic.[2] There is no doubt that the firm benefited substantially from the crisis, but although its business was certainly larger than that of either the General Credit or the United Discount, it was definitely smaller than the National's.[3] As the table below reveals, for nearly twenty years the supremacy of the National remained unchallenged. The only other change in its capital occurred in 1877,[4] when the house was joined by Messrs. Cunliffe and Fowler, to whom 9,333 shares were issued, credited with £5 paid. These gentlemen came from Alexander's, the partnership into which they had entered with the Alexander family having terminated by effluxion of time.[5] Four years later, Alexander's connections were increased by the absorption of the firm of H. D. Anderson.[6]

It is worth noting that in the opinion of the *Economist* [7] the three discount companies were at this period responsible for approximately 30 per cent. of the aggregate business of the

[1] In the first 11 years of its existence, the company discounted bills to the amount of £194,738,859, with average losses of 10¼*d*. per £100. In the second half of this period, the discounts were £123,798,152, and the average losses were 3¼*d*.

[2] See advertisement in *The Times*, City of London No., Nov. 8, 1927.

[3] Alexander's *net* portfolio, as shown by records still in the possession of the house, fluctuated generally between £4,000,000 and £5,000,000 during the late 'seventies and 'eighties.

[4] No further addition was made until 1925.

[5] See *Economist*, 1877, p. 210.

[6] See *ante*, p. 258.

[7] See *Economist*, 1877, pp. 121–3, 1455; and 1870, pp. 188–9.

DISCOUNT COMPANIES' PROGRESS, 1867–84*

Year.	National.			General Credit.			United.		
	Deposits † £000s.	Capital £000s.	Div. %	Deposits † £000s.	Capital £000s.	Div. %	Deposits † £000s.	Capital £000s.	Div. %
1867 .	6,935	797	16	763	1,500	5	1,053	134	5·1
1868 .	7,946	,,	15	2,491	,,	5	2,038	138	6
1869 .	8,057	,,	15¾	3,576	,,	5	1,555	140	6
1870 .	9,152	,,	16½	4,608	,,	5	2,175	,,	7
1871 .	10,774	,,	18	7,432	,,	7	2,471	,,	8½
1872 .	11,051	800	15	6,366	,,	7	3,090	237	8
1873 .	9,661	,,	14½	6,335	,,	6	2,335	300	5½
1874 .	9,569	,,	14½	5,105	,,	10	2,273	,,	6
1875 .	8,201	,,	10	4,050	,,	5	3,873	,,	6
1876 .	7,785	,,	10	4,797	,,	5	4,424	,,	7
1877 .	8,860	847	10	5,657	,,	5	3,609	,,	7
1878 .	6,749	,,	10	‡	,,	4	2,042	,,	Nil.§
1879 .	11,070	,,	12	4,083	,,	4	3,862	,,	5
1880 .	11,470	,,	13	6,085	700‖	6	4,757	,,	6
1881 .	12,815	,,	12½	7,428	,,	5	5,496	,,	6
1882 .	12,885	,,	13	6,662	,,	5⅜	5,265	,,	6
1883 .	11,646	,,	13	5,582	,,	5¾	4,929	,,	6
1884 .	10,153	,,	12	5,325	,,	5	5,625	,,	7

* Compiled from *Economist* and *Bankers' Magazine*. † Including re-discounts.

‡ Figure not obtainable. § Company was involved in City of Glasgow Bank failure.

‖ Capital reduced from £2,000,100 in £10 shares, £7 10*s*. paid, to £1,200,060 in £6 shares, £3 10*s*. paid, by returning £1 10*s*. per share in cash and writing-off £2 10*s*., represented by assets locked up in B. A. & Campana Railway and returnable to shareholders as and when realized.

market. On this basis, the *total* running liabilities on loans, deposits and re-discounts at any one time must have ranged in the 'seventies from about £54 to £69 millions, rising to as much as £86 millions in 1881, but dropping steeply to £70 millions by 1884. The *Economist* estimated the annual market *turnover* at between £475 and £550 millions for the period 1871–6.

DISCOUNT COMPANIES FROM 1885 TO 1913

Down to 1885, therefore, the National Discount was by far the most important institution in the market. In April of that year, however, its dominant position was challenged by the decision of its two joint stock rivals to join forces. The merger was the work of W. T. Brand,[1] a director of the General Credit Co., who realized that the capital of the United Discount Corporation, like that of his own company, was excessive, and who saw that a fusion would make possible both a reduction of capital and an increase in the joint business. On May 12, 1885, the two businesses were taken over by the Union Discount Company of London, with a capital of £1,000,000 in £10 shares, credited with £5 paid, and with a reserve fund of £100,000. The paid-up capital of £500,000 was thus only half of that of the two constituent companies combined, and the superfluous resources were returned to shareholders. The General Credit contributed three-fifths of the new company's resources (£300,000 of the capital and £60,000 of the reserve), but the two concerns secured equal representation on the new board,[2] while the smaller concern actually supplied the first manager—Christopher R. Nugent,[3] who was to guide the fortunes of the company for thirty-seven years.[4] The new company's resources were much smaller than the National's, whose capital and reserve totalled £1,306,665; but the merger was such a success that in 1888 the paid-up capital was raised to £650,000 by an issue at a premium. The company's turnover then passed that of its rival, but it did not take the lead in deposits until 1894. Thereafter,

[1] See W. T. Brand's speech at the meeting on June 12, 1924.

[2] The initial board comprised W. T. Brand, E. Blount, G. F. Mewburn, G. H. Oppenheim of the General Credit; and A. Deacon, W. Dunn, J. D. Hill, and R. P. Laurie, M.P., of the United Discount.

[3] He had succeeded T. Fraser Sandeman as manager of the United Discount a few years previously. The first assistant manager of the Union was J. R. MacDonald, previously manager of the General Credit.

[4] For many years the house was widely known among bankers as "Nugent's".

despite its smaller capital, the Union Discount became, and remains to this day, the largest house in the market.[1]

With the National and the Union so strongly organized, and with the growing public preference for houses which published accounts, it is not surprising that the third big house—Alexander's—decided in February, 1891, to adopt the limited company form. It was not until 1911, however, that it became a *public* company, and its initial subscribed capital of £900,000, in £100,000 of fully-paid preference shares (a novel feature for the bill market) and £800,000 of £10 Ordinary shares, £5 paid, was taken up wholly by members of the old firm.[2]

Upon Alexander's registration, the bill market assumed in general structure the form which it retained down to the War period, comprising three large limited companies and rather more than a score of private firms. Of the latter, four were formed in the decade after the "Union" merger—in 1886, King & Foà (which recently merged with White & Shaxson, to form King & Shaxson); in 1888, Vaile, Allen & Co. (which later became Allen, Harvey & Ross); in 1891, Smith, St. Aubyn & Co.; and, in 1895, William P. Bonbright & Co. But although the structure of the market sustained no outstanding changes from the early 'nineties until 1914,[3] this period witnessed very marked expansion in its operations. As the following table reveals, the aggregate deposits of the three largest houses rose from £22½ millions in 1890 to no less than £31 millions in 1895; and while there was a sharp contraction in the ensuing two years, after 1903 the total began to rise steeply, touching £46½ millions in 1913.[4]

[1] It took over the private firm of Green, Tomkinson & Co. in 1891, and later absorbed the business of Harwood, Knight and Allen.

[2] The first board was R. H. Alexander (chairman), W. C., R. E., and W. G. Alexander, and H. D. Anderson.

[3] Four modern firms were, however, formed in the early years of the century: Henry Sherwood & Co. (1901), Ryder, Parker & Co. (as Ryder, Mills & Co., in 1903), Cater & Co. (as C. E. Cater, in 1908), and Daniell, Cazenove & Co. (1913).

[4] See also App. IV, for separate figures for *net* portfolios, re-discounts and deposits for each of the companies, and for aggregates under each head (*post*, pp. 330–1).

DISCOUNT COMPANIES' LOANS AND DEPOSITS, 1885–1913 [1]

(Excluding Re-discounts)

At Dec. 31.	Alexander's.	National.	Union.	Aggregate.
	£	£	£	£
1885 .	*	8,698,014	3,697,831	—
1886 .	*	8,397,591	4,854,406	—
1887 .	*	9,417,192	6,266,785	—
1888 .	*	9,350,445	8,738,826	—
1889 .	*	10,198,383	9,564,294	—
1890 .	5,933,892†	9,543,731	7,028,531	22,506,154
1891 .	7,287,719†	8,775,368	7,517,952	23,581,039
1892 .	6,970,813	9,807,423	8,271,338	25,049,574
1893 .	6,249,142‡	7,963,568	7,762,600	21,975,310
1894 .	7,217,217	9,230,210	10,679,980	27,127,407
1895 .	8,238,422	10,452,724	12,390,264	31,081,410
1896 .	6,377,725	8,932,608	9,695,301	25,005,634
1897 .	6,588,630	8,025,861	10,087,491	24,701,982
1898 .	6,894,839	9,350,743	9,925,953	26,171,535
1899 .	6,160,204	8,987,697	10,865,506	26,013,407
1900 .	6,066,545	8,757,155	12,483,918	27,307,618
1901 .	6,345,473	8,647,126	13,383,341	28,375,940
1902 .	6,208,886	9,061,058	12,502,037	27,771,981
1903 .	6,229,551	8,569,653	12,431,186	27,230,390
1904 .	6,748,309	10,116,496	13,683,012	30,547,817
1905 .	7,537,820‡	10,355,847	14,849,382	32,743,049
1906 .	7,780,781	12,003,999	15,641,509	35,426,289
1907 .	7,764,233	13,495,948	17,573,288	38,833,469
1908 .	7,279,596‡	12,324,699	17,206,482	36,810,777
1909 .	8,321,952‡	14,280,562	17,765,630	40,368,144
1910 .	8,531,052‡	14,312,200	17,163,143	40,006,395
1911 .	9,311,741	15,208,208	17,112,160	41,632,109
1912 .	9,731,880	15,871,902	18,913,711	44,517,493
1913 .	10,134,947	15,757,480	20,662,330	46,554,757

* No figures were published, and records are no longer available.
† Based on an estimate of the relevant re-discounts total.
‡ Figure for the preceding June 30, as the re-discounts' total is not available for Dec. 31.

[1] This table, together, with the more comprehensive one in App. IV, was compiled with the assistance of the companies concerned. In the published accounts, the Union combined re-discounts with loans and deposits until 1888; the National did so until 1900; and Alexander's did so until 1911. The author is therefore indebted to each of the companies for the re-discount figures before these dates.

CHAPTER VIII

GROWTH OF THE INTERNATIONAL MONEY MARKET

THE collapse of Overend, Gurney, as has been shown, wrought great changes in the constitution of the discount market. These changes, however, were mainly changes of personnel, which, though purging and strengthening the market, did not fundamentally alter its structure. Unlike the crises of 1847 and 1857, both of which had led to radical alterations in the relationships between the discount houses and the Bank of England, the crisis of 1866 left the broad framework of the market unchanged. Nevertheless, during the 'fifties and 'sixties, and especially after 1866, new tendencies of more far-reaching change were becoming steadily more marked: the market was becoming dominated more and more by credit conditions abroad, and proportionately less by purely domestic needs.

The London money market had, of course, long been susceptible to international influences, and British investors and British financial houses had long been heavily committed in foreign securities and enterprises. As early as 1832 Nathan Rothschild had declared [1] that "this country in general is the Bank for the whole world; . . . all transactions in India, in China, in Germany, in the whole world, are guided here and settled through this country"; and he had shown that drafts on London were widely used to finance even trade which never touched British shores. Acceptances of the big London houses had long been employed as a kind of international currency which, thanks to the freedom and extent of the London discount market, could be turned into gold at a moment's notice. In the 'thirties the system of "open" credits granted by British houses had been extensively used to finance not only international trade, but also (though surreptitiously) all kinds of capital development projects in America, for the credits were supported by remittances of American securities, which were

[1] 1832 Committee, Minutes, QQ. 4799, 4802, 4866.

subsequently " introduced " by the acceptance houses to the British investor.[1] In 1846 it had been remarked that a British private banking firm was to be found in every one of forty Mediterranean ports.[2] In the 'forties and 'fifties British capital had financed, and British contractors had arranged, the building of railways in many parts of the world. At the time of the 1857 crisis, it had been estimated that no less than £80 millions of American securities alone were held in this country[3]; while a few years later investment in America had received a new stimulus from the very high yields obtainable on North American bonds during the American Civil War. In this period, too, the craze for the formation of Anglo-foreign and Anglo-Colonial banks, and of finance companies, had provided a new, and peculiarly efficient, means of tapping British savings for use overseas.[4] " The trade of the world," it had been said in 1858,[5] " could hardly be carried on without the intervention of English credit . . . a man in Boston cannot buy a cargo of tea in Canton without getting a credit from Messrs. Matheson or Messrs. Baring."

This internationalization of the London market necessarily implied that in the long run there had to be a definite equilibrium between London rates and rates in leading foreign centres. As early as 1819, it had been recognized that a marked differential between Continental and London rates could at certain times exert an important effect on London credit conditions[6]; and Rothschild had explained a decade later that the premium on gold on the Continent " levelled itself " within $\frac{1}{4}$ per cent. between Hamburg, Amsterdam and Paris.[7] Nevertheless, in days when mails to New York took at least a fortnight (as they did even in 1866), and when cable transfers were unknown,[8] a rapid adjustment of rates was impossible. Even in the late 'fifties, it is clear that international influences upon the discount market were seldom felt except at moments of special stress, or when the differential between London and foreign discount rates had become abnormally wide: there was no regular or sustained relationship between the different rates, and in the short run the importance of foreign factors as London rate

[1] See Jenks, *Migration of British Capital*, pp. 73–98, and *ante*, p. 95.
[2] *Ibid.*, p. 188. [3] *Ante*, p. 197.
[4] See especially Goschen, *Essays*, *op. cit.*
[5] 1858 Committee, Minutes, QQ. 1699–1792. [6] *Ante*, p. 74.
[7] 1832 Committee, Minutes, Q. 4811.
[8] See Luke Hansard before Manchester and District Bankers' Institute, Jan., 1901. (*Bankers' Magazine*, 1901, I, p. 412.)

determinants was probably not great. Wide rate disparities were common between London and even the more highly developed Continental commercial centres, such as Hamburg and Paris. Nor was there in foreign centres any very large volume of mobile balances, so that foreign-owned short-term funds in London were only exceptionally sufficient to provide any important menace to market stability. It was well recognized that extreme stringency or crisis abroad was bound to have its reactions upon London, but even as late as 1859 the idea that there must be *day-to-day* sympathetic movements between the various markets, in normal as well as abnormal times, was still regarded as comparatively new.[1] Chapman declared in 1857 that differential rates did not greatly stimulate the flow of funds internationally, as " capital is not disturbed so very easily "; although he agreed that any noteworthy fall in the London market rate below the Hamburg rate would lead a Hamburg banker to remit his English acceptances for immediate discount, instead of holding them to maturity, as was customary.[2] Moreover, it is clear that at this period foreign bills formed only a small proportion of the total outstanding at any one time—for the middle 'forties the proportion had been estimated (by Newmarch) at under 14 per cent.[3]

The Mania for Foreign Loans

From the early 'sixties, however, various new influences, and a general quickening of the tempo of economic life, contributed to a great expansion of international trade and international finance, and to a growing economic interdependence of nations which, within very few years, made each of the leading money markets simply a part of a great international market.[4] Possibly the most important single cause of this change was a new develop-

[1] See *Economist*, 1859, p. 530.

[2] 1857 Committee, Minutes, Q. 5079.

[3] *Ante*, p. 192 *n*.

[4] The drawing together of the different financial markets was undoubtedly stimulated by the more rapid dissemination of financial intelligence, both internationally and among investors in each country. In this connection, the most important development was the rise of the financial press. The *Money Market Review* was published weekly after 1859, and about 1870 its proprietors launched the *Financier*, issued five times weekly. Under the same auspices there appeared in the early 'seventies the *Bondholders' Register*, devoted to new issues, maturities, coupon dates, etc. The *Bullionist*, a weekly, appeared in 1866, while from 1863 the *Economist* published the *Investors' Monthly Manual*. (See Jenks, *op. cit.*, p. 254, for further details.)

ment of the system of foreign Government loans.[1] Such flotations had been common in London for at least half a century,[2] and had provided one of the major causes of the 1825 crisis; but, in general, it was not until the 'fifties (and, more particularly, the 'sixties) that they assumed very large proportions. Development at this period sprang from a wave of enthusiasm on the Continent for public works, improvement of public buildings and city sanitation; from preparations for war and from war itself; from demands for lower taxes; and from a new attitude towards Government borrowing, formerly considered as purely an emergency expedient and strongly opposed by economists. The large funds required for such purposes could rarely be raised in the local markets, while such international centres as Paris and Berlin were strictly controlled by their Governments, who sought always to impose political conditions upon prospective borrowers. Hence the foreign Governments came to the only extensive "free" market (Amsterdam and Brussels were also "free", but small), to London, where public sentiment, reacting violently after 1866 from limited liability and from companies in general, was then even more ready to receive them than it had been in the 'fifties and early 'sixties.

The technical equipment of the London capital market had, however, been severely damaged by the crisis, and for several years many of the surviving finance companies were fully engaged in nursing their bad assets. This gave the foreigner his opportunity, and brought a fresh influx of cosmopolitan bankers and financiers, whose ramified connections increased the internationalism of the market.[3] Moreover, the scale of borrowings became too large for one house or even one market to handle, and there arose the practices of "syndicating"[4] and of placing *tranches* of each loan simultaneously in different financial centres. The new technique was devoted first to persuading a government that it ought to borrow, and only secondarily to persuading lenders to lend, for the second task could be readily achieved by an engineered press campaign and by judicious preparatory

[1] An excellent account of the growth of Britain's overseas lending will be found in Jenks, *op. cit.*, to which work the writer is especially indebted for much of the material in the first half of this section.

[2] The first issue, for Austria, had been placed in 1794.

[3] See Jenks, p. 271, *et seq.*, and 1875 *Committee on Loans to Foreign States*.

[4] A form of underwriting whereby the various issuers guaranteed subscription of a given proportion of an issue, receiving frequently a sliding-scale commission, in cash or scrip at a discount.

market manipulation, even though (as frequently happened) the problem were aggravated by the organized " bear " opposition of disappointed issuers. Thus there arose in the late 'sixties a new mania for foreign loans, and in the early 'seventies, when the boom reached its height, any government, no matter how impecunious, could find buyers in London for its bonds, so long as it were ready to add liberal commissions to the capital of its debt, and later to meet a crippling interest bill by new borrowing on the same system. In the decade after 1866 foreign bonds eclipsed in public interest and fluctuations all other securities on the London Stock Exchange; between 1871 and 1875 alone the new issues exceeded £280 millions, and, in addition, there were large-scale London purchases of the internal issues of foreign states, especially of American securities.[1]

Development on such a scale, and particularly the practice of simultaneous issue in different centres (which frequently gave an option to the holder of bonds to take payment in several centres at stated rates of exchange), brought a new sensitiveness of markets to foreign conditions. There arose a vast block of international securities (Van Oss estimated in 1872 that of European public debts of some £4,600 millions, about £1,700 millions was held internationally), with a proportionate increase in the means of making international remittances, and a marked growth of arbitrage in coupons and bonds.[2]

By far the greatest part of this international business was secured by London. Her position as the leading international market was definitely confirmed by the Franco-German War,[3] which not only removed the rivalry of Paris, but greatly increased the volume of foreign funds in London. The Bank of France suspended gold payments, exercising its option to pay in silver, thereby directing all demands for gold to London, the only remaining free gold market; while the subsequent payment of the huge War indemnity to Germany literally created a new phenomenon—a large volume of international balances held at call. The reason for this was that the bulk of the French payments was made in commercial bills of exchange, which could actually be tendered in subscription for the French £120 millions loan of 1872, with the result that the amount was heavily oversubscribed. These bills, mainly bills on London, were handed over to the German Government, which throughout the 'seventies

[1] See *Bankers' Magazine*, 1876, pp. 424, 519. [2] Jenks, *op. cit.*
[3] See Bagehot, *Lombard Street*, pp. 35–6, 214, 310 *et seq.*, and Giffen, *Essays in Finance* (1886), Vol. I, pp. 55–74.

thus secured command of enormous floating balances in London, which balances were lent on the market pending their repatriation in gold.[1]

Internationalization of Commerce

These various financial influences upon internationalism were paralleled by developments in the commercial sphere. Down to the late 'sixties Britain could herself supply the bulk of her needs for essential raw materials and food, with the notable exception of cotton. The " great commerce ", says Jenks, was still of the nature of adventure, and few areas had fundamentally close economic ties with Britain.[2] The ensuing decade, with its 10 per cent. growth of population, accompanied by a noteworthy rise in the standard of living, the general adoption of steam transport, and the maturity of railway schemes abroad, revolutionized trade in raw materials and food. In 1868 Britain had supplied four-fifths of her demands for such products as grain, meat, dairy produce and wool; by 1878 the proportion had fallen to only one half.[3] With this new dependence upon external supplies came an additional inter-locking of the world's markets, and, from the bill market standpoint, there came also a great increase in international acceptances, stimulated in particular by the growing regional connections of the London issuing-cum-acceptance houses.

On all sides, therefore, there were powerful influences at work to bring the nations closer together. But not even these influences could have produced real internationalism in the money markets had it not been for the simultaneous development of speedy telegraphic communication. The first Atlantic telegraph line had been opened for traffic in August, 1858, but not until about eight years later were New York foreign exchange rates regularly advised by cable.[4] Thereafter, use of the cable transfer became increasingly more widespread, and by 1877 the *Economist* was remarking that telegraphic transfers, together with international coupons, were superseding the bill as a means of remittance.[5]

[1] See Giffen, *op. cit.*; *Bankers' Magazine*, 1872, pp. 555, 742; and Arthur Ellis, *Rationale of Market Fluctuations* (1879).

[2] Jenks, *op. cit.*, p. 329.

[3] James Caird, *The Landed Interest and the Supply of Food* (1880), p. 127; and see Knowles, *Industrial and Commercial Revolutions in Great Britain* (Part IV).

[4] Luke Hansard, *loc. cit.*

[5] *Economist*, 1877, p. 1006.

Within a decade from the 1866 crisis these various factors had completed London's transformation into a true international market, making it more closely sensitive than ever before to external influences. " London," declared a partner in Smith, Payne & Co. in 1875,[1] " is the centre of the commerce of the world, and each accident that happens on the Continent, or a bad harvest in any quarter, or any material cause that renders money cheaper or dearer on the Continent, *instantly affects us*, and much more rapidly than it used to." London interest rates, it was said, were " practically in relation " to those on the Continent; there were many classes of bills which could be discounted " either in Paris, or in Frankfort, or in London ", and would flow quickly to the cheapest centre; and English bankers were constantly asked whether they had bank bills to sell to meet demands from the Continent.[2] Seyd estimated in 1878 that between £50 and £60 millions of London acceptances were regularly held on the Continent; so that there was at all times a substantial volume of claims which would crystallize, and be sent for immediate discount in London, at the first sign of stringency in any Continental market or upon any sudden ease in London. As Bagehot forcibly pointed out, the existence of these claims, added to the mass of internationally-owned bonds and coupons, made London liable to violent and sudden fluctuations in discount rates. To a great extent, this acute sensitivity was attributable to the existence of a specialized discount market, for the discount houses, unlike the bankers in London or any other market, paid interest on virtually the whole of their resources. They were compelled therefore always to employ the whole, and as their profits depended upon the *margin* between borrowing and lending rates, it was a matter of indifference to them that their search for bills depressed rates unduly, so long as there was an appropriate fall in short money costs; and if keen competition narrowed the profit-margin, the loss on that account would be small compared with the loss on keeping balances idle. Conversely, in times of stringency, it was of little consequence to the discount houses that their competition forced money rates up abruptly, for discount rates would also rise. Thus even a small increase in the credit supply, from whatever cause, often produced a very marked

[1] 1875 Committee, evidence of Jervoise Smith, Q. 7285; and see also Giffen, *op. cit.*

[2] 1875 Committee, evidence of Thomas Cooke, chairman of Manchester and Liverpool District Bank, Q. 6647.

fall in rates, and a small decrease brought an equally marked rise.[1]

The increase in sensitivity was not, however, the only or even the most important consequence for the bill market of the growing internationalism of finance. During the last three decades of the century there was proceeding a fundamental, though very gradual, change in the basic function of the discount houses. At the time of the 1857 crisis, the bill market was an integral and vital part of the mechanism of domestic finance, the sole means which enabled a unit banking system to supply efficiently and at reasonable rates the needs of domestic borrowers. What had been almost the sole function of the market in Thomas Richardson's day was still its primary function in Barclay Chapman's. Thereafter, its function as an essential link between purely domestic borrowers and lenders steadily diminished in importance, and its resources were devoted more and more to the finance of overseas trade and that of trade in which Britain was neither seller nor buyer. By the close of the century, the market had become primarily an instrument of external finance, and only secondarily one of domestic finance.

Decline of the Domestic Bill

The first cause of this vital transition was, necessarily, the growth of international influences in general and the expansion of world trade in primary commodities in particular. But this increase in overseas trade, while it inevitably increased the volume of "external" bills with which the market had to deal, would not have led to such a marked preponderance of "external" paper in Lombard Street had there not been a simultaneous decline in the importance of the internal bill.

This decline may be said to have begun shortly after the 1857 crisis, although it was not until the 'seventies that it became at all marked. Its first cause, in point of time, was the diminution of country bank re-discounting, the abuse of which had caused so much distress, and attracted so much censure, in 1857 that regular re-discounting came to be regarded as the practice of only second-rate banks.[2] The larger provincial banks there-

[1] See Bagehot, *op. cit.*, p. 157.

[2] "After the panic of 1857 was over, I remember particularly well there was a great change in the management of the banks all over England, and I knew it in this way: The great business of our house about 1857 was re-discounting for country banks. That business rapidly reduced after 1857, because banks felt the imprudence of having

fore sought to avoid it at all normal times, and were enabled to do so, without seriously contracting their turnover, by the rapid growth of the banking habit and by the competitive effectiveness of their deposit allowances, which rendered bank deposits simply an alternative means of private investment.[1] By 1875, the Liverpool banks, which, by reason of their preponderantly industrial connections, had formerly been the largest re-discounters, were regularly very large lenders in the London market,[2] and re-discounting was "practically never done".[3] The decline of bank re-discounting did not, of course, necessarily involve a reduction in the total supply of domestic paper, but it did involve a reduction in the quantity sold in Lombard Street. The bill market made intensive efforts to make good the gap, and the result was a substantial increase in the provincial trade connections of the bigger discount houses. By 1865 several houses had agencies even in Glasgow,[4] and ten years later George Rae was complaining that the Liverpool banks had to compete "day by day" with the London bill brokers,[5] and were obliged to cut rates in order to obtain discounts at all.[6]

such a mass of bills that they could not hold themselves, and therefore they kept more money in London than they previously had had. But that process went on far more rapidly after 1866. . . . Those lessons have never been forgotten, and the great banks in the country that were large [re-] discounters in 1866 are now large depositors in London."—William Fowler, before Institute of Bankers, Nov. 4, 1891 (*Journal*, 1891, p. 618). For many years after 1857, however, a few prominent authorities contended that reasonable re-discounting, safeguarded by proper reserves against the contingent liability, was entirely legitimate when conducted by banks in industrial districts. See, for example, George Rae, *The Country Banker*, pp. 222–4, 253.

[1] *Economist*, 1877, p. 914.

[2] See George Rae before 1875 Committee, Minutes, Q. 5285.

[3] 1875 Committee, Minutes, Q. 7171.

[4] 1875 Committee, Minutes, QQ. 6360, 2064. [5] *Ibid.*, QQ. 5372–83.

[6] In thus competing, the market was assisted by the large commissions charged by many country banks on current account turnover, which led many business men virtually to use the brokers as bankers, discounting their bills with a discount house (with whom they kept a regular account, and a balance at interest), and instructing the discounters to remit Bank of England notes, as and when required, to meet their local payments. (See 1875 Committee, *loc. cit.*) For Scottish business, too, the discount houses were helped by the practice of the Scottish banks of fixing uniform discount rates, applicable for all banks and for all classes of paper, the principle being that the rate applied to sound bills, and that no bills should be taken unless they were sound. All second-grade bills were therefore sent for discount to London. (See 1875 Committee, especially QQ. 2064 and 1402.)

This active search for bills enabled the market for some time to offset the effect on its domestic bill portfolios of the reduction in bank re-discounting, but in the 'sixties and 'seventies new factors began to diminish the internal bill circulation itself.

By far the most important of these new influences was the bank amalgamation movement, bringing with it a great expansion of branch banking, and enabling many banks each to perform within its own organization the " equalizing " function for which the bill market had previously been indispensable. In a few isolated cases, branch banking had indeed begun many years earlier to reduce the banks' dependence on the bill market, as Vincent Stuckey's evidence [1] in 1841 revealed; but the early instances of " balanced " branch systems were rare. For a bank to equalize within its own area the credit surpluses and deficits of different districts required generally a large organization, so that down to the 'seventies such effects as bank amalgamations and extending branch systems produced upon the bill supply were completely obscured by the general expansion of trade. After 1878, however, when the scandal of the City of Glasgow Bank failure led to the adoption of the principle of " reserve liability ", and thus removed the principal deterrent to the formation of limited liability banking companies, the era of really large-scale banking began. In consequence, the number of branch banks, which had risen by some 35 per cent. to 2,413, in the nine years to 1881, increased by a further 40 per cent., to 3,383, in the ensuing decade.[2] This development, by enabling the bigger banks to finance from the deposits of their " agricultural " branches the demands at their " industrial " branches, removed one of the principal reasons for the use of the bill as the standard instrument of accommodation. From many points of view, it became a matter of indifference to the banks whether they financed their customers by discounting their bills or by granting loans or advances, and to the customers the flexibility of the overdraft system had definite attractions. Thus the spread of branch banks was accompanied in many trades by a gradual displacement of the internal bill by the " open credit " system as the standard means of finance.

Meanwhile, other influences were working in the same direction. The improvement in communications, accelerating the speed with which goods moved to market and into final con-

[1] 1841 Committee, Minutes, Q. 641.

[2] See Joseph Sykes, *Amalgamation Movement in British Banking*, p. 113. Palgrave estimated the total for 1858 at 1,195.

sumption, was shortening the customary credit terms; the growth of the industrial combine, making it increasingly difficult for the head office of a business to watch the many bills of its retailer customers, and to ensure due payment at maturity, was producing a marked preference for cash payments, or at least for credit by ledger accounts; and a new and vigorous business competition was popularizing a system of cash rebates which made payment by bill definitely unprofitable. At the same time, the growth of the banking habit, and the availability of banking facilities in every important town, put an end to the use of bills as local currency.

For these various reasons there proceeded during the last quarter of the century a steady decline in the importance of the internal bill, both in the general trade of the country and in the portfolios of the discount market. This tendency, comparatively slow until the last decade, was sharply accentuated in the 'nineties, for the Baring Crisis gave a new stimulus to the movement for the absorption of private banks, while the subsequent prolonged spell of acute monetary ease in London drew special attention to the advantages of geographical extension by the Metropolitan banks, for country rates remained comparatively attractive. During this period there were on the average eleven bank amalgamations yearly, while between 1891 and 1901 the number of bank branches rose from 3,383 to 4,762.[1] By 1900, the decay of the domestic bill was attracting widespread attention. In 1902 it was remarked [2] that the separate accounting of the fourth of each month in the Clearing House returns was a "survival of a feature in banking now far from important, but at one time of great consequence . . . Nowadays . . . the volume of bills due on the fourth of the month [3] is distinctly less in proportion, owing to the extension of open credit —called ledger accounts—and the increased use of payments of cash by means of cheques passed through the country clearing." [4]

So striking a change in banking and trade methods, and in the size of the banking unit, as occurred after about 1875 might

[1] See Sykes, *op. cit.*

[2] By J. H. Tritton, before London Chamber of Commerce, on Jan. 30, 1902 (*Institute of Bankers' Journal*, 1902, p. 213).

[3] Domestic bills were generally dated on the first of the month and thus, with the addition of days of grace, usually matured on the 4th of the month.

[4] The decline in the relative importance of the "fourths" had first become noticeable after about 1877. (See *Institute of Bankers' Journal*, 1891, p. 114.)

have been expected to have had violent repercussions on bill market structure and prosperity. That it did not do so was attributable very largely to the great expansion of " external " discounts, already discussed. Moreover, while the decline of country bank re-discounting removed one form of bank dependence on the bill market, even the banks whose branch systems were best balanced remained dependent on the market for a supply of securities for reserve purposes,[1] for local bills were no alternative to first-class " brokers' bills "; and as bank deposits grew and a quickening of trade made bank accounts more " active ", a sound bill portfolio became more than ever important. Finally, the gap in the market's domestic bill portfolios was to some extent made good by the introduction of Treasury bills. The origin and early history of these demand some attention.[2]

The Birth of the Treasury Bill

Down to 1877, the sole marketable instrument of Government floating debt was the Exchequer bill, which, for reasons already discussed,[3] had many years earlier ceased to be popular with either the banks or the investing public. It was even less attractive to the discount market, owing to its peculiarly cumbersome form. The Exchequer bill, in the 'sixties and 'seventies,[4] generally had a maximum currency of five years, and was issued only twice a year—in March and June. It carried half-yearly interest coupons, but the rate of interest was never known for more than six months ahead, being fixed half-yearly by the Treasury. For the first half of each year of the bill's life, a holder had no remedy against an unsatisfactory interest rate, but in each second half-year the bills were accepted at par by the Treasury in payment of taxes or other sums due to the Government, and during these periods, too, the holder could *ask* for repayment. This, however, the Treasury had the right to refuse, save only when the bills were presented on an anni-

[1] See, for example, 1875 Committee, Minutes, Q. 4226.

[2] Only brief reference is made here, for the pre-War position of the Treasury bill in the discount market was insignificant in contrast with the enormous importance it has assumed since 1914. Detailed treatment of the pre-War history of the Treasury bill is therefore most appropriately considered in relation to its modern history, and such treatment has been deferred to a further volume, in course of preparation, on the discount market during and after the War.

[3] See *ante*, pp. 115–17.

[4] Then governed by the Exchequer Bills and Bonds Act, 1866.

versary of the date of their issue. In that case, payment could be *demanded*.[1] It is hardly surprising that so strange a security had far less appeal to the bill market than had commercial bills; and early in 1877 the anomaly was noted [2] that the British Government was paying on its short obligations as much as 2 per cent., while market rate was barely 1½ per cent., and while the French Government, in a comparatively rudimentary money market, was borrowing at ½ per cent. on *Bons du Tresor* of 3 to 5 months and at no more than 1 per cent. for 12 months.

In such circumstances, the Exchequer bill was little used, except for issue to Government departments. The only alternative means of financing Government short-term needs at that time was by borrowing at the Bank—on Deficiency Advances (these replaced Deficiency " Bills " after 1866) for Consolidated Fund Services, and on Ways and Means Advances for Supply Services.[3] Such borrowing, although it inevitably caused considerable and unnecessary disturbance in the market, answered sufficiently well so long as floating debt needs were not large. When, however, in the middle 'seventies the purchase of the Suez Canal shares, and large advances to local authorities for public works, brought a sharp increase in the floating debt,[4] some other means of finance had to be devised. The Chancellor of the Exchequer, Sir Stafford Northcote, through Lord Welby, sought the advice of Bagehot, then at the height of his fame. Bagehot promptly advised the use of a short security " resembling as nearly as possible a commercial bill of exchange . . . issued under discount, and falling due at certain intervals ".[5] The advice was followed, and by the Treasury Bills Act, 1877, and the regulations made in pursuance of it,[6] there was created the Treasury bill—a Government promissory note, issued by tender under discount, and having a fixed currency not exceeding twelve months.

The new security proved a great success, and rapidly super-

[1] See Hansard, Third Series, Vol. CCXXXII, Cols. 1583–7, and Joseph Burn, *Stock Exchange Investments*, pp. 112–15.

[2] See *Economist*, 1877, p. 182.

[3] See Burn, *op. cit.*, pp. 30–1. Supply Services are those the expenditure on which requires the *annual* sanction of Parliament, as opposed to the Consolidated Fund Services, the expenditure upon which is made under a permanent authorization. Most important of Consolidated Fund Services is the service of the National Debt.

[4] Hansard, *loc. cit.* The debt had risen in 1877 to £9 millions.

[5] See Lord Welby's letter to the *Economist* (1909, p. 1045).

[6] The first regulations were embodied in a Treasury Minute dated March 16, 1877. (See *Bankers' Magazine*, 1877, pp. 651–5.)

seded the Exchequer bill, which was finally abolished in 1897. As, however, the Treasury bill (like the Exchequer bill) could be used only for Consolidated Fund purposes, for the first twenty-five years the amount in issue was always small, judged by modern standards, and never surpassed about £20 millions. In this period, too, individual issues were usually between only £2 and £3 millions (in the whole pre-War period the figure never exceeded £5 millions), and only about three or four were made each year, although after 1889 private issues were made to the National Debt Commissioners, in addition to the public tender issues. In 1902, however, when power was given[1] to use Treasury bills for Ways and Means purposes (*i.e.*, for temporary finance for Supply, as well as Consolidated Fund, Services), the bills came to be an instrument of everyday Government finance. Thereafter, public issues became much more frequent, averaging about fifteen each year, and reaching a pre-War maximum of twenty-two in 1910, while the volume of tender bills outstanding frequently exceeded £25 millions, and in April, 1910, touched a peak of £36,700,000.[2] In considering these figures in the light of post-1914 experience, it must be remembered that Ways and Means bills (which after 1902 formed the bulk of the total) had to be paid off entirely within the financial year in which they were issued. This limitation prevented any very large growth in the outstanding total, for, so long as it remained, Treasury bills were, in the strict sense of the term, instruments of short-term finance, and not merely a means of carrying permanent or semi-permanent debt in short-dated form. It was only when the War brought an abandonment of all restrictions upon Government borrowing that issues on the grand scale became possible.

With this limitation in mind, it will be seen that the contrast between the pre-War and the post-War volume of Treasury bills does not afford a reliable measure of the relative importance of the Treasury bill in *normal* Government finance, even if account be taken of the different scale of the Budget. In fact, the period from 1877 to 1913 witnessed an enormous growth in the importance of the Treasury in the market, especially

[1] By the year's Appropriation Act, thereafter renewed annually.

[2] A curious feature of all pre-War issues was that six months' bills were by far the most popular. Twelve month bills were largely used in 1902–4, and throughout the period there were occasional issues of nine, four, two, and one month bills; but in the period 1902–13, six months' issues totalled 116, in contrast with only 32 issues of three months' bills.

after 1902. But while the growth of Treasury bills provided a valuable addition to the market's "domestic" paper, and while their volume was at times sufficiently large to exert a strong effect upon the credit position, the increased scale of Government operations did not prevent the domination of the market by external influences, nor did it compensate for more than a part of the decline in internal trade paper.

Foreign Balances and Sensitivity

The availability of Treasury bills did, in fact, actually increase the sensitiveness of the market to external influences, for while the small trade bill (as opposed to the acceptances of big merchant banking houses) had never been negotiable abroad, the Treasury bill came to be eagerly sought by Continental bankers, and often figured largely in foreign portfolios. Thus by 1900 it was remarked [1] that the fact that London was the one really free gold market in which bills were readily negotiable at all times had led most Continental bankers "of any position" regularly to hold London bills "as a gold reserve"; and that in consequence foreign bankers were keen buyers of English Treasury bills whenever the rate was attractive. Indeed, in the autumn of that year a sudden rise of London rates led to French purchases of bills estimated at £30 millions, of which about one half was believed to consist of Treasury bills; while at the same time part of an issue of Exchequer Bonds was placed in New York.[2] Felix Schuster estimated [3] that in 1901 French balances alone, including security holdings, totalled between £50 and £70 millions, and considered that the influx of French money was the principal cause of a marked discrepancy between Bank and market rates. Foreign balances, he declared, "must have an important bearing on the future of our money market". Their importance was to be stressed over and over again [4] in

[1] See Luke Hansard, *loc. cit.*, p. 412.

[2] This transaction was hailed as the first in which America, reversing the traditional order, had financed "Europe". Exchequer bonds, however, like Consols, were not popular with foreigners, owing to the deduction of income-tax at source, and it was said that the Americans regretted their purchase. See Cornelis Rozenraad, *The International Money Market*. (*Institute of Bankers' Journal*, 1902, p. 174.)

[3] At the meeting of the Union Bank of London, Jan. 15, 1902.

[4] Especially in 1905, when Japanese balances became prominent. Important Japanese participation in the London market dated from 1895, when the Bank of England was made the temporary depository of the Chinese war indemnity proceeds.

the ensuing few years, when the vulnerability of London's position in the event of any calamity abroad became increasingly recognized, and gave added point to the generation-old clamour for a larger gold reserve.

This vulnerability was forcibly demonstrated at the time of the American crisis, which for the first time brought home the extent of London's transformation into an international centre. In that year the panic demands for gold which swept America, and almost those demands alone (for the U.K. domestic position was comparatively sound), imposed tremendous strain on the Bank's reserve, and forced Bank rate up from 4½ to 7 per cent.—its highest since 1873—in little over a week. So violent an impact inevitably led to condemnations [1] of the system which permitted the market to be thus susceptible to foreign influences. But several prominent bankers, and, with them, the *Economist*,[2] rejoiced in that susceptibility, holding it an indication that "the London market is a live market, and that nothing should be done to remedy what is not a defect but a virtue . . . the absence of sensitiveness in Paris, which Sir Felix Schuster dwelt upon with admiration, affects us with a precisely opposite feeling. So long as Paris is comparatively dead and nerveless, with a gold trap instead of a gold market, so long is the supremacy of London assured." The notion of a "cast-iron" gold reserve the *Economist* thought preposterous, comparing its advocates with those who would "beggar the tax-payer in time of peace by frantic preparations for war". And there was much to be said for the *Economist* view, for the crisis had revealed a surprising strengthening in the effectiveness of Bank rate,[3] whose vigorous increase had within a few weeks attracted large amounts of gold from all quarters, despite the protective rate increases on the Continent. The strain, it was remarked, had disclosed both the strength and the excellence of the market, and had shown "how London, the capital of Free-trade and the great emporium of gold, plays its lucrative part as the distributor and collector of credit, the clearing-house of the world . . . London is sensitive but safe, because our basis is automatic, and we respond freely to foreign demands".[4]

[1] See *Institute of Bankers' Journal*, 1907, p. 469 *et seq.*

[2] *Economist*, 1907, p. 2070.

[3] The Governor of the Bank attributed this strengthening wholly to the "increased and more rapid means of intercommunication between financial centres". (See evidence before United States Monetary Commission, 1910, Senate Document No. 405, 61st Congress, 2nd Session.)

[4] *Economist*, 1907, p. 2286.

One other powerful cause of the increased internationalization of the market after about 1900 remains to be noted. This was the marked expansion of first-class acceptance business. For very many years, as has been shown, acceptances granted by London houses had played a vital part in the financing of world trade. In the last quarter of the nineteenth century their use was greatly stimulated, first by the new influx of cosmopolitan financiers which began after the 1866 crisis, and later by a rapid increase in the number of foreign banks which found it necessary, especially in the closing years of the century, to open offices in London.[1] London offices of foreign banks could not, of course, engage in first-class acceptance business themselves, for their bills ranked as " agencies " on the London market; but their advent, by strengthening the links between London and foreign centres, undoubtedly brought a great deal of additional business to the great merchant banking houses and to the newer " foreign " bankers, in whose hands London's acceptance business was largely concentrated.

In this sphere, the supremacy of these houses remained unchallenged by the big London joint stock banks until the early years of the present century. The traditional attitude of the English deposit banks to acceptance business, as several witnesses explained to the 1875 Committee,[2] was that it ought to be left to the merchants—it was considered to be the duty of a banker to avoid the " greater risks " of the merchant, and to

[1] See Luke Hansard, *loc. cit.*, p. 418. The German banks came to London after 1870, the Deutsche Bank in 1874, the International Bank of Hamburg in 1871, the German Bank of London in 1872, and the British and Foreign Exchange Investment (Englisches Band und Wechsler Geschaft) in 1873. The Crédit Lyonnais opened in 1872, followed by the Banque Française et Italienne and the Bank of Belgium and Holland in 1873. The Comptoir d'Escompte de Paris opened in 1881, and the Société Générale in 1890. Other banks to open in London during this period were the Russian Bank for Foreign Trade (1872), Bank of Constantinople (1873), the Russian Bank (1876), and the Commercial Bank of Alexandria (1881). Among the Anglo-American banks were the Mercantile Bank of the River Plate (1873), the Anglo-Californian Bank (1874), Banco Internacional de Brasil (1888), Anglo Argentine Bank, Banco Nacional de la Republica, Oriental del Uruguay (1889), Banco Sud Americano (1892), and Banco da Republica do Brazil (1894). The Yokohama Specie Bank opened in 1885, and the National Bank of China in 1892. Some of the more important merchant banking houses to set up in London after about 1850 were Bischoffsheims (1850), Blydensteins (1858), Erlangers (1859), Japhets (1880), and Grace Bros. (1889).

[2] See especially QQ. 7030–5, 7318.

refrain from all transactions " the results of which were dependent upon the rise and fall of goods ". Thus, although the newly opened London offices of the Scottish banks did a large acceptance business, in 1875 and for many years after, the London banks generally refused all acceptances whose primary security was represented by goods. In practice, this meant that they avoided acceptances for private customers, and ordinarily accepted only on behalf of other banks, for in that case the bank's name was regarded as the primary security. Early in the twentieth century, however, owing partly to the powerful competition which resulted from large-scale amalgamations, and partly to the fact that amalgamation tended to break down old traditions (some of the absorbed country banks had well-established acceptance connections [1]), the London banks turned their attention increasingly to general acceptance business,[2] though they usually required the customer to deposit negotiable securities.

The result was a welcome expansion in the supply of really first-class " external " paper available to the discount market, and from that time onwards clearing bank acceptances came to take pride of place in the market portfolios, always commanding very fine rates. By the eve of the War, the supply of purely internal paper had become an almost insignificant factor. " A study of the bills lodged by the London discount houses as security for loans," it was said even in 1907,[3] " is a lesson in commercial geography . . . they are drawn from all parts of the world and are based on every conceivable type of produce." The big discount houses still sent their agents " all over the country " in search of ordinary trade bills,[4] but neither the bills thus obtained, nor the few which were still re-discounted by the rapidly dwindling number of purely country banks, provided any important part of the market's bill supply. The bulk now came from direct connections overseas, and above all from

[1] See Sykes, *op. cit.*, p. 171.

[2] The minimum pre-War charge was ¼ per cent. on a 90-day bill, with higher rates charged on produce shipments, where the bank had to watch the " margin ". (See Schuster before U.S. Monetary Commission, *loc. cit.*)

[3] J. Russell French, of Bank of New South Wales, before Australian Institute of Bankers, cited by Powell, *op. cit.*

[4] See evidence of Schuster and Charles Gow before 1910 Commission, *loc. cit.* These trade bills became re-discountable with the London banks after endorsement by the bigger discount houses. Gow considered this endorsement " very valuable ".

the re-discounts [1] of the big specialists in the finance of overseas trade, the merchant bankers and the London offices of the Eastern, colonial and foreign banks, which received from their agents or branches (or parent institutions) abroad bills negotiated at the point of shipment, and which poured into Lombard Street an incessant stream of paper of all descriptions.[2]

In the few years before the War, London had become in every sense a true international market, in daily, even hourly, contact with foreign centres, which constantly studied its variations, followed its tendency, and took its bills.[3] Its working capital, which had formerly been " almost entirely native, is now more than half foreign . . . the most active and powerful factors in it are of foreign origin . . . they have foreign interests to serve which may frequently clash with British interests ". " Lombard Street," it was remarked, " is no longer a purely English or even a British institution ; it belongs to all nations." [4]

[1] For a classification of the various types of paper, see Tritton, in the *Institute of Bankers' Journal*, 1902, pp. 209–19.

[2] It was in this field that the displaced " true " bill broker found his opportunity, by acting as agent for the marketing of these bills, especially for the Eastern banks.

[3] See Rozenraad, *loc. cit.*

[4] See W. R. Lawson, in *Bankers' Magazine*, 1906, II, p. 20. The *discount* market, however, remained in *personnel* predominantly British.

CHAPTER IX

THE MORAL SUPREMACY OF THE BANK OF ENGLAND

" For fully a year," wrote Lawson in 1906,[1] " Lombard Street has been more under the control of the Japanese banks than of the Bank of England." That was an exaggeration; but it forcibly illustrates the extent of the problem which the internationalization of the money market raised for its central institution. To steer a safe course amid the swirling cross-currents of international finance would, indeed, have been a difficult and delicate task even for a body already in supreme and unchallenged command of the vessel which it sought to navigate. The Bank of England's was no such command: at the very time when international influences first became really powerful, the Bank was facing a potent challenge in the domestic market. As early as the 'fifties, as has been seen,[2] the Bank had lost its quantitative supremacy; yet the growth of banking resources which the 1858 Committee had found so remarkable was small beside the vast increase of the next few decades. In the twenty years to 1877, the total volume of commercial bank deposits was certainly almost trebled, and, according to figures cited by Palgrave,[3] was actually more than quadrupled; while the Bank's resources rose by barely two-thirds. So striking a difference inevitably produced a marked change in the balance of power in the money market, and a threat to every traditional relationship within it. Of the many factors which shaped central bank policy in the forty odd years before the War, these two—London's gradual internationalization, and the growth in the power of the joint stock banks—were by far the most important. Together, they raised problems which nothing less than a complete remodelling of technique could solve.

Even before the 1857 crisis, as has been shown, the Bank was certainly aware that it was powerless to check the rise of

[1] See W. R. Lawson, *loc. cit.* [2] *Ante*, pp. 191–2.

[3] *Bank Rate and the Money Market*, p. 41.

its joint stock rivals, and had already learnt the dangers of competition with them. But it had not then discovered any means of market control which might replace its waning quantitative power. In various ways, the Bank did, it is true, seek to keep market activities within the bounds of prudence; but the measures which it took to this end, such as the drastic regulation of March, 1858, were inspired rather by a desire to prevent the growth of outside resources from menacing its own safety than by consideration for the broad interests of the commercial world.

There is, however, an interesting paradox here: in normal times, the true central bank motive was clearly not the mainspring of Bank policy; yet the Bank's anxiety to check the new influences which threatened its position arose very largely from recognition of its responsibilities. It realized that in time of stress it would again be, and ought to be, the general refuge, and was acutely aware that the greater the scale of the outside market, the greater would be the burden of emergency demands. In bad times, the Bank's power was evident enough; the problem was how to exercise a similar power in good times, and to impose upon the market then a caution which otherwise might not be exercised until it was too late. No evident progress towards solution of this problem was made for many years, and not until the time of the Baring crisis did the Bank seem even within sight of its goal.

Abandonment of the Rule of "Following" the Market

The third quarter of the nineteenth century was, indeed, a period of "drift" so far as central bank evolution was concerned: changes in Bank technique were dictated mainly by the needs of the moment, and seemed devoid of any fundamental underlying aim. And the Bank was reluctant to abandon traditional principles and methods until they had become demonstrably obsolete.[1] Thus the rule that Bank rate should follow, and not lead, the market rate—a rule which was supposed to emphasize a virtuous abstention from competition—remained a

[1] Bagehot noted one instance, the only one of which he was aware, in which the Bank made a change "which was not exacted by contemporary opinion, and which was in advance of it". This was the adoption of Goschen's suggestion that Bank rate ought always to be raised by steps of 1 per cent., instead of the customary ½ per cent., whenever the object was to affect the foreign exchanges. The change was made in 1860.

guiding principle until about 1875, or for some years after it had become a bewildering inconvenience to both the market and the commercial world, and a danger to the Bank itself. Rationally interpreted, the rule was sound enough. But whereas it had been evolved simply to ensure that the Bank would never repeat the dangerous mistakes of 1844–7, it was later construed to mean that Bank rate must conform more or less closely to market rate, and that the Bank ought never to initiate rate changes. It was, of course, desirable from many points of view that the Bank should maintain a sufficiently close contact with the market to ensure that its portfolio was reasonably well stocked with commercial bills [1]; and, as already indicated, the cessation of bill market re-discounts after March, 1858, had made it impossible for the Bank ordinarily to secure more than a few bills unless its rate was virtually attuned to market rate. This was probably the main reason for the reluctance to change the rule; but the advantages of market contact were far outweighed by the disadvantages. It was clearly undesirable that the Bank should seek to follow every major downward move in market rate, and at least equally undesirable that it should refrain from raising its rate until a rise in the market virtually compelled it to do so.

By the early 'seventies, it was clear that the rule would have to be abandoned. Market rate, influenced by a host of external factors, had become highly variable, and in one year the Bank's convulsive efforts to keep its own rate effective had necessitated no less than twenty-four changes. And not even so elastic a rate policy as this could ordinarily achieve the result intended. At all normal times, competition between outside lenders, who paid interest (at relatively high rates) for practically the whole of their resources, was bound to force market rate below Bank rate,[2] for such lenders dare not have balances unemployed. Thus, early in 1870, when a new method of collecting direct taxes caused stringency in the outside market,[3] the fact that market rate had approached closely to Bank rate was noted

[1] See Thomas Hankey, *Principles of Banking*, for the views of the Bank board on this point in the 'seventies.

[2] The impossibility of Bank competition with the market had been stressed as early as 1864 (see *Bankers' Magazine*, 1864, p. 57). The bill brokers, it was said, would always "cut under" Bank rate: the Bank could never increase its business by reducing its rate.

[3] In the Budget of 1869 it had been provided that the "assessed" taxes should be paid in one sum in advance, instead of in two instalments.

with some surprise by the financial press, the *Bankers' Magazine* remarking that it was " a circumstance which does not usually happen ".[1] Nevertheless, until 1871 the differential was usually substantially less than 1 per cent. But the Bank's efforts to maintain a narrow differential were seriously accentuating the disconcerting instability of market rates, for as both bank and discount market deposit allowances were regulated by Bank rate, every reduction in the latter stimulated a new competition between outside lenders, and forced a fresh decline in market rate, making the eventual reaction the more severe. Moreover, so long as its own rate was ineffective, the Bank was prone to assume that no increase could be necessary, however threatening the international prospect ; yet, when foreign balances in London were large, it often happened that rates were unduly depressed at the very time when the potential threat to the Bank's reserve was greatest, and when, therefore, a precautionary increase in Bank rate was peculiarly necessary. In the 'sixties and early 'seventies, the Bank was criticized almost as often for undue delay in raising the rate as for its too frequent alteration.[2]

The first sign of divergence from the traditional rule occurred in the autumn of 1871, when the Bank aroused widespread comment by maintaining its rate at 5 per cent. for several weeks after market rate had dropped to 3½ per cent., and when one of its directors suggested that it was no longer advisable to publish a " minimum " rate.[3] No permanent change was then made, however, and Bagehot, writing in 1873, was still attacking the Bank for adjusting its rate to market rate, describing the rule as a " recipe for making a large number of panics ".

> This rule [he declared] was never so erroneous as now, because the number of sudden demands upon the reserve was never formerly so great. The market rate . . . is not influenced by those demands. . . . The probable efflux of bullion from the Bank scarcely affects it at all ; even the real efflux affects it but little ; if the open market did not believe that the Bank rate would be altered in consequence of such effluxes the market rate would not rise. If the Bank choose to let its bullion go unheeded, and is seen to be going so to choose, the value of money in Lombard Street will remain unaltered. The

---

[1] 1870, p. 65. [2] See, for example, Bagehot, *op. cit.*, p. 187.

[3] See *Bankers' Magazine*, 1878, p. 570, and Arthur Crump, *The Key to the London Money Market* (1872), pp. 20, 40. The suggestion of abandonment of the minimum rate had first been made as far back as 1863, at the meeting of the Bank Court and Proprietors. (*Bankers' Magazine*, 1863, pp. 235, 250.)

more numerous the demands on the Bank for bullion, and the more variable their magnitude, the more dangerous is the rule. . . .[1]

The Bank was, in fact, facing a complex conflict of interests in the money market. The interests of its proprietors, as well as of its own customers, demanded that its rate should remain reasonably close to market rate; but its own safety, and the ultimate interests of both the market and the commercial world, demanded that it should take early and vigorous measures to counter any threatened attack upon its reserve, whatever the position in the domestic money market. In the last resort, the interests of all parties were virtually identical, and Bagehot was wrong in asserting that a decline in the reserve could not affect market rate unless the Bank raised its rate; but an unco-ordinated money market could not be expected to see that its best interests might be served by precautionary measures in advance of a coming stringency, and an over-keen competition kept rates down until their increase was literally inevitable. And if an irresponsible market would not take precautionary measures voluntarily, it was clear that the Bank would have to take the initiative, and seek to compel the necessary action.

Bagehot's criticisms apparently made an impression, for on several occasions in 1874 Bank rate was raised to ward off impending foreign demands at times when strict adherence to traditional practice of "following" the market might have dictated a reduction,[2] and on at least one occasion the Bank sought to impose its own rate on the market by "borrowing" on Consols. Thereafter, it became less precipitate in its efforts to follow market rate downwards, frequently allowing the differential to reach 1 per cent. before making a change. In consequence, its bill portfolio began to show a marked decline. The portfolio in 1874 averaged no more than £4,665,000, in contrast with £7,737,000 in 1873 and an average of £7,103,000 for the preceding decade; while the average of £4,402,000 for 1875 [3] was actually the lowest since 1852, and represented only 23 per cent. of the "Other" securities, a new low record percentage. By 1875 it was clear that the rule had been definitely abandoned, and from that time onwards the average differential between Bank rate and market rate became steadily wider.

[1] Bagehot, *op. cit.*, pp. 321–2.
[2] See *Bankers' Magazine*, 1874, p. 1002, and 1875, p. 73.
[3] No details of the constituents of the "other" securities were available after 1875.

Deposit Allowances and Excessive Competition

This change in the Bank's policy raised in an acute form a problem which had for some years troubled the outside market—the problem of maintaining an adequate profit-margin between the rates allowed on deposits and the yields obtainable by their employment in bills ; for deposit rates were still rigidly regulated by Bank rate, whereas market rate was not only often far below Bank rate, but had ceased to move at all closely in sympathy with it. The vigorous competition created in the discount market by the fact that the bulk of the resources seeking employment were themselves interest-bearing had been steadily accentuated by the failure of the supply of bills to keep pace with the enormous growth in deposits. Palgrave estimated [1] that between 1856 and 1873 the aggregate volume of bank deposits had risen from £200 to £800 millions, and that at the later date the normal bill supply was around £300 to £350 millions, compared with Newmarch's figure of £180 to £200 millions for 1851. No exactitude can be claimed for these figures, and indeed the *Economist* [2] put the total of bank deposits even for 1877 at not more than between £550 and £650 millions ; but the estimates leave no room for doubt that there was a marked difference between the growth in the volume of bills and the volume of funds seeking employment in them.

The resultant aggressive scramble for bills inevitably presented opportunities to the creators of bad paper, for some discount houses, forced to find prompt employment for costly deposits, became all too ready to take any bills they could get ; and the banks, often relying unduly upon the bill dealer's guarantee or endorsement, were hardly more cautious. The ease with which the unscrupulous trader could secure accommodation in certain quarters enabled him to build up discount accounts whose very size gave the impression (to all who had no direct dealings with him) that his business must be both strong and prosperous. Moreover, competition in the market had engendered a jealousy which frustrated all attempts to achieve co-operative measures for the checking of abuses : no bank would ever admit that it held any paper which offered grounds for suspicion, and could never know what volume of paper bearing the same " names " was locked in the portfolios of its rivals. The money market, declared Ellis, was a conspicuous instance of lack of co-operation.

[1] Palgrave, *op. cit.*, pp. 41, 66. [2] *Economist*, 1877, p. 1273.

" The lenders of money in Lombard Street," he said, " are all within a stone's throw of one another, but the Channel might run between, instead of a dark, narrow little street, for all the interchange of information or assistance that goes on . . . indeed, it is their business, or they conceive it to be so, to have as little to do with one another as possible." [1] Many dealers, it was said, were glad to sift out their bad bills, and unload them on their fellows ; and the banks were in the hands of the dealers, who, if they chose, could " sort " their bills, and " ration " the names to each bank.

It was the notorious accommodation bill frauds of June, 1875, which brought matters to a head.[2] The trouble started at end-May and early June with the default of the Aberdare Iron Co. on fictitious bills. The failure of this concern, together with its convenient satellite, the Plymouth Iron Co., with liabilities of well over a million, revealed the enormous accommodation system which had been built up, with the aid of one of the smaller discount houses (Young & Borthwick), by Alexander Collie & Co., which collapsed later in the month with liabilities of about £3,000,000. In the bill market, R. M. Sanderson & Co. and Young & Borthwick both suspended payment, with aggregate commitments of about £9 millions, and it was estimated that the many mercantile failures which followed brought the total defaults up to £21 millions. Several discount houses were involved, apart from the two which failed, and nearly all the London banks. Four of the joint stock banks, among which the London & Westminster figured prominently, held no less than £1,000,000 of Collie's drafts as collateral for market loans.

In the general outcry which followed, the methods of both the banks and the discount market were strongly criticized.[3] The main sources of the trouble were, first, the excessive competition engendered by the fact that the banks allowed liberal interest both on current and deposit accounts, and, secondly, the undue secrecy which surrounded all discount operations. Neither evil, however, could be removed without a more fundamental change

[1] Arthur Ellis, *op. cit.*, pp. 47–53.

[2] See *Economist*, 1875, p. 665 ; *Bankers' Magazine*, 1875, pp. 597–600, 941–7 ; 1876, pp. 65–72 ; and Ellis, *op. cit.*

[3] See, for example, 1875 Committee, Minutes, QQ. 6697–702, 4959–4965, 8092, 8093. The *Economist* argued that the banks' organization had not progressed with the growth of their resources ; some of them, it was said, " appear to have done a bill broker's business without a good bill broker's expert knowledge ", and the high rates they allowed on balances at call left no margin available to meet bad debts.

in outlook than the market was then prepared to face. The suggestion of *The Times* for the establishment of a "credit" clearing house at which, with adequate safeguards to ensure secrecy, the banks and discount houses could "register" the amounts of the bills which they held on particular names, was ridiculed in many quarters; and, despite its strong backing from the financial press, the scheme was not adopted.

Efforts to solve the problem of deposit allowances were at first almost equally unsuccessful. In August, 1875, representatives of the London joint stock banks had met to consider a widening of the margin between deposit rates and Bank rate, but separated without reaching agreement.[1] It seemed that nothing would be done, but in the following October the London & Westminster decided to act alone, announcing that its allowance on current accounts (interest was allowed on the minimum monthly balance, provided that a given minimum was retained throughout each half-year) would in future be 1½, instead of 1 per cent. below Bank rate, and expressing the hope that a more substantial change would later prove possible.[2] That this hope was fulfilled was attributable very largely to the alteration in the practice of the Bank of England, for during the depression of 1876 the increasing ineffectiveness of Bank rate, despite its repeated reduction, added greatly to the burden of excessive deposit allowances. So long as deposits could be employed at even a fractional margin over the rates allowed upon them there was no prospect of reform, but in the middle of 1876, when Bank rate stood at 2 per cent. and the scarcity of bills was such that no outlet for short-term money could be found even at 1 per cent.[3] (the existing deposit allowance), a change became imperative. Even so, the banks could reach no general agreement, and some of them, rather than make a move which their rivals might not follow, actually began to refuse deposits. In July, however, several banks compromised by refusing interest altogether on current account balances of under £200, while retaining the traditional "1 per cent. under" for larger sums.[4] This paved the way for more sweeping changes, and by 1877 all the London banks had abolished all current account allowances.[5]

Meanwhile, strenuous efforts had been made to secure agree-

[1] See *Bankers' Magazine*, 1875, pp. 772–3.

[2] *Ibid.*, p. 928; 1876, p. 96.

[3] *Ibid.*, 1876, p. 709–14 (and citation from *The Times*).

[4] *Ibid.*, pp. 664, 671, 691–2, for announcements by the various banks.

[5] *Ibid.*, 1876, p. 1063; 1877, pp. 54–5, 108–9, 117; and *Economist*, 1877, p. 1455.

ment upon a reduction of allowances on deposit accounts. The discount houses had already succeeded in doing so. Their usual practice had been to allow 1 per cent. below Bank rate for deposits at call, and $\frac{3}{4}$ per cent. below for those at 7 days' notice; but during the extreme ease of 1876 they "prudently disregarded entirely the exploded notions of regulating allowances of interest by the Bank minimum", and increased their margins to $1\frac{1}{4}$ per cent.[1] By this step, declared the *Economist*,[1] they proved themselves "better traders than the Joint Stock Banks".

A few banks had in fact reduced their rates,[2] but the general contention was that the wide differential between market rate and Bank rate was simply a passing phase, attributable to the depression, and that an alteration in the time-honoured margins was not desirable. For the banks, once they had abated or abandoned their allowances on current accounts, there was of course less urgency for a widening of the margin than there was for the discount market, where all funds were interest-bearing, so that the *Economist's* verdict was not altogether justified. But in principle the journal's argument for a wider margin was unassailable, as the banks realized in 1877 when a rise in Bank rate proved only momentarily effective. Then, at last, it was recognized that what had been dismissed as a purely transitory phenomenon was in reality an indication of fundamental change in the whole money market situation; and upon this recognition, it was questioned whether even the desired increase in the deposit rate differential could solve the banks' problem.

The "Private and Personal" Rate of the Bank of England

The only ultimate solution, it was argued, lay in a complete abandonment of Bank rate as the basis of market rates. For a time, it seemed that the new forces would result eventually in rejection of Bank leadership, and disappearance of its power. "There are now, and have been for some time," wrote Bonamy Price in July, 1877,[3] "two money markets in London, two rates of interest, one—the true one—that of the trade of the nation, the other, the private and personal one of the Bank of England."

> . . . The motives which influence the Bank in fixing its terms are not identical with those which make bankers lend on totally different terms in the true money market of trade. Why then

[1] *Economist*, 1877, pp. 121–3; *Bankers' Magazine*, 1876, p. 694.
[2] *The Times*, cited by *Bankers' Magazine*, 1876, p. 710.
[3] In a letter to the *Economist*, July 22, 1877 (1877, p. 887).

should these private and personal views of the Bank of England be proclaimed in every organ of the Press, every City article of every newspaper, and, strange to say, by every man who lives on discount, as the rulers of those loans of our banks on which every great commercial business of the country depends ? The ratio of its cash reserve to its liabilities is the Bank's individual affair ; why should a change in that ratio be hoisted up on every flagstaff as the signal of what rate of discount ought to be charged by bankers in a wholly different money market . . . why should other bankers . . . concern themselves with the internal affairs of the Bank ?

The difficulty was, of course, that the Bank's cash ratio was *not* merely its own " individual affair ". Upon the adequacy of that ratio there depended the solvency of every bank in the country, for there had been no attempt to dispute the Bank's position as the ultimate refuge in time of stringency; and although in its rate policy the outside market had shown a persistent disobedience to the traditional ruler, the Bank had become more than ever before the acknowledged custodian of the other banks' reserves, as the following table [1] reveals :

BANK OF ENGLAND DEPOSITS AND RESERVE
(Annual Averages)

Year.	London Banks' Balances at Bank.		Bank's Total Deposits.	Banking Department Reserve.	Banking Department Reserve Ratio.
	Actual.	% of Bank's Reserve.			
	£		£	£	%
1844	977,000	11	13,300,000	8,500,000	59
1850	1,656,000	15	17,597,000	11,219,000	59
1855	3,065,000	37	16,716,000	8,366,000	47
1860	4,283,000	51	20,164,000	8,451,000	40
1865	5,038,000	63	20,707,000	8,089,000	38
1870	6,618,000	53	25,735,000	12,435,000	47
1871	8,390,000	59	28,393,000	14,162,000	48
1872	7,609,000	63	28,861,000	12,122,000	41
1873	8,586,000	71	28,495,000	12,051,000	41
1874	8,341,000	75	25,098,000	11,035,000	43
1875	10,324,000	89	26,413,000	11,597,000	43
1876	11,851,000	74	30,286,000	15,962,000	52
1877	9,543,000	77	28,412,000	12,478,000	43

[1] Based on figures compiled by Palgrave, *op. cit.*, pp. 12–13. Separate figures for bankers' balances at the Bank were not published after 1877.

To abandon the one permanent link between Bank rate and market rate, by fixing deposit allowances independently of the former, would, therefore, have been a fatal step so long as the Bank remained the custodian of the reserve; for, with the decline in the Bank's quantitative importance, market rate had superseded Bank rate as the regulator of demands upon that reserve.[1] On the other hand, if it was true (as many believed) that the Bank had lost all power to compel market rate to adjust itself to a Bank rate determined by the needs of the reserve, then to increase the differential between Bank rate and deposit rate, while still regulating the latter by the former, would merely have aggravated the problem, by tending to force market rate still further below Bank rate. Responsibility for the reserve and responsibility for fixing the rate by which it could be regulated had become divided,[2] although clearly the two should have been in the same hands. Recognition of this anomaly led many to contend that, unless the Bank could devise means of controlling market rate, measures should be taken to transfer control of the primary bankers' reserve from the Bank of England to the banks themselves.[3] Thus a suggestion made in 1874 [4] for the establishment of an independent clearing bankers' reserve was revived, and with it was coupled a scheme for the fixing by the Committee of Clearing Bankers of a "market rate" by which deposit allowances should be governed.[5]

Suggestions such as these plainly struck at the heart of the

[1] See *Bankers' Magazine*, 1877, pp. 983, 1037, and *Economist*, 1877, pp. 813, 817, 913–14.

[2] *Cf. Bankers' Magazine*, 1877, pp. 983–4, 890. [3] *Ibid.*

[4] "Suggestions for the Formation of a Cash Reserve by the Clearing Bankers to take the place of their present Balances in the Bank of England," set out in a letter, signed "*B*", to the *Economist* (1874, pp. 1449–50). (See also *Bankers' Magazine*, 1875, pp. 1–7.) One reason for this suggestion, apart altogether from the rate problem, was, of course, the growing opinion among the banks that the Bank of England failed to keep an adequate reserve; that it treated bankers' balances as ordinary deposits; and that, by so doing, it was able to employ them in competition with the banks which provided them. In particular, it was pointed out that the banks contributed the bulk of the reserve. Palgrave discovered that on 61 separate occasions between 1844 and 1877 (48 between 1866 and 1877) these balances had actually exceeded the reserve. It is worth noting that a similar suggestion for an independent reserve and rate had been discussed in 1847; then, however, the reason was the Bank's aggressive competition.

[5] See letters to *Economist* from a "Bill Broker" and a "Banker" (*Economist*, 1877, pp. 1281–2, 1339–40); also *Bankers' Magazine*, 1877, p. 981.

traditional constitution of the money market; and it is very questionable whether the scheme could have been worked successfully so long as the Bank retained control of the note issue on the one hand, and management of the Government account on the other. In any case, there was not the slightest prospect of agreement among the contesting parties. This was fortunate, for it was hardly conceivable that the banks under the proposed system would suddenly have moderated their competition so as to avoid pressure upon rates, and in that event the menace to the reserve would not have been diminished, and might well have been increased, by the change. Nevertheless, there was a cold logic about the plan which for a time escaped even the *Economist*; and this paper, supported by the *Bankers' Magazine*, strongly advocated the fixing of an independent rate, while rejecting the proposal for a separate reserve.[1]

> Old feeling, old tradition [it declared] all claim the pre-eminence of the Bank. But the tide of affairs now seems to turn in the contrary direction, and though it must be a subject of regret, we have to record the facts as they stand. It is undeniable that the Bank rate is no longer the index of the value of money which it used to be. It is not that anyone desires to dethrone the Bank, far from it; but if the Bank rate ceases to be a sure guide, is not there a close approach to an abdication of the position?

A few months' later, however, the *Economist* was shifting its ground. It admitted the inevitability of the Bank's retention of the final reserve, and then reiterated its plea for abolition of a published Bank rate—but on this occasion because it thought that such a step might strengthen the Bank's control, "an eminently desirable thing". "Publication of a fixed rate," it contended, "is as much an anachronism now as a permanently fixed rate was in 1844. The Bank loses the power of delicate adjustment over the market: it cannot feel the pulse of its customers as closely as if its rate were not advertised, since when the rate is above market rate people do not even come to the Bank at all."[2]

There can be no doubt that the acute controversy aroused by these many suggestions for far-reaching reform added greatly to

[1] See *Economist*, 1877, p. 1274, and *Bankers' Magazine*, 1877, pp. 981–4.

[2] *Economist*, 1878, pp. 173–5. (This article, as Professor Gregory has pointed out in his *British Banking Statutes*, p. xxxv., was quite evidently written by Palgrave; *cf. Bank Rate and the Money Market*, pp. 48–54.)

the difficulty of securing agreement upon the original, and less fundamental, proposal—that of widening the deposit rate margin. A temporary agreement was, in fact, reached on November 9, 1877, when the London joint stock banks decided to fix deposit allowances at $3\frac{1}{2}$ per cent. although Bank rate remained at 5 per cent.[1] This, however, was a wholly exceptional unanimity, compelled by the fact that for some weeks it had actually been possible to raise money by discounts at $3\frac{1}{4}$ per cent. (and even less), and place it on deposit at 4 per cent.[1]; when Bank rate was later reduced, the old differential was restored. Thereafter, realization of the impossibility of securing agreement thrust the controversy into the background, but dissatisfaction with the anomalous relationship between market rate and deposit rate necessarily remained, and was increased by the knowledge that a favourable opportunity for reform had been lost.

A few months' later, in early June, 1878, the market was startled to learn that the Bank had intimated that it would no longer feel bound to adhere to its published rate when discounting for its own exclusive customers, but would discount for them at or near market rate. This step was widely interpreted as an attempt to revive aggressive competition; and the "latent discontent at once burst into flame".[2] Actually, as the *Economist* pointed out,[3] the Bank had acted "with utmost delicacy in avoiding anything like competition": the change was nothing more than a recognition that under the old system the Bank's customers had a legitimate grievance. In a sense, it was even designed to *avoid* competition, for unless the Bank were to relinquish discount business entirely, it could not continue to charge rates often far removed from the market charge; and the alternative to quoting different rates for customers would have been to make Bank rate—the public rate—a competitive quotation. Nevertheless, the decision was of very real significance, for it proved that the Bank did not regard the ineffectiveness of its published rate as any merely passing phase; and, by some, it was read as an admission by the Bank of its inability to discipline the market.

In consequence, the controversy of the previous year was revived with re-doubled intensity, and in the indignation of the

[1] See *Bankers' Magazine*, 1877, pp. 965, 1037, and *Economist*, 1877, pp. 1273, 1329. The discount houses had already made a similar change on October 22, and the London and Westminster had done so on Nov. 5.

[2] See *Bankers' Magazine*, 1878, pp. 569–74.

[3] *Economist*, 1878, pp. 693–4.

moment there were repeated threats of immediate withdrawal of the bankers' balances from the Bank. After heated discussion, the London joint stock banks decided to await a hurriedly summoned meeting of the Clearing House Committee, in order that the views of the private banks might be canvassed.[1] The rival schemes, as before, were that for a wider deposit rate margin and that for an independent rate and an independent reserve [2]; but the cleavage of opinion was no less violent than it had been in 1877, and two meetings of the Committee separated without reaching agreement upon either plan.[1] Once again, the jealousy among the London bankers had proved to be the Bank's most valuable ally; had the banks shown a more co-operative spirit, the discussions and schemes of the middle 'seventies might indeed have produced a complete re-casting of the traditional constitution of the market. As it was, the Bank retained at least the opportunity for re-establishing its supremacy.

Bank's Struggle for Mastery: Ineffectiveness of Bank Rate in the 'Eighties

The whole responsibility for finding a solution to the problem was thus thrown upon the Bank; but not until 1890 was any perceptible progress made.[3] In the 'eighties, therefore, the Bank was obliged to resort more and more frequently to the ancient, but unsatisfactory, expedient of "borrowing" on Consols whenever the disobedience of the outside market became especially dangerous. In one respect only was its task easier than it had been in the middle 'seventies: after the introduction of the Treasury bill, it was confronted less frequently by those temporary (and highly embarrassing) inflations of credit which were caused by its own advances to the Government, and it also gained in power from the increasing importance of the Treasury in the market. Especially in the last quarter of the financial year, which since 1869 [4] had become the period of maximum revenue

[1] *Bankers' Magazine*, 1878, pp. 569–74.

[2] Both the *Economist* and the *Bankers' Magazine* opposed withdrawal from the Bank, but advocated publication of a separate rate, and establishment of a *second* reserve which should be kept at the Bank but should not be shown in the Bank Return.

[3] The *Economist* argued that, if the Bank could not control market rate, it ought to hold foreign securities in order that it could operate directly upon the exchanges. Similar proposals had been made over fifty years before, notably by Gilbart (see 1841 Committee, Minutes, QQ. 1211–67), but the plan was never adopted.

[4] See *ante*, p. 285 *n*.

collections, the Bank often found itself in quite unaccustomed command of the market, and sudden spasms of stringency recurred frequently at such times. One consequence of this was that the market began to seek advances at the Bank at other times than the periods before the dividend dates; and the Bank, at its discretion, came to extend beyond the "shuttings" the periods during which advances would be made.[1] There was at no time any definite abandonment of the 1858 rule, but this relaxation of it paved the way to an admission of the principle that, if necessary, the Bank ought to lend at all times at which the Government balances were unduly high.[2] Thus, almost imperceptibly, the bill market reverted to the practice of the 'fifties, and came to assume that it could count upon the Bank's assistance, not only in time of real crisis, but at the first sign of temporary stringency.

Early in the 'eighties it seemed that this assumption might have the same consequences as it had done a quarter of a century before, as the following passage reveals:

> There can be no doubt that of late brokers have come to rely far too much upon the Bank. They have reckoned upon getting advances there almost as a matter of course whenever they have applied for them, and in this belief they have entered into engagements which if they had not thought the Bank was behind them they possibly would not have risked. The belief, too, that the resources of the Bank would always be available at ordinary rates if necessary has enabled the brokers to borrow more freely than they otherwise would have been able to do, because the outside lender had, or thought he had, the assurance that if he called in his money the broker would be able to fall back upon the Bank.[3]

Thus, once again, an undue reliance upon the Bank was tending to produce over-trading in the discount market. It was certainly

[1] *Cf. Bankers' Magazine*, 1883, pp. 565–9.

[2] Palgrave asserted that in 1878 the Bank abandoned the 1858 rule, by informing the market that it could have advances whenever it desired. This is definitely incorrect: between 1858 and 1890 there was no official change in the relationships between the Bank and the discount houses in this respect. The advances granted at times other than the shuttings were brought within the category of "special" advances mentioned in 1858, while no market discount accounts were permitted at all. Palgrave also states incorrectly the date on which the Bank abandoned the minimum rate, giving this as Feb., 1878, possibly because he was reproducing an article (written by himself) which appeared in that month. (*Cf.* Palgrave, *Bank Rate and the Money Market*, pp. 48–54, and *Economist*, 1878, pp. 173–5.) And see *ante*, p. 294 *n*.

[3] *Economist*, 1883, p. 485, and see also Giffen, *op. cit.*, p. 111.

responsible for a growing practice of discounting bills "forward"[1]—buying bills for delivery at some date in the future—a practice which not only introduced a new element of instability into the market, but further accentuated the tendency for market rate to fall substantially below Bank rate. In the second half of 1882 the *average* differential was no less than 17*s*. per cent.[2] The existence of so unprecedented a disparity brought home to the Bank the extent to which its leniency towards the market was aggravating its own problem; and in April, 1883, it took steps to regularize the position in the light of the 1858 rule, by intimating that in future it would ordinarily refuse advances save during the shuttings for the Consol dividends.[3]

This tightening of control was warmly approved by the financial press, especially by the *Economist*, which argued (apparently interpreting what it thought to be the Bank's opinion) that the market ought to stand on its own feet at times when it had command of all the "usual" resources. "This view," it said, "was the habitual view of the older discount houses, and used to be generally acted upon." Its general re-adoption was expected to do something to check "that overkeen competition which has made it so difficult for the Bank of late years to make its rate effective".[1] The change, it was hoped, would help the Bank in three ways—first, by imposing caution on the discount market, thereby preventing the unnatural depression of discount rates; secondly, by diminishing the market demands upon the Bank; and, thirdly, by compelling the outside banks to keep larger reserves.[4]

The immediate consequence of the decision was to force market rate right up to Bank rate; and, for a time, to judge from the trend of Bank return figures, each of the three expected results was at least partially achieved. Action far more drastic, however, was required to outweigh the force of cut-throat bank competition: in times of comparative calm in the money market the possibility that call loans might become frozen at the very moment when their liquidity was most necessary seemed a remote danger, especially as all were well aware that in the last resort the support of Threadneedle Street could never be withheld. The Bank's

[1] *Economist*, 1883, p. 485.

[2] See *Bankers' Magazine*, 1885, p. 21, for margins from 1882 to 1884.

[3] *Economist*, *loc. cit.*, and *Bankers' Magazine*, 1883, p. 565.

[4] The *Bankers' Magazine* pointed out that the surplus of the commercial banks had for some years tended to be employed at call rather than in purchases of bills; and that the fact that the market was to be refused regular recourse to the Bank was bound to make the banks chary of holding too much money at call.

scheme therefore failed to produce the desired narrowing of the disparity between Bank rate and market rate. The differential, it is true, was smaller in 1883 and 1884 than it had been in 1882, but in the first half of 1885 its average reached a new record of 17*s*. 4*d*. per cent., and even for the full year the figure was well over 15*s*. per cent.

Meanwhile, the banks' so-called " profit-margin "—the excess of the average market rate over the average deposit rate—had declined from around 10*s*. per cent. in 1883 and 1884 to only 4*s*. per cent. for the first half of 1885, and 5*s*. 4*d*. per cent. for the full year. On many occasions, as the smallness of the *average* implies, deposit rate actually exceeded market rate. Realization that this relationship was becoming a more or less permanent feature of the market thus compelled the banks to the action which had been postponed in 1878. On May 6, 1886, when Bank rate was raised from 2 to 3 per cent., the banks increased their London deposit allowances by only ½ per cent., and thus widened the margin under Bank rate to 1½ per cent.[1] The new rule of " 1½ per cent. under " was consistently followed thereafter, save only when Bank rate dropped to 2 per cent. or rose above 5 per cent., when the margin became 1 per cent. and generally 2 per cent. respectively.[2]

Unfortunately, while the banks had sunk their differences upon this point, they did not abate in the slightest their aggressive competition. In consequence, the easing of deposit allowances merely intensified the pressure upon the short money rate. The result was a new decline in bill rates, which quickly became so marked as to deprive the banks of practically the whole of the advantage which the new rule should have brought. This is revealed by the following table [3] :

[1] Except in 1876, when a few banks had temporarily adopted a margin of 1¼ per cent., while Bank rate stood at 2 per cent., this was the first occasion on which the margin had been over 1 per cent. with a Bank rate of less than 5 per cent. The 1½ per cent. margin was maintained until 1921, when increased costs (notably salaries) led the banks to increase the margin to 2 per cent. ; this must now be considered the normal margin, although with the abnormal period of ease which began in 1932, when Bank rate dropped to 2 per cent., the margin has been 1½ per cent.

[2] An allowance of 1 per cent. was regarded as a minimum by the banks, but the discount houses sometimes went lower.

[3] Based on the half-yearly averages computed by the *Bankers' Magazine* ; Palgrave made similar calculations (yearly averages), but if the two sets of figures be compared it will be seen that Palgrave cites bill rates which were appreciably above the fine " competitive " rates. His tables thus understate the disparities.

Relationships Between Bank Rate, Market Rate and Deposit Rate (Half-yearly Averages)

Half-Year.	Bank Rate (*a*). %	Market Rate (*b*). %	Deposit Rate (*c*). %	Excess of (*a*) over (*b*). %	Excess of (*b*) over (*c*). %
	£ *s.* *d.*	£ *s.* *d.*	£ *s.* *d.*	£ *s.* *d.*	£ *s.* *d.*
1883:					
1st . .	3 14 3	3 4 3	2 12 11	0 10 0	0 11 4
2nd . .	3 8 10	2 17 1	2 8 10	0 11 9	0 8 3
1884:					
1st . .	2 16 4	2 5 5	1 16 4	0 10 11	0 9 1
2nd . .	3 2 4	2 10 7	1 19 3	0 11 9	0 11 4
1885:					
1st . .	3 9 7	2 12 3	2 8 3	0 17 4	0 4 0
2nd . .	2 7 1	1 13 1	1 6 4	0 14 0	0 6 9
1886:					
1st . .	2 12 6	1 15 0	1 6 1	0 17 6	0 8 11
2nd . .	3 9 7	2 10 1	1 19 7	0 19 6	0 10 6
1887:					
1st . .	3 4 1	2 0 0	1 4 1	1 4 1	0 2 5
2nd . .	3 9 9	2 16 2	2 1 5	0 13 7	0 14 9
1888:					
1st . .	2 13 2	1 12 4	1 6 6	1 0 10	0 5 10
2nd . .	3 19 6	3 3 0	2 9 6	0 16 6	0 13 6
1889:					
1st . .	3 1 0	2 3 0	1 11 0	0 18 0	0 12 0
2nd . .	4 3 0	3 4 6	2 13 0	0 18 6	0 11 6
1890:					
1st . .	4 4 0	3 1 0	2 11 0	1 3 0	0 10 0

These figures demonstrate very forcibly the extent to which the action of the banks had complicated the Bank's task: Bank rate was frequently ineffective by 2 per cent., while even the average margin was little under 1 per cent.

So long as there was no violent threat to the reserve on foreign account, the incentive to devise corrective measures was small, for the Bank had long since abandoned all hope of earning an income from commercial discounts. In 1887, indeed, when the Bank was gaining gold, it was suggested that there was no longer the need for the authorities to endeavour to "sustain" the market; and the *Bankers' Magazine* thought that the proper corrective of so anomalous a position was for the Bank to follow Lombard Street more closely.[1] This argument was based on

[1] *Bankers' Magazine*, 1887, pp. 610–11.

the belief that the maintenance of Bank rate far above market rate was an indication to the outside market that the Bank assumed all responsibility for safeguarding the reserve. It was thought that, if the two rates were in harmony, the market would " feel more responsibility " and would itself take precautionary measures in good time, and avoid the reckless beating-down of rates. The flaw in this argument was that while bankers individually were responsible persons, fully conscious of the dangers of the position, collectively they became wholly irresponsible, and in day-to-day competition with one another ignored entirely the sound principles which they preached at the animated sessions of the Institute of Bankers, and elsewhere. Always, it was the " other fellow " who was to blame.

The Vigour of William Lidderdale

Clearly, there was no solution along this road. This was generally realized in 1888 and 1889, when a new boom in finance and trust companies, stimulated partly by the famous Goschen conversion of Consols, and a fresh mania for foreign investment, especially in the " Brazils " and the Argentine,[1] brought a rise in money rates and foreign demands for gold. Several leading bankers thereupon made strenuous efforts to achieve an agreement with their colleagues upon a minimum short loan rate,[2] while the Bank, it was believed, endeavoured to induce the banks to restore their deposit rate margin to 1 per cent.[3] Neither scheme met with any success,[4] and when, in the autumn of 1889, successive increases in Bank rate failed to check a menacing gold efflux, it became evident that only exceptional measures could avert serious trouble. A sharp break in the Stock Exchange, especially in finance company shares and South

[1] See Burn, *op. cit.*, p. 54 ; Andréades, *History of the Bank of England*, p. 362 ; *Institute of Bankers' Journal*, Jan., 1891, p. 1.

[2] *Bankers' Magazine*, 1890, pp. 1641–3.

[3] *Ibid.*

[4] The *Bankers' Magazine* remarked that if a short-loan agreement was informally reached, it was immediately abandoned afterwards. Similar efforts to achieve a short loan minimum were revived on many subsequent occasions during the ensuing 20 years, but always without success. During the War, however, the virtual control of the market by the Bank of England and the Treasury established a *de facto* minimum, which later became a permanent feature. It was not, however, until 1921 that any formal resolution, embodying the pre-existing agreement, was taken by the Committee of Clearing Bankers. The minimum then formally adopted, of 1 per cent. below Bank rate, was maintained until late in 1934.

American securities, had revealed the under-current of nervousness; yet market rate persistently underbid the Bank. And in early December the position was further complicated by the sudden disbursement of nearly £2,000,000 of Treasury funds "in aid" of local authorities under the Local Government Act, forcing market rate down to only 3¼ per cent.—1¾ per cent. under Bank rate.[1]

The device of "borrowing" on Consols was clearly inadequate to meet so difficult a situation, and the Bank, under the strong guidance of William Lidderdale, the then Governor, took unusual steps to secure control of the surplus balances. According to the first reports, it offered to receive the balances of the County Councils on deposit; actually, the arrangement was that, subject to the retention of a certain minimum balance, the Bank would on its own responsibility lend on the market the funds of the bodies concerned, paying to them the resultant interest, less commission.[2] Thanks to an arrangement of this kind with several County Councils, the market rate was levered up to 3¾ per cent. by the end of the month. But this laborious improvement was insufficient to stop the gold efflux; and on December 30—a Monday—the Bank, faced with year-end demands and the imminence of the Consol dividends, raised its discount rate to 6 per cent., and its charge for advances to 7 per cent. These rates were maintained for nearly eight weeks, but, despite stringency caused by tax demands, which kept short money around 6 per cent., market rate never rose above 4¾ per cent., and in February, 1890, dropped below 4¼ per cent.[3]

The signal failure of this effort to discipline the market, notwithstanding the psychological effect of a Bank rate increase to a penal level on a "non-Court" day, forced the Bank to a more

[1] See *Bankers' Magazine*, 1890, pp. 63, 328 (speech of chairman at meeting of Union Bank of London).

[2] See resolution adopted by Hampshire County Council in Feb., 1890, and Lidderdale's speech at Bank meeting in March. (*Bankers' Magazine*, 1890, pp. 395, 602–3.) The arrangement bore some resemblance to that which had been adopted in the middle 'thirties for the East India Co.'s deposits. (See *ante*, p. 87 *n*.)

[3] See *Bankers' Magazine*, 1890, p. 232, and *Economic Journal*, 1891, p. 193. The banks were vigorously attacked for this lack of co-operation; they had got into the habit, it was said, of "regarding the amount of the reserve of the Bank as of no importance, although it is the sole fund in existence to enable them to meet their liabilities if called upon. They fully believe that, if the worst comes to the worst, the Bank will not be allowed to fail, as an ordinary bank would fail, if the whole of its cash were gone, and the experience of more than one commercial crisis has shown that this calculation is a safe one" (*Ibid.*).

general adoption of its new plan; and its determination was increased by the fact, which the financial press was repeatedly emphasizing, that the level and quality of speculative activity from about 1887 onwards was presenting close parallels to the period before 1866.[1] No official details were ever made available, but by the middle of the year it was believed that the Bank had secured control of the balances of most of the public and semi-public bodies which were ordinarily large lenders, and especially of the important India Council balances, which formerly had been employed extensively in daily and weekly market loans.[2] As the table given on an earlier page reveals, these measures at first had little effect on discount rates; but the effect on short money rates was very marked, for during the first half of 1890 these were frequently well above the market rate. Thus in the bill market there were bitter complaints[3] at the effects of the Bank's policy, especially when it was found that the Bank was frequently refusing to re-lend even at Bank rate the funds it had secured, and was charging ½ per cent. or even 1 per cent. over the published rate.

The Bank had, in fact, struck at the roots of the evil, the evil which had arisen from the "throwing of unemployed money at the heads of the bill brokers . . . for any wretched rag of interest that might be got from day to day". Even a small surplus, an odd £50,000, it was said, had often acted "like a steam-hammer" on rates, creating a veritable paradise for bill brokers, "who reckoned on borrowing money from day to day on terms which left a wide margin between the rate borrowed and the rate at which they took in bills . . ."

> . . . The business of bill-broking grew to be quite a mechanical and blind business. It was found best to ignore outside influences, to disregard political or economical events, to do nothing but shut one's eyes and buy bills in the belief, justified by experience, that the average value of short money would always leave a profit on the business so done.[4]

These conditions had created a number of men of straw who were hard hit by the short loan stringency.[5] Legitimate bill dealers, however, could not complain of unfair treatment, for

[1] See, for example, *Bankers' Magazine*, 1890, pp. 534–7.

[2] See Arthur Ellis, in *Economic Journal*, 1891, pp. 198–9, and *Bankers' Magazine*, 1890, p. 1641–3.

[3] *Ibid.* [4] *Ibid.*

[5] Several small firms went out of business; others turned largely to high-yielding but precarious business in loans to the Stock Exchange.

on July 24, 1890, the Bank took the wholly unexpected, but very important, step of re-admitting the discount houses to re-discount facilities, intimating to them that in future it would be willing *at all times* to discount approved bills of 15 days or under at " not less than " Bank rate. [1]

In that the greater leniency as to bill market advances before 1883 had been one cause of the ineffectiveness of Bank rate at that time, this decision to abandon the rule of 1858 might seem at first sight to be at variance with the Bank's main policy. Actually, it was a powerful buttress for that policy. Lidderdale had perceived the fundamental fact, which James Morris and many successive Governors had failed to do, that it was impossible for the Bank to control the market so long as it remained aloof from it. Contact with the market in any competitive sense was no longer feasible, and had never been desirable ; but the alternative form of contact, achieved in the decade to 1858 (by allowing the market liberal re-discount and loan facilities at all times, and at moderate rates), was at least equally objectionable. Yet if the Bank, in seeking to avoid these two evils, both maintained ordinarily a non-competitive rate and also refused to lend to the market except in times of emergency, it followed that it was only at such times (and sometimes also during the " shuttings ") that it could with certainty impose its will upon the market. At all other times, the market could stray far from the Bank, and could build up speculative commitments which the Bank was powerless to check and which the dealers themselves, with their eyes glued on their own individual " books ", would hardly notice until the dangerous consequences were both imminent and inevitable. What was wanted was not a divorce of the market from the Bank, but a regular, or at least frequent, intercourse between the two which would not at the same time stimulate market over-trading.

The immediate and superficial reason for Lidderdale's decision was to save legitimate bill dealers from the loss and inconvenience caused by his " dear money " policy of absorbing surplus floating balances ; but the ultimate and fundamental reason was that the new system of limited re-discount facilities would afford a basis for that rational contact with the market which had for so long been wanting. If the Bank relied solely upon " borrowing " on Consols to make its rate effective, the most

[1] See *Economist*, 1890, pp. 949–50, and *Bankers' Magazine*, 1890, p. 1665. The actual rate was varied from time to time, but was usually below the charge for advances.

it could do was to screw rates up to Bank rate until the next Consol settlement; thereafter, unless it were prepared to repeat the (often costly) operation, outside rates would subside. Under the new system, however, by depleting the money supply sufficiently to force the market to send in bills for discount at whatever rate the Bank thought fit to charge, it not only could produce a much more direct (and therefore greater) effect on market rate, but could extend the period of its control by refusing to renew the bills as they matured. Lidderdale, in fact, was encouraging the market to borrow at the Bank, because he knew that the more it did so, the greater would be the Bank's power, and the greater its knowledge of the types of paper afloat and of the extent of commitments outstanding. Thus, so long as accommodation were given only on penal terms—Bank rate or over—against first-class, short-dated [1] securities, and only to houses whose commitments were in reasonable relation to their capital, the restoration of re-discount facilities, far from encouraging market over-trading, would actually enable the Bank to detect and check it. These were the principles upon which Lidderdale worked. He thereby laid the foundations of a qualitative control which alone could restrain the ill effects of over-free competition. As the discount houses came to use the new facilities more frequently, so they gave increasing preference to those bills which were re-discountable at the Bank, and so, too, did they seek to avoid any such extension of their commitments as might involve the risk of exclusion from the Bank, or any such decline in rates as might make re-discounting unduly costly.

THE BARING CRISIS AND AFTER

Thanks to Lidderdale's vigorous policy, which received wholehearted approval from the banks (and discriminating approval from the bill market), the Bank even before the Baring crisis had thus gone far towards solving its problem. [2] Indeed, the

[1] The actual resolution approved by the Bank board in 1890 did not specify short bills, but empowered the Governor to take any bills of up to three months. The regulations made under this authority were altered from time to time, mainly by extensions of the maximum permitted currency. The limit was raised to 60 days in 1895, and later the modern practice was adopted of taking bills of up to 3 months.

[2] For discussion of the effects of the new policy, see *Economist*, 1890, pp. 949–50, 964; *The Times*, July 25, 1890; *Bankers' Magazine*, 1890, pp. 1641–3; F. E. Steele, *On Changes in the Bank Rate* (1891), p. 17. "Under Mr. Lidderdale," wrote Ellis, "there have been fewer complaints than for many years past, as to the banking system being out of joint."

success of its policy very largely explains why the crisis of 1890 was accompanied by no such panic or subsequent distress as was that of 1866. At the time, it was widely asserted that the reason for this satisfactory contrast was that the crisis was wholly attributable to the embarrassment of one firm, which was not allowed to fail. In fact, the " Baring " crisis was no more exclusively due to the difficulties of Barings than the " Overend, Gurney " crisis was to the rottenness of Gurney's.

Its causes lay in a five-year wave of rising prices, of stock exchange and company speculation, and over-investment in illiquid and distant securities. In 1888 and 1889 the official returns of new companies' capital reached £354 millions and £241 millions respectively, while new investment in the Argentine alone amounted to no less than £36 millions in 1888 and £29 millions in 1889.[1] In this same period there was a craze for the conversion of private businesses—especially breweries—into limited companies,[2] which usually took over the properties at grossly inflated prices, and whose no less overvalued shares were eagerly sought after by the many newly-formed trust companies. The formation of " trusts ", indeed, became part of the big speculator's technique, enabling him, and others who followed him, to " ride on the back " of the institutional investor.[3] It was in foreign investment, however, that the worst excesses occurred. The issuing houses, following the same reckless methods which had caused so much distress in the 'seventies, poured funds into the exchequers of governments who were all too ready to " borrow " what they could never hope of repaying. That the sponsors of the loans succeeded in firing public imagination with the vastness of the riches of these borrowing countries is clearly shown by the fact that in the six years to 1890 *net* immigrants into the Argentine totalled no less than 1,000,000, increasing the population by roughly one-third.[4] The issuing houses, having prepared the investment market thus effectively, did not stop at Government securities, but introduced loans for municipal bodies, and the equities of public utility undertakings of every description. In the Argentine market a favourite security was the *cedulas*, or bonds, of the many Argentine land mortgage " banks ", which bonds were placed in London in large blocks, and unloaded by the financing houses without the

[1] *Institute of Bankers' Journal*, 1891, p. 1.
[2] *Economic Journal*, 1891, p. 192.
[3] See *Economist*, 1890, pp. 1470–1.
[4] *Economic Journal*, 1891, p. 535.

issue of any sort of prospectus.[1] By such means, the aggregate external debt of the Republic (including private indebtedness) was raised to some £200 millions, carrying an annual service of some £12,000,000—roughly 60 per cent. of the total exports ! [2]

Speculation and over-investment on such a scale could have but one end. It was hastened by the fact that in mid-1890 revolution broke out in the Argentine,[3] revealing the utter corruption of the administration (and the extent to which loan monies had been diverted to politicians' pockets), and precipitating a violent financial crisis in the leading towns. Though many other houses were heavily involved, the effect in London was most acutely felt by Barings, who were carrying, among gross liabilities of about £34 millions,[4] large quantities of Argentine securities "left" with them as underwriters,[5] and had to meet an extravagant volume of acceptances in the course of the ensuing few months. Heavy sales of securities, estimated at £4 millions, enabled them to keep afloat until November 8. On that day, when it became evident that they could not continue without assistance, they placed their position before the Bank of England. Lidderdale, realizing the extent of the danger, took prompt measures, first, by instituting a thorough but strictly private inquiry into the firm's affairs, and, secondly, by arranging, with the co-operation of the French and Russian authorities, for the importation of £4,500,000 of gold.

The investigation revealed that the firm was not insolvent. Immediately this was known, Lidderdale summoned a meeting of representatives of all the City banks and leading houses, to whom he proposed that the Bank should shoulder the Baring commitments as they matured, provided that the banks and market collectively agreed to bear any loss which might arise. The response was immediate : a guarantee of over £5 millions was furnished at the outset, and by the following day (November 15), when news of the plan became public, the total had reached £9 millions, eventually exceeding twice that sum.[6] Not

[1] See *Economic Journal*, 1891, p. 192, and *Bankers' Magazine*, 1890, pp. 1673–9.

[2] *Economic Journal*, 1891, p. 191.

[3] For detailed accounts of the progress of the Argentine crisis, see *Bankers' Magazine*, 1890, pp. 775–9, 1126–7, 1508.

[4] See *The Times*, Nov. 25, 1890.

[5] *Economic Journal*, 1891, p. 192, and *Bankers' Magazine*, 1890, p. 1936.

[6] There is no doubt that its amount was swollen by the adherence of minor houses who, after the danger was past, thought that it would "look well" to co-operate. The text of the guarantee will be found in the *Economist* (1890, p. 1482).

until that day, when all danger of collapse had been averted, did the general public (and many even in the City) learn that Barings was in serious difficulties, although they had known of the special gold transactions several days before. In consequence, there was no panic, no run on the Bank from the country, and not even any extreme calling in of loans.[1] Within a week, arrangements had been made for a reconstruction of the firm by the transfer of its business to a limited company, financed by the Baring family and its friends.[2] Then, indeed, within a fortnight of the first intimation of a threatened disaster, was all risk of alarming repercussions past.[3]

The Baring crisis thus marked the appearance of a new spirit in the money market. Despite the intense rivalries of the preceding decade, the London banks had shown that in emergency they could sink their differences, and pool their resources, for the common good. In every previous crisis, the one guide to action had been a frenzied *sauve qui peut*. In 1866 the panic had been magnified a hundredfold by wholesale withdrawals from the bill market both from London and from the country, and by the banks' blank refusal to discount; in 1890 the few banks which started to call in loans, and to refuse accommodation for the Stock Exchange settlement, immediately desisted when requested by the Bank to do so. The banks had grasped the fundamental truth that the interests of one were the interests of all; that the failure of one would precipitate a crisis from which none could escape. But this inter-bank solidarity was not the only new feature which emerged from the crisis: the banks collectively and individually gave full support to the Bank of England, and thereby implicitly acknowledged its leadership. In 1866, by contrast, they had threatened open revolt and a withdrawal of their balances, declaring that they "would not allow the Bank to go on while they failed".[4]

Thanks to the new spirit of co-operation, for which the forceful personality of the Governor of the Bank had been largely responsible, the banking system had been dragged from the

[1] For full details of the crisis see *The Times*, Nov. 14–25, 1890; *Bankers' Magazine*, 1890, pp. 1933–8; *Institute of Bankers' Journal*, 1891, pp. 1–10.

[2] Full details of the reconstruction were given in the *Economist* (1890, p. 1482).

[3] Bank rate was never raised above 6 per cent., though up to 8 per cent. was charged to prevent an unloading of Barings' paper by foreign holders. (See *The Times*, Nov. 19, 1890.)

[4] *Economist*, 1866, p. 582.

very verge of the precipice. But it was evident that what Crump called the new principle of "commercial salvage"[1] could not be applied to insolvent firms; had Barings been really insolvent, and not merely imprudently illiquid, they must have failed, and their failure must have involved a stress which the banking system was ill-equipped to withstand. It is to the credit of the banks that they made no attempt to minimize the danger which had threatened. Thus the lesson of the crisis proved salutary; and the fresh outcry[2] against the inadequacy of commercial bank reserves evoked a surprisingly general response. After 1890 the banks' cash ratios were progressively strengthened,[3] and the tendency continued right down to the eve of the War.

So far as the Bank's control of the market was concerned, this movement had two important consequences. First, it blunted the sharp edge of bank competition in the short loan market, and thus tended to check the beating-down of discount rates. Secondly, by strengthening the position of the Bank, it provided a "cushion" between demands on the reserve and market rate, thus making a constantly effective Bank rate less imperative. In any case, a day-to-day contact between market rate and Bank rate was of much less importance than the ability of the Bank to achieve such contact at short notice. Indeed, so long as the outside market was conscious of its responsibilities, and could be trusted to respond quickly to an official hint (backed by the threat of vigorous action should it fail to do so) at the first sign of danger, it was a matter of small consequence that at other times market rate might fall substantially below the Bank. There was, in fact, one definite advantage of such a divergence in quiet times: the existence of a relatively high Bank rate, implying that forced borrowing, should it prove necessary, would be costly, tended to check the over-trading which low rates might otherwise have produced. That the banks could be trusted to remember, and act upon, the lesson of 1890 was demonstrated three years later when, in the Australian banking "crisis", they substantially increased their reserves, and enabled

[1] See *Economic Journal*, 1891, pp. 388–94.

[2] The financial press in 1891 and 1892 was filled with discussions of the problem, and numerous pamphlets and books appeared. See, especially, Goschen's speeches, and the writings of Pownall, Stanley Cobb, Gairdner. Goschen's proposals were ably summarized by Foxwell in the *Economic Journal* (1892, pp. 138–62).

[3] See Drummond-Fraser before British Association, Aug. 3, 1906, and *cf. Economist*, 1890, p. 1467.

the Bank to make its rate effective. "The banks," it was said, "have done their duty."[1]

Recognition of these principles, and the moderation of the more extreme forms of inter-bank competition, proved a valuable reinforcement of Lidderdale's more direct measures. Together they provided an adequate solution of the Bank's problem of making its rate effective at moments of danger to the reserve, without necessitating an unduly tight hold on the market situation at other times. The effects of this important advance were not, however, immediately apparent in the average rate differentials, for the liquidation of the enormous boom commitments of 1886–90 brought a period of monetary ease of unprecedented duration and intensity.[2] During this period, market rate, necessarily, dropped far below the Bank; and the differential was widened in and after 1894 when the banks met a 2 per cent. Bank rate by a London deposit rate of only ½ per cent.,[3] thereby affording yet another indication of their changed attitude towards competition. The average margins are shown below[4]:

RATE MARGINS IN TIME OF MONETARY EASE
(Yearly Averages)

Year.	Bank Rate (a). %	Market Rate (b). %	Deposit Rate (c). %	Excess of (a) over (b). %	Excess of (b) over (c). %
	£ s. d.	£ s. d.	£ s. d.	£ s. d.	£ s. d.
1890 . .	4 10 0	3 13 3	2 17 9	0 16 9	0 15 6
1891 . .	3 6 8	2 12 6	1 16 8	0 14 2	0 15 10
1892 . .	2 10 0	1 8 6	1 4 6	1 1 6	0 4 0
1893 . .	3 2 0	2 2 6	1 12 0	0 19 6	0 10 6
1894 . .	2 2 4	0 19 5	0 16 5	1 2 11	0 3 0
1895 . .	2 0 0	0 15 11	0 10 0	1 4 1	0 5 11
1896 . .	2 9 8	1 9 5	0 19 8	1 0 3	0 9 9
1897 . .	2 13 1	1 15 8	1 1 10	0 17 5	0 13 10

[1] *Bankers' Magazine*, 1893, Vol. II, p. 12.

[2] For 931 days from February 22, 1894, Bank rate was unchanged at 2 per cent. This duration of a 2 per cent. rate has only once been exceeded—in the period which followed the War Loan conversion announced on June 30, 1932.

[3] The Scottish banks were much less prudent, maintaining a minimum deposit rate of 1½ per cent., and reducing it to the unprecedented level of 1 per cent. only in 1896.

[4] The averages are compiled from the computations of the *Bankers' Magazine*.

It will be noted that in 1895, when the average market rate touched a fresh low record,[1] the margin below Bank rate even exceeded the previous maximum (18*s.* 10*d.* per cent.) reached in 1887.[2] These very wide margins did not, however, cause any inconvenience to the Bank, for there was no external menace to the reserve, which rose rapidly to record figures.[3]

Control Regained: The Effectiveness of Bank Rate

That the abnormal relationships of the middle 'nineties represented no defiance of the Bank's wishes, but resulted simply from the fact that there was then no need for rigid control, was forcibly demonstrated when the spell of ease drew to its close. In 1898, when reviving trade and the opening up of Africa and the Far East brought increasing demands for money,[4] the average margin between Bank rate and market rate dropped to under ½ per cent., and two years' later, when the stringency was intensified by the Boer War, barely exceeded ¼ per cent. Indeed, in the second half of 1899, the Bank had held so strong a grip upon the market that for some considerable time it was said to have " monopolized " discount business.

During the ensuing decade there were, it is true, occasional complaints that the Bank was finding difficulty in making its rate effective. In 1901, for example, Luke Hansard was begging the clearing banks to restrain their " eagerness to beat down discount rates ", and questioned whether the state of the exchanges influenced " in any marked degree the minds of the principal boards . . . in their lendings or discounts ". The Bank, he declared, had " for some years past " been alive to its duty; but why should it " pawn its Government securities

[1] The lowest *half*-yearly average ever recorded before the recent slump was that of 13*s.* 2*d.* per cent., in the second half of 1894. The average margin under Bank rate then was £1 6*s.* 10*d.* per cent., also a record.

[2] It is worth noting that in the middle 'nineties, despite the extreme plethora of money, and the relative scarcity of bills, discount rates remained on the average perceptibly above the short money rate; so that throughout the period the bill market was able to " run " bills at a profit. This is in marked contrast to the experience since 1932 (the only comparable period of prolonged ease before or after the 'nineties) when the existence of a clearing banks' short loan minimum has kept money costs persistently above the level of discount rates.

[3] In 1894 the reserve *ratio* averaged no less than 63 per cent., and was only fractionally lower in 1895.

[4] See Rozenraad, *loc. cit.*, pp. 165–75.

for the purpose of taking up surplus market supplies?"[1] Again, in 1909, Edward Holden made a strong plea[2] for clearing bank co-operation with the Bank, for the purpose of keeping Bank rate effective.

These and similar protests, however, were provoked much less by any really deep-seated disharmony in the market than by the special and temporary conditions ruling at the periods at which they were made. In contrast with the experience of earlier years, and especially of that of the 'eighties, the grounds for complaint about strained relations between the Bank and the clearing banks, and about the margin between Bank rate and market rate, were insignificant. There was no longer any doubt that the Bank *could* control the market; and the average differentials revealed that, despite occasional spasms of unusually fierce competition or of pronounced monetary ease, the Bank in general *did* control it. The trend of rates in the immediate pre-War years is shown below:

DISCOUNT RATES ON THE EVE OF THE WAR[3]
(Yearly Averages)

Year.	Bank Rate (*a*). %	Market Rate (*b*). %	Deposit Rate (*c*). %	Excess of (*a*) over (*b*). %	Excess of (*b*) over (*c*). %
	£ *s.* *d.*	£ *s.* *d.*	£ *s.* *d.*	£ *s.* *d.*	£ *s.* *d.*
1898 . .	3 3 0	2 13 3	1 13 0	0 9 9	0 19 3
1899 . .	3 14 1	3 3 7	2 3 5	0 10 6	1 0 2
1900 . .	3 18 10	3 13 2	2 8 7	0 5 8	1 4 7
1901 . .	3 14 6	3 3 2	2 4 5	0 11 4	0 18 9
1902 . .	3 6 7	2 19 5	1 16 7	0 7 2	1 2 10
1903 . .	3 15 10	3 8 3	2 5 10	0 7 7	1 2 5
1904 . .	3 6 0	2 13 7	1 16 0	0 12 5	0 17 7
1905 . .	3 0 0	2 11 3	1 10 0	0 8 9	1 1 3
1906 . .	4 5 1	3 19 9	2 13 7	0 5 4	1 6 2
1907 . .	4 18 6	4 9 4	3 3 6	0 9 2	1 5 10
1908 . .	3 0 3	2 6 4	1 9 9	0 13 11	0 16 7
1909 . .	3 1 11	2 5 9	1 11 11	0 16 2	0 13 10
1910 . .	3 14 6	3 3 3	2 4 6	0 11 3	0 18 9
1911 . .	3 9 6	2 18 5	1 19 6	0 11 1	0 18 11
1912 . .	3 15 5	3 12 0	2 5 5	0 3 5	1 6 7
1913 . .	4 15 5	4 7 5	3 5 5	0 8 0	1 2 0

[1] See *Bankers' Magazine*, 1901, Vol. I, p. 415.

[2] At the meeting of the London, City and Midland Bank (*Economist*, 1909, p. 209).

[3] Compiled from the computations of the *Bankers' Magazine*.

The narrowness of the margin between Bank and market rate during this period is the more noteworthy in view of the further contraction in the volume of bills relatively to the volume of bank deposits. While the latter rose rapidly, it is doubtful whether the volume of bills was more than maintained. Palgrave thought that in 1902 the normal bill supply was about £300 millions, compared with his own estimate of £300–350 millions for 1873 [1]; while by the outbreak of War the figure was generally put at around £325–350 millions, excluding Treasury bills.

One important reason for the Bank's better grip upon the market, despite the increasing scarcity of bills, was the rapid growth in the importance of Treasury operations. These assisted the Bank in two ways. First, because the increase in the Treasury's needs for short-term finance led in 1902 to the authorization of the use of Treasury bills to finance Supply Services and not merely Consolidated Fund Services; and, secondly, because of the higher level of the Government balances, especially at certain seasons.

The change in Treasury practice was of great significance, for prior to 1902 the Treasury had been obliged to meet all Supply deficiencies, which sometimes were very large, by borrowing on Ways and Means at the Bank.[2] As these borrowings involved an equivalent addition to clearing bank cash, and a much more than proportional increase in the volume of bank credit, their effect was to produce an artificial, and often very pronounced, ease in the money market. Ways and Means borrowings therefore undermined the Bank's control, and, moreover, did so most noticeably at the most critical season of the year, for the leanest Exchequer quarter coincided with the period of the autumnal " drain " caused by payments for raw material imports (chiefly cotton and grain) from America. By the substitution of Treasury bills for Ways and Means advances the effects of Treasury borrowings were virtually reversed; not only was there then no artificial flooding of the market by newly-created credit, but each issue of bills correspondingly *reduced* the available credit supply, which was restored to its former

[1] Palgrave, *op. cit.*, p. 66.

[2] See report of Chancellor of Exchequer's explanation (*Economist*, 1902, p. 1243); and Tritton in *Institute of Bankers' Journal* (1902, pp. 102–3, 492–3). The rate charged by the Bank for Ways and Means Advances was half the published Bank rate, so that the change was expensive to the Treasury.

level only as Government disbursements gradually filtered back to the market through the banks. In consequence, Treasury operations tended to increase the power of the Bank not only in the last quarter of the financial year, when heavy tax-payments normally created stringency, but also in the third quarter, when the Treasury was a large borrower. Indeed, in 1904 and 1905, when a large increase in Government expenditure had been financed principally by the income-tax, the bulk of which was collected in the fourth quarter, it was remarked that the " financing of the Exchequer during the first nine months of the year is becoming one of the chief factors in determining the course of money rates in Lombard Street ".[1]

Another factor which in the early years of the century was throwing the market more and more into the hands of the Bank was the growing practice of clearing bank " window-dressing ",[2] not merely for the half-yearly balance sheets, but also for the monthly statements, which then related to a single day towards the end of the month.[3] " Window-dressing " has always been regarded as objectionable, but at this period it had the quite definite, though unintentional, advantage that the market, threatened with the possibility of comparatively frequent borrowings at the Bank,[4] was thereby afforded very real grounds for endeavouring to prevent its own rate from falling far below Bank

[1] See *Economist*, 1905, p. 1376. At this period " Supply " needs had involved the issue of £15 millions of bills, bringing the total issue up to nearly £32 millions, a " gigantic total ". The *Economist* declared, " to put it mildly ", that this was " unwieldy finance ", which raised serious dangers through foreign ownership of the bills, and imposed needlessly jerky conditions upon the market when the bills were issued or repaid.

[2] For contemporary discussion of the problem, see especially *Economist*, 1902, pp. 1, 80 ; Schuster at Union Bank of London meeting, Jan. 15, 1902 ; Tritton before Institute of Bankers, Nov. 5, 1902 ; and other bank meetings in January, 1902. It was from this practice that the system of " night " money arose—the system of one-day loans, for repayment on the following day.

[3] The practice of publishing monthly averages of four weekly figures was begun in 1908 in the hope that this would relieve the strain on the market and would lead eventually to abandonment of all window-dressing, which, however, continues to this day.

[4] Borrowing at the half-year-ends was often very large. For example, at the end of 1901 it exceeded £12 millions. On that occasion, the National Discount Co. complained that it was called upon to repay call loans of £1,200,000 on one day. (See E. T. Doxat's speech at the meeting on Jan. 22, 1902.)

rate, especially as the Bank was quite commonly charging rates above its published minimum.[1]

That these various influences had greatly eased the Bank's task of securing control of the market was plainly shown by its smaller reliance upon the practice of " borrowing " on Consols : it was said in 1908 that such " borrowing " had not occurred for " several years ".[2] Indeed, after the close of the nineteenth century, the problem of market control fades into the background. From about 1900 onwards, the main concern of the Bank seems to have been, not how to impose its own rate on the market, but how to avoid imposing upon the trade of the country a rate often dictated solely by external influences. Thus, early in the century, to avoid undue increases in Bank rate, the authorities, following the example of several Continental central banks, began to allow importers of gold the use of money for up to a fortnight *free of interest*, against an undertaking to repay the loan in gold, thereby attracting bullion before the normal gold point was reached.[3] The same motive, clearly, lay behind the practice in times of stringency of charging rates above the published rate, for this avoided the rise in commercial bank loan and overdraft charges which would have followed a formal increase in Bank rate.[4] Other measures were taken to the same end, but by far the most striking was that introduced in the autumn of 1905, when an easing of money caused by the maturity of Exchequer Bonds unfortunately coincided with a threat of gold demands from Paris. The authorities then took the unusual step of inviting the leading clearing banks to place their surplus balances on deposit with the Bank ; and although it was said that only a " low " rate of interest was to be allowed, the response was so general that market rate was quickly screwed right up to Bank rate, thereby avoiding an increase above 4 per cent. throughout the autumn.[5]

[1] For discounts, rates varying from Bank rate to 1 per cent. over were charged to the market, while for advances the usual charge was 1 per cent. over ; after 1906, however, the advances' charge became generally, as now, $\frac{1}{2}$ per cent. over. No loans would be made for less than seven days, and no repayment would be accepted on a Saturday. The maximum period of an advance was three months.

[2] Burn, *op. cit.*, p. 39.

[3] Luke Hansard, *loc. cit.*

[4] N. E. Neill, " History and Basis of Modern Discount Policy " (*Bankers' Magazine*, 1901, Vol. II, p. 467 ; see also 1906, Vol. II, pp. 565–6, 605).

[5] See J. Spencer Phillips at the meeting of Lloyds Bank, Jan. 26, 1906 ; and Ernest Sykes, address to Chartered Institute of Secretaries, on " The Circulation of Small Notes ".

At the time, the policy behind these various expedients created a very favourable impression, and is significant as a proof that the Bank was beginning to take a very broad view of its obligations, not only to the money market, but also to the general trade of the country. Such a policy, however, could be justified only when the external influences which menaced the reserve were no more than transitory, for otherwise the maintenance of a discount rate below the "natural" level was merely bolstering up an unstable equilibrium which was bound to collapse eventually. This principle was ignored in 1905 and 1906, but was brought home to the authorities in forcible and unpleasant fashion a year later, when it became apparent that the Bank's consideration for the interests of trade had been partly to blame for the violence of the repercussions of the American crisis of 1907 upon the London market: for the maintenance of comparatively low discount rates in the two years before the crisis had led to the renewal of many American finance bills which otherwise would have been paid off.[1] It was then perceived that the Bank's policy, which had seemed so successful at the time, offered no solution to the problem of reconciling the frequently divergent interests of domestic trade and international finance.

It is not too much to say that the problem remains unsolved to this day. The most serious disadvantage of an international standard is that the domestic trade of any country which boasts an international money market must be subjected to jolts and jars arising purely from conditions abroad. By a skilful open market technique, almost unknown before the War, it is indeed possible for a central bank to smooth out the more violent and extreme fluctuations; but post-War experience has shown that it is highly difficult, and often impossible, for the authorities in any market to determine at any given moment whether a sudden movement of international balances is a fortuitous disturbance or part of a major trend. Yet an incorrect diagnosis may have disastrous results; and even when a short-term disturbance is correctly diagnosed, it may be impossible for a central bank successfully to take "neutralizing" steps in the absence of co-operation from the authorities in the centre from which the disturbance emanates.

[1] This had been pointed out by the financial press in the autumn of 1906. (See, for example, *Bankers' Magazine*, 1906, Vol. II, pp. 565–6, 605–7.) The Bank had, however, made some sort of attempt to discriminate between finance paper and legitimate bills, by discounting for its own customers (which included the Eastern banks) at 4 per cent., but charging 4½ or 5 per cent. to other applicants.

Co-operation: the End of the Struggle

Since the War there has been some progress towards inter-central bank co-operation of this type, but the results so far achieved are not wholly reassuring. Before the War such co-operation, which involves day-to-day intercourse between central banks, was almost non-existent. Thus the authorities, once they had realized the dangers of attempting to resist the consequences of foreign-imposed influences, had no practicable alternative[1] but to pursue a so-called automatic policy, regulating Bank rate almost mechanically by gold movements and the trend of the leading exchanges. They were not then troubled by what may be described, for lack of a better phrase, as the "domestic ineffectiveness" of Bank rate, for there was then no serious rigidity in the internal price- and wage-structure, and changes in short-term interest rates necessitated by an unbalanced external position quickly brought an appropriate adjustment in the internal position. The Bank's major task, therefore, was to ensure that Bank rate could always be made speedily and completely effective in the money market. Performance of this task, as has been shown, had been greatly facilitated by the development of a sound market technique, and by such influences as the growth of Treasury operations, for these influences gave the Bank very great power at certain seasons. Really rapid control at other times, however, would not have been possible had there been any serious conflict of interests in the money market; and even at seasons of maximum power the disciplining of an unruly market would have required measures so drastic as to cause grave inconvenience to trade. That these difficulties were not important in the decade before the War was attributable very largely to a growing spirit of co-operation between the various elements of the market, and especially between the clearing banks and the Bank of England.

There were, it is true, occasional indications of disharmony, but the few much-quoted expressions of dissatisfaction on the part of the clearing banks were in marked contrast to the policy which they actually followed. For example, both Felix Schuster, of the Union Bank of London and Smiths, and Charles Gow, of the London Joint Stock Bank, in evidence before the U.S. Monetary Commission of 1910 (the interviews took place in 1906),

[1] The only available alternative, the substitution of a pure managed currency for an international standard, was unthinkable before the War.

complained bitterly of competition from the Bank, which, they said, sought to increase its business and make a profit just as any other bank did. Yet the one regretted that there was no " official way of communication, no regular meeting, between the banks and the Bank of England ", and the other admitted that the Bank was " absolutely indispensable ".[1] And almost at the very time this evidence was given, the clearing banks as a whole were co-operating freely with the Bank, offering what the *Bankers' Magazine* described as " loyal support " [2] for the scheme to take surplus money off the market, and voluntarily placing their balances at the disposal of the authorities *at low rates*.

This plan, indeed, while creating " consternation and considerable ill-feeling " [3] in the bill market, was whole-heartedly approved by the banks, as the following remarks [4] from Spencer Phillips revealed :

> I think I may state for ourselves that we welcome, and cordially welcome, this new departure of the Bank ; and, although I have no authority for saying so, I am perfectly certain that I am voicing the opinion of the rest of the bankers in stating that they are equally pleased. *The more the Bank co-operates with the leading bankers the better for everybody. We are in a certain way interdependent upon each other, although, so long as the Bank retains its present privileges and is the keeper of the ultimate reserve—and the system is not likely to be changed in our time—I think we perfectly recognize that they are the pre-dominant partner.*

Again, the *Bankers' Magazine*, discussing the question of the gold reserve, declared that it could not be solved by mere informal co-operation, because of the " excessive jealousy and competition which exists between banking institutions, bankers personally, and also between the bankers and the Bank of England " ; although the paper noted with satisfaction " one or two indications that the Bank of England and the banks are coming into somewhat closer connection ".[5] Despite these assertions, in 1907 it was remarked that the Bank's control had been increased by the fact that the clearing banks had restricted their loans to the bill market, " from the feeling that some of the troubles of the past have been occasioned by allowing the market to compete too freely for bills ".[6]

[1] See U.S. Monetary Commission, *loc. cit.*
[2] *Bankers' Magazine*, 1906, Vol. II, p. 3.
[3] See Ernest Sykes, *loc. cit.*
[4] At the meeting of Lloyds Bank, Jan. 26, 1906.
[5] *Bankers' Magazine*, 1906, Vol. II, pp. 6–8.
[6] *Ibid.*, 1907, Vol. I, pp. 30–4.

The banks, clearly, were beginning to follow a far more responsible policy than might have been anticipated from the somewhat militant speeches of a few of their general managers; such speeches, more or less inevitably, received more publicity than the sober facts of everyday practice which revealed the change of policy, and in consequence the comments of the press were not always in true perspective. One example of false perspective arose in the autumn of 1905, when much attention was attracted by a remark from A. C. Cole, a director of the Bank, that " it is no business of the Bank during any time of crisis to take care of the other banks . . . all that the Bank is called upon to do is to take care of itself ".[1] This remark, as construed by most commentators, gave a wholly misleading impression of the Bank's attitude, and brought a strong reply from the Governor, A. F. Wallace, a few months later.[2] For years, as has been shown, the Bank had been thoroughly alive to its responsibilities, in normal times as well as in emergency, and was fully conscious of the advantages of free co-operation with the market. " There can be no question," declared Wallace, " of the Bank's competing with the other banks, and this is no doubt well understood by those who are really on top of the subject. . . . The Bank of England is the one institution in the country whose main aims are anything but that of serving its own interest . . . the interests of proprietors have invariably to give way when national or more important issues are at stake." [3]

Wallace, indeed, did much to foster the spirit of co-operation, and throughout his period of office worked intensively to secure among the various elements of the money market realization of the essential principle of identity of interests. That these efforts met with very real success was demonstrated unmistakably in 1911, when the clearing banks, with a view to closer co-operation both among themselves and with the Bank, actually took the initiative in proposing regular quarterly meetings between their representatives and the Governor. By a strange irony, it fell to A. C. Cole to make the first public announcement of the scheme, at the Bankers' Dinner at the Mansion House [4]:

> . . . I am one of those [he declared] who have always refused to believe that the interests of the bankers are opposed to the interests

[1] Quoted by Palgrave in speech before British Association, Aug. 3, 1906.

[2] At the Bankers' Dinner at the Mansion House, June 20, 1906.

[3] *Bankers' Magazine*, 1906, Vol. II, pp. 66, 326–7.

[4] On July 1, 1911.

of the Bank of England. While the Bank of England naturally keeps in view the interests of its shareholders, still, the first consideration of the Bank, in its decisions as to Bank rate, is the welfare of the trade of the country. We reduce our rate so far as we can, keeping in view that the gold reserve at the Bank must be maintained. In the prosperity of the trade of the country every banker is directly interested, and all bankers are also interested in the maintenance of the gold reserve. There is no conflict of interest between the bankers and the central institution, and I have hailed with the utmost satisfaction a proposal which has unanimously been made by the representatives of the clearing bankers that will bring the Governor of the Bank into more direct personal relations with the clearing banks.

The significance of this agreement, as the press of the day was not slow to observe, could hardly be over-estimated. Its importance lay, not so much in the actual arrangements made—though the value of these was evident—as in the spirit which had prompted them; for behind the clearing banks' proposal lay a formal acknowledgment of the Bank's mastery.

Close of an Epoch

From this point of view, it is hardly too much to say that the Bankers' Dinner of 1911 marked the close of an epoch, the end of eighty years and more of violent, and often bitter, struggle between the two great powers in the money market. Until the 'nineties, there had been no decisive indication of where eventual victory would lie. Thereafter, the issue was never in doubt; and by the close of the century both bill market and banks were fully, at times painfully, aware of the Bank's power. They had learnt that the authorities, despite the persistent decline in their resources relative to the whole volume of credit, would always hold the last trump. They knew that any open disobedience could be only temporarily effective; that in the long run it must defeat its own ends and make the ultimate corrective action the more unpleasant. With this recognition of the Bank's capacity eventually to punish the insubordinate there had come naturally a new consideration for its wishes. Instead of using recklessly the freedom afforded at seasons when the Bank's grip was light, the banks and discount houses began to watch closely the trend of official policy, anxiously scanning the Bank returns, the trend of money rates abroad, and, above all, the exchanges, for any clue as to what the action of Threadneedle Street would be when its full power was restored. And at such times a helpful hint from the authorities that there might be breakers ahead came to be almost as effective in Lombard Street as even the most direct disciplinary attempts had often been in the past. For the old "quantitative" control there had been substituted a more benevolent, and yet more effective, "moral" control.

By the eve of the War, therefore, the various elements in the market, formerly contesting parties with interests often violently divergent, had become merged into one organic whole around the nucleus of the Bank. Yet the unification, upon which the War itself set the final seal, had been accomplished without any impairment of the elasticity of the discount market or any real sacrifice of the freedom of its individual members: never before had the market been more sensitive, or discount rates more "fine". In that freedom, so strangely blended with a speedy and effective control and discipline, lay the real foundations of London's strength and supremacy. Both were to be subjected to supreme test in the years immediately to come. But the War, while it wrought great changes in market portfolios, added new functions, and subjected the whole organism to a Treasury domination unknown in the past, merely demonstrated anew the extraordinary elasticity, adaptability and superiority of a market whose distinguishing characteristic was the possession of a specialized discount mechanism. It was through that mechanism, which in a century of growth had made London the banker, and Britain the financier, of the world, that the whole vast expenditure of the War was in the first instance to be financed, and financed with an ease and expedition which was the envy of every foreign centre. It was through that mechanism, too, that a central bank faced with new problems and new forces was to exercise smoothly and efficiently a control of the credit situation and of the general price-structure upon a scale and in a manner without precedent in the pre-War years. In 1914, if not also to-day, it could with justice be said that London without its specialized discount market would be London without its greatness.

APPENDICES

1. Chronological Table of Discount Companies.
2. Prospectus of the National Discount Company, Ltd.
3. Prospectus of Overend, Gurney & Co., Ltd.
4. Discount Companies, 1885–1913.

APPENDIX No. I

CHRONOLOGICAL TABLE OF DISCOUNT COMPANIES

Company.	Date of Formation.	Initial Paid-up Capital.*	Description.	Date of Liquidation.
National . .	Feb., 1856	£200,000	New business.	—
London . .	Oct., 1856	£178,235	New business.	Nov., 1860
General . .	Nov., 1857	£11,543	New business.	1860
Mercantile . .	May, 1859	£43,000	New business.	Jan., 1861
London & Provincial	Early 1861	Very small	New business.	1861
Joint Stock . .	Feb., 1863	£200,000	Bought business of J. F. Wilkinson.	Mar., 1866
Discount Corporation	Oct., 1863	£168,235	Bought businesses of Bruce & Co. & Weston & Laurie.	1867 : see below
Consolidated .	Dec., 1863	£91,180	Bought business of Fraser Sandeman.	1866 : see below
Financial . .	Mar., 1864	£30,000	Bought a private business.	1866 : see below
London Mercantile	Mar., 1864	£50,000	Bought business of Womersley & Burt.	Nov., 1865
Overend, Gurney	July, 1865	£1,500,000	Refinancing of existing business.	May, 1866
New Consolidated	1866	£44,921	Reconstruction of Consolidated Co.	May, 1869
City . . .	1866	£37,970	Reconstruction of Financial Co.	No trace after 1869
United Discount Corporation	1867	£134,109	Reconstruction of Discount Corporation.	May, 1885: see below
General Credit & Discount Co. of London	1867	£1,500,000	Reconstruction of General Credit & Finance Co. of London.	May, 1885 : see below
Union Discount Co. of London	1885	£500,000	Fusion of General Credit & United Discount Cos.	—
Alexanders .	Feb., 1891	£500,000	Conversion of firm into private company.	—

* In some instances the figures are those at the date of the first accounts.

APPENDIX No. II

COPY OF THE PROSPECTUS OF THE NATIONAL DISCOUNT COMPANY, LIMITED

(ISSUED ON FEBRUARY 9, 1856)

THE

NATIONAL DISCOUNT COMPANY, LIMITED

(PROVISIONALLY REGISTERED.)

Capital, £1,000,000 (with power to increase to £2,000,000) in 40,000 Shares of £25 each. Deposit, £5 per Share.

DIRECTORS.

WILLIAM PATRICK ANDREW, Esq. Chairman of the Scinde Railway Company, 26, Montague Square.
ARCHIBALD BOYD, Esq. Director of the Union Bank of London, 115, Westbourne Terrace.
MATTHEW HUTTON CHAYTOR, Esq. Deputy Chairman of the General Iron Screw Collier Company, 3, Adelaide Place, London Bridge.
JOHN UTLAY ELLIS, Esq. 13, Craven Hill Gardens, Hyde Park.
EDWARD HALES, Esq. North Frith, Hadlow, Kent.
ALEXANDER MACKENZIE, Esq. Director of the Oriental Bank Corporation, 43, Sussex Square, Brighton.
FRANCIS WILLIAM RUSSELL, Esq., M.P. 18, Cannon Street.
JOHN ROBERT THOMSON, Esq. (J. R. Thomson and Co.), St. Peter's Chambers, Cornhill.
HENRY HEYMAN TOULMIN, Esq. Great St. Helen's.
EDWARD WARNER, Esq., M.P. 49, Grosvenor Place.
FREDERICK CHARLES WILKINS, Esq. 31, Gt. Winchester Street.
(With power to add to their number.)

BANKERS.

THE UNION BANK OF LONDON, 2, Princes Street.

SOLICITORS.

Messrs. MARTEN, THOMAS, and HOLLAMS. Messrs. SEWELL, FOX, and SEWELL.

BROKERS.

Messrs. GEORGE BURNAND & CO. 69, Lombard Street. Messrs. HUGGINS & ROWSELL, 14A, Austin Friars.

TEMPORARY OFFICES.

14A, AUSTIN FRIARS.

A Joint Stock Company has been formed, and provisionally registered, under the above title, for carrying on a general Discount Business.

The circumstances of the times are peculiarly favourable to the establishment of such a Company, and the commercial exigencies of the country require it.

The foreign trade alone of the United Kingdom has trebled itself within the last twenty-five years; the exports, which, in the year 1832, amounted to £32,000,000, having, in the year 1854, risen to over £97,000,000. The home trade has received a proportionate impetus and development, and the aggregate transactions of the country, in exchangeable products, have multiplied to an extent which it is difficult to estimate; whilst the monetary facilities for carrying on these transactions have not kept pace with this rapid and gigantic increase.

A Company, which from its ample resources offers additional facilities for commercial operations, will, it is believed, be favourably received by the trading community and prove a useful auxiliary to the Banking Establishments throughout the kingdom; at the same time affording to all classes a safe and remunerative investment, either permanent or temporary, for their surplus funds.

The principles on which the Company is based are simple and familiar.

The foundation is a large subscribed capital, of which a considerable proportion will be at once paid up; and money will be received on deposit, at rates and upon terms of repayment, to be specially agreed on with the depositors.

These means will be employed in discounting, and in loans, on approved securities.

The Company will not open drawing accounts with their customers, nor act in any respect as a bank.

The Capital is to be £1,000,000, divided into 40,000 shares of £25 each, upon which a deposit of £5 per share shall be paid, on the acceptance of the letters of allotment. Power will be taken by the deed to increase the Capital to £2,000,000, with the assent of three-fourths of the Proprietors specially convened.

It will be the duty of the Directors to select a General Manager, whose ability and experience shall assure to the Shareholders and the Public a vigilant and prudent administration.

The Company is constituted within the provisions of the Limited Liability Act.

Each application for shares must be accompanied by a payment to the Bankers of the Company of £1 per share on the number of shares applied for, and for which a voucher will be given. Should no allotment be made to the applicant, the money thus lodged with the Bankers will be returned free of charge; if an allotment be made, it will be applied towards the deposit of £5 per share then payable.

Applications for shares to be addressed to the Provisional Directors' at the Temporary Offices of the Company, No. 14A, Austin Friars; or to the Brokers, in the form set forth on the fly-leaf.

N.B.—In Scotland, deposits will be received by the National Bank of Scotland, in Edinburgh and Glasgow.

London, 8*th February*, 1856.

APPENDIX No. III

COPY OF THE PROSPECTUS OF OVEREND, GURNEY AND CO., LTD.

(Issued on July 13, 1865)

OVEREND, GURNEY AND CO. (LIMITED)

(Incorporated under "The Companies Act", 1862)

Capital, £5,000,000, in 100,000 shares of £50 each, of which it is not intended to call up more than £15 per share.

Deposit on application, £2 per share; £5 per share on allotment; £4 per share on the 15th of September, and the same on the 15th of November.

Directors.—Henry Edmund Gurney, Esq., 65, Lombard Street; John Henry Gurney, Esq., 9, St. James's Square, and Catton Hall; Robert Birkbeck, Esq., 65, Lombard Street, and Norwich; Henry Ford Barclay, Esq., Monkhams, Woodford, Essex; Thomas A. Gibbs, Esq. (Messrs. T. A. Gibbs and Co.), 72, Old Broad Street; Harry G. Gordon, Esq. (Chairman of the Oriental Bank); William Rennie, Esq. (Messrs. Cavan, Lubbock and Co.), 16, Leadenhall Street.

Bankers.—Bank of England, Messrs. Barclay, Bevan, Tritton, Twells and Co.

Brokers.—Messrs. Sheppards, Pelly and Allcard, 28, Threadneedle Street.

Solicitors.—Messrs. Young, Jones, Vallings and Roberts.

Offices.—65, Lombard Street.

Temporary Offices for allotment and the registration of shares.—51, Lombard Street.

The Company is formed for the purpose of carrying into effect an arrangement which has been made for the purchase from Messrs. Overend, Gurney and Co., of their long established business as bill brokers and money dealers, and of the premises in which the business is conducted, the consideration for the goodwill being £500,000, one half being paid in cash and the remainder in shares of the company with £15 per share credited thereon—terms which, in the opinion of the directors, cannot fail to ensure a highly remunerative return to the shareholders.

The business will be handed over to the new company on the 1st of August next, the vendors guaranteeing the company against any loss on the assets and liabilities transferred.

Three of the members of the present firm have consented to join the board of the new company, in which they will also retain a large pecuniary interest. Two of them (Mr. Henry Edmund Gurney and Mr. Robert Birkbeck) will also occupy the position of managing directors and undertake the general conduct of the business.

The ordinary business of the company will, under this arrangement, be carried on as heretofore, with the advantage of the co-operation of the board of directors, who also propose to retain the valuable services of the existing staff of the present establishment.

The directors will give their zealous attention to the cultivation of business of a first-class character only, it being their conviction that they will thus most effectually promote the prosperity of the company and the permanent interests of the shareholders.

Copies of the company's Memorandum and Articles of Association, as well as the Deed of Covenant in relation to the transfer of the business, can be inspected at the offices of the solicitors of the company.

Applications for shares must be accompanied by the payment of a deposit of £2 per share, which will be received by Messrs. Barclay, Bevan, Tritton, Twells and Co., 54, Lombard Street. In the event of no allotment being made, the deposit will be returned in full. Should a less number of shares be allotted than are applied for, the deposit will, so far as required, be appropriated towards the payment due upon allotment.

LONDON, July 12, 1865.

APPENDIX No. IV

DISCOUNT COMPANIES, 1885–1913

	Alexanders.			National.		
At Dec. 31.	Net Discounts.	Re-discounts.	Deposits.	Net Discounts.	Re-discounts.	Deposits.
	£	£	£	£	£	£
1885 . .	*	*	*	7,109,655	2,594,283	8,698,014
1886 . .	*	*	*	6,385,663	3,501,428	8,397,591
1887 . .	*	*	*	7,000,354	2,976,791	9,417,192
1888 . .	*	*	*	7,185,823	3,120,609	9,350,445
1889 . .	*	*	*	7,586,559	3,420,154	10,198,383
1890 . .	5,121,802	910,000‡	5,933,892	7,515,521	4,561,291	9,543,731
1891 . .	5,952,186	1,050,000‡	7,287,719	6,772,212	2,634,480	8,775,368
1892 . .	5,631,767	1,239,103	6,970,813	7,671,750	2,986,592	9,807,423
1893 . .	4,901,783†	952,558†	6,249,142†	6,329,885	3,321,635	7,963,568
1894 . .	6,060,051	1,011,508	7,217,217	7,117,883	2,786,093	9,230,210
1895 . .	6,905,113	608,567	8,238,422	8,464,777	2,196,881	10,452,724
1896 . .	4,942,071	735,011	6,377,725	6,627,602	2,816,635	8,932,608
1897 . .	5,237,149	749,039	6,588,630	5,887,194	2,388,347	8,025,861
1898 . .	5,587,559	965,424	6,894,839	6,974,325	1,973,159	9,350,743
1899 . .	4,836,074	1,130,656	6,160,204	7,015,728	2,269,488	8,987,697
1900 . .	4,816,880	911,555	6,066,545	6,429,532	2,833,197	8,757,155
1901 . .	5,108,174	1,887,756	6,345,473	6,391,530	2,353,468	8,647,126
1902 . .	4,550,002	782,679	6,208,886	6,320,322	2,059,229	9,061,058
1903 . .	4,992,377	365,277	6,229,551	6,355,654	3,753,612	8,569,653
1904 . .	4,927,786	1,970,500	6,748,309	6,995,048	3,346,453	10,116,496
1905 . .	5,375,556†	933,994†	7,537,820†	7,185,055	3,263,484	10,355,847
1906 . .	6,454,572	976,634	7,780,781	8,901,861	3,514,343	12,003,999
1907 . .	7,454,076	1,801,120	7,764,233	11,364,875	3,309,062	13,495,948
1908 . .	6,518,538	1,613,000‡	7,279,596	9,795,256	6,048,107	12,324,699
1909 . .	7,340,973	1,758,000‡	8,321,952	11,426,626	4,160,791	14,280,562
1910 . .	7,692,262	1,451,000‡	8,531,052	11,127,638	3,051,121	14,312,200
1911 . .	8,290,742	1,587,997	9,311,741	12,580,989	3,982,888	15,208,208
1912 . .	8,731,209	1,685,154	9,731,880	12,817,078	4,179,346	15,871,902
1913 . .	9,301,419	1,497,231	10,134,947	14,128,857	5,656,538	15,757,480

* No figures were then published, and records are no longer available. † At previous June 30. ‡ Estimated.

DISCOUNT COMPANIES, 1885–1913—*continued*

	Union.			Aggregate.		
At Dec. 31.	Net Discounts.	Re-discounts.	Deposits.	Net Discounts.	Re-discounts.	Deposits.
	£	£	£	£	£	£
1885 . .	2,992,211	4,714,128	3,697,831	—	—	—
1886 . .	3,351,981	4,691,512	4,854,406	—	—	—
1887 . .	4,485,817	5,060,903	6,266,785	—	—	—
1888 . .	6,278,269	6,347,864	8,738,826	—	—	—
1889 . .	7,520,908	9,083,119	9,564,294	—	—	—
1890 . .	5,544,759	7,561,075	7,028,531	18,182,082	13,032,366	22,506,154
1891 . .	5,376,683	4,280,126	7,517,952	18,101,081	7,964,606	23,581,039
1892 . .	6,029,558	4,989,084	8,271,338	19,333,075	9,214,779	25,049,574
1893 . .	6,982,400	5,229,817	7,762,600	18,214,068	9,504,010	21,975,310
1894 . .	8,705,658	4,764,439	10,679,980	21,883,592	8,562,040	27,127,407
1895 . .	10,542,132	5,283,155	12,390,264	25,912,022	8,088,603	31,081,410
1896 . .	7,784,782	6,210,933	9,695,301	19,354,455	9,762,579	25,005,634
1897 . .	7,951,235	5,779,051	10,087,491	19,075,578	8,916,437	24,701,982
1898 . .	7,724,721	6,945,740	9,925,953	20,286,605	9,884,323	26,171,535
1899 . .	9,286,407	3,812,811	10,865,506	21,138,209	7,212,955	26,013,407
1900 . .	9,269,286	6,414,149	12,483,918	20,515,698	10,158,901	27,307,618
1901 . .	9,778,885	4,699,812	13,383,341	21,278,589	8,941,036	28,375,940
1902 . .	9,432,459	5,436,561	12,502,037	20,302,783	8,278,469	27,771,981
1903 . .	9,605,659	3,333,719	12,431,186	20,953,690	7,452,608	27,230,390
1904 . .	9,972,843	4,230,074	13,683,012	21,895,677	9,547,027	30,547,817
1905 . .	9,950,699	5,865,486	14,849,382	22,511,310	9,962,964	32,743,049
1906 . .	11,210,849	6,113,397	15,641,509	26,567,280	10,604,374	35,426,289
1907 . .	14,202,014	7,100,448	17,573,288	33,020,965	12,210,630	38,833,469
1908 . .	12,020,374	8,664,071	17,206,482	28,334,168	16,325,178	36,810,777
1909 . .	13,021,614	8,919,387	17,765,630	31,789,213	14,838,178	40,368,144
1910 . .	12,531,758	6,321,697	17,163,143	31,351,658	10,823,818	40,006,395
1911 . .	14,052,181	6,260,182	17,112,160	34,923,912	11,831,067	41,632,109
1912 . .	16,011,890	8,248,458	18,913,711	37,560,177	14,112,958	44,517,493
1913 . .	18,397,062	8,966,329	20,662,330	41,827,338	16,120,098	46,554,757

BIBLIOGRAPHY

OF PRINCIPAL REFERENCES

Books, Pamphlets and Papers

A Catechism of the Currency, by John Taylor. (1836.)
A Defence of the Joint Stock Banks, by David Salomons. (1837.)
A New Discourse on Trade, by Sir Josiah Child. (1690.)
A Practical Essay on Banking, by Joseph Macardy. (1834.)
A Practical Treatise on Banking, by J. W. Gilbart. (1828.)
Amalgamation Movement in British Banking, by Joseph Sykes. (1926.)
An Examination of the Report of the Joint Stock Bank Committee, by T. Joplin. (1837.)
An Inquiry into the Currency Principle, by Thomas Tooke. (1844.)
Annals of an East Anglian Bank, by W. H. Bidwell. (1900.)
Bank Rate and the Money Market, by R. H. Inglis Palgrave. (1903.)
Bank Rate in England, France, and Germany, 1844–1878, by R. H. Inglis Palgrave. (1880.)
British Banking Statutes and Reports, by Prof. T. E. Gregory. (1929.)
Byles on Bills.
Calendar of Early Mayors' Court Rolls, by A. H. Thomas. (1924.)
Currency Reform : Improvement not Depreciation, by T. Joplin. (1844.)
Depredations ; or Overend, Gurney & Co., and the Greek and Oriental Steam Navigation Company, by Stefanos Xenos. (1869.)
Early History of Banking in England, by R. D. Richards. (1928.)
English Banking, etc., by G. H. Pownall. (1914.)
English Merchants, by H. R. Fox Bourne. (1866.)
Enquiry into the Currency Principle, by Thos. Tooke. (1844.)
Essay on Banking, by T. Joplin. (1822.)
Essay on the Condition of the National Provincial Bank of England, etc., by its Founder, by T. Joplin. (1843.)
Essays and Addresses on Economic Questions, by Viscount Goschen. (1905.)
Essays in Finance, by Robert Giffen. (1886.)
Europe the World's Banker, 1870–1914, by Herbert Feis. (1930.)
Evolution of the Money Market, by Ellis T. Powell. (1915.)
Financial and Commercial Crisis Considered, by Lord Ashburton. (1847.)
Further Reflections on the State of the Currency and the Action of the Bank of England, by S. J. Loyd. (1837.)
Handbook of London Bankers, by Hilton Price. (1890.)
Hints by way of Encouraging the Formation of a Joint Stock Banking Company in London, etc., Anon. (1834.)

Hints, by way of Warning, on the . . . Foundation of Joint Stock Banks, by George Farren. (1833.)
History of Banking, by W. J. Lawson. (1850.)
History of Barclays Bank, by Matthews and Tuke. (1926.)
History of Prices, Vols. III and IV, by Thos. Tooke. (1840 and 1848.)
History of Prices, Vols. V and VI., by Tooke and Newmarch.
History of the Bank of England, by A. Andréadès. (1909.)
Imperial Banks, by A. J. S. Baster. (1929.)
Industrial and Commercial Revolutions in Great Britain, by L. C. A. Knowles. (1922.)
Journal of Thomas Raikes.
Letter to Lord Melbourne on the Causes of the Recent Derangement of the Money Market and on Bank Reform, by R. Torrens. (1837.)
Letters to William Raynor Wood, On the Currency, by William Leatham. (1841.)
Local Issues—Joint Stock Banks and Bank of England Notes, etc., Contrasted, by " A Merchant ". (1834.)
Logic of Banking, by J. W. Gilbart. (1859.)
Lombard Street, by W. Bagehot. (1873.)
Management of the Circulation and Prices, Anon. (1840.)
Memorials of Samuel Gurney, by Mrs. T. Geldart.
Migration of British Capital, by L. H. Jenks. (1927.)
Minutes of Evidence on Banks of Issue, 1875, by R. H. Inglis Palgrave. (1876.)
Money, the Servant of the People, etc.—A Letter to William Leatham, by James Taylor. (1842.)
On Changes in the Bank Rate, by F. E. Steele. (1891.)
On Currency, Anon. (1840.)
Origin and Historical Development of the Profession of Notaries Public, by H. C. Gutteridge.
Plan for the Establishment of a National Bank, by David Ricardo. (1824.)
Principles of Banking, by Thos. Hankey. (1st edition, 1873 ; and 4th edition, 1887.)
Rationale of Market Fluctuations, by Arthur Ellis. (1879.)
Rise and Growth of Joint Stock Banking, by S. E. Thomas. (1934.)
Rise of the London Money Market, 1640–1826, by W. R. Bisschop. (1910.)
Stock Exchange Investments, by Joseph Burn. (1909.)
Stories of Banks and Bankers, by F. Martin. (1865.)
System of London Clearances, etc., by W. Tate. (1841.)
The Advantages of the Proposed National Bank of England, by T. Joplin. (1833.)
The Bank of England and the Discount Brokers, by *A.B.C.* (1860.)
The Bank of England from Within, by W. M. Acres. (1931.)
The Commercial Crisis of 1847–8, by D. Morier Evans. (1848.)
The Country Banker, by George Rae. (1885.)
The Grievance of the Discount Houses, by *X.* (1860.)
The History of the Commercial Crisis of 1857–8, by D. Morier Evans. (1859.)
The History, Principles and Practice of Banking, by J. W. Gilbart. (1866.)
The International Money Market, by Cornelis Rozenraad. (1902.)

The Key to the London Money Market, by Arthur Crump. (1872 and later editions.)
The Landed Interest and the Supply of Food, by James Caird. (1880.)
The Money Pressure of 1836, by T. Joplin. (1837.)
The System of National Finance, by E. Hilton Young, M.P. (1915.)
Thoughts on the Separation of the Departments, by S. J. Loyd. (1844.)
Wealth of Nations, by Adam Smith. (1776.)

Official Publications

1797. *Committee of Secrecy on the Total Amount of Outstanding Demands on the Bank of England and the Funds for discharging the Same.*
House of Commons' Committees (1803 Collected Edition), Vol. 11.

1797. *Lords' Committee of Secrecy on the Causes which produced the Order of Council on the 26th of February, 1797.*
B.P.P. 1810. Vol. 3 (Reprinted).

1810. *Select Committee on the High Price of Gold Bullion.*
B.P.P. 1810 (349) III. 1.—[48].

1819. *Secret Committee on the Expediency of the Bank resuming Cash Payments.*
B.P.P. 1819 (202) III. i.—[46] and 1819 (282) III. i.—[46].

1819. *Lords' Committee on the State of the Bank of England with reference to the Expediency of the Resumption of Cash Payments.*
B.P.P. 1819 (291) III. 363.—[47].

1832. *Secret Committee on the Expediency of renewing the Charter of the Bank of England, and the System on which Banks of Issue in England and Wales are conducted.*
B.P.P. 1831–2 (722) VI. 1.

1836. *Secret Committee on the Operation of the Act of the 7 Geo. IV, c. 46, permitting the establishment of Joint Stock Banks.*
B.P.P. 1836 (591) IX. 411.

1837. *Secret Committee on the Operation of the Acts permitting the Establishment of Joint Stock Banks in England and Ireland.*
B.P.P. 1837 (531) XIV. 1.

1838. *Secret Committee on the Operation of the Acts permitting the Establishment of Joint Stock Banks in England and Ireland.*
B.P.P. 1837–8 (626) VII. 1.

1840. *Select Committee on the effects produced on the Circulation of the Country by the various Banking Establishments issuing Notes payable on Demand.*
B.P.P. 1840 (602) IV. 1.

1841. *Select Committee of Secrecy on the effects produced on the Circulation of the Country by the various Banking Establishments issuing Notes payable on Demand.*
B.P.P. 1841 (366) V. 1 and 1841 (410) V. 5.

1848. *Secret Committee on the Causes of the recent Commercial Distress and how far it has been affected by the Laws for regulating the Issue of Bank Notes payable on Demand.*
B.P.P. 1847–8 (395) VIII. Part I. 1; 1847–8 (584) VIII. Part I. 505; and 1847–8 (395–584) VIII Part II. 1 and 379.

1848. *Secret Committee of the House of Lords on the Causes of the Distress which has for some time prevailed among the Commercial Classes and how far it has been affected by the Laws for regulating the Issue of Bank of England Notes payable on Demand.*
B.P.P. 1847–8 (565) VIII. Part III. 1 and 537.

1857. *Select Committee on the Operation of the Bank Act of 1844 (7 and 8 Vict., c. 32) and of the Bank Acts for Ireland and Scotland (8 and 9 Vict., c. 37 and 38).*
B.P.P. 1857 (220, Sess. 2) X. Part I. 1, and Part II. 1.

1858. *Select Committee on the Operation of the Bank Act of 1844 (7 and 8 Vict., c. 32) and of the Bank Acts for Ireland and Scotland (8 and 9 Vict., c. 37 and 38), and the Causes of the recent commercial Distress and how far it has been affected by the Laws for Regulating the Issue of Bank Notes payable on Demand.*
B.P.P. 1857–8 (381) V. 1.

1875. *Select Committee on the Restrictions imposed and Privileges conferred by Law on Bankers authorized to make and issue Notes in England, Scotland and Ireland respectively.*
B.P.P. 1875 (351) IX. 1.

House of Commons' Debates.

Periodicals

Circular to Bankers.
Economica.
The Bankers' Almanack.
The Bankers' Magazine.
The Daily News.
The Economic Journal.
The Economist.
The Edinburgh Review.
The Financial News.
The Journal of the Institute of Bankers.
The Journal of the Royal Statistical Society.
The London Directory.
The Manchester Guardian.
The Mark Lane Express.
The Money Market Review.
The Observer.
The Statist.
The Times.

INDEX